BATMAN

ARKHAM KNIGHT

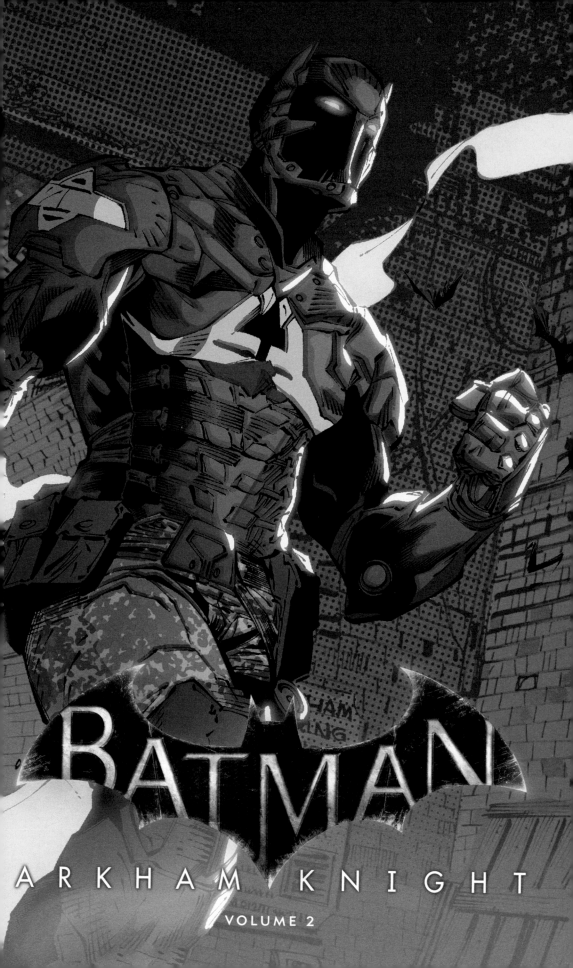

BATMAN

ARKHAM KNIGHT

VOLUME 2

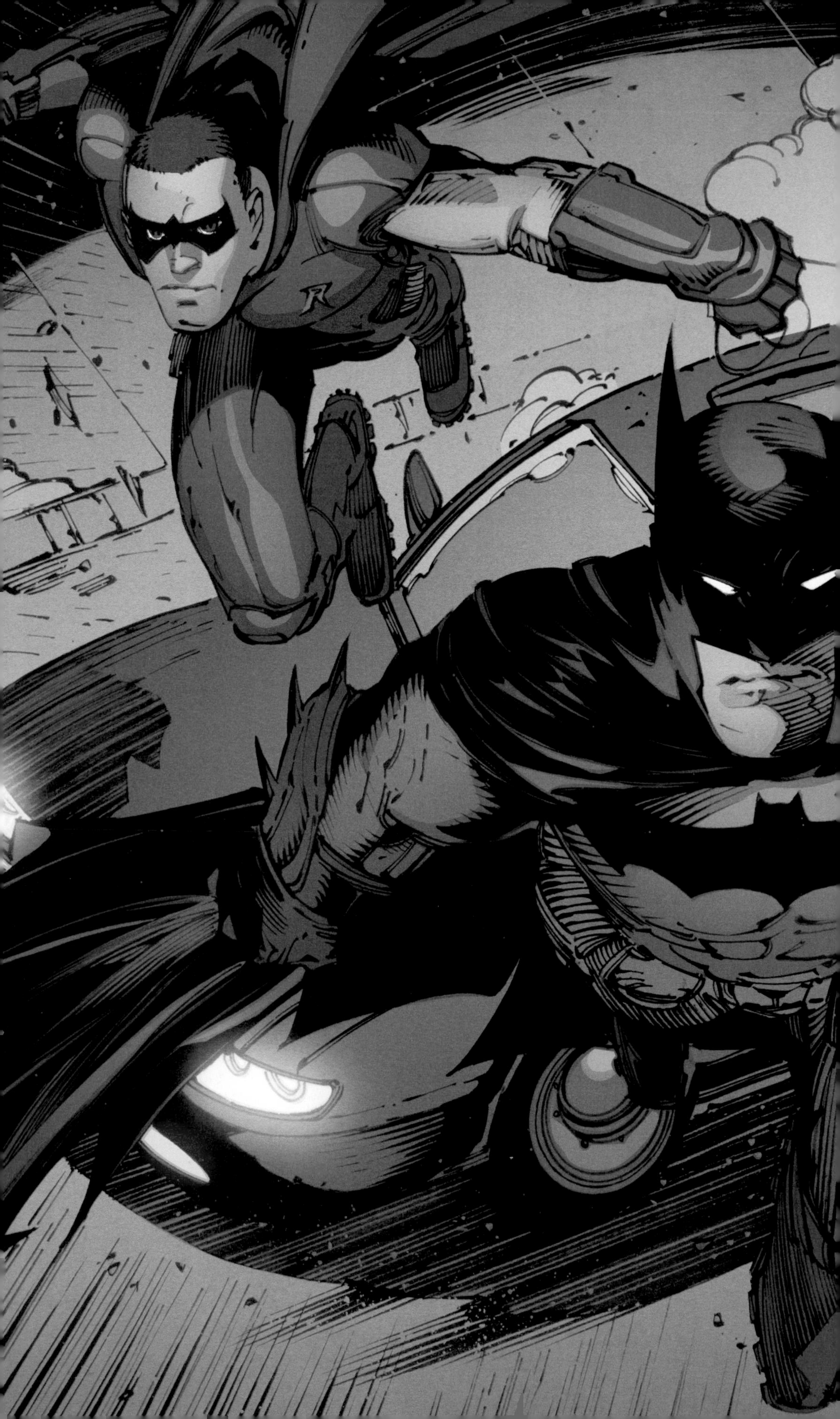

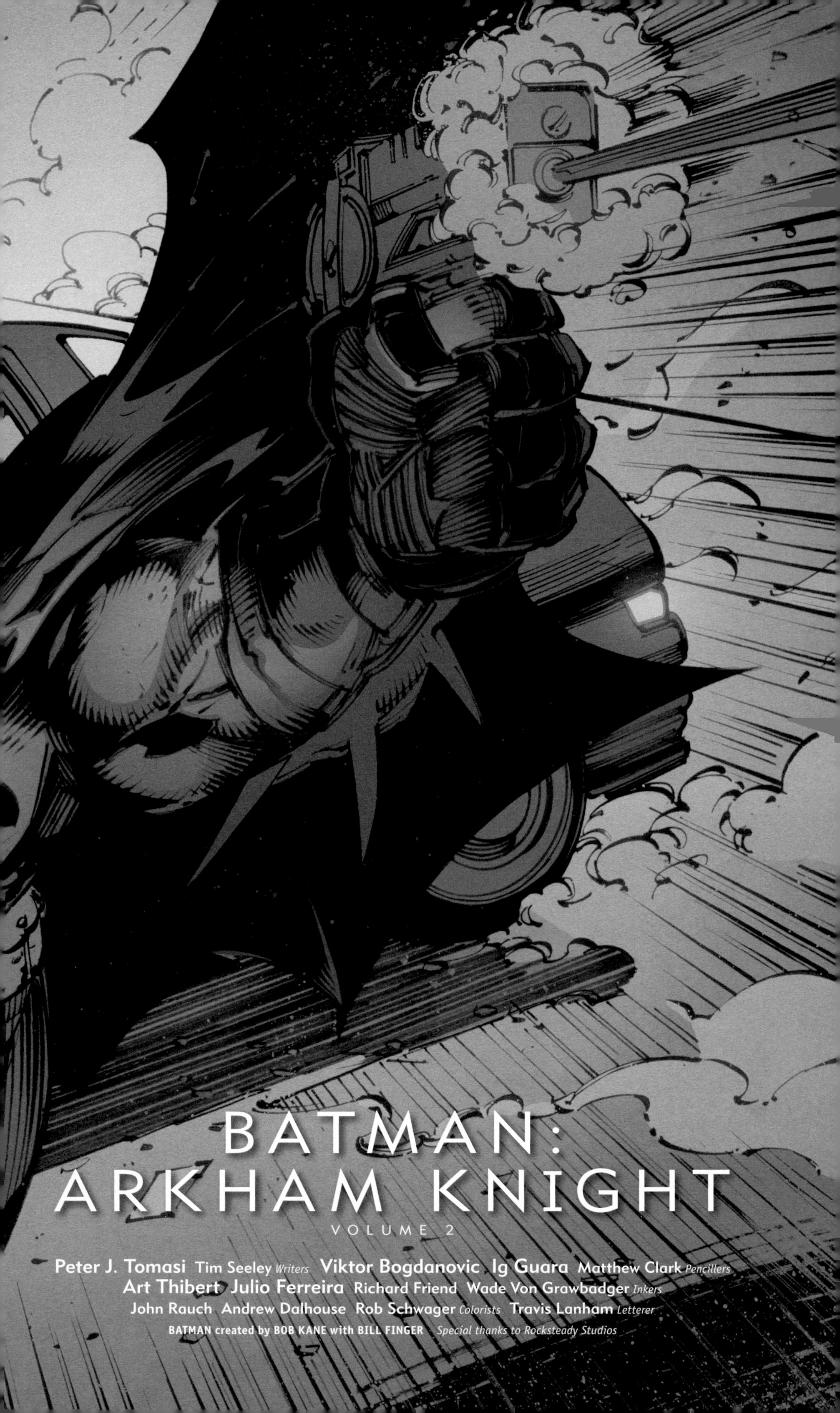

BATMAN: ARKHAM KNIGHT

VOLUME 2

Peter J. Tomasi Tim Seeley *Writers* Viktor Bogdanovic Ig Guara Matthew Clark *Pencillers*
Art Thibert Julio Ferreira Richard Friend Wade Von Grawbadger *Inkers*
John Rauch Andrew Dalhouse Rob Schwager *Colorists* Travis Lanham *Letterer*

BATMAN created by BOB KANE with BILL FINGER *Special thanks to Rocksteady Studios*

BATMAN: ARKHAM KNIGHT VOLUME 2

Published by DC Comics. Compilation and all new material
Copyright © 2016 DC Comics. All Rights Reserved.

Originally published in single magazine form in BATMAN: ARKHAM KNIGHT
5-9, BATMAN: ARKHAM KNIGHT: BATGIRL BEGINS and online as BATMAN:
ARKHAM KNIGHT Digital Chapters 13-26, BATMAN: ARKHAM KNIGHT: BATGIRL
BEGINS Copyright © 2015 DC Comics. All Rights Reserved. All characters,
their distinctive likenesses and related elements featured in this publication
are trademarks of DC Comics. The stories, characters and incidents featured
in this publication are entirely fictional. DC Comics does not read or accept
unsolicited ideas, stories or artwork.

DC Comics, 2900 West Alameda Ave., Burbank, CA 91505
Printed by RR Donnelley, Salem, VA, USA. 1/22/16. First Printing.
ISBN 978-1-4012-6067-5

Library of Congress Cataloging-in-Publication Data is available.

PEFC Certified
Printed on paper from
sustainably managed
forests and controlled
sources
PEFC/29-31-75   www.pefc.org

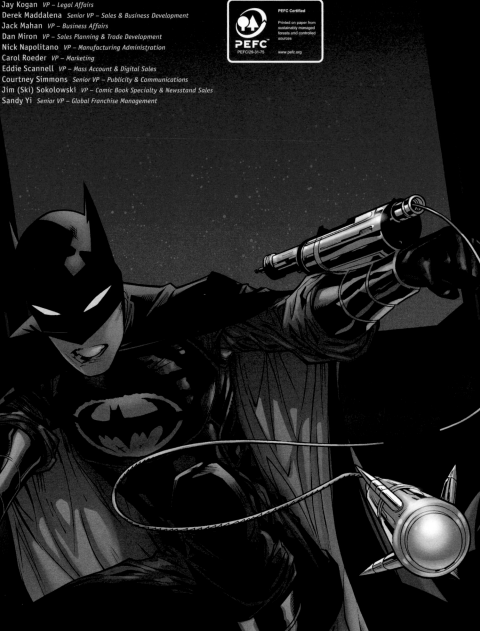

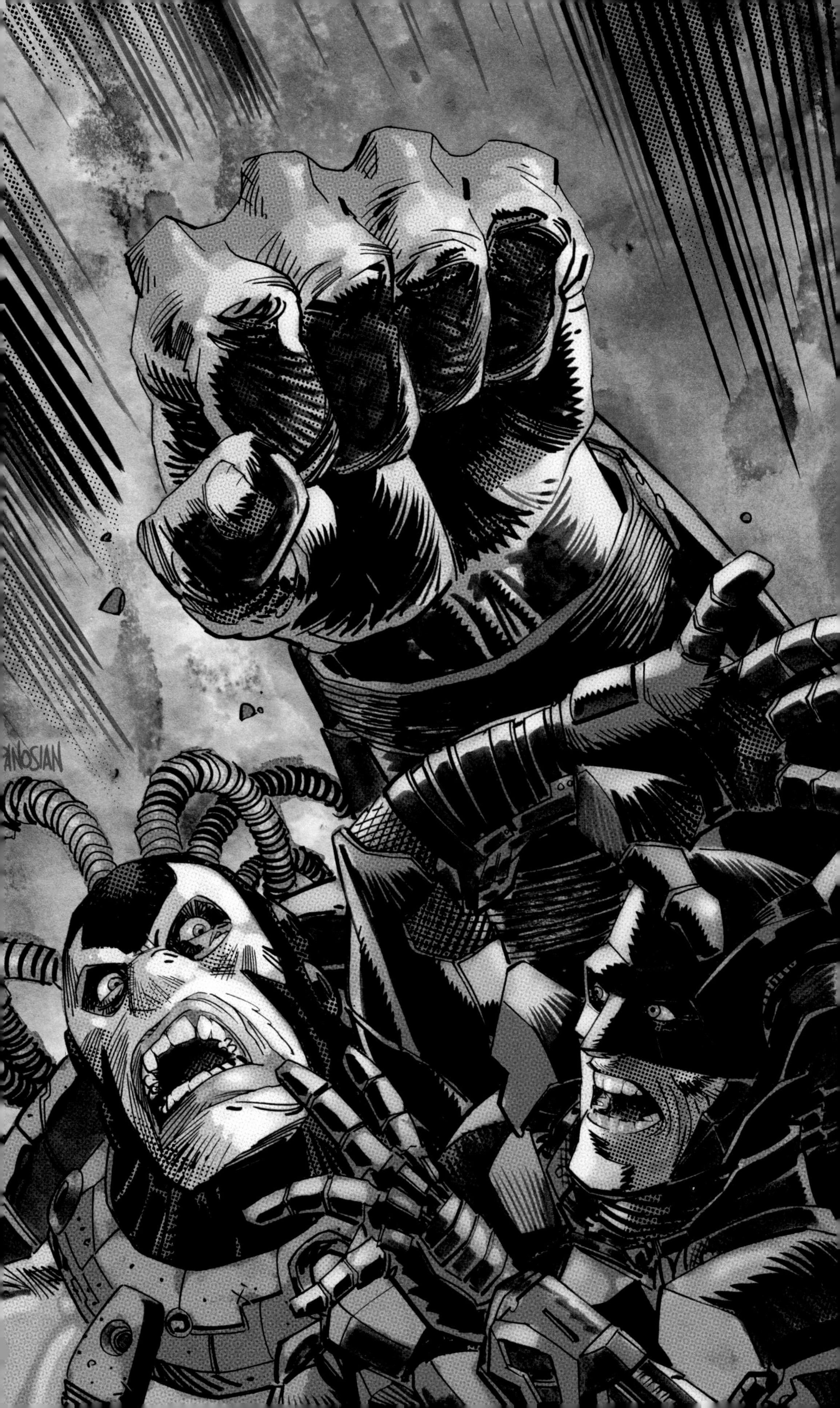

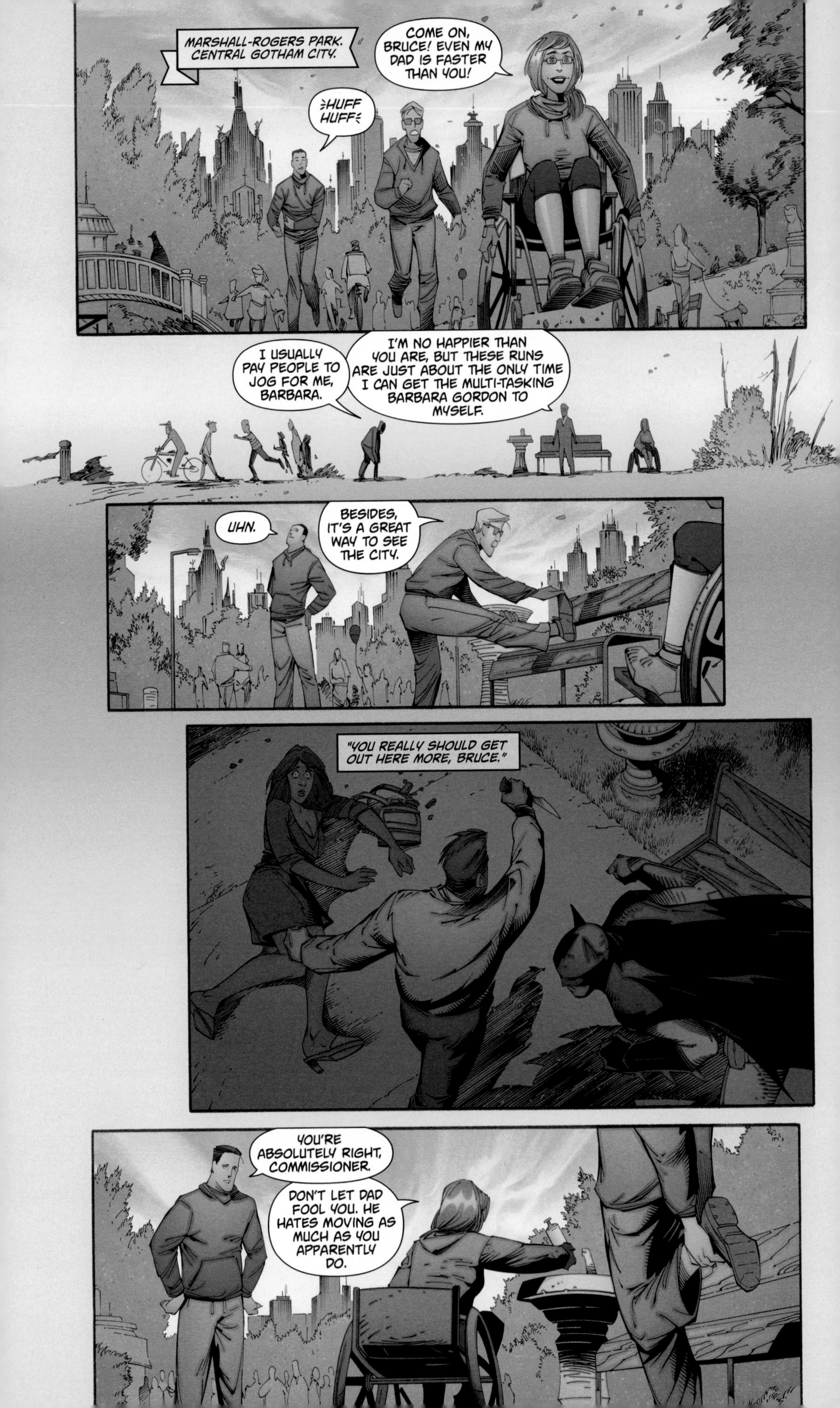

MARSHALL-ROGERS PARK. CENTRAL GOTHAM CITY.
COME ON, BRUCE! EVEN MY DAD IS FASTER THAN YOU!
HUFF HUFF
I USUALLY PAY PEOPLE TO JOG FOR ME, BARBARA.
I'M NO HAPPIER THAN YOU ARE, BUT THESE RUNS ARE JUST ABOUT THE ONLY TIME I CAN GET THE MULTI-TASKING BARBARA GORDON TO MYSELF.
UHN.
BESIDES, IT'S A GREAT WAY TO SEE THE CITY.
"YOU REALLY SHOULD GET OUT HERE MORE, BRUCE."
YOU'RE ABSOLUTELY RIGHT, COMMISSIONER.
DON'T LET DAD FOOL YOU. HE HATES MOVING AS MUCH AS YOU APPARENTLY DO.

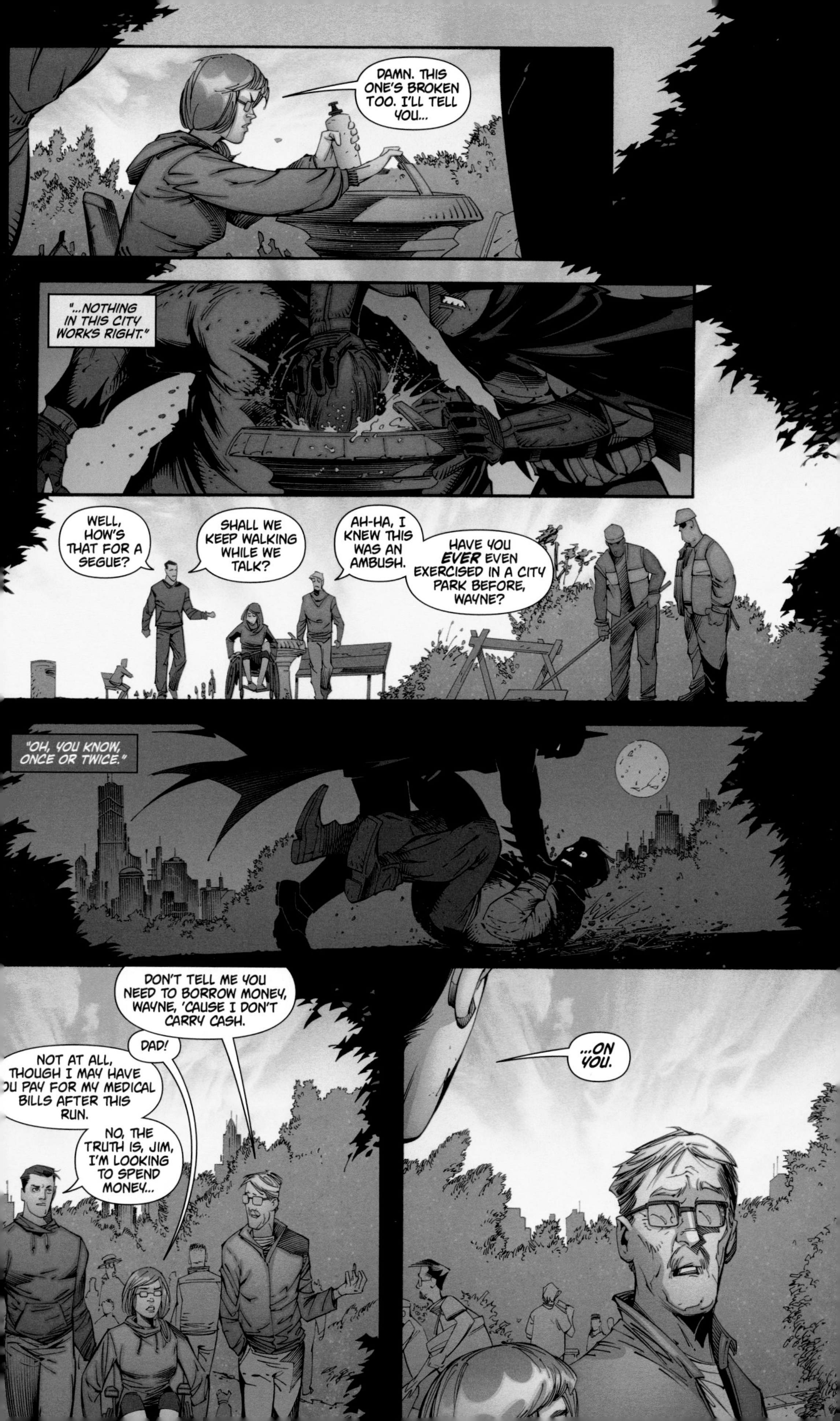
DAMN. THIS ONE'S BROKEN TOO. I'LL TELL YOU...
"...NOTHING IN THIS CITY WORKS RIGHT."
WELL, HOW'S THAT FOR A SEGUE?
SHALL WE KEEP WALKING WHILE WE TALK?
AH-HA, I KNEW THIS WAS AN AMBUSH.
HAVE YOU EVER EVEN EXERCISED IN A CITY PARK BEFORE, WAYNE?
"OH, YOU KNOW, ONCE OR TWICE."
DON'T TELL ME YOU NEED TO BORROW MONEY, WAYNE, 'CAUSE I DON'T CARRY CASH.
DAD!
NOT AT ALL, THOUGH I MAY HAVE OU PAY FOR MY MEDICAL BILLS AFTER THIS RUN.
NO, THE TRUTH IS, JIM, I'M LOOKING TO SPEND MONEY...
...ON YOU.

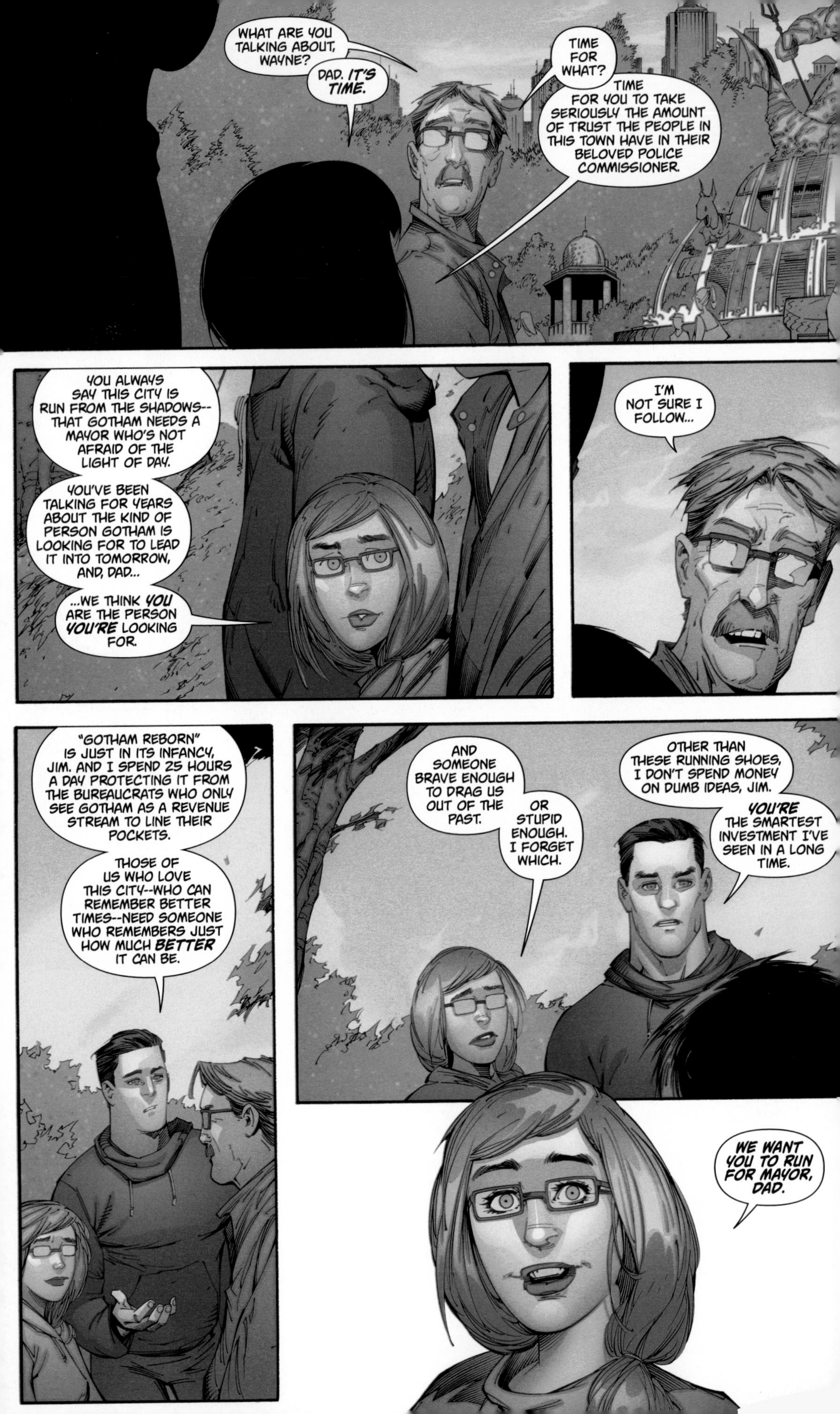
WHAT ARE YOU TALKING ABOUT, WAYNE?
DAD. IT'S TIME.
TIME FOR WHAT?
TIME FOR YOU TO TAKE SERIOUSLY THE AMOUNT OF TRUST THE PEOPLE IN THIS TOWN HAVE IN THEIR BELOVED POLICE COMMISSIONER.
YOU ALWAYS SAY THIS CITY IS RUN FROM THE SHADOWS--THAT GOTHAM NEEDS A MAYOR WHO'S NOT AFRAID OF THE LIGHT OF DAY.
YOU'VE BEEN TALKING FOR YEARS ABOUT THE KIND OF PERSON GOTHAM IS LOOKING FOR TO LEAD IT INTO TOMORROW, AND, DAD...
...WE THINK YOU ARE THE PERSON YOU'RE LOOKING FOR.
I'M NOT SURE I FOLLOW...
"GOTHAM REBORN" IS JUST IN ITS INFANCY, JIM. AND I SPEND 25 HOURS A DAY PROTECTING IT FROM THE BUREAUCRATS WHO ONLY SEE GOTHAM AS A REVENUE STREAM TO LINE THEIR POCKETS.
THOSE OF US WHO LOVE THIS CITY--WHO CAN REMEMBER BETTER TIMES--NEED SOMEONE WHO REMEMBERS JUST HOW MUCH BETTER IT CAN BE.
AND SOMEONE BRAVE ENOUGH TO DRAG US OUT OF THE PAST.
OR STUPID ENOUGH. I FORGET WHICH.
OTHER THAN THESE RUNNING SHOES, I DON'T SPEND MONEY ON DUMB IDEAS, JIM.
YOU'RE THE SMARTEST INVESTMENT I'VE SEEN IN A LONG TIME.
WE WANT YOU TO RUN FOR MAYOR, DAD.

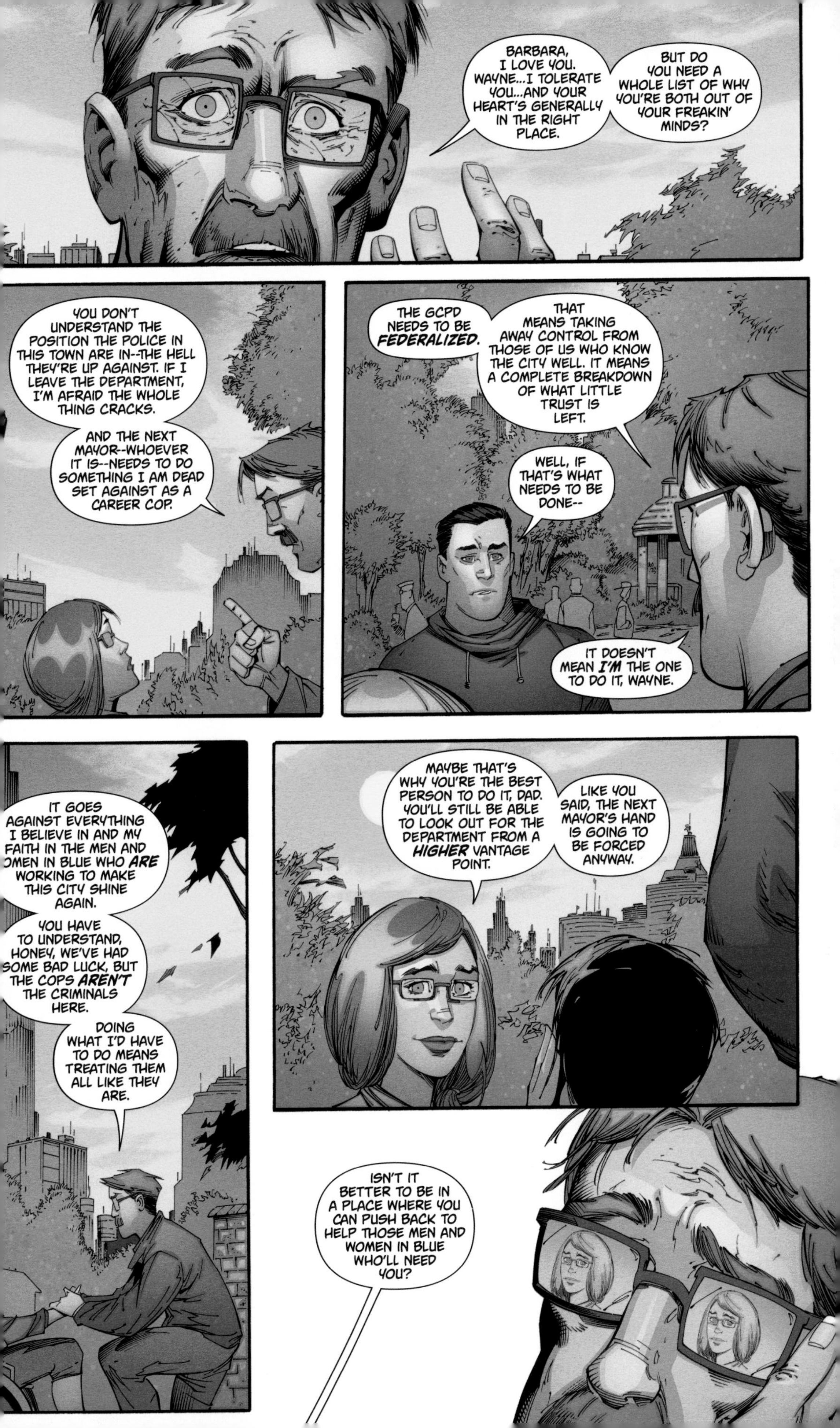
BARBARA, I LOVE YOU. WAYNE...I TOLERATE YOU...AND YOUR HEART'S GENERALLY IN THE RIGHT PLACE.
BUT DO YOU NEED A WHOLE LIST OF WHY YOU'RE BOTH OUT OF YOUR FREAKIN' MINDS?
YOU DON'T UNDERSTAND THE POSITION THE POLICE IN THIS TOWN ARE IN--THE HELL THEY'RE UP AGAINST. IF I LEAVE THE DEPARTMENT, I'M AFRAID THE WHOLE THING CRACKS.
AND THE NEXT MAYOR--WHOEVER IT IS--NEEDS TO DO SOMETHING I AM DEAD SET AGAINST AS A CAREER COP.
THE GCPD NEEDS TO BE FEDERALIZED.
THAT MEANS TAKING AWAY CONTROL FROM THOSE OF US WHO KNOW THE CITY WELL. IT MEANS A COMPLETE BREAKDOWN OF WHAT LITTLE TRUST IS LEFT.
WELL, IF THAT'S WHAT NEEDS TO BE DONE--
IT DOESN'T MEAN I'M THE ONE TO DO IT, WAYNE.
IT GOES AGAINST EVERYTHING I BELIEVE IN AND MY FAITH IN THE MEN AND OMEN IN BLUE WHO ARE WORKING TO MAKE THIS CITY SHINE AGAIN.
YOU HAVE TO UNDERSTAND, HONEY, WE'VE HAD SOME BAD LUCK, BUT THE COPS AREN'T THE CRIMINALS HERE.
DOING WHAT I'D HAVE TO DO MEANS TREATING THEM ALL LIKE THEY ARE.
MAYBE THAT'S WHY YOU'RE THE BEST PERSON TO DO IT, DAD. YOU'LL STILL BE ABLE TO LOOK OUT FOR THE DEPARTMENT FROM A HIGHER VANTAGE POINT.
LIKE YOU SAID, THE NEXT MAYOR'S HAND IS GOING TO BE FORCED ANYWAY.
ISN'T IT BETTER TO BE IN A PLACE WHERE YOU CAN PUSH BACK TO HELP THOSE MEN AND WOMEN IN BLUE WHO'LL NEED YOU?

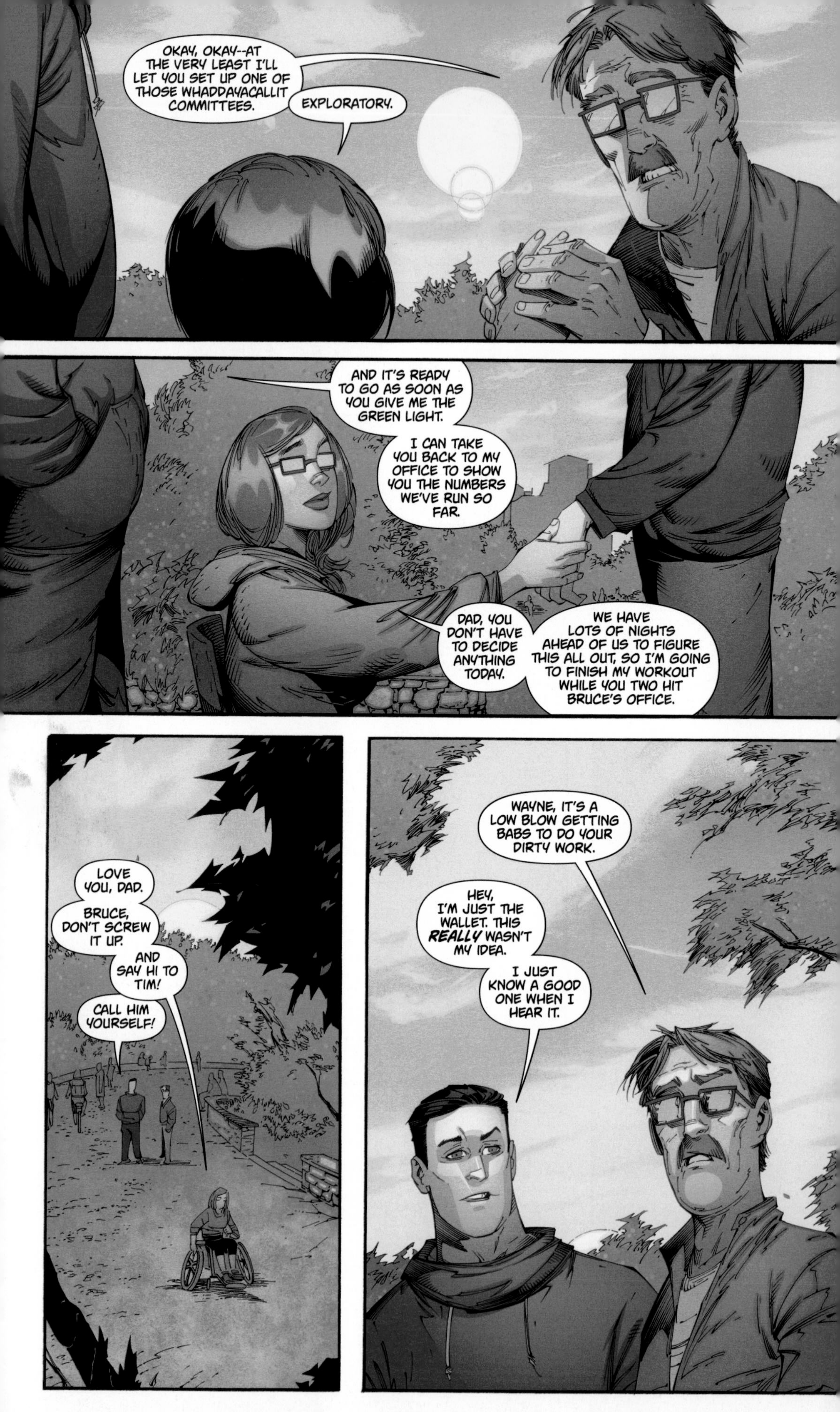
OKAY, OKAY--AT THE VERY LEAST I'LL LET YOU SET UP ONE OF THOSE WHADDAYACALLIT COMMITTEES.
EXPLORATORY.
AND IT'S READY TO GO AS SOON AS YOU GIVE ME THE GREEN LIGHT.
I CAN TAKE YOU BACK TO MY OFFICE TO SHOW YOU THE NUMBERS WE'VE RUN SO FAR.
DAD, YOU DON'T HAVE TO DECIDE ANYTHING TODAY.
WE HAVE LOTS OF NIGHTS AHEAD OF US TO FIGURE THIS ALL OUT, SO I'M GOING TO FINISH MY WORKOUT WHILE YOU TWO HIT BRUCE'S OFFICE.
LOVE YOU, DAD.
BRUCE, DON'T SCREW IT UP.
AND SAY HI TO TIM!
CALL HIM YOURSELF!
WAYNE, IT'S A LOW BLOW GETTING BABS TO DO YOUR DIRTY WORK.
HEY, I'M JUST THE WALLET. THIS *REALLY* WASN'T MY IDEA.
I JUST KNOW A GOOD ONE WHEN I HEAR IT.

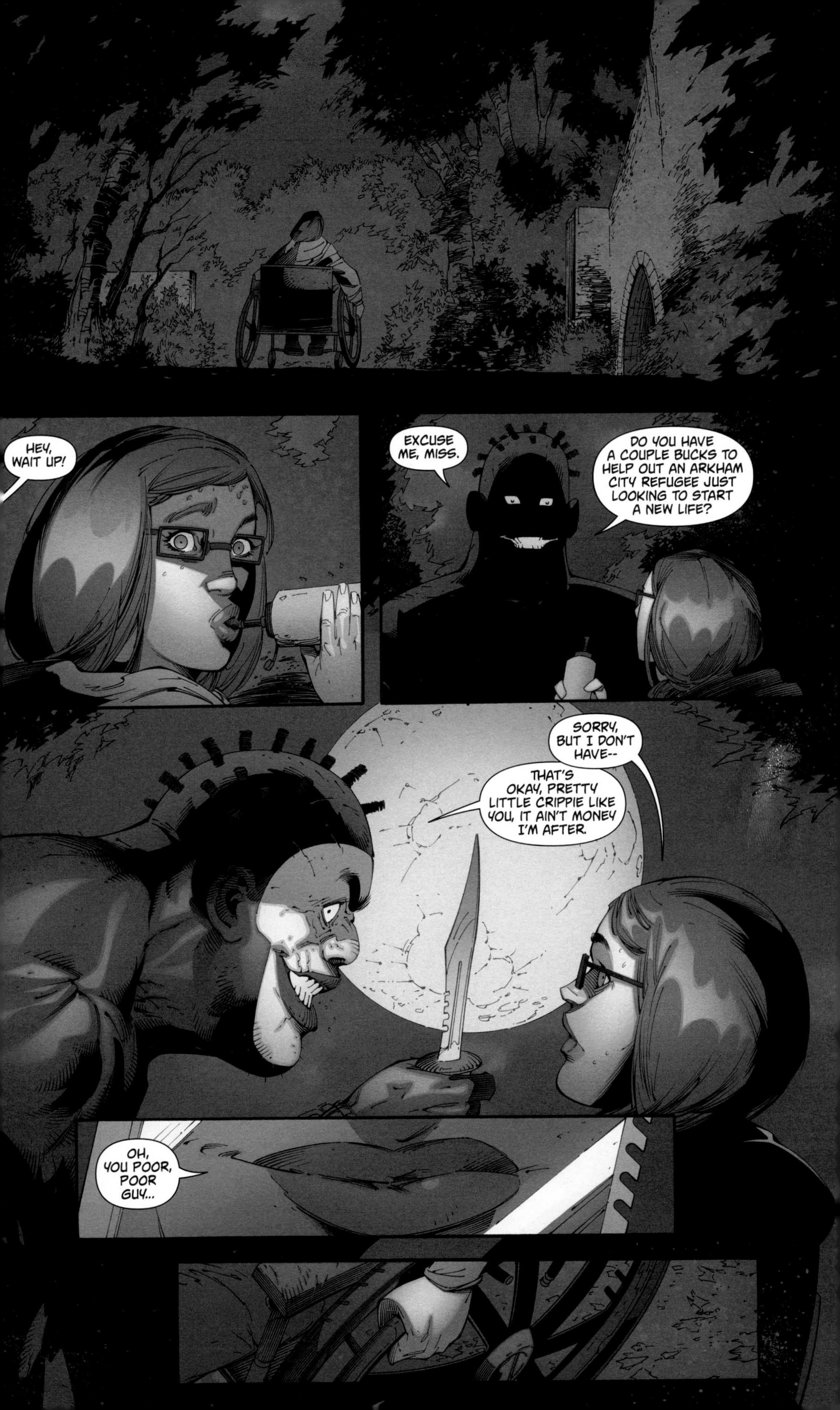
HEY, WAIT UP!
EXCUSE ME, MISS.
DO YOU HAVE A COUPLE BUCKS TO HELP OUT AN ARKHAM CITY REFUGEE JUST LOOKING TO START A NEW LIFE?
SORRY, BUT I DON'T HAVE--
THAT'S OKAY, PRETTY LITTLE CRIPPIE LIKE YOU, IT AIN'T MONEY I'M AFTER.
OH, YOU POOR, POOR GUY...

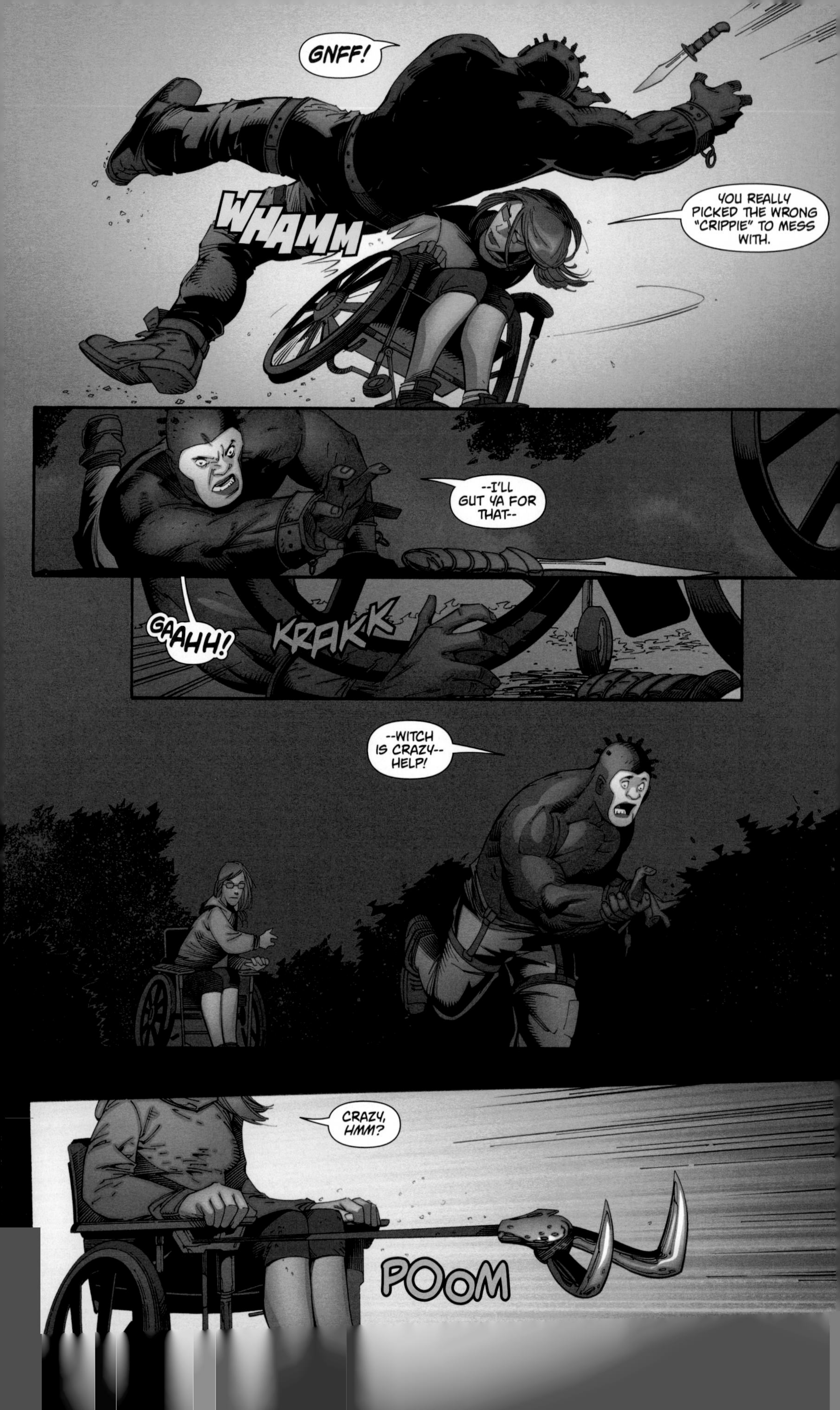
GNFF!
WHAMM
YOU REALLY PICKED THE WRONG "CRIPPIE" TO MESS WITH.
--I'LL GUT YA FOR THAT--
GAAHH!
KRAKK
--WITCH IS CRAZY-- HELP!
CRAZY, HMM?
POOM

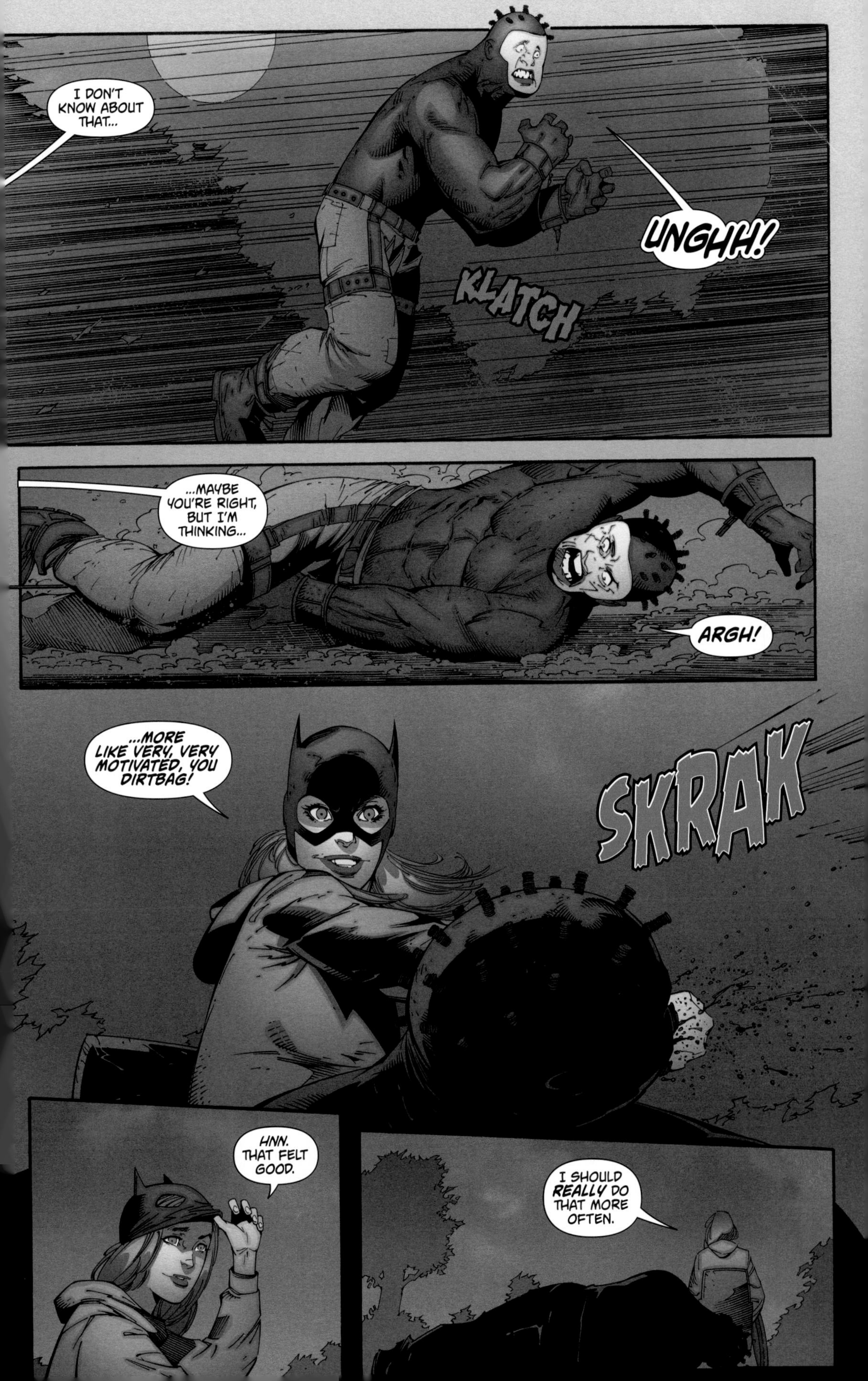
I DON'T KNOW ABOUT THAT...
UNGHH!
KLATCH
...MAYBE YOU'RE RIGHT, BUT I'M THINKING...
ARGH!
...MORE LIKE VERY, VERY MOTIVATED, YOU DIRTBAG!
SKRAK
HNN. THAT FELT GOOD.
I SHOULD REALLY DO THAT MORE OFTEN.

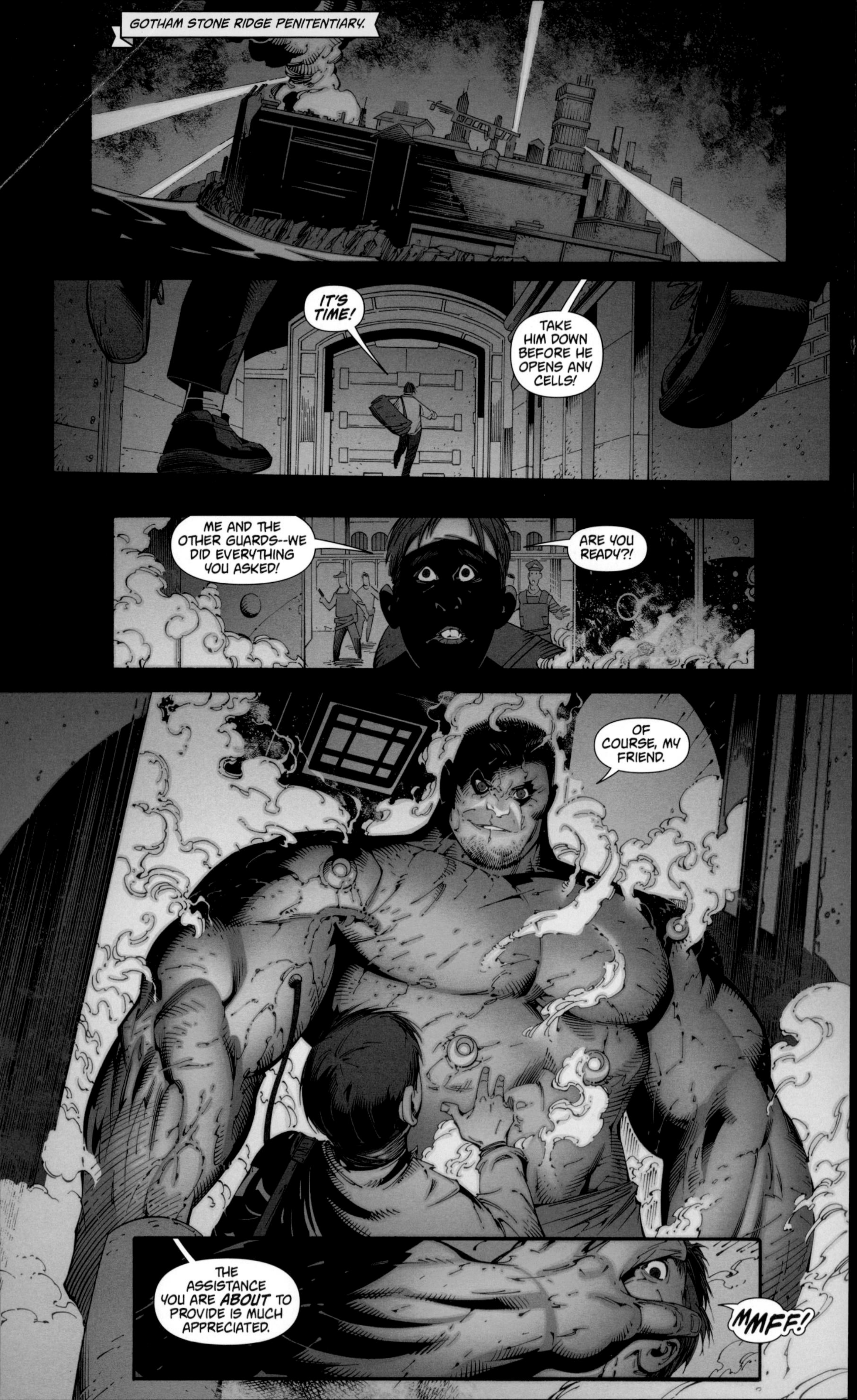
GOTHAM STONE RIDGE PENITENTIARY.
IT'S TIME!
TAKE HIM DOWN BEFORE HE OPENS ANY CELLS!
ME AND THE OTHER GUARDS--WE DID EVERYTHING YOU ASKED!
ARE YOU READY?!
OF COURSE, MY FRIEND.
THE ASSISTANCE YOU ARE ABOUT TO PROVIDE IS MUCH APPRECIATED.
MMFF!

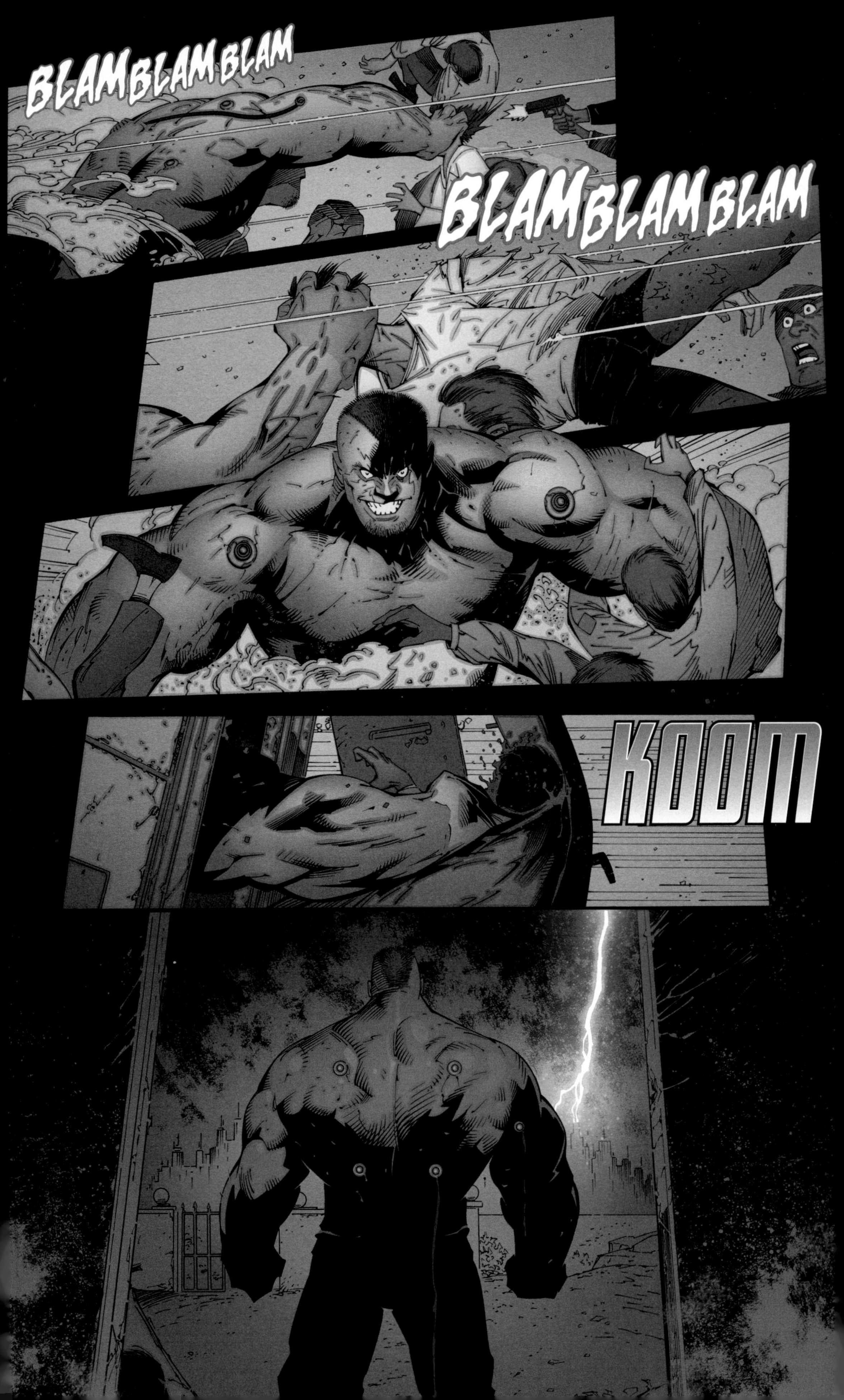
BLAM BLAM BLAM
BLAM BLAM BLAM
KOOM

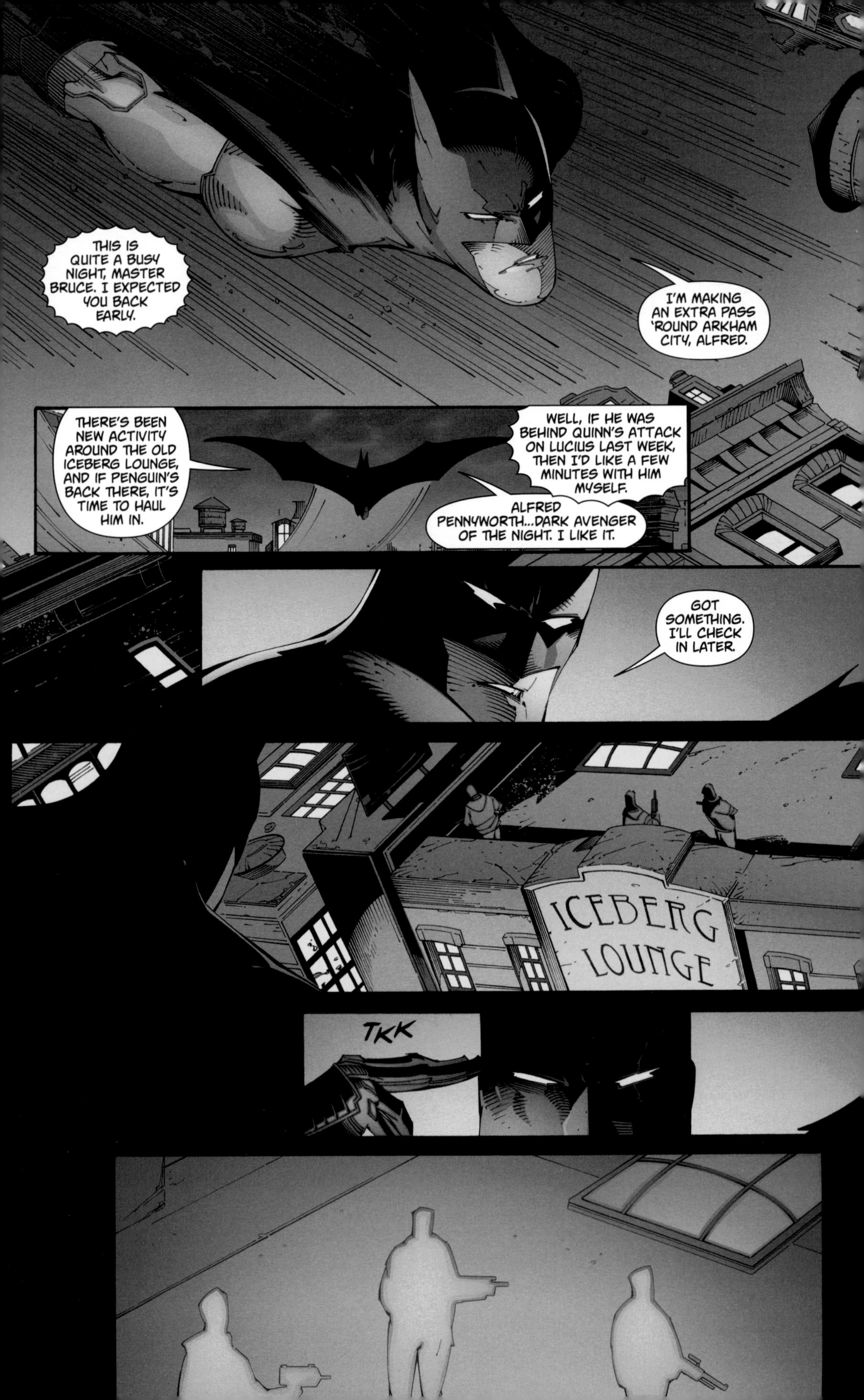
THIS IS QUITE A BUSY NIGHT, MASTER BRUCE. I EXPECTED YOU BACK EARLY.
I'M MAKING AN EXTRA PASS 'ROUND ARKHAM CITY, ALFRED.
THERE'S BEEN NEW ACTIVITY AROUND THE OLD ICEBERG LOUNGE, AND IF PENGUIN'S BACK THERE, IT'S TIME TO HAUL HIM IN.
WELL, IF HE WAS BEHIND QUINN'S ATTACK ON LUCIUS LAST WEEK, THEN I'D LIKE A FEW MINUTES WITH HIM MYSELF.
ALFRED PENNYWORTH...DARK AVENGER OF THE NIGHT. I LIKE IT.
GOT SOMETHING. I'LL CHECK IN LATER.
ICEBERG LOUNGE
TKK

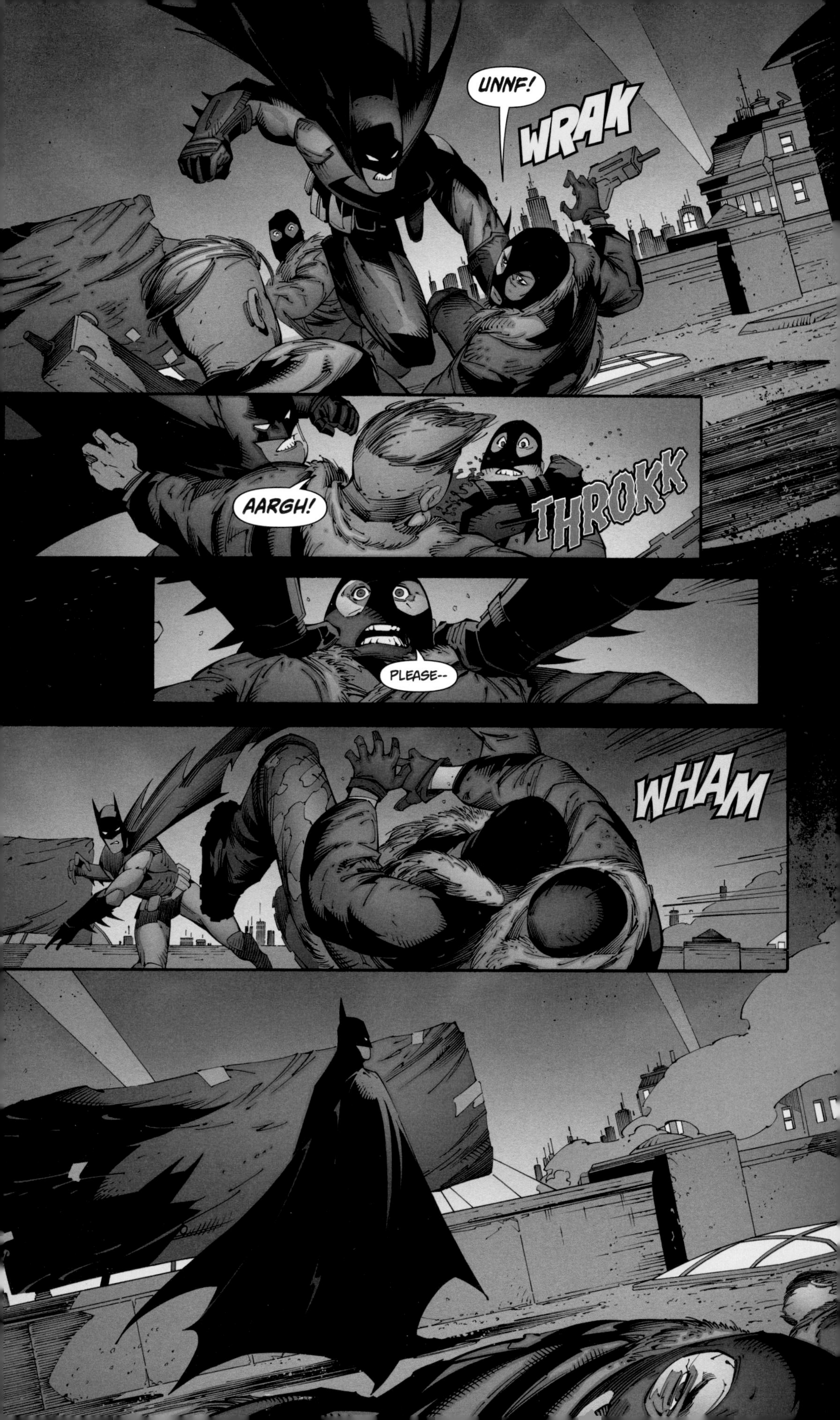
UNNF!
WRAK
AARGH!
THROKK
PLEASE--
WHAM

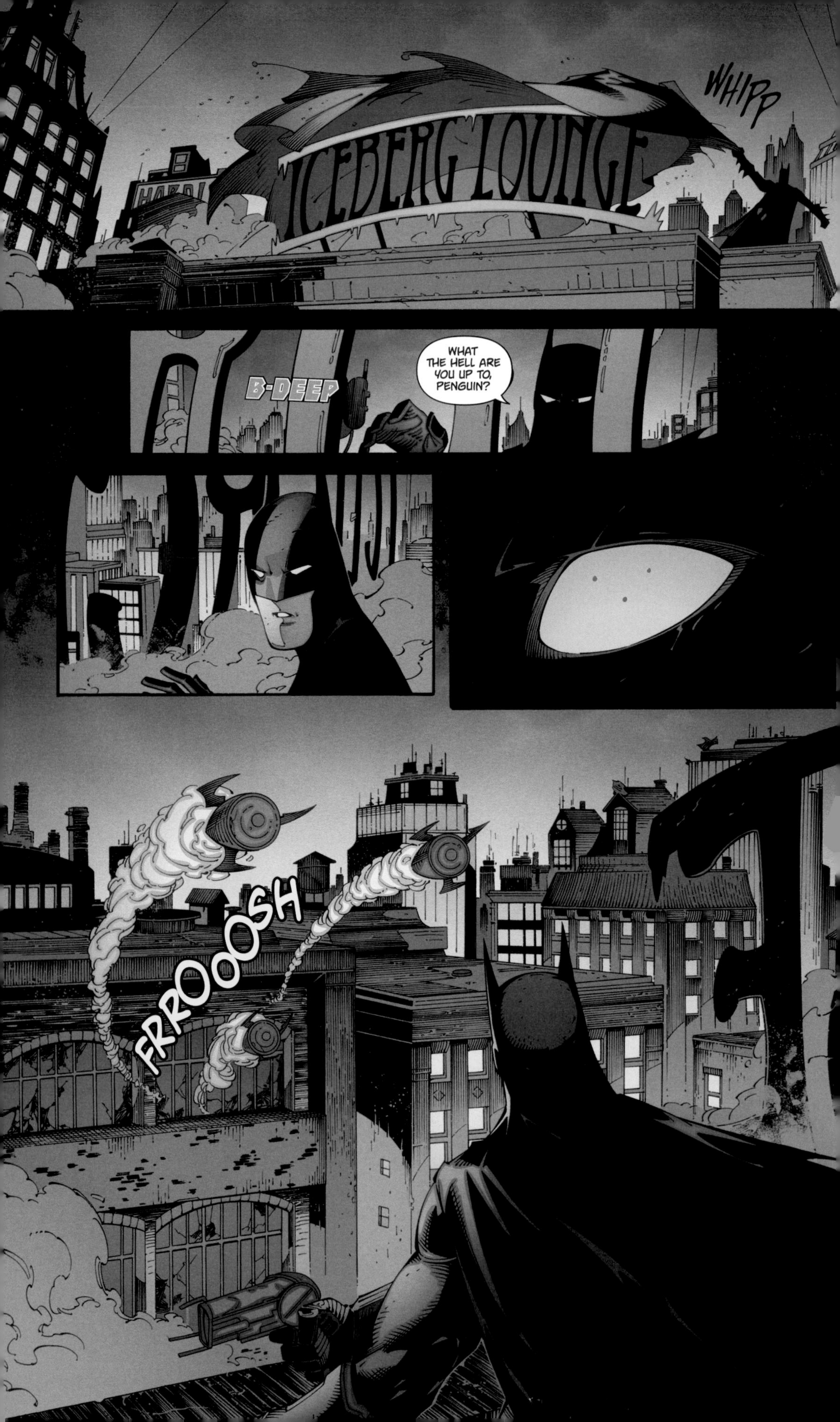
ICEBERG LOUNGE
WHIPP
B-DEEP
WHAT THE HELL ARE YOU UP TO, PENGUIN?
FRROOOSH

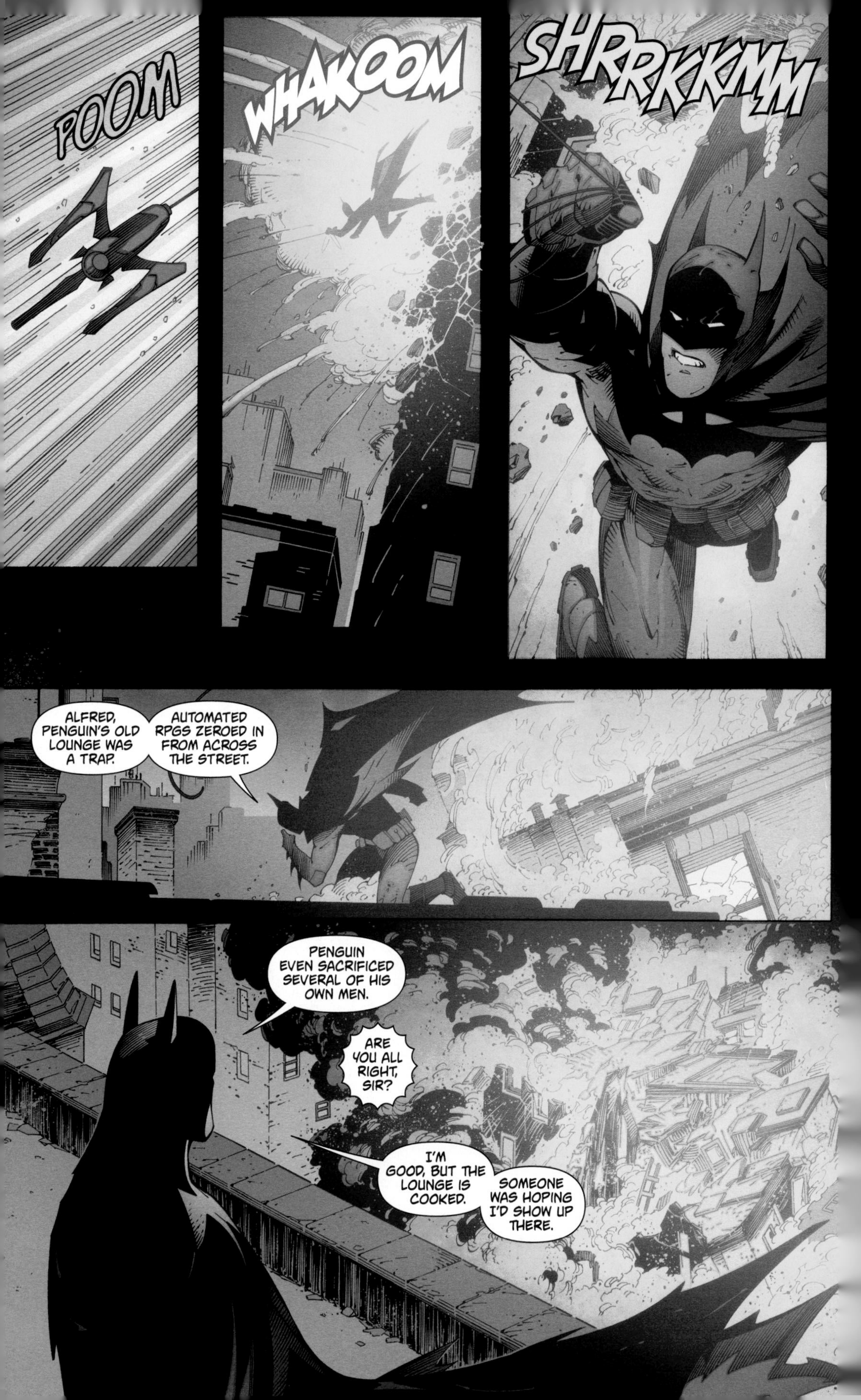
POOM
WHAKOOM
SHRRKKMM
ALFRED, PENGUIN'S OLD LOUNGE WAS A TRAP.
AUTOMATED RPGS ZEROED IN FROM ACROSS THE STREET.
PENGUIN EVEN SACRIFICED SEVERAL OF HIS OWN MEN.
ARE YOU ALL RIGHT, SIR?
I'M GOOD, BUT THE LOUNGE IS COOKED.
SOMEONE WAS HOPING I'D SHOW UP THERE.

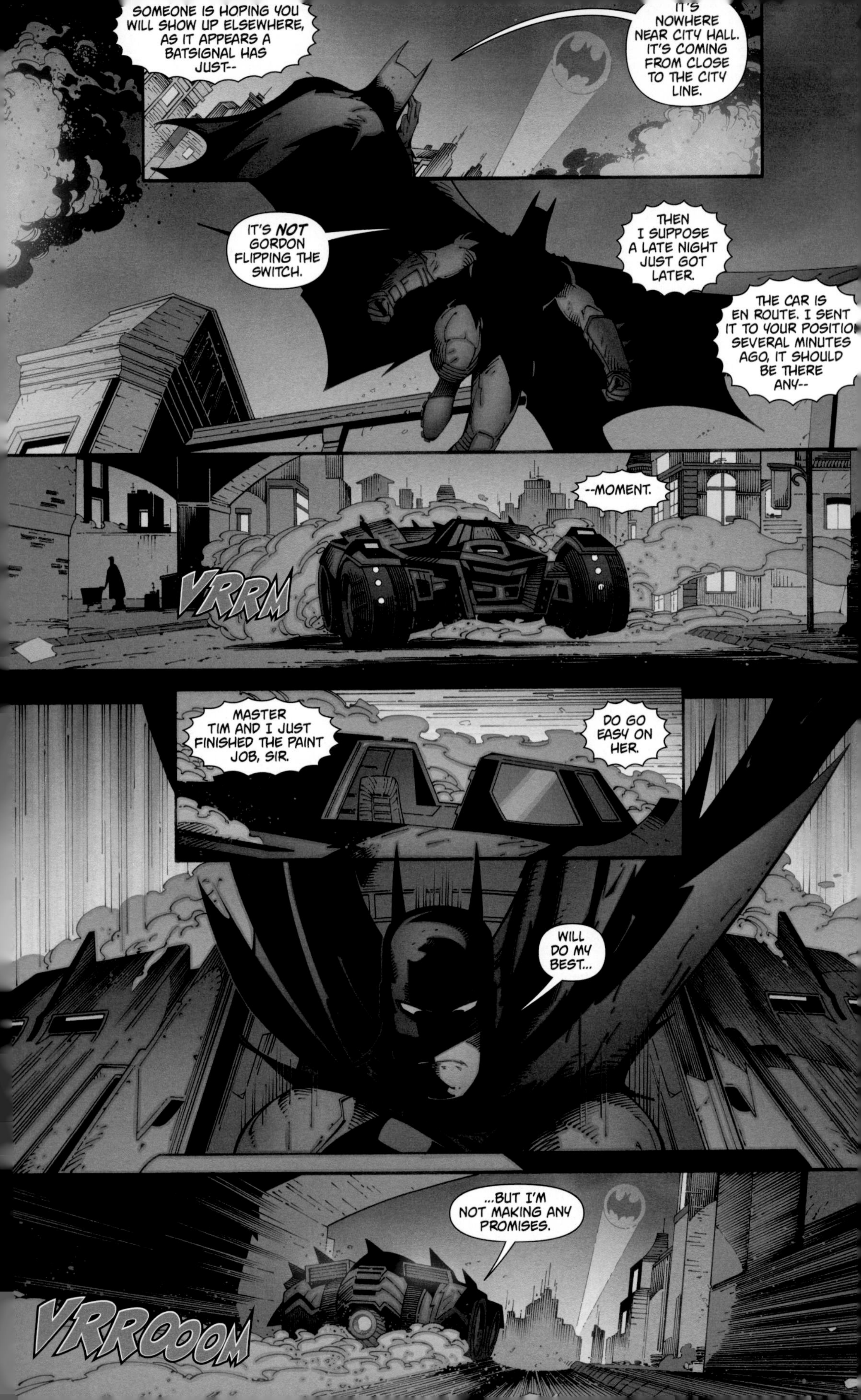
SOMEONE IS HOPING YOU WILL SHOW UP ELSEWHERE, AS IT APPEARS A BATSIGNAL HAS JUST--
IT'S NOWHERE NEAR CITY HALL. IT'S COMING FROM CLOSE TO THE CITY LINE.
IT'S NOT GORDON FLIPPING THE SWITCH.
THEN I SUPPOSE A LATE NIGHT JUST GOT LATER.
THE CAR IS EN ROUTE. I SENT IT TO YOUR POSITIO SEVERAL MINUTES AGO, IT SHOULD BE THERE ANY--
--MOMENT.
VRRM
MASTER TIM AND I JUST FINISHED THE PAINT JOB, SIR.
DO GO EASY ON HER.
WILL DO MY BEST...
...BUT I'M NOT MAKING ANY PROMISES.
VRROOOM

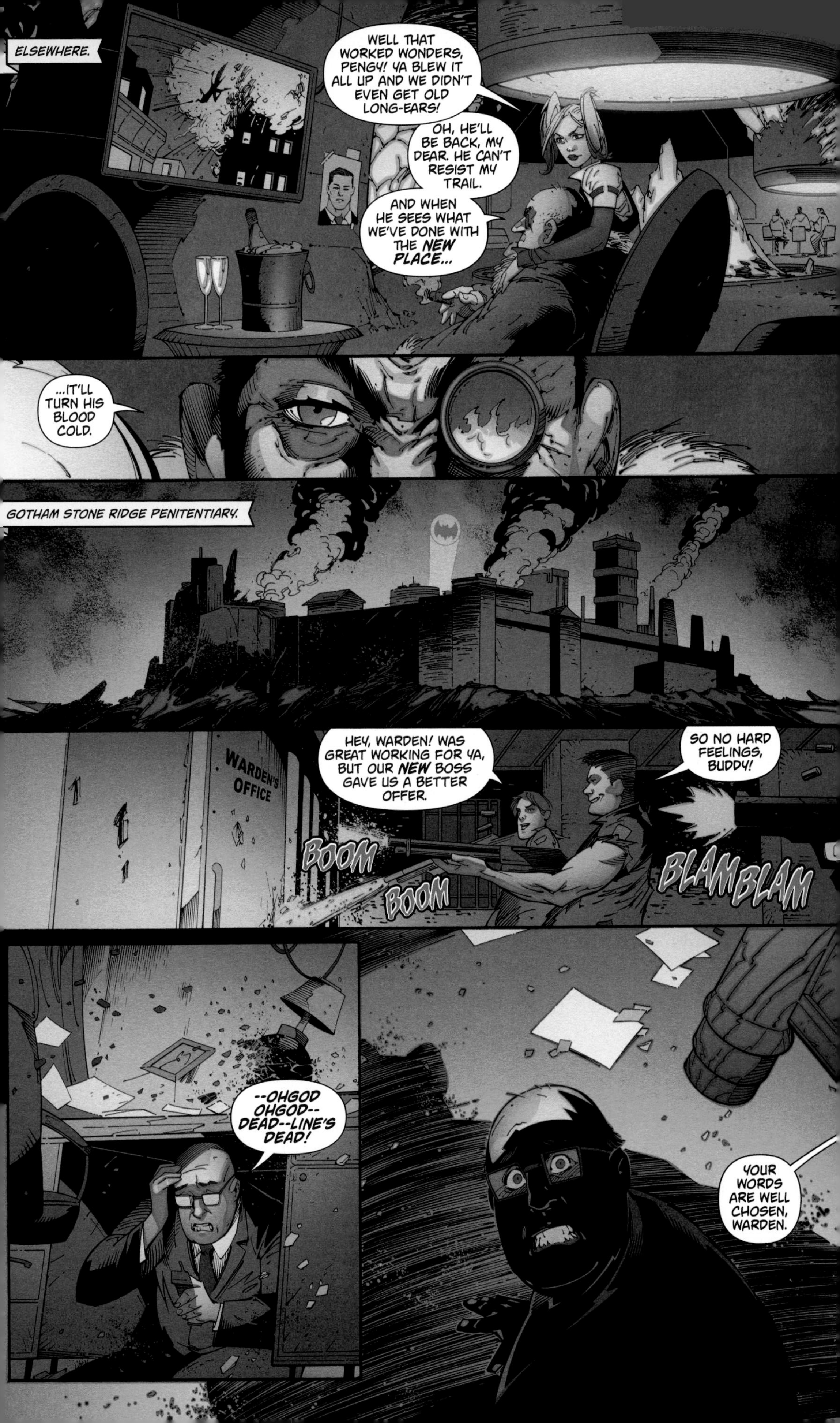
ELSEWHERE.
WELL THAT WORKED WONDERS, PENGY! YA BLEW IT ALL UP AND WE DIDN'T EVEN GET OLD LONG-EARS!
OH, HE'LL BE BACK, MY DEAR. HE CAN'T RESIST MY TRAIL.
AND WHEN HE SEES WHAT WE'VE DONE WITH THE NEW PLACE...
...IT'LL TURN HIS BLOOD COLD.
GOTHAM STONE RIDGE PENITENTIARY.
WARDEN'S OFFICE
HEY, WARDEN! WAS GREAT WORKING FOR YA, BUT OUR NEW BOSS GAVE US A BETTER OFFER.
SO NO HARD FEELINGS, BUDDY!
BOOM
BOOM
BLAMBLAM
--OHGOD OHGOD--DEAD--LINE'S DEAD!
YOUR WORDS ARE WELL CHOSEN, WARDEN.

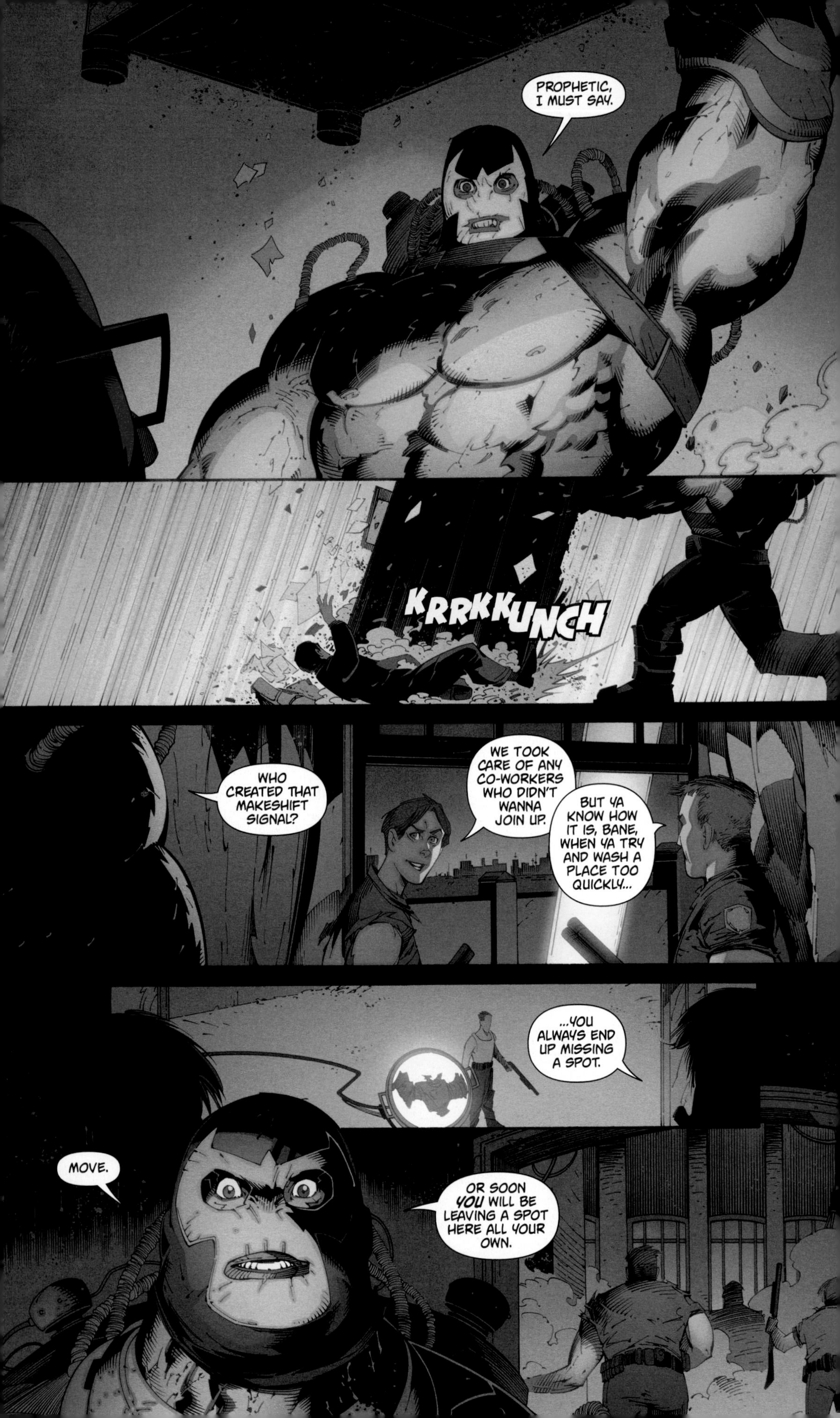
PROPHETIC, I MUST SAY.
KRRKKUNCH
WHO CREATED THAT MAKESHIFT SIGNAL?
WE TOOK CARE OF ANY CO-WORKERS WHO DIDN'T WANNA JOIN UP.
BUT YA KNOW HOW IT IS, BANE, WHEN YA TRY AND WASH A PLACE TOO QUICKLY...
...YOU ALWAYS END UP MISSING A SPOT.
MOVE.
OR SOON YOU WILL BE LEAVING A SPOT HERE ALL YOUR OWN.

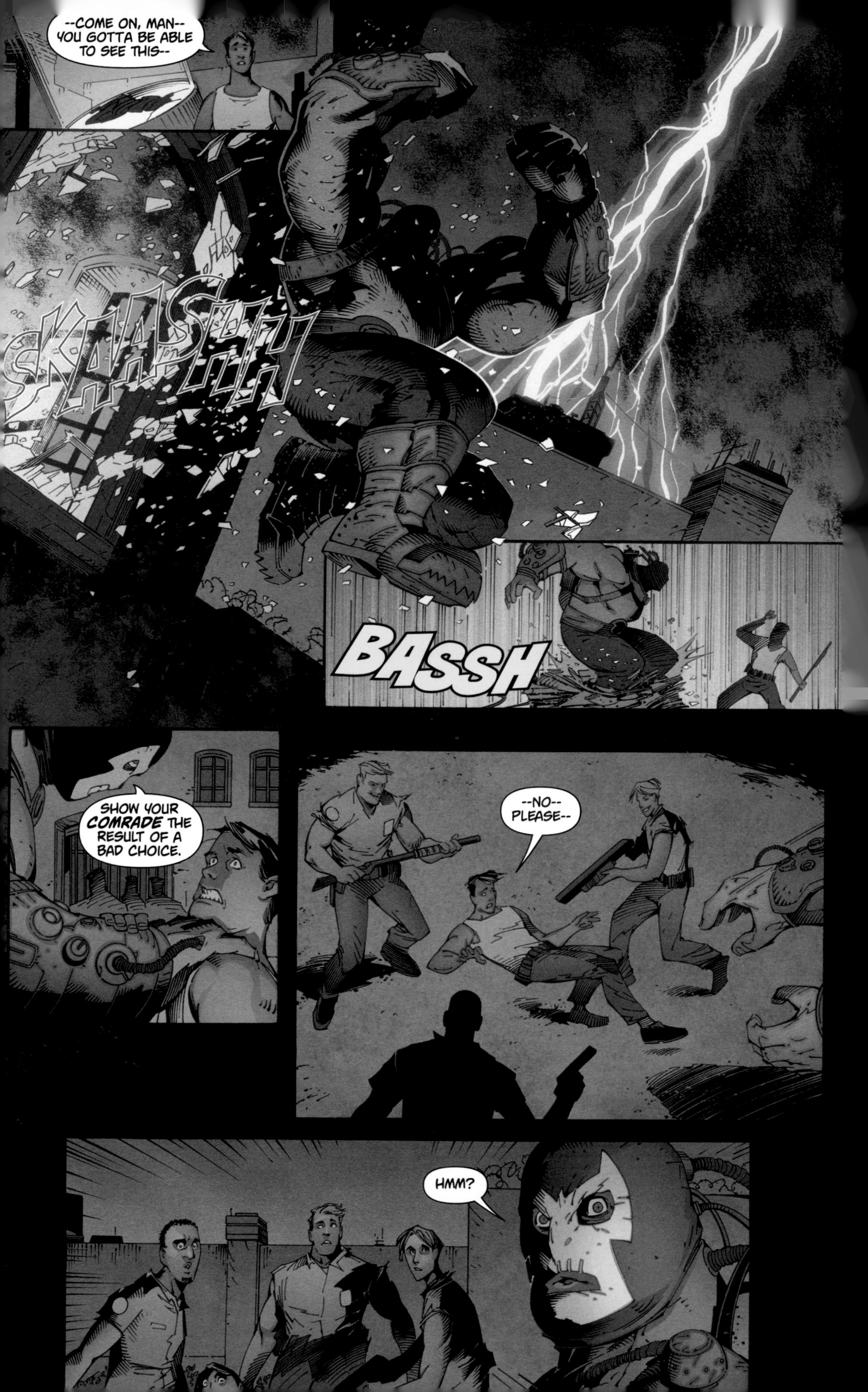
--COME ON, MAN-- YOU GOTTA BE ABLE TO SEE THIS--
SKAASHH
BASSH
SHOW YOUR COMRADE THE RESULT OF A BAD CHOICE.
--NO-- PLEASE--
HMM?

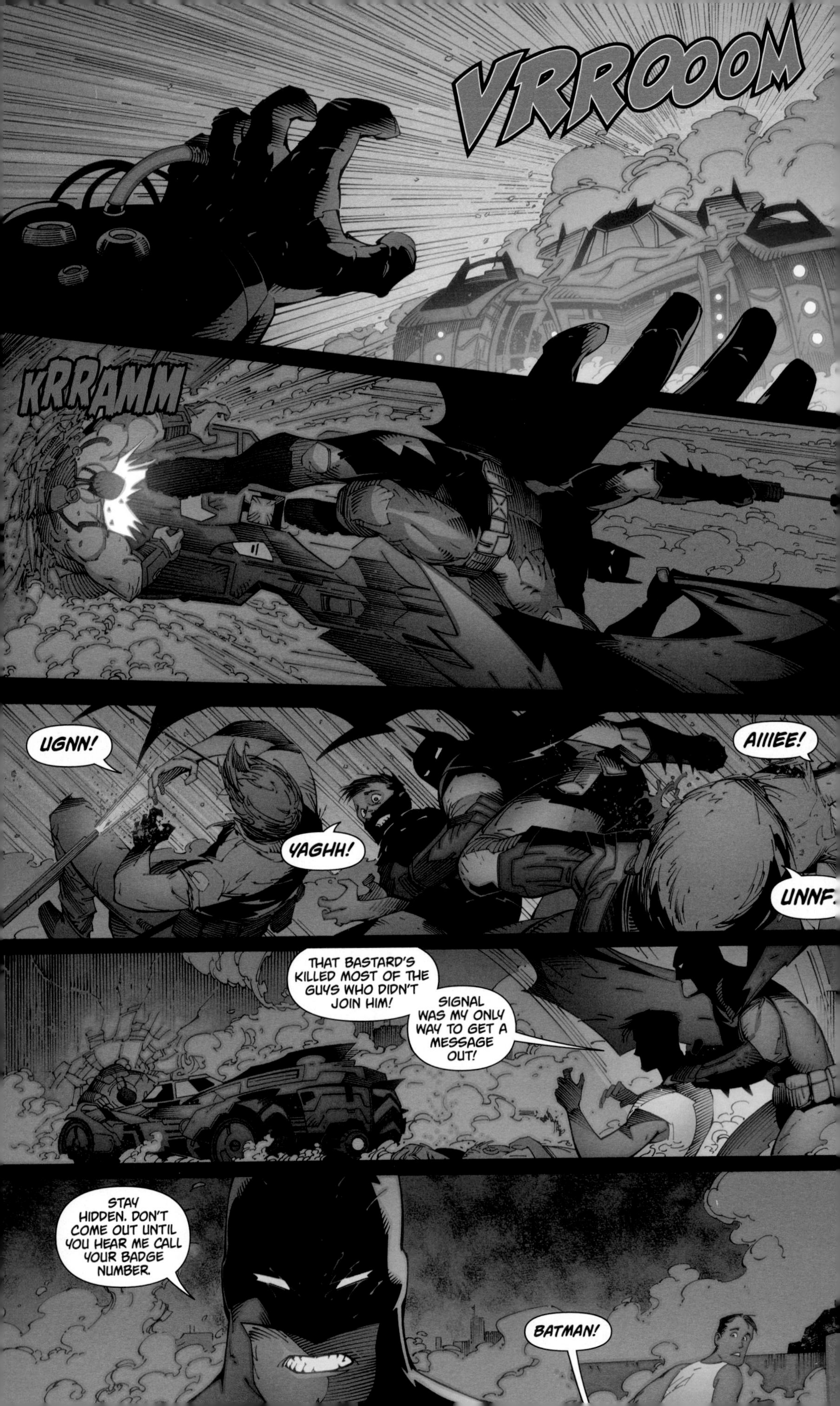
VRROOOM
KRRAMM
UGNN!
YAGHH!
AIIIEE!
UNNF.
THAT BASTARD'S KILLED MOST OF THE GUYS WHO DIDN'T JOIN HIM!
SIGNAL WAS MY ONLY WAY TO GET A MESSAGE OUT!
STAY HIDDEN. DON'T COME OUT UNTIL YOU HEAR ME CALL YOUR BADGE NUMBER.
BATMAN!

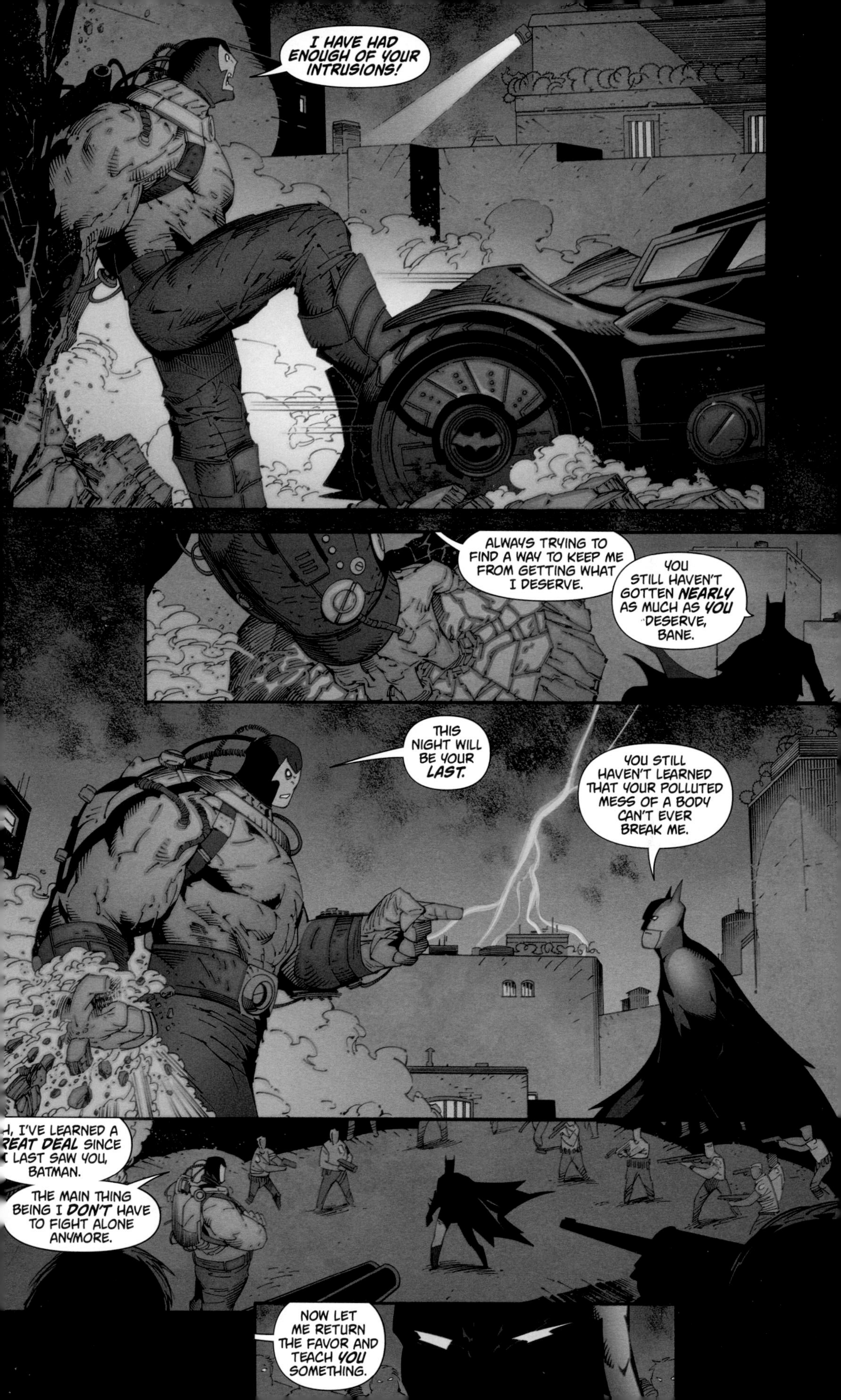
I HAVE HAD ENOUGH OF YOUR INTRUSIONS!
ALWAYS TRYING TO FIND A WAY TO KEEP ME FROM GETTING WHAT I DESERVE.
YOU STILL HAVEN'T GOTTEN NEARLY AS MUCH AS YOU DESERVE, BANE.
THIS NIGHT WILL BE YOUR LAST.
YOU STILL HAVEN'T LEARNED THAT YOUR POLLUTED MESS OF A BODY CAN'T EVER BREAK ME.
H, I'VE LEARNED A REAT DEAL SINCE LAST SAW YOU, BATMAN.
THE MAIN THING BEING I DON'T HAVE TO FIGHT ALONE ANYMORE.
NOW LET ME RETURN THE FAVOR AND TEACH YOU SOMETHING.

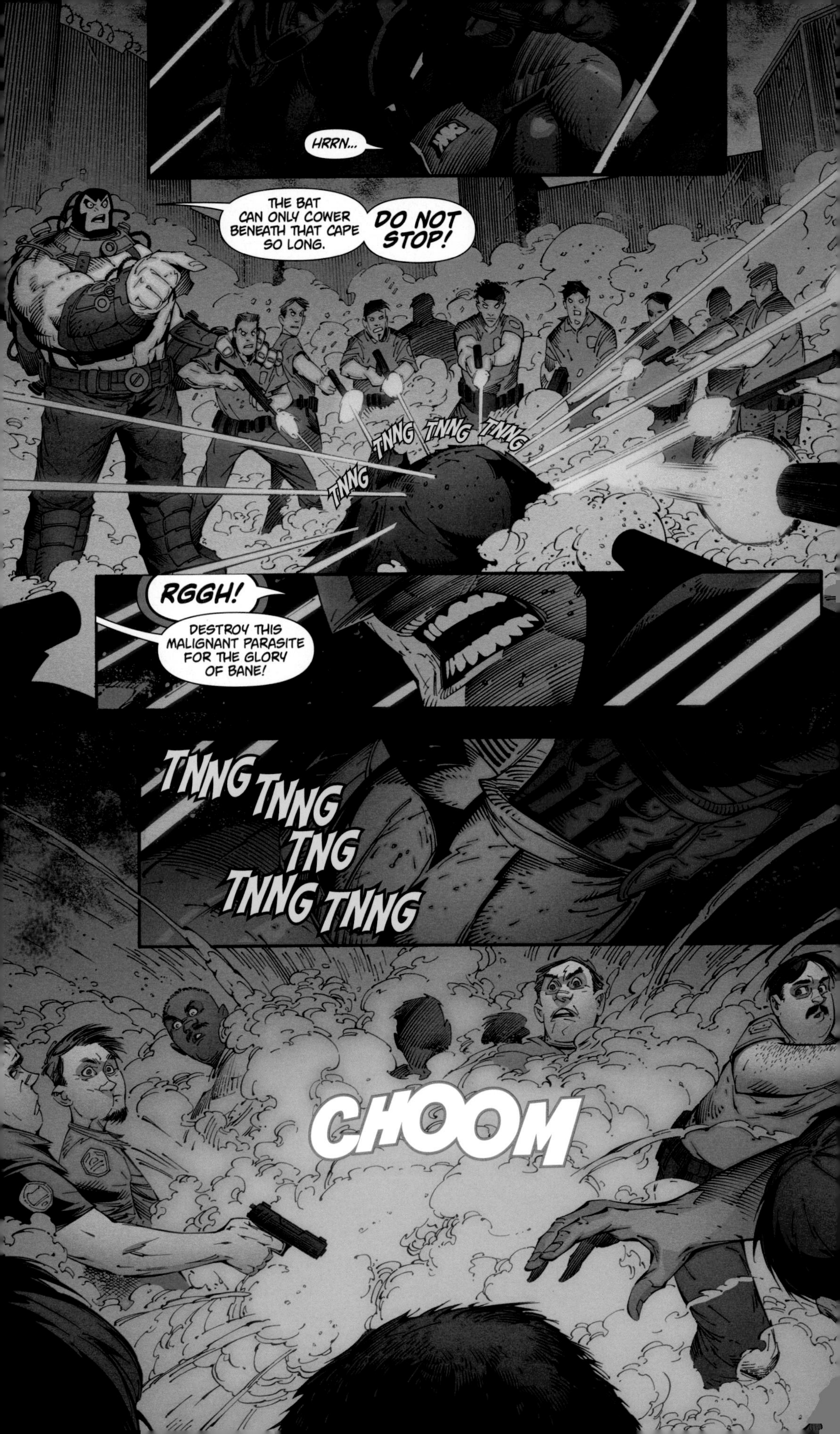
HRRN...
THE BAT CAN ONLY COWER BENEATH THAT CAPE SO LONG.
DO NOT STOP!
TNNG TNNG TNNG
TNNG
RGGH!
DESTROY THIS MALIGNANT PARASITE FOR THE GLORY OF BANE!
TNNG TNNG TNG TNNG TNNG
CHOOM

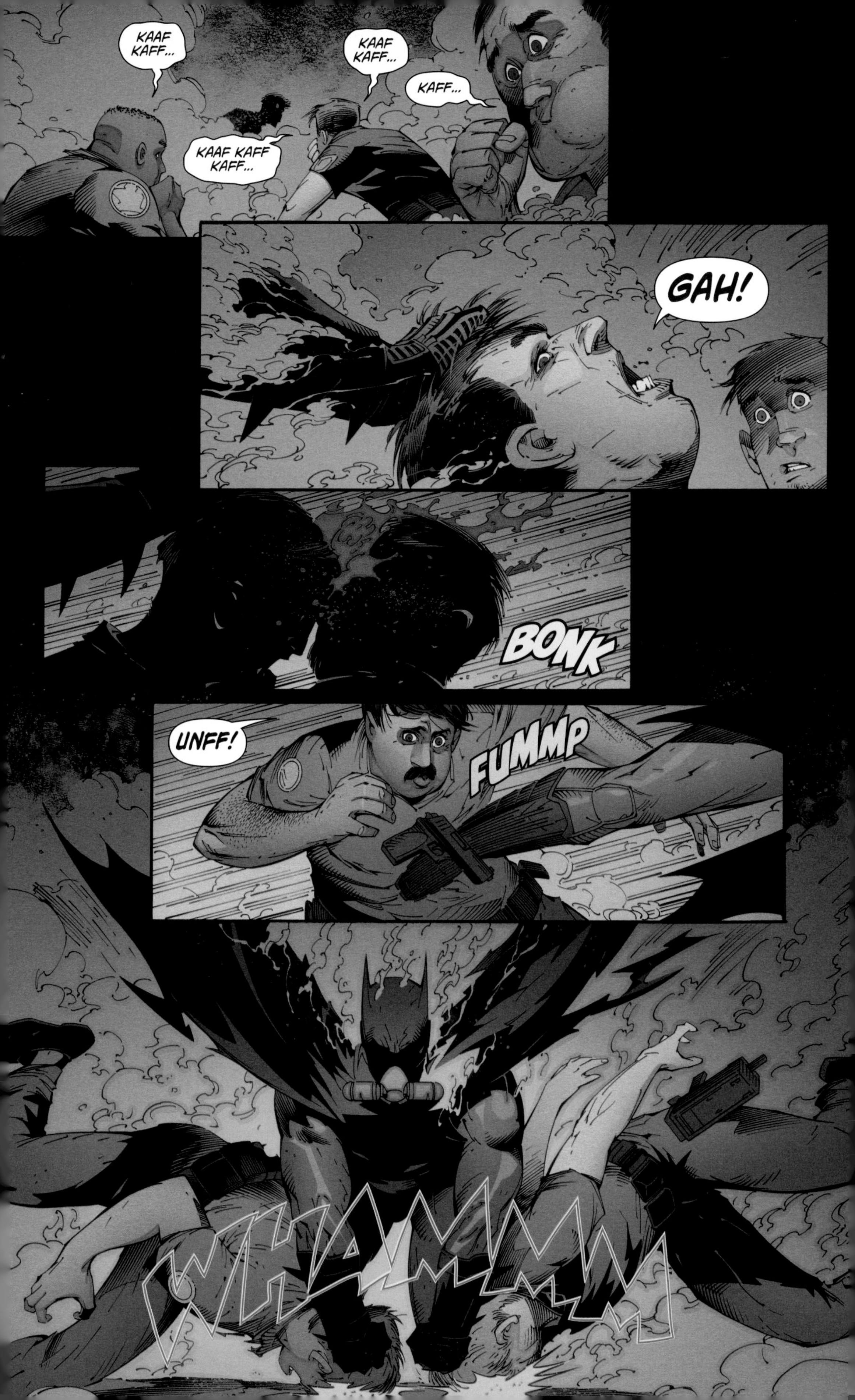
KAAF KAFF...
KAAF KAFF...
KAFF...
KAAF KAFF KAFF...
GAH!
BONK
UNFF!
FUMMP
WHAMMM

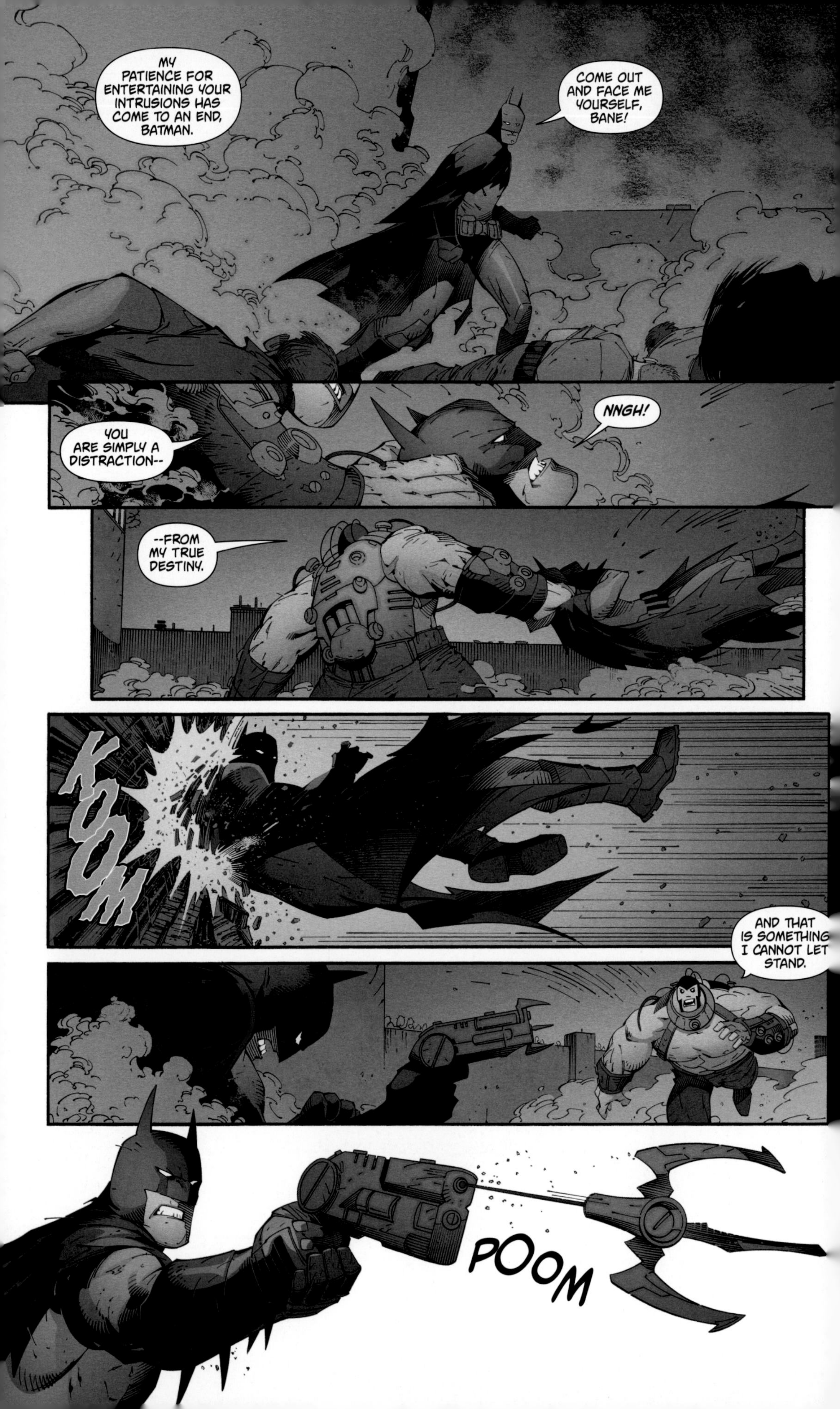

MY PATIENCE FOR ENTERTAINING YOUR INTRUSIONS HAS COME TO AN END, BATMAN.
COME OUT AND FACE ME YOURSELF, BANE!
YOU ARE SIMPLY A DISTRACTION--
NNGH!
--FROM MY TRUE DESTINY.
KOOM
AND THAT IS SOMETHING I CANNOT LET STAND.
POOM

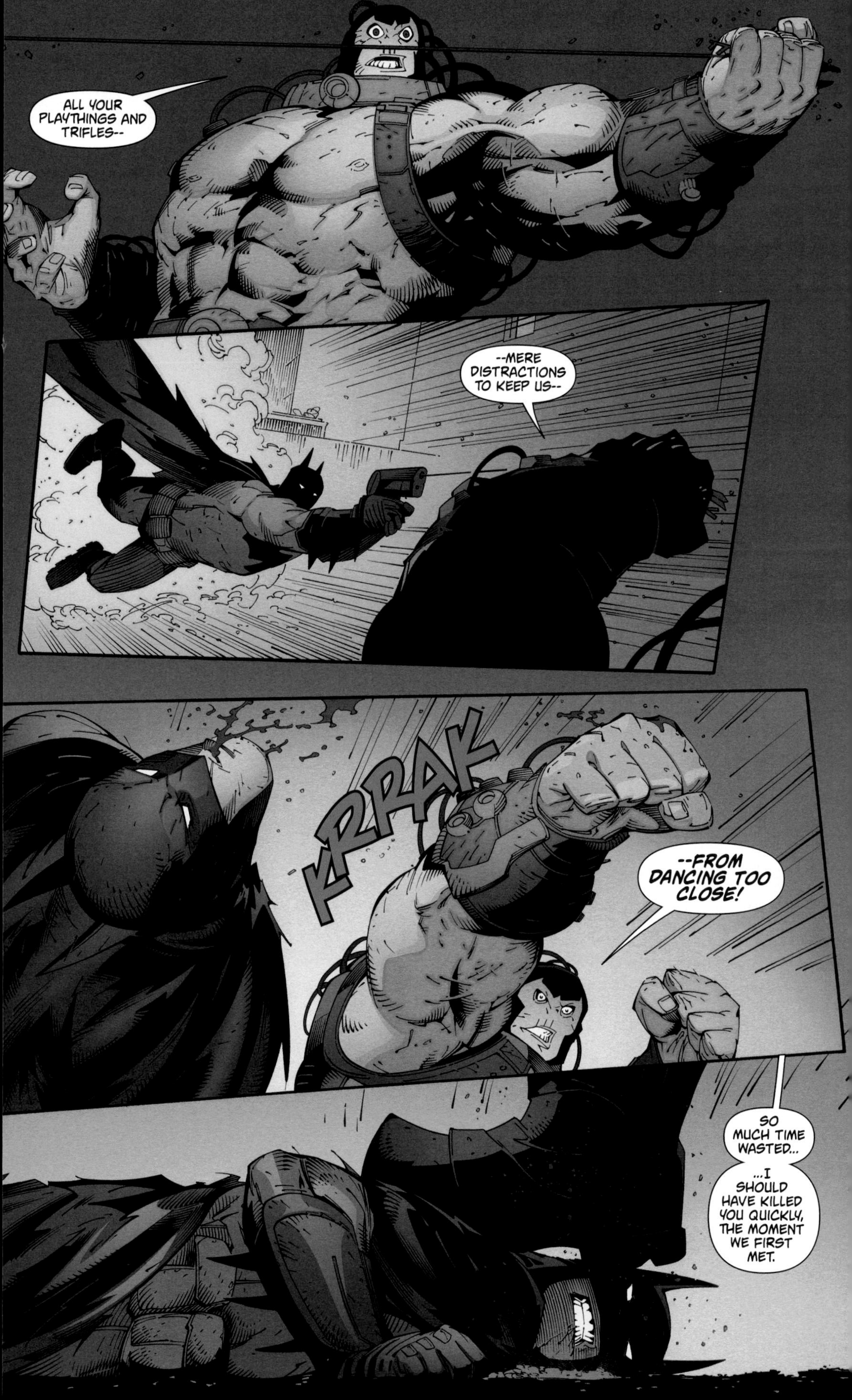
ALL YOUR PLAYTHINGS AND TRIFLES--
--MERE DISTRACTIONS TO KEEP US--
KRRAK
--FROM DANCING TOO CLOSE!
SO MUCH TIME WASTED...
...I SHOULD HAVE KILLED YOU QUICKLY, THE MOMENT WE FIRST MET.

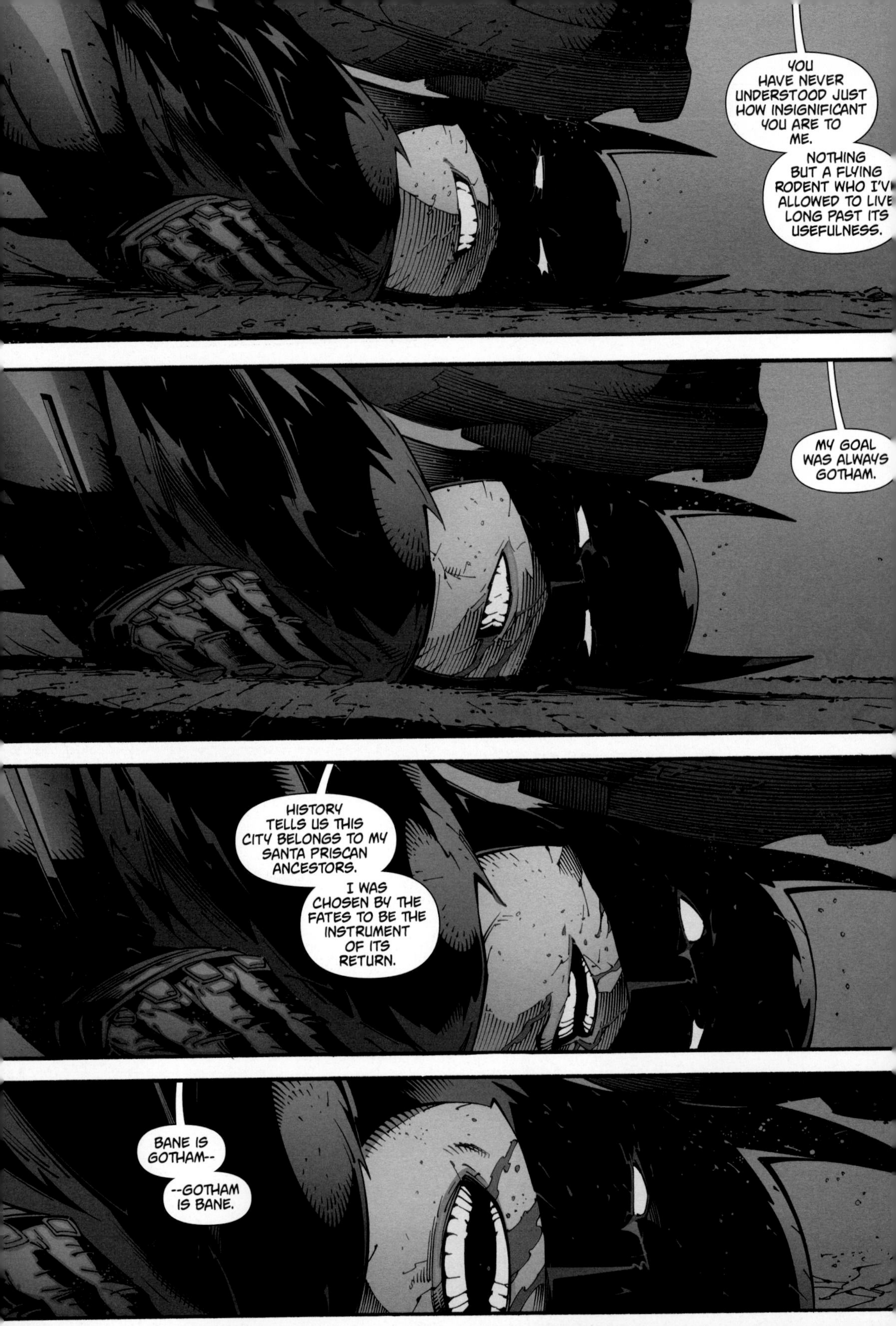
YOU HAVE NEVER UNDERSTOOD JUST HOW INSIGNIFICANT YOU ARE TO ME.
NOTHING BUT A FLYING RODENT WHO I'VE ALLOWED TO LIVE LONG PAST ITS USEFULNESS.
MY GOAL WAS ALWAYS GOTHAM.
HISTORY TELLS US THIS CITY BELONGS TO MY SANTA PRISCAN ANCESTORS.
I WAS CHOSEN BY THE FATES TO BE THE INSTRUMENT OF ITS RETURN.
BANE IS GOTHAM--
--GOTHAM IS BANE.

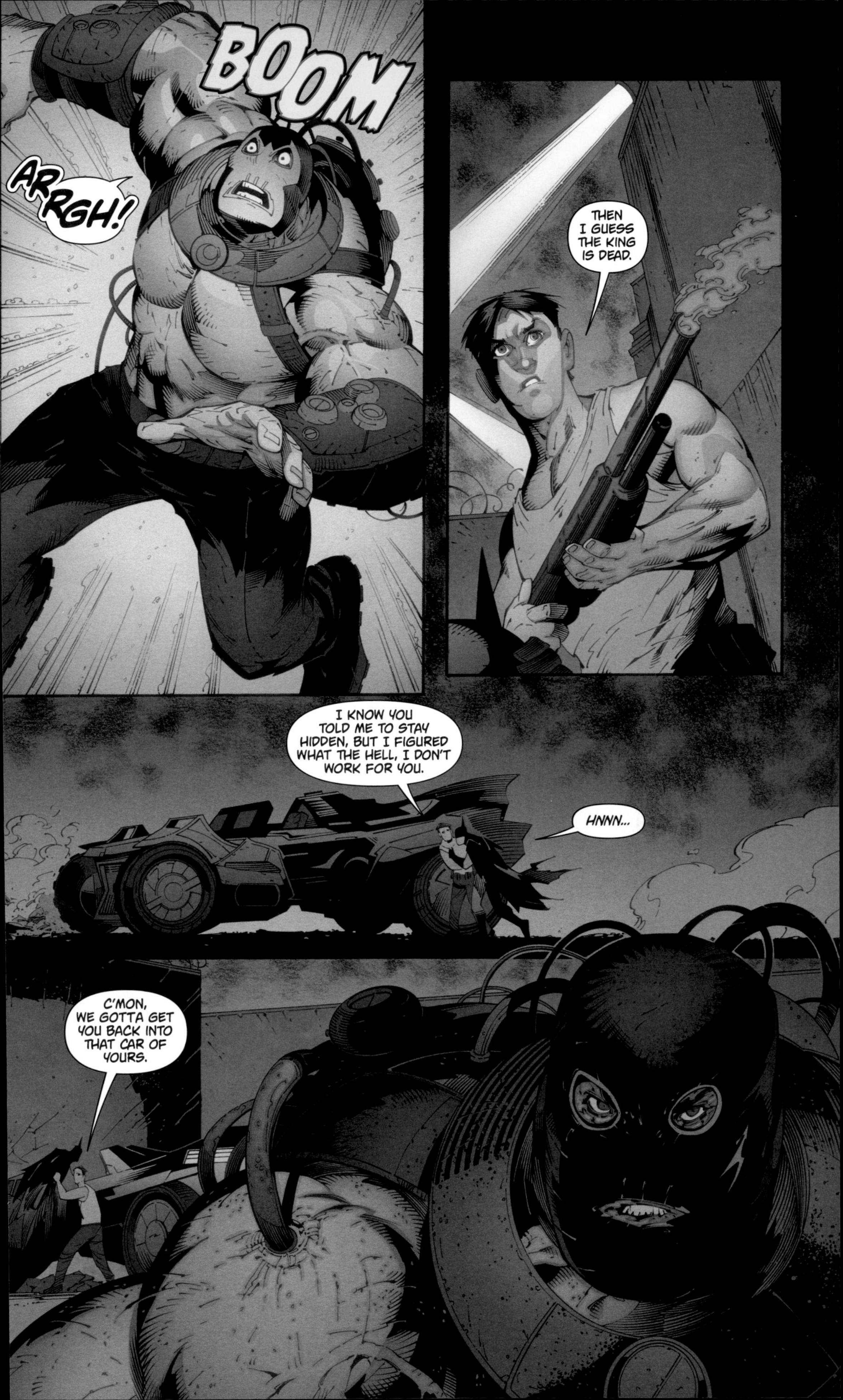
BOOM
ARRGH!
THEN I GUESS THE KING IS DEAD.
I KNOW YOU TOLD ME TO STAY HIDDEN, BUT I FIGURED WHAT THE HELL, I DON'T WORK FOR YOU.
HNNN...
C'MON, WE GOTTA GET YOU BACK INTO THAT CAR OF YOURS.

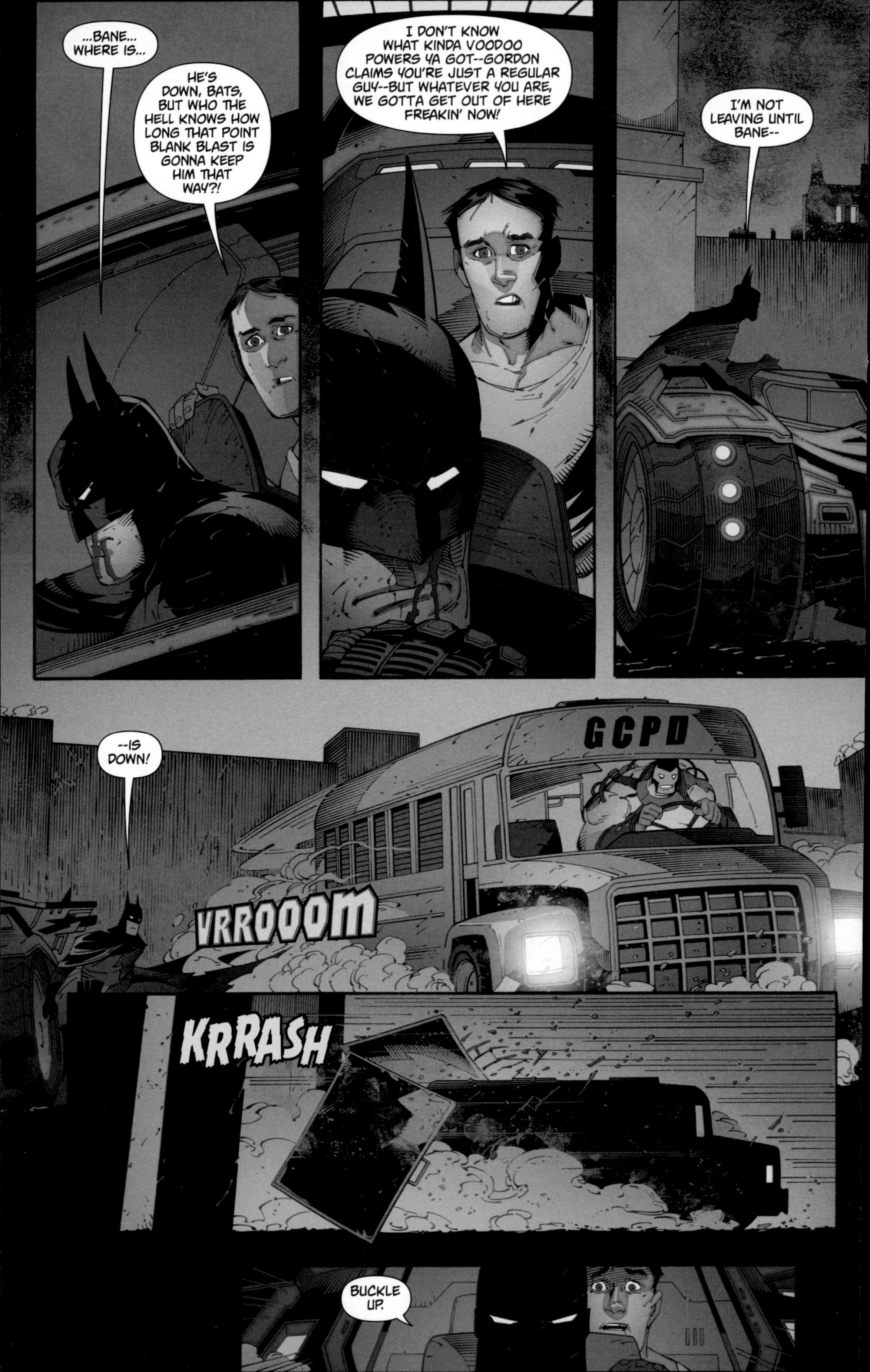
...BANE... WHERE IS...
HE'S DOWN, BATS, BUT WHO THE HELL KNOWS HOW LONG THAT POINT BLANK BLAST IS GONNA KEEP HIM THAT WAY?!
I DON'T KNOW WHAT KINDA VOODOO POWERS YA GOT--GORDON CLAIMS YOU'RE JUST A REGULAR GUY--BUT WHATEVER YOU ARE, WE GOTTA GET OUT OF HERE FREAKIN' NOW!
I'M NOT LEAVING UNTIL BANE--
--IS DOWN!
GCPD
VRROOOM
KRRASH
BUCKLE UP.

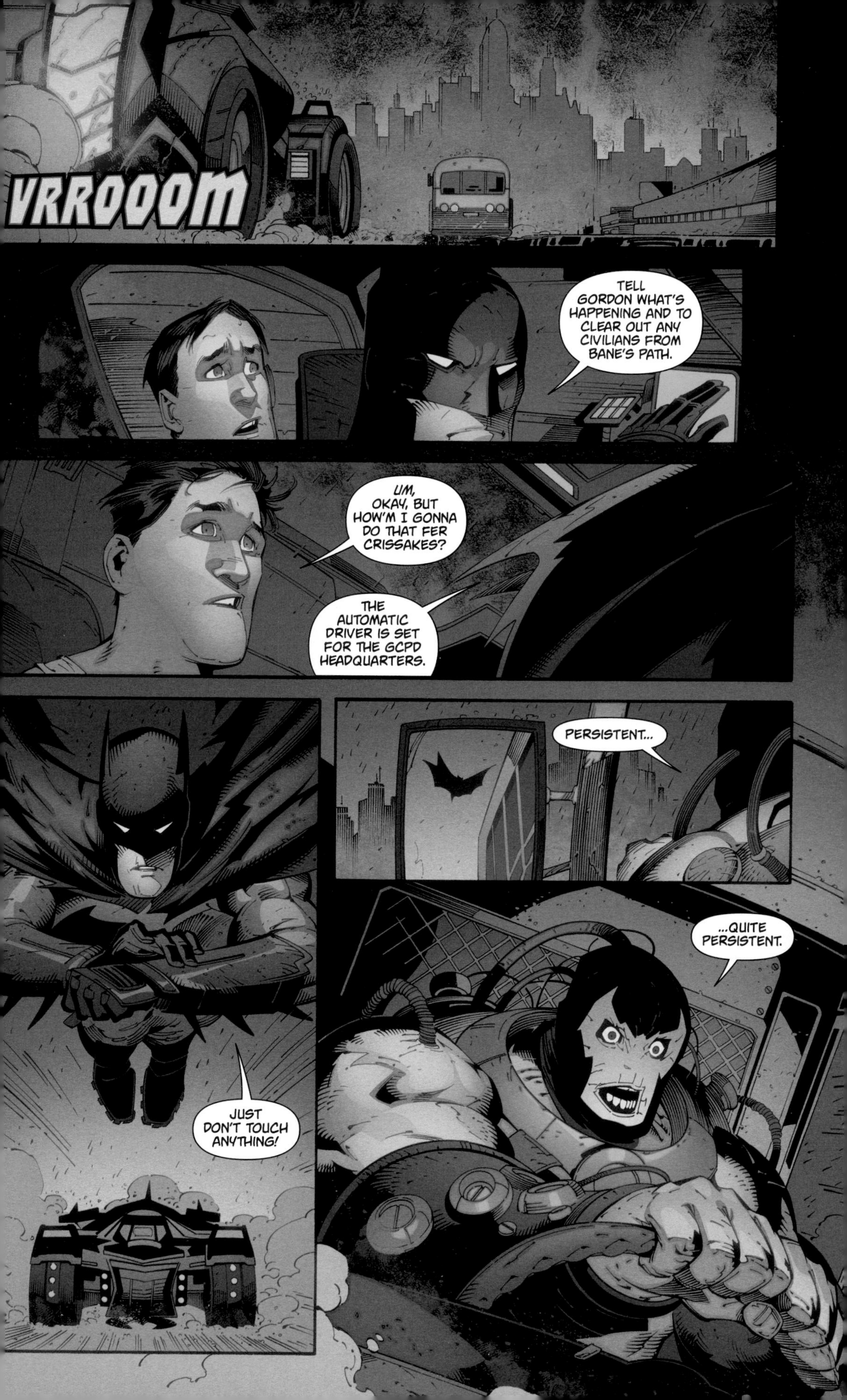
VRROOOM
TELL GORDON WHAT'S HAPPENING AND TO CLEAR OUT ANY CIVILIANS FROM BANE'S PATH.
UM, OKAY, BUT HOW'M I GONNA DO THAT FER CRISSAKES?
THE AUTOMATIC DRIVER IS SET FOR THE GCPD HEADQUARTERS.
JUST DON'T TOUCH ANYTHING!
PERSISTENT...
...QUITE PERSISTENT.

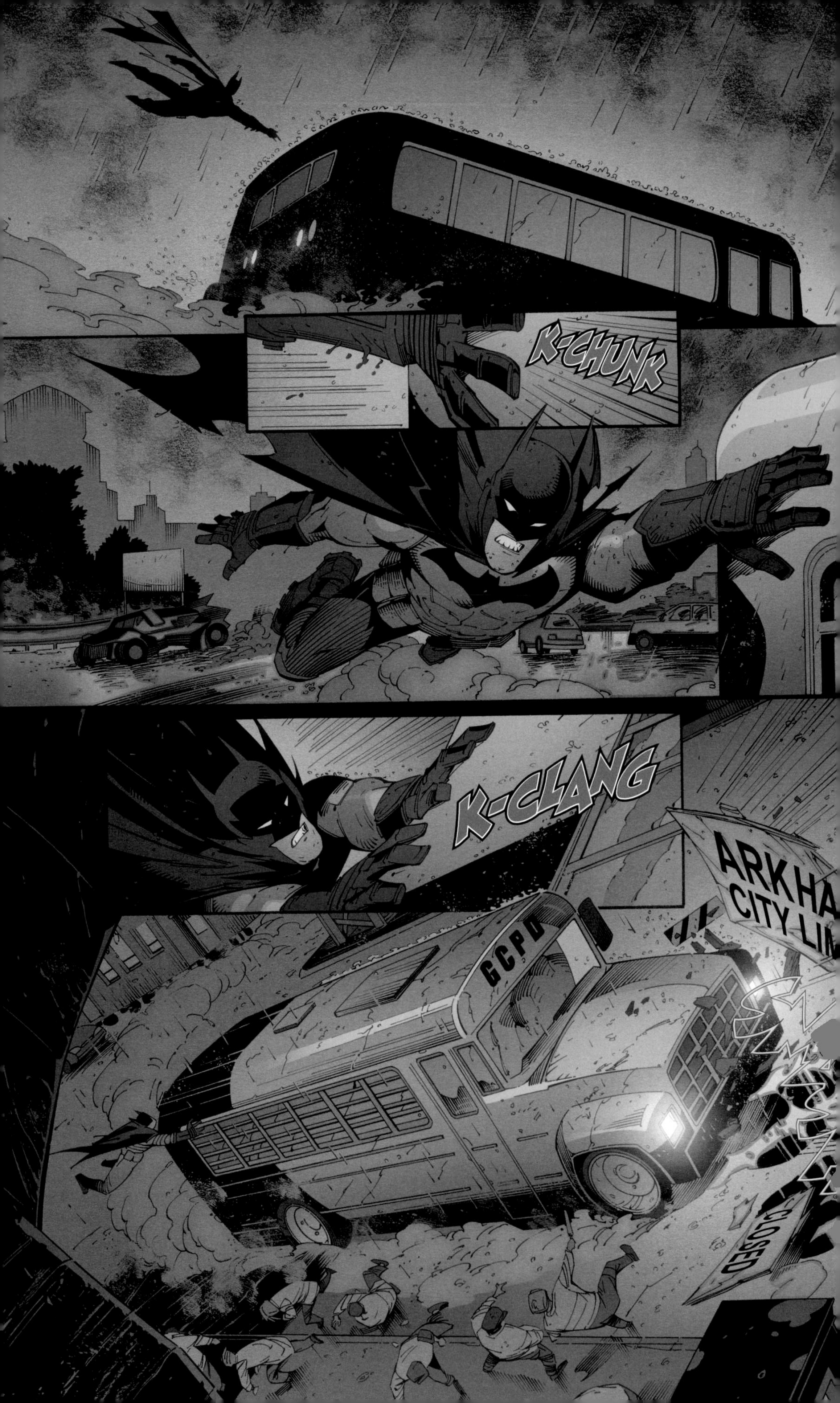
K-CHUNK
K-CLANG
ARKHA
CITY LIM
GCPD
CLOSED

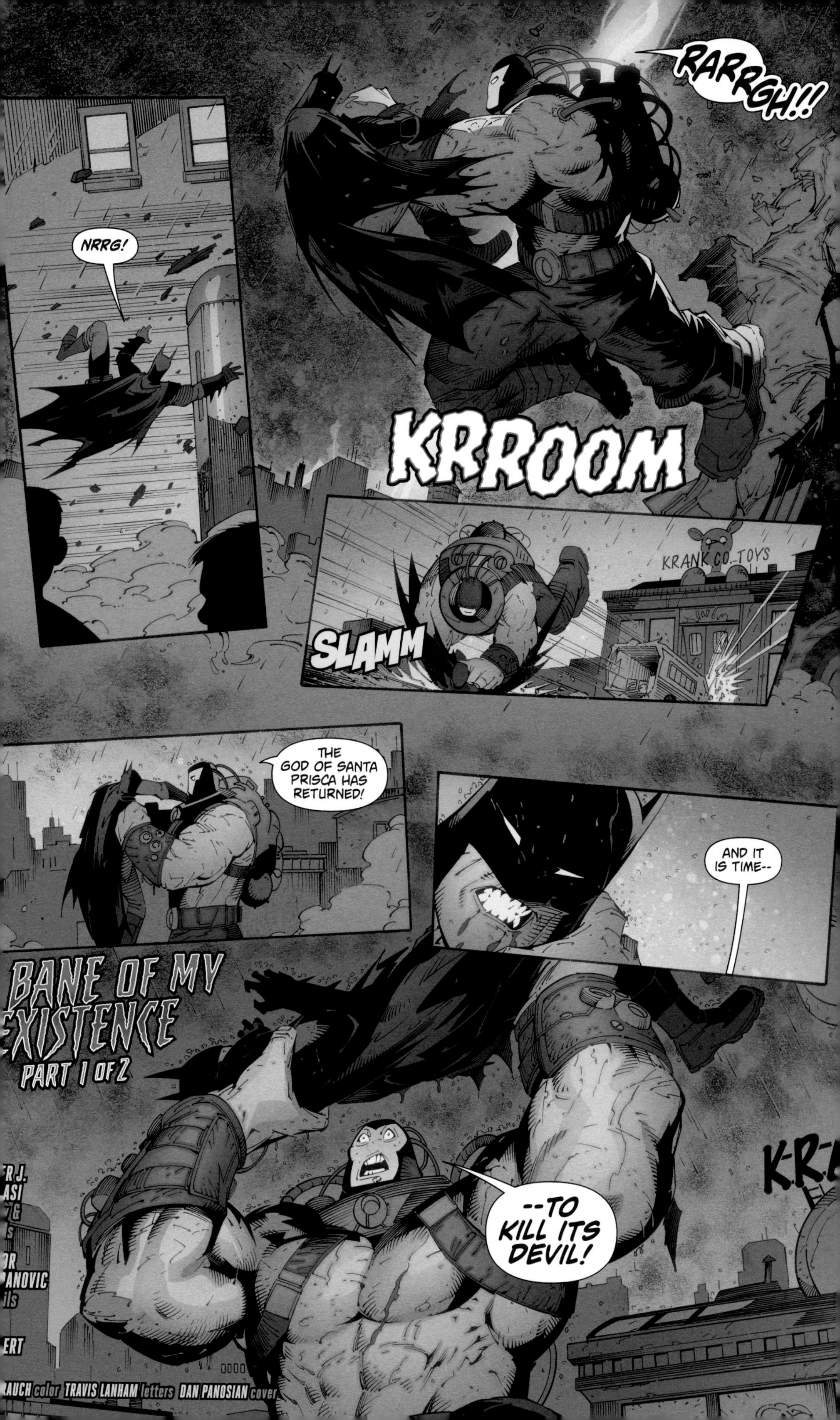
RARRGH!!
NRRG!
KRROOM
KRANK CO. TOYS
SLAMM
THE GOD OF SANTA PRISCA HAS RETURNED!
AND IT IS TIME--
BANE OF MY EXISTENCE
PART 1 OF 2
--TO KILL ITS DEVIL!
RAUCH color TRAVIS LANHAM letters DAN PANOSIAN cover

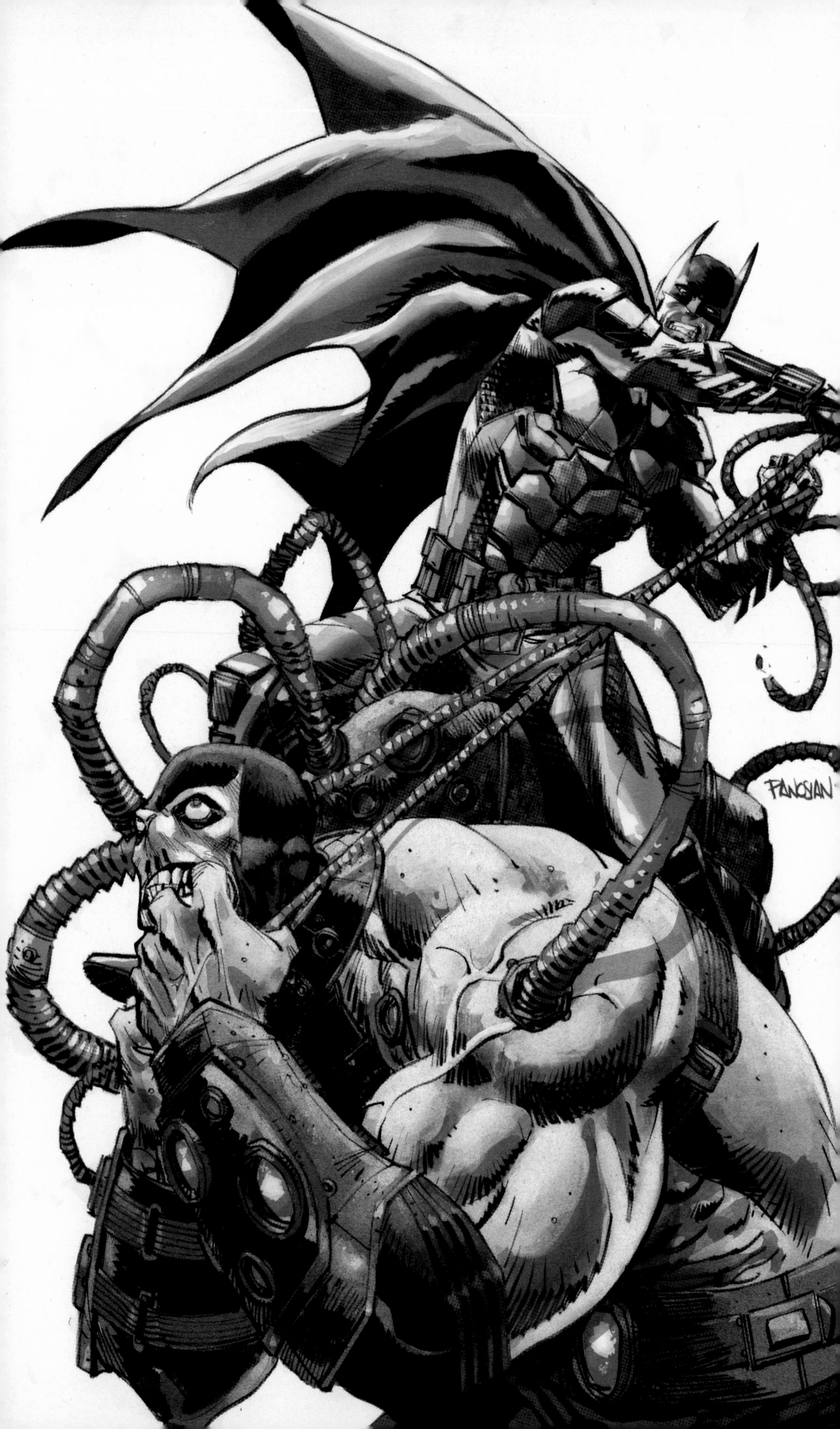
PANOSIAN

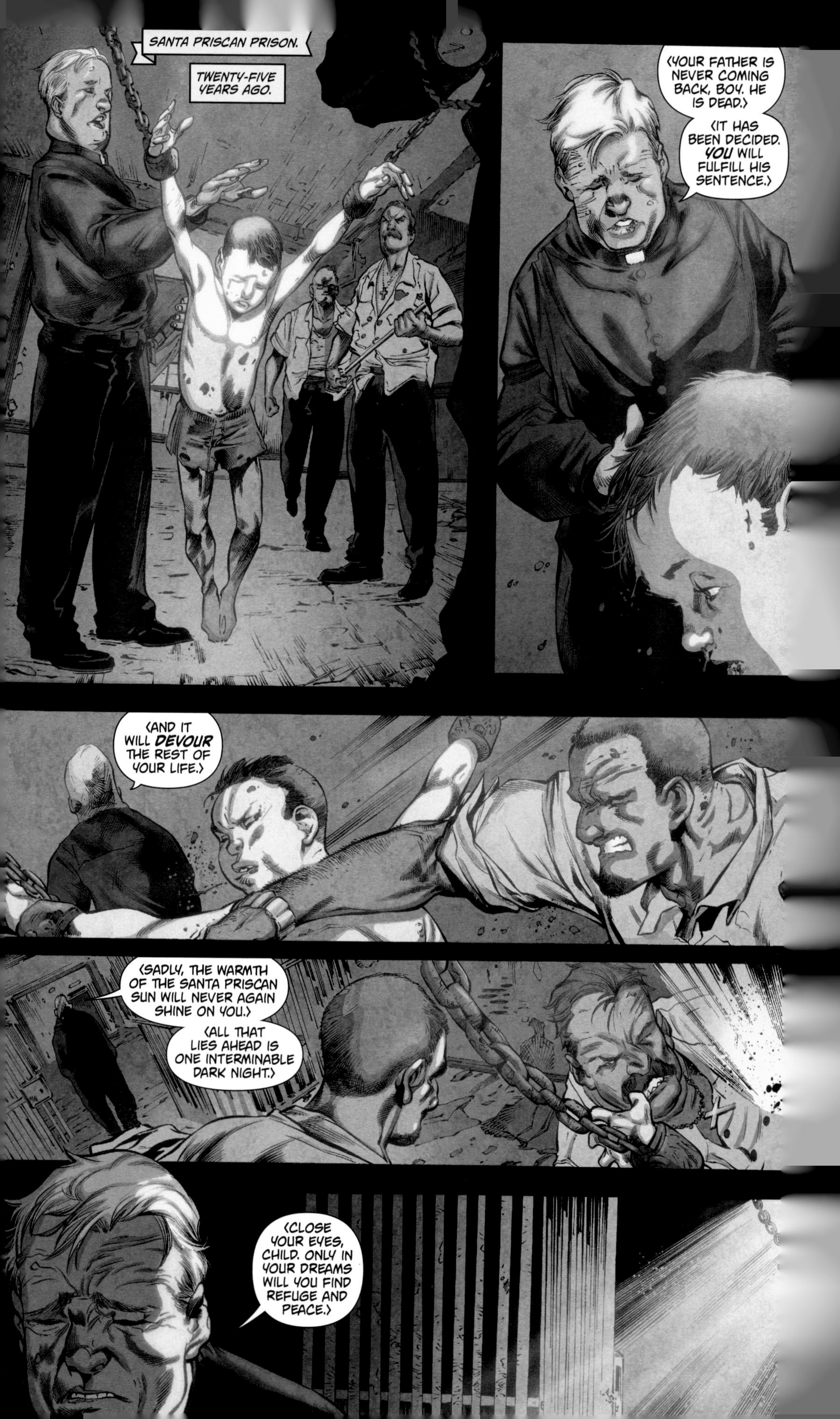
SANTA PRISCAN PRISON.
TWENTY-FIVE YEARS AGO.
‹YOUR FATHER IS NEVER COMING BACK, BOY. HE IS DEAD.›
‹IT HAS BEEN DECIDED. YOU WILL FULFILL HIS SENTENCE.›
‹AND IT WILL DEVOUR THE REST OF YOUR LIFE.›
‹SADLY, THE WARMTH OF THE SANTA PRISCAN SUN WILL NEVER AGAIN SHINE ON YOU.›
‹ALL THAT LIES AHEAD IS ONE INTERMINABLE DARK NIGHT.›
‹CLOSE YOUR EYES, CHILD. ONLY IN YOUR DREAMS WILL YOU FIND REFUGE AND PEACE.›

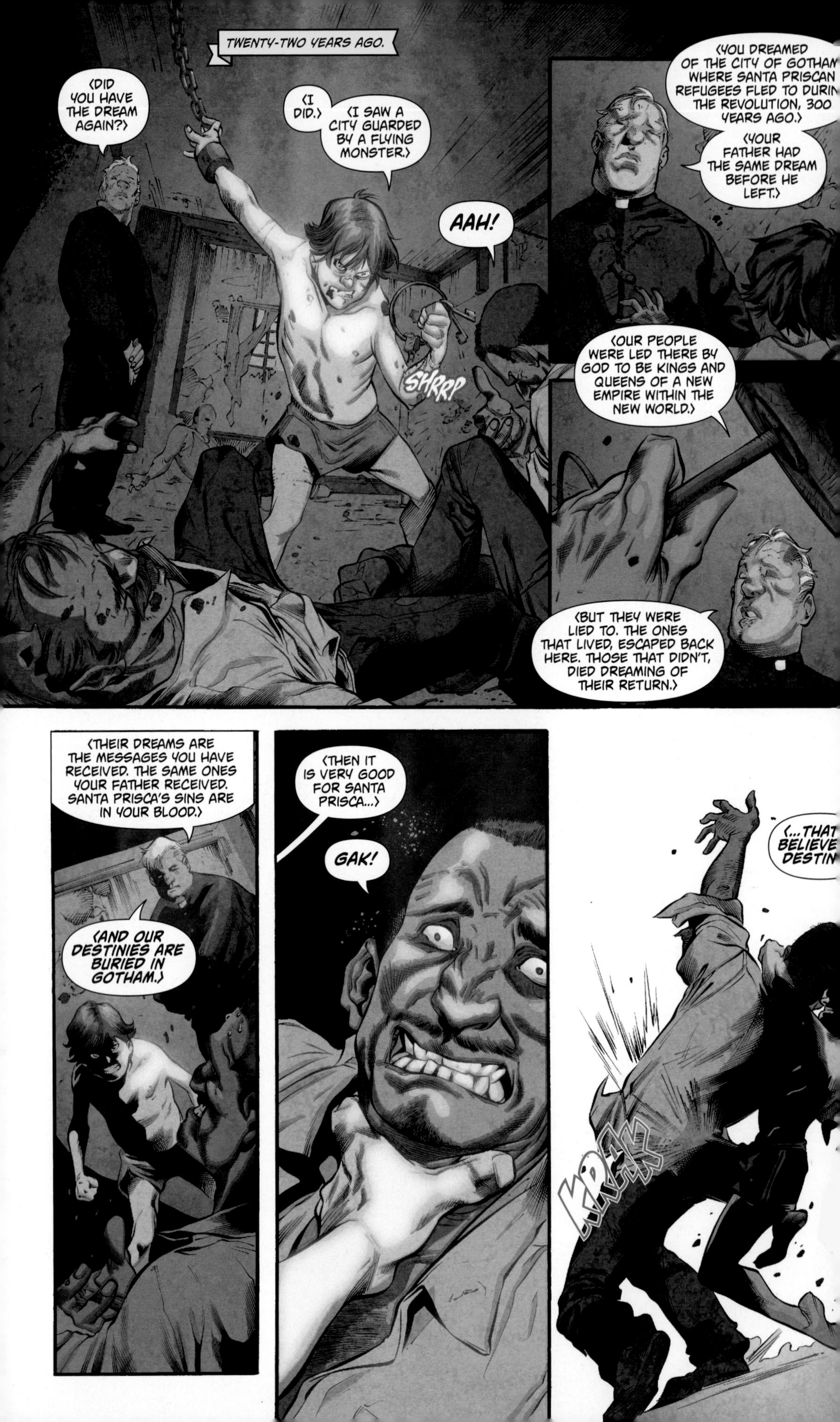
TWENTY-TWO YEARS AGO.
‹DID YOU HAVE THE DREAM AGAIN?›
‹I DID.›
‹I SAW A CITY GUARDED BY A FLYING MONSTER.›
AAH!
SHRRP
‹YOU DREAMED OF THE CITY OF GOTHAM WHERE SANTA PRISCAN REFUGEES FLED TO DURIN THE REVOLUTION, 300 YEARS AGO.›
‹YOUR FATHER HAD THE SAME DREAM BEFORE HE LEFT.›
‹OUR PEOPLE WERE LED THERE BY GOD TO BE KINGS AND QUEENS OF A NEW EMPIRE WITHIN THE NEW WORLD.›
‹BUT THEY WERE LIED TO. THE ONES THAT LIVED, ESCAPED BACK HERE. THOSE THAT DIDN'T, DIED DREAMING OF THEIR RETURN.›
‹THEIR DREAMS ARE THE MESSAGES YOU HAVE RECEIVED. THE SAME ONES YOUR FATHER RECEIVED. SANTA PRISCA'S SINS ARE IN YOUR BLOOD.›
‹AND OUR DESTINIES ARE BURIED IN GOTHAM.›
‹THEN IT IS VERY GOOD FOR SANTA PRISCA...›
GAK!
‹...THAT BELIEVE DESTIN

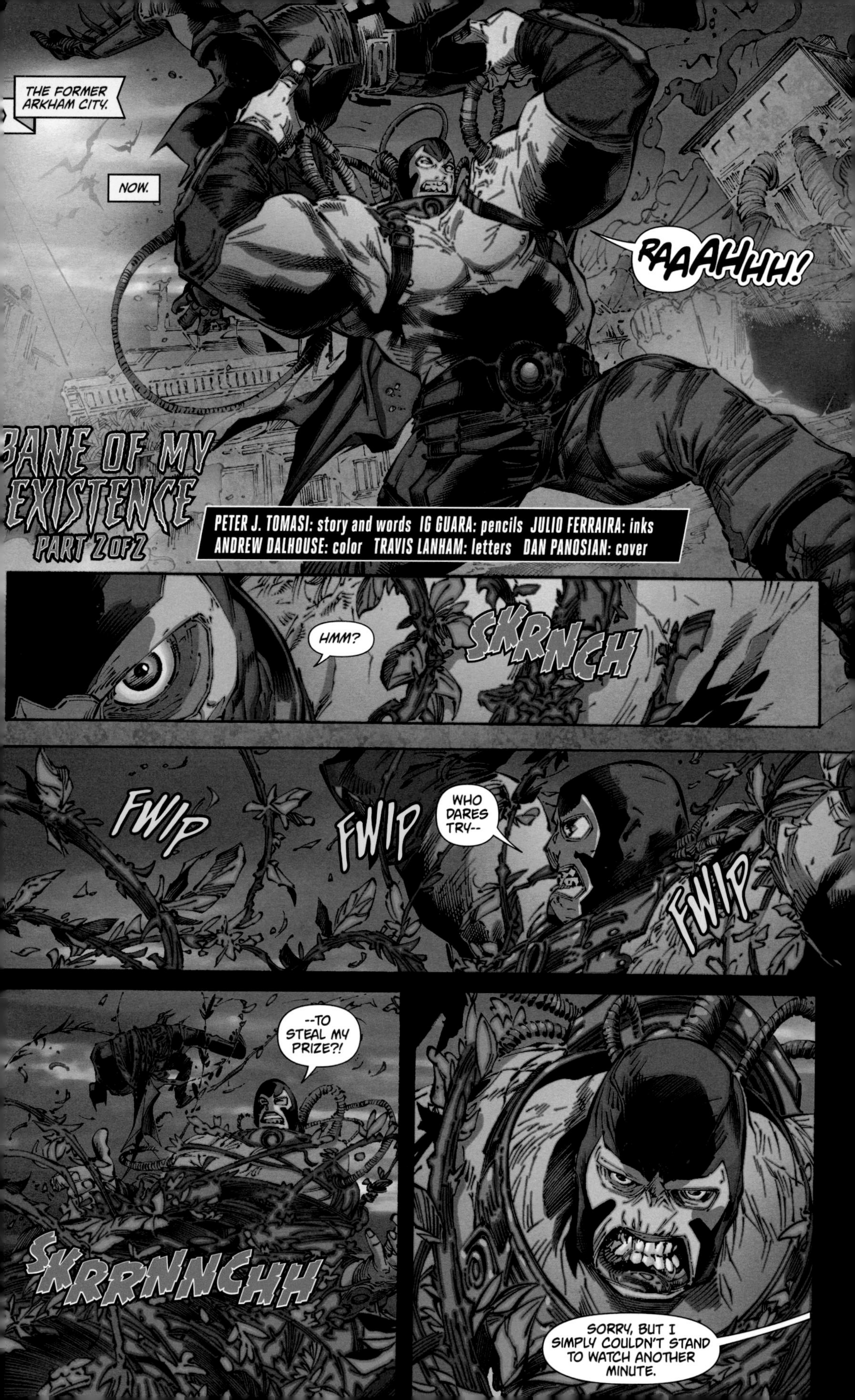
THE FORMER ARKHAM CITY.
NOW.
RAAAHHH!
BANE OF MY EXISTENCE
PART 2 OF 2
PETER J. TOMASI: story and words IG GUARA: pencils JULIO FERRAIRA: inks
ANDREW DALHOUSE: color TRAVIS LANHAM: letters DAN PANOSIAN: cover
HMM?
SKRNCH
FWIP
FWIP
WHO DARES TRY--
FWIP
--TO STEAL MY PRIZE?!
SKRRNNCHH
SORRY, BUT I SIMPLY COULDN'T STAND TO WATCH ANOTHER MINUTE.

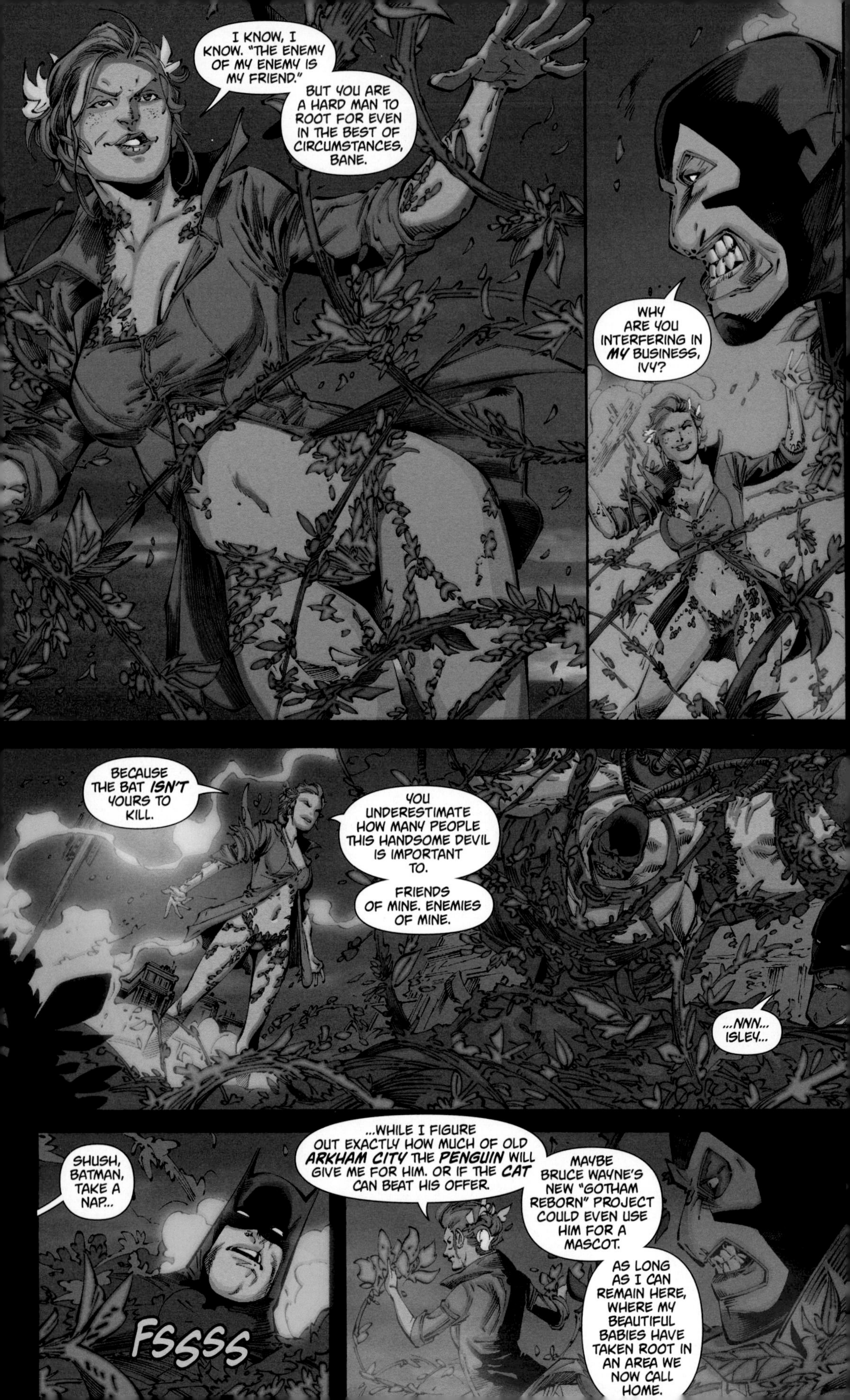
I KNOW, I KNOW. "THE ENEMY OF MY ENEMY IS MY FRIEND."
BUT YOU ARE A HARD MAN TO ROOT FOR EVEN IN THE BEST OF CIRCUMSTANCES, BANE.
WHY ARE YOU INTERFERING IN *MY* BUSINESS, IVY?
BECAUSE THE BAT *ISN'T* YOURS TO KILL.
YOU UNDERESTIMATE HOW MANY PEOPLE THIS HANDSOME DEVIL IS IMPORTANT TO.
FRIENDS OF MINE. ENEMIES OF MINE.
...NNN... ISLEY...
SHUSH, BATMAN, TAKE A NAP...
FSSSS
...WHILE I FIGURE OUT EXACTLY HOW MUCH OF OLD *ARKHAM CITY* THE *PENGUIN* WILL GIVE ME FOR HIM. OR IF THE *CAT* CAN BEAT HIS OFFER.
MAYBE BRUCE WAYNE'S NEW "GOTHAM REBORN" PROJECT COULD EVEN USE HIM FOR A MASCOT.
AS LONG AS I CAN REMAIN HERE, WHERE MY BEAUTIFUL BABIES HAVE TAKEN ROOT IN AN AREA WE NOW CALL HOME.

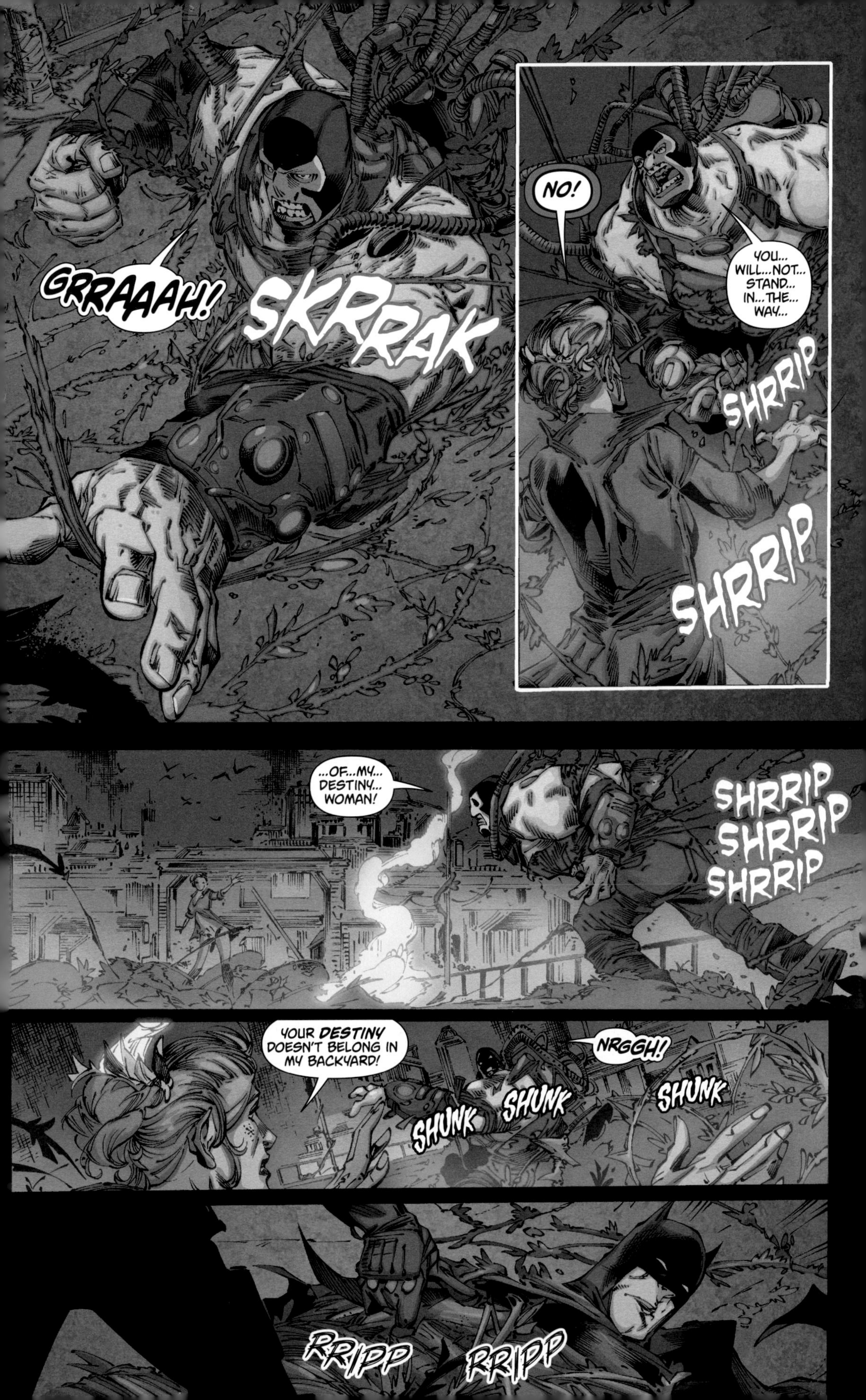
GRRAAAH!
SKRRAK
NO!
YOU... WILL...NOT... STAND... IN...THE... WAY...
SHRRIP
SHRRIP
...OF...MY... DESTINY... WOMAN!
SHRRIP
SHRRIP
SHRRIP
YOUR DESTINY DOESN'T BELONG IN MY BACKYARD!
NRGGH!
SHUNK
SHUNK
SHUNK
RRIPP
RRIPP

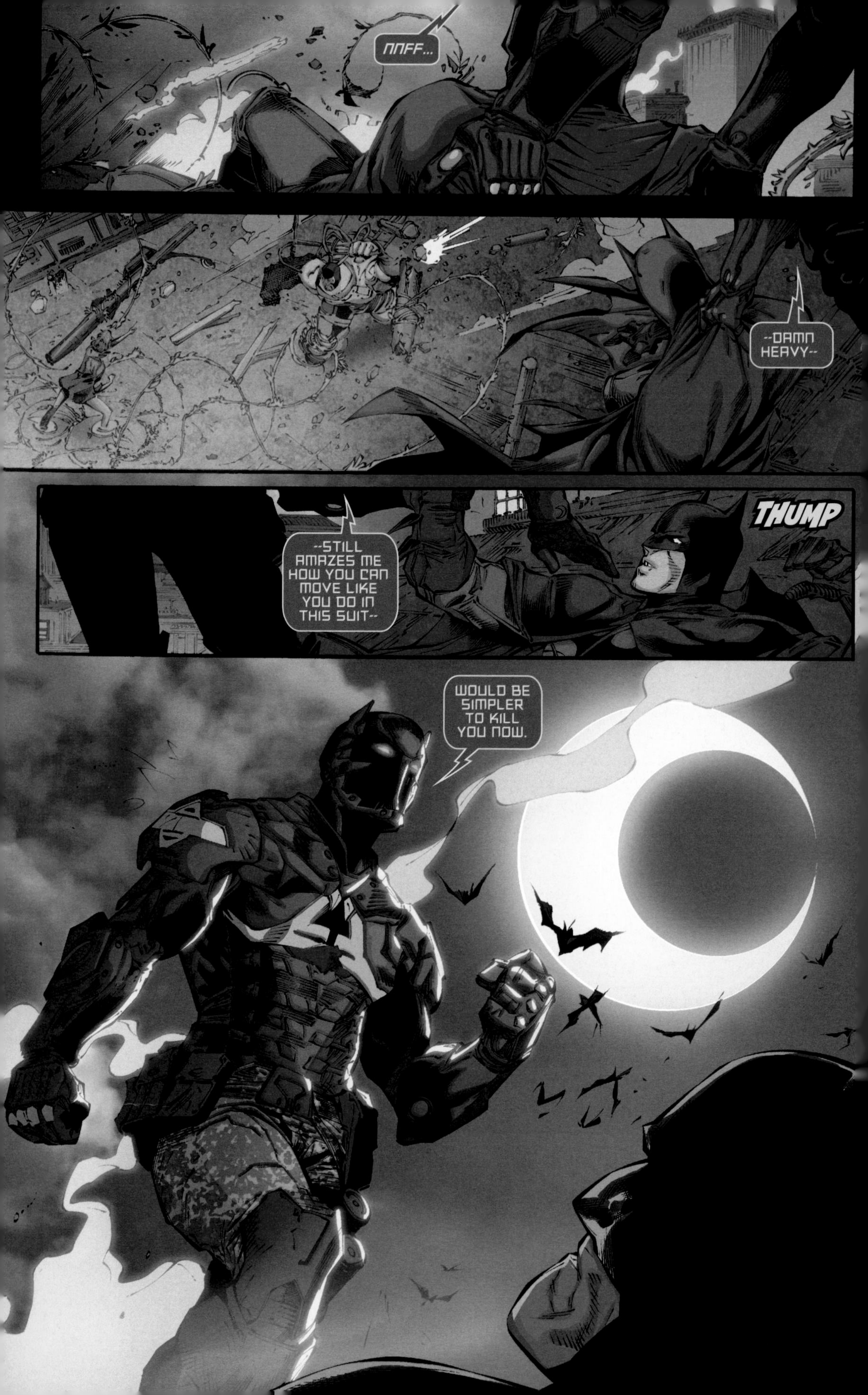

NNFF...
--DAMN HEAVY--
--STILL AMAZES ME HOW YOU CAN MOVE LIKE YOU DO IN THIS SUIT--
THUMP
WOULD BE SIMPLER TO KILL YOU NOW.

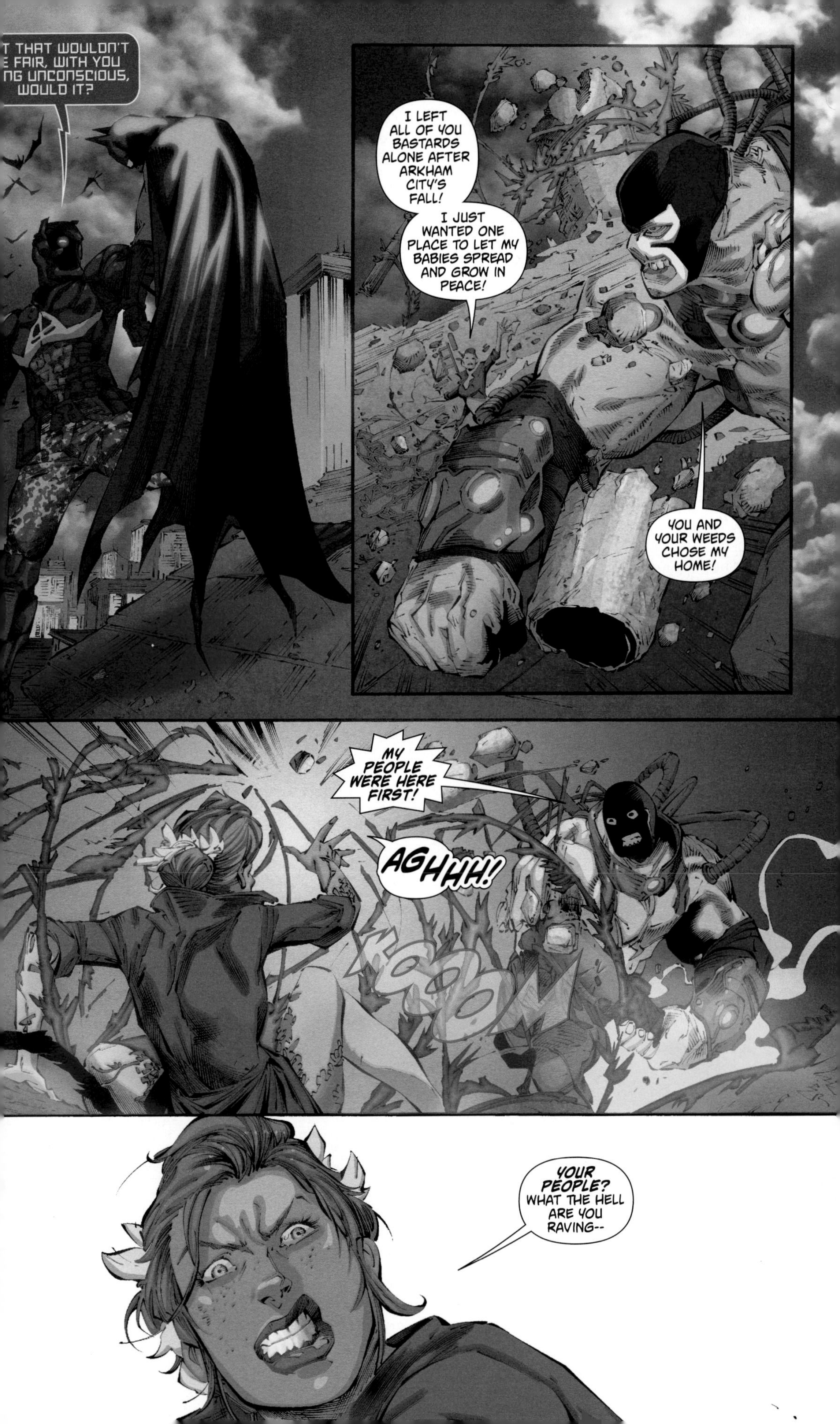
T THAT WOULDN'T
E FAIR, WITH YOU
NG UNCONSCIOUS,
WOULD IT?
I LEFT ALL OF YOU BASTARDS ALONE AFTER ARKHAM CITY'S FALL!
I JUST WANTED ONE PLACE TO LET MY BABIES SPREAD AND GROW IN PEACE!
YOU AND YOUR WEEDS CHOSE MY HOME!
MY PEOPLE WERE HERE FIRST!
AGHHH!
KOOOOM
YOUR PEOPLE? WHAT THE HELL ARE YOU RAVING--

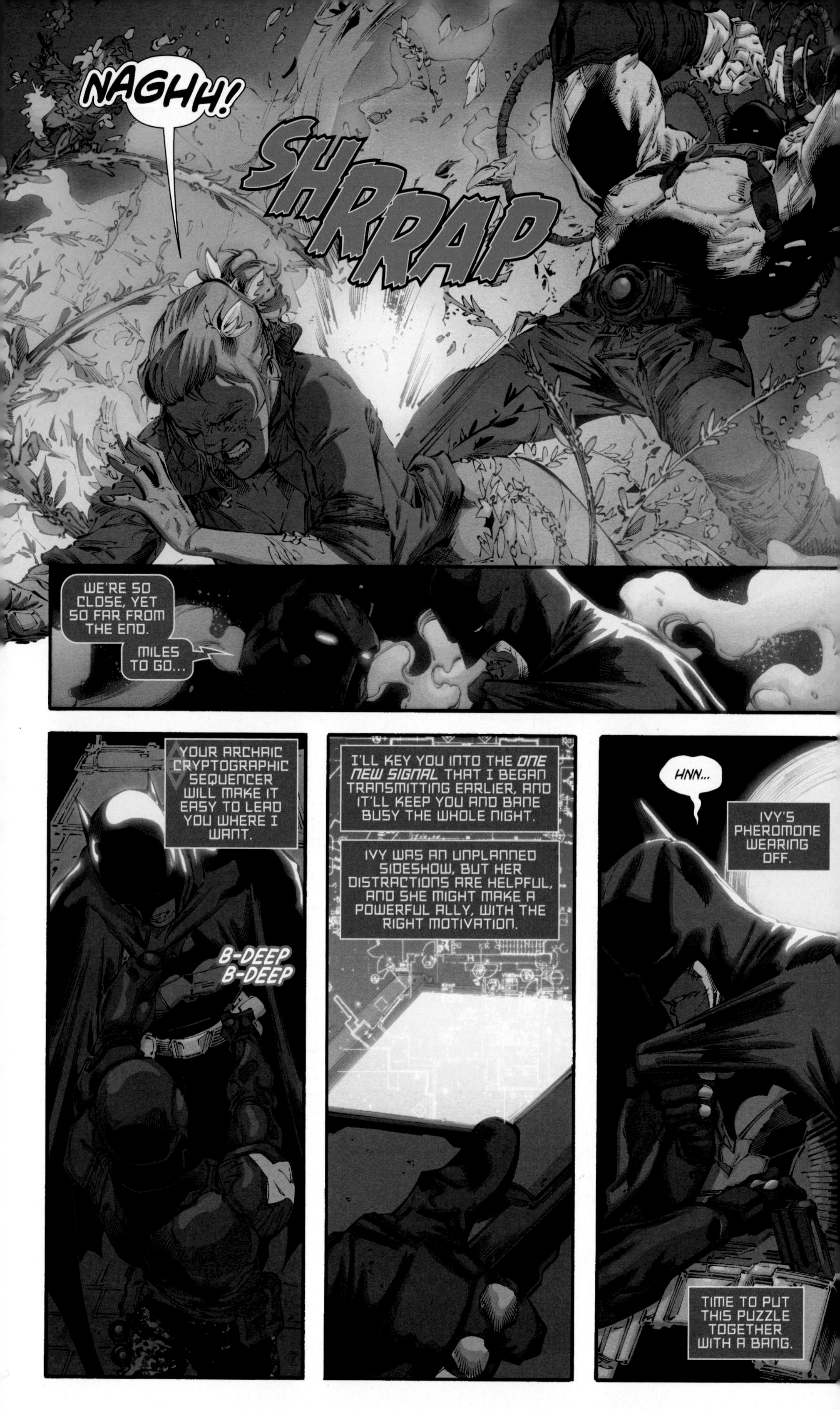
NAGHH!
SHRRAP
WE'RE SO CLOSE, YET SO FAR FROM THE END.
MILES TO GO...
YOUR ARCHAIC CRYPTOGRAPHIC SEQUENCER WILL MAKE IT EASY TO LEAD YOU WHERE I WANT.
B-DEEP B-DEEP
I'LL KEY YOU INTO THE ONE NEW SIGNAL THAT I BEGAN TRANSMITTING EARLIER, AND IT'LL KEEP YOU AND BANE BUSY THE WHOLE NIGHT.
IVY WAS AN UNPLANNED SIDESHOW, BUT HER DISTRACTIONS ARE HELPFUL, AND SHE MIGHT MAKE A POWERFUL ALLY, WITH THE RIGHT MOTIVATION.
HNN...
IVY'S PHEROMONE WEARING OFF.
TIME TO PUT THIS PUZZLE TOGETHER WITH A BANG.

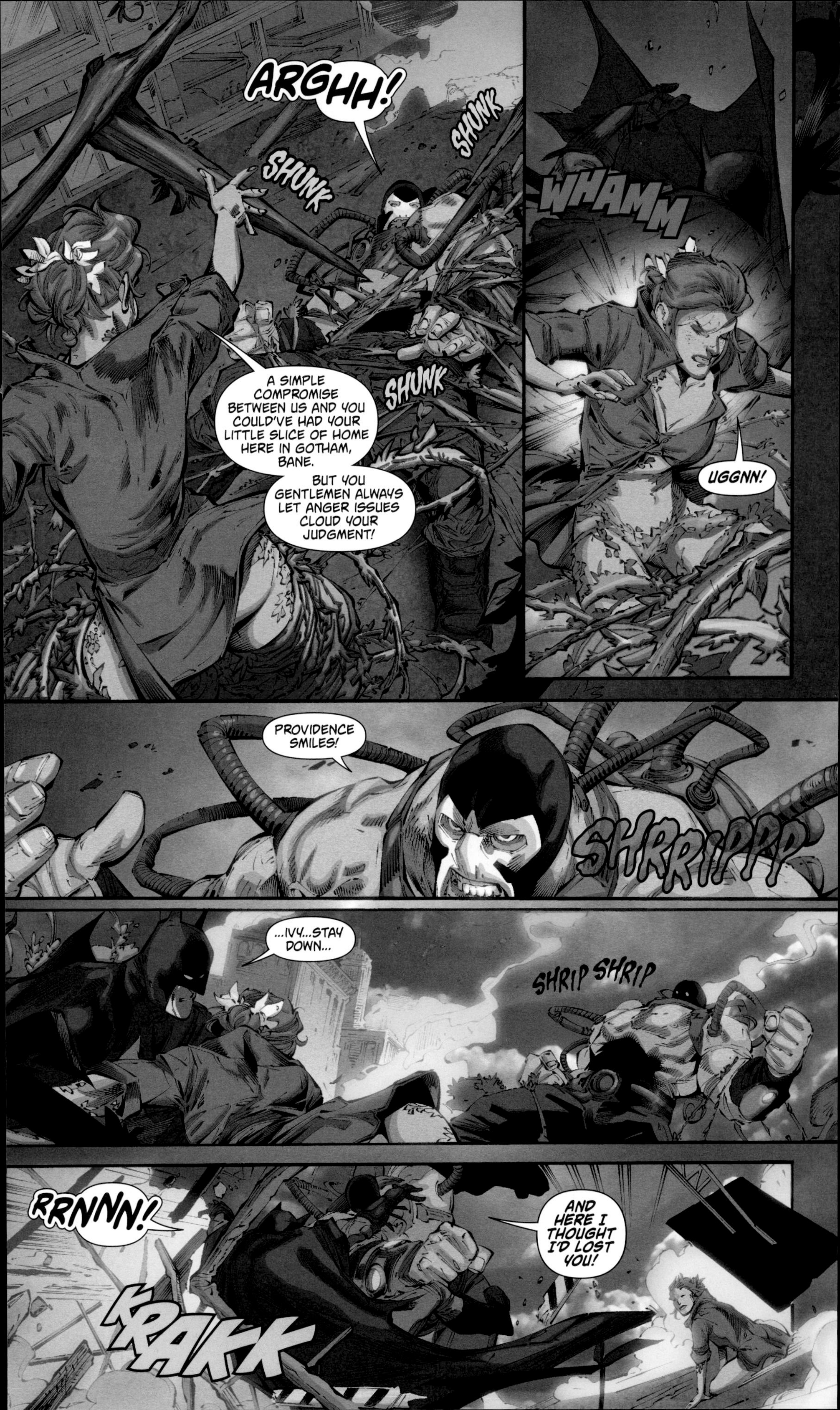
ARGHH!
SHUNK
SHUNK
A SIMPLE COMPROMISE BETWEEN US AND YOU COULD'VE HAD YOUR LITTLE SLICE OF HOME HERE IN GOTHAM, BANE.
BUT YOU GENTLEMEN ALWAYS LET ANGER ISSUES CLOUD YOUR JUDGMENT!
SHUNK
WHAMM
UGGNN!
PROVIDENCE SMILES!
SHRRIPPP
...IVY...STAY DOWN...
SHRIP SHRIP
RRNNN!
AND HERE I THOUGHT I'D LOST YOU!
KRAKK

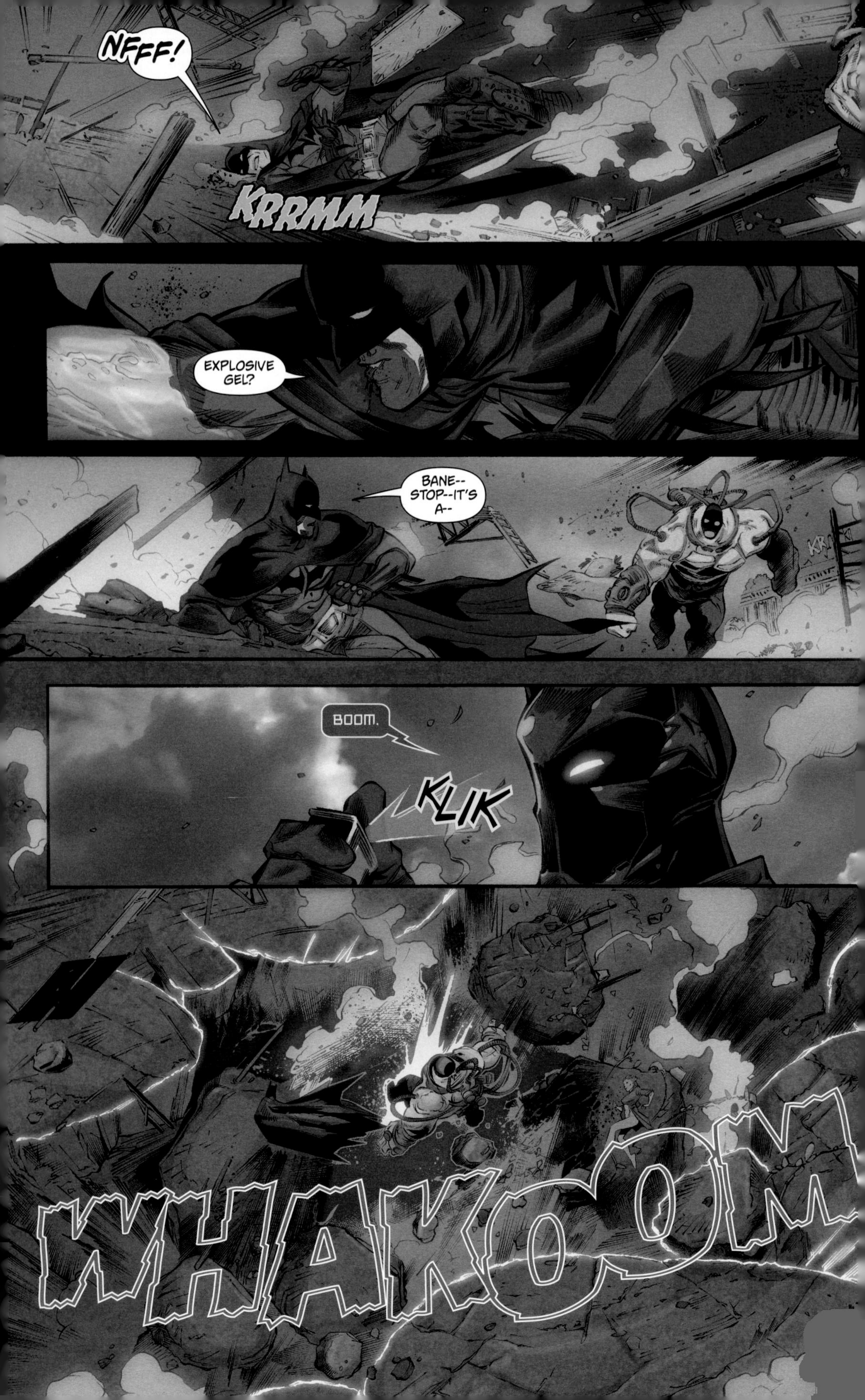
NFFF!
KRRMM
EXPLOSIVE GEL?
BANE--STOP--IT'S A--
BOOM.
KLIK
WHAKOOM

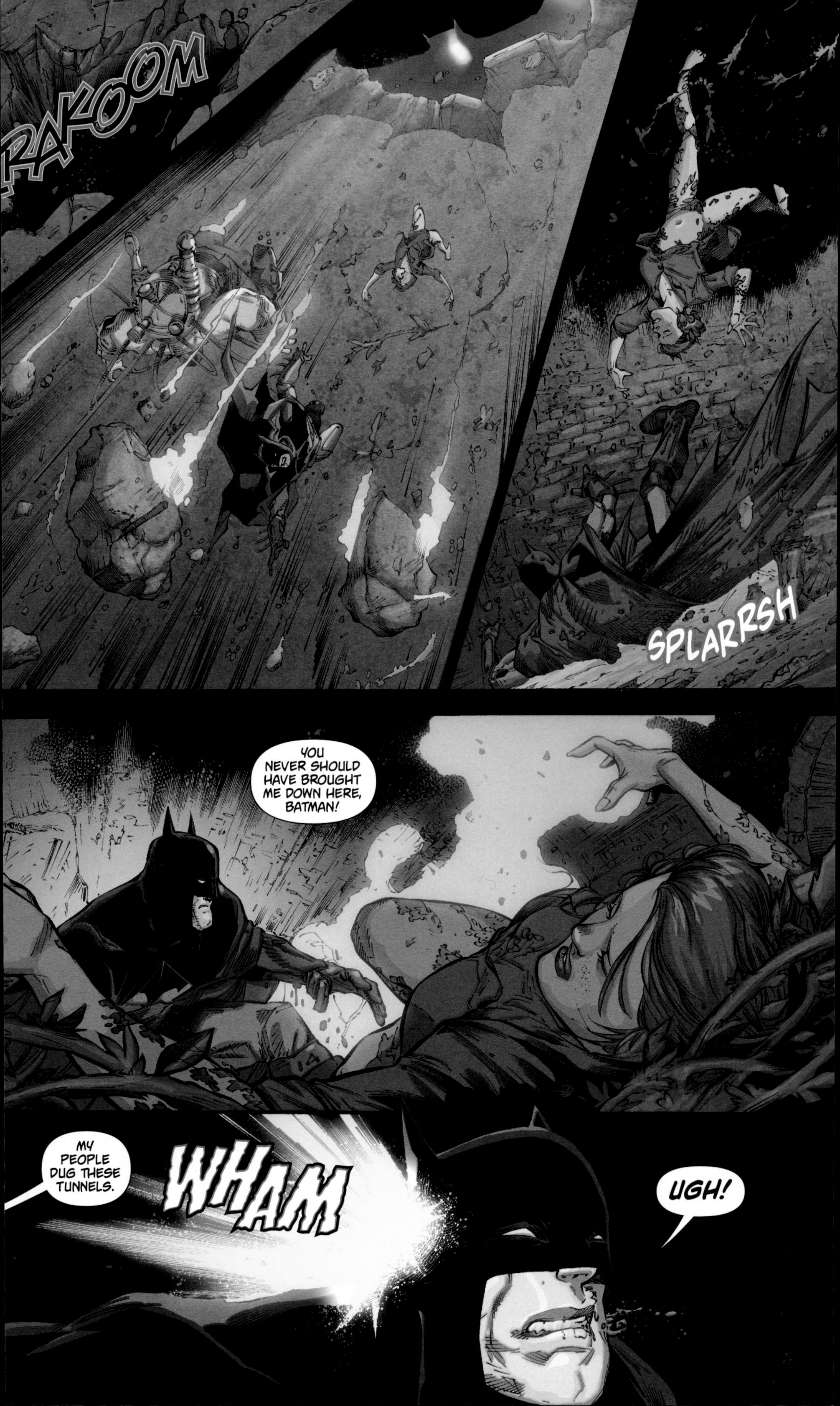
RAKOOM
SPLARRSH
YOU NEVER SHOULD HAVE BROUGHT ME DOWN HERE, BATMAN!
MY PEOPLE DUG THESE TUNNELS.
WHAM
UGH!

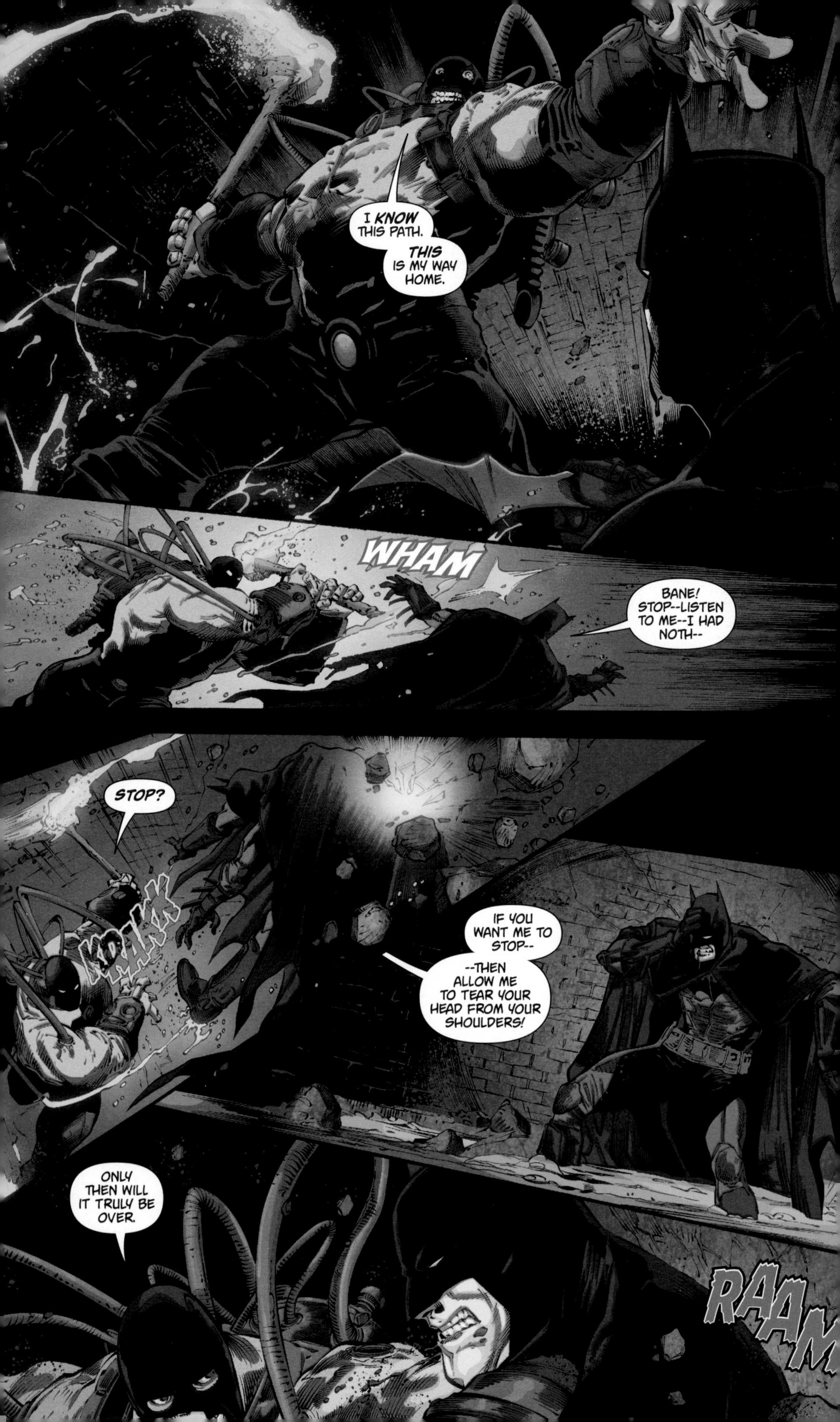
I KNOW THIS PATH.
THIS IS MY WAY HOME.
WHAM
BANE! STOP--LISTEN TO ME--I HAD NOTH--
STOP?
KRAKK
IF YOU WANT ME TO STOP--
--THEN ALLOW ME TO TEAR YOUR HEAD FROM YOUR SHOULDERS!
ONLY THEN WILL IT TRULY BE OVER.
RAAM

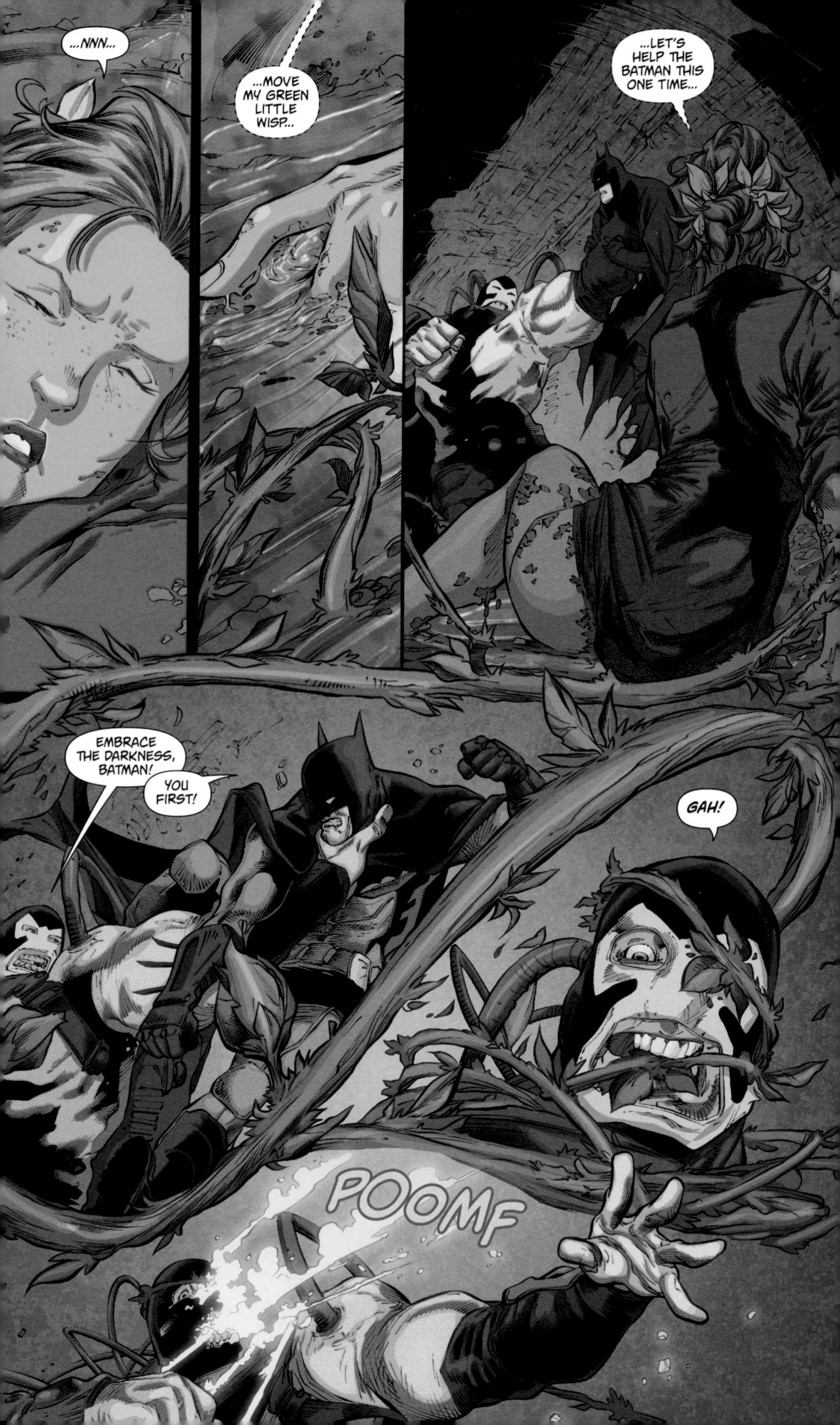
...NNN...
...MOVE MY GREEN LITTLE WISP...
...LET'S HELP THE BATMAN THIS ONE TIME...
EMBRACE THE DARKNESS, BATMAN!
YOU FIRST!
GAH!
POOMF

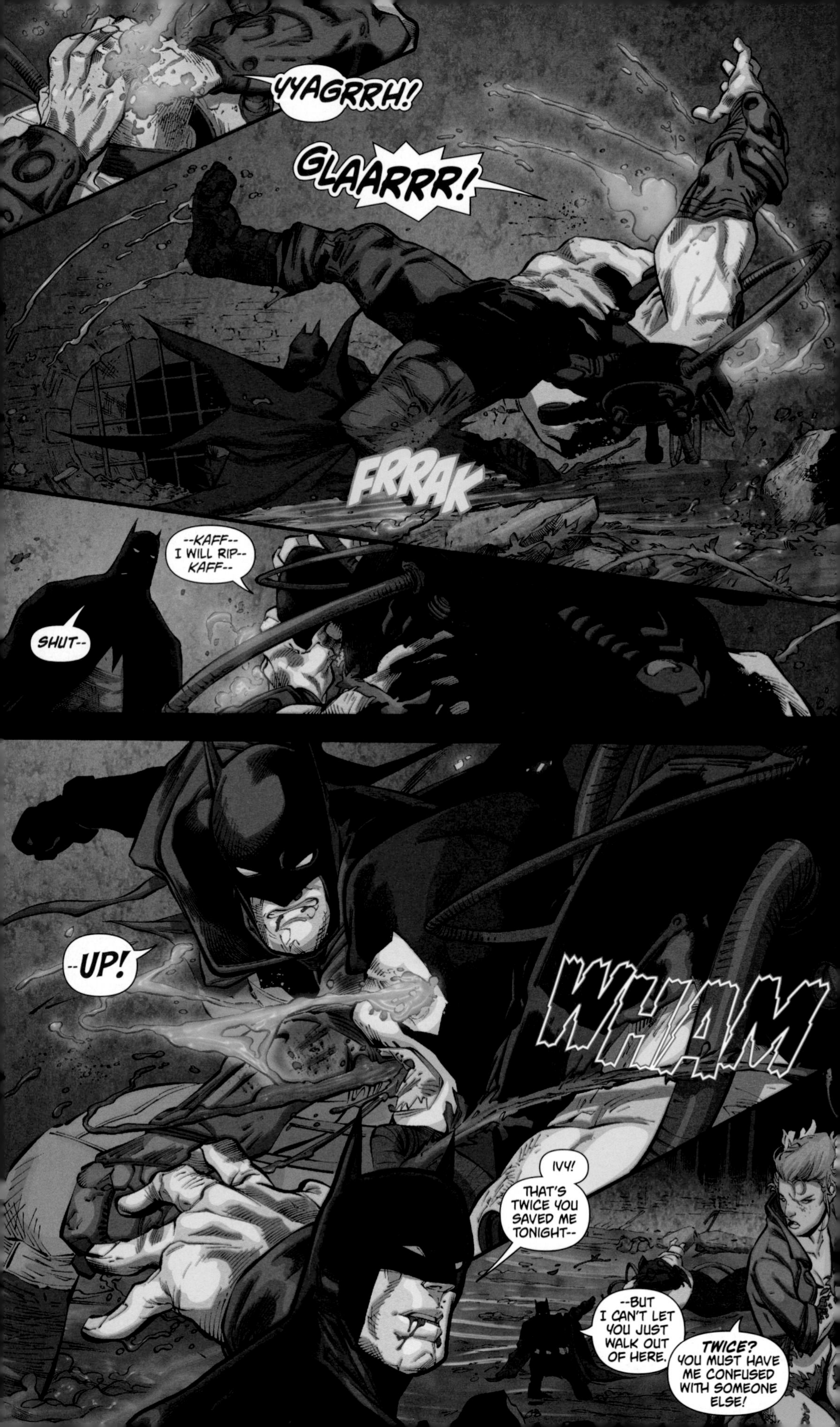
YYAGRRH!
GLAARRR!
FRRAK
--KAFF-- I WILL RIP-- KAFF--
SHUT--
--UP!
WHAM
IVY!
THAT'S TWICE YOU SAVED ME TONIGHT--
--BUT I CAN'T LET YOU JUST WALK OUT OF HERE.
TWICE? YOU MUST HAVE ME CONFUSED WITH SOMEONE ELSE!

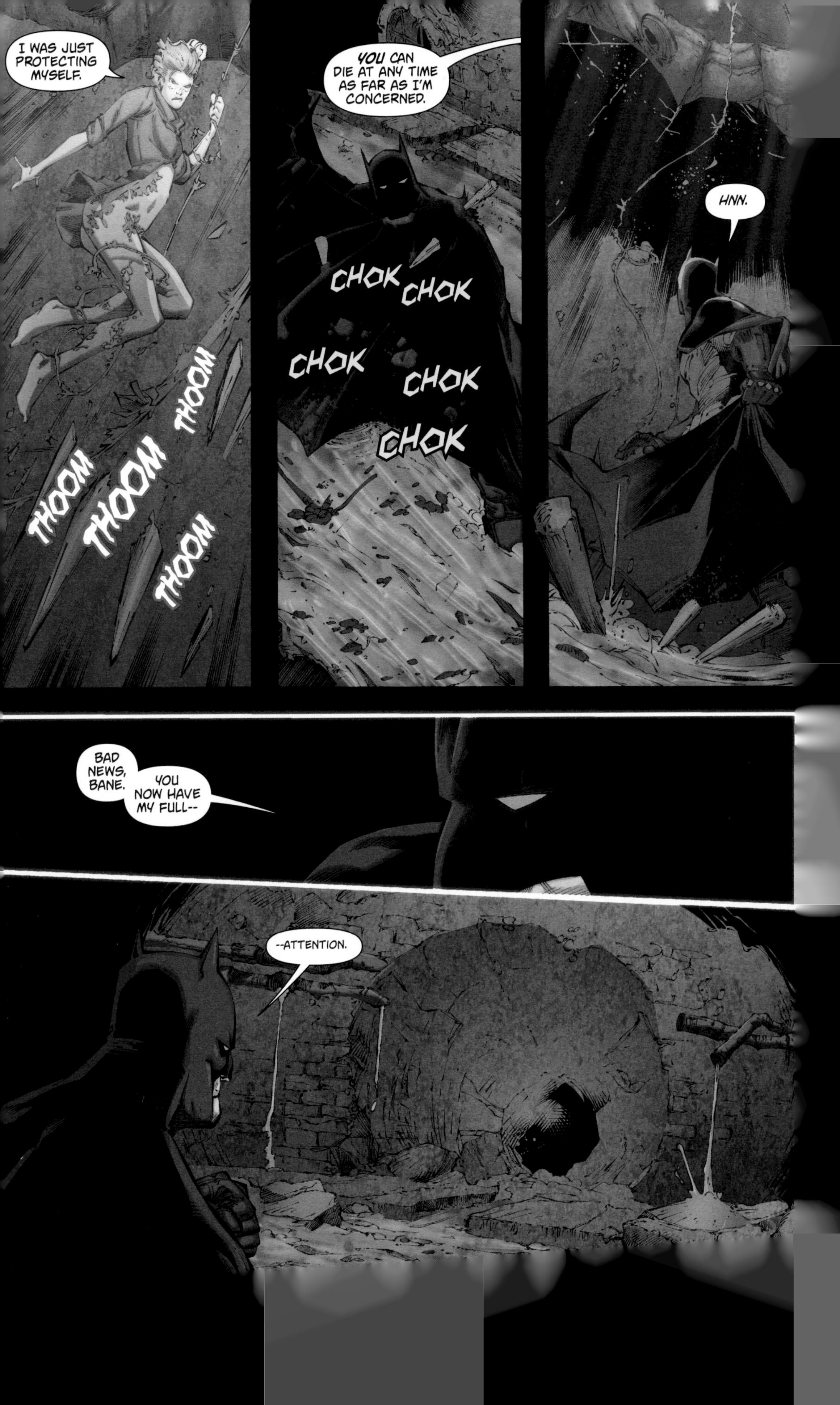
I WAS JUST PROTECTING MYSELF.
THOOM THOOM THOOM THOOM
YOU CAN DIE AT ANY TIME AS FAR AS I'M CONCERNED.
CHOK CHOK
CHOK CHOK
CHOK
HNN.
BAD NEWS, BANE.
YOU NOW HAVE MY FULL--
--ATTENTION.

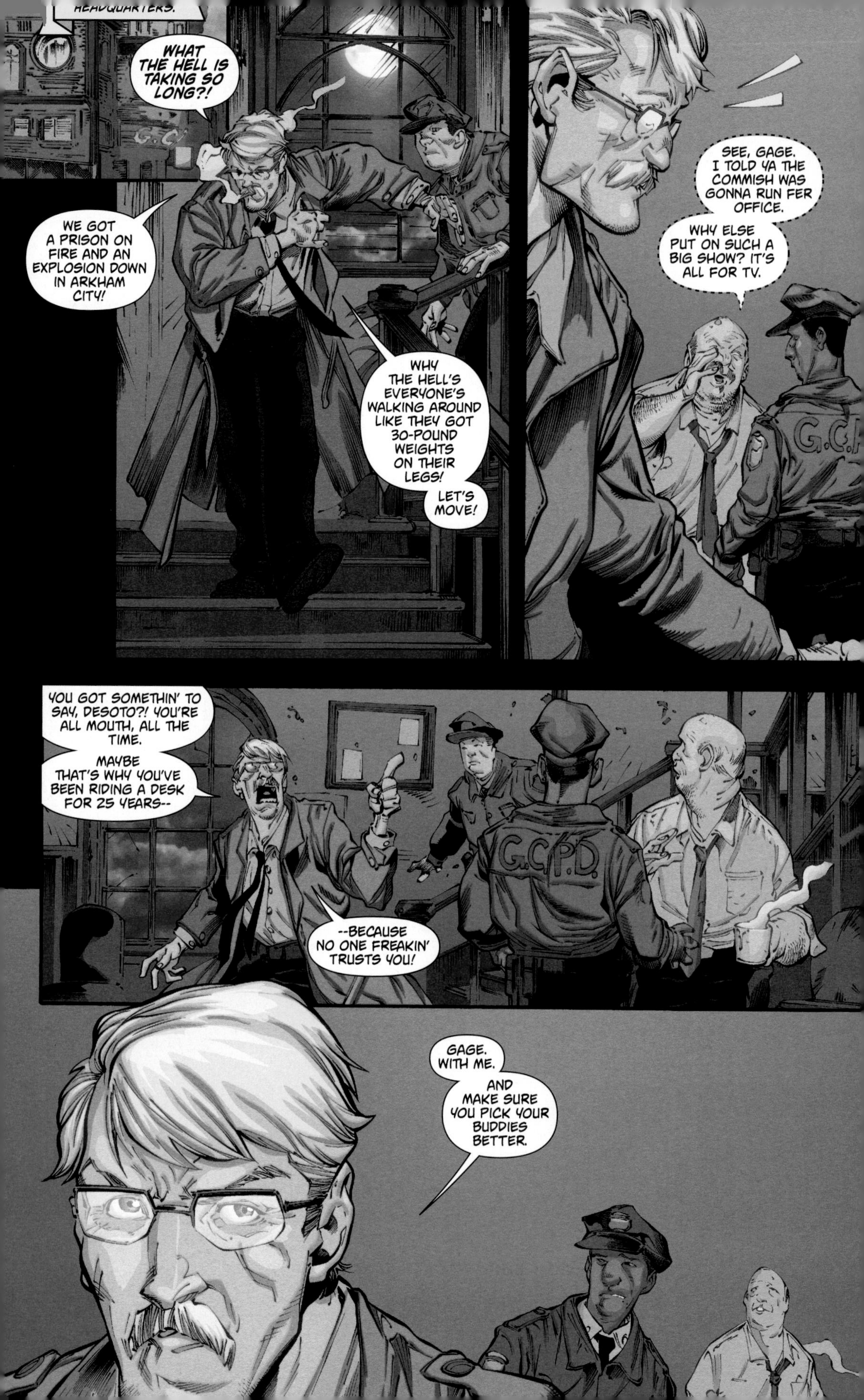
HEADQUARTERS.
WHAT THE HELL IS TAKING SO LONG?!
WE GOT A PRISON ON FIRE AND AN EXPLOSION DOWN IN ARKHAM CITY!
WHY THE HELL'S EVERYONE'S WALKING AROUND LIKE THEY GOT 30-POUND WEIGHTS ON THEIR LEGS!
LET'S MOVE!
SEE, GAGE. I TOLD YA THE COMMISH WAS GONNA RUN FER OFFICE.
WHY ELSE PUT ON SUCH A BIG SHOW? IT'S ALL FOR TV.
G.C.
YOU GOT SOMETHIN' TO SAY, DESOTO?! YOU'RE ALL MOUTH, ALL THE TIME.
MAYBE THAT'S WHY YOU'VE BEEN RIDING A DESK FOR 25 YEARS--
G.C.P.D.
--BECAUSE NO ONE FREAKIN' TRUSTS YOU!
GAGE. WITH ME.
AND MAKE SURE YOU PICK YOUR BUDDIES BETTER.

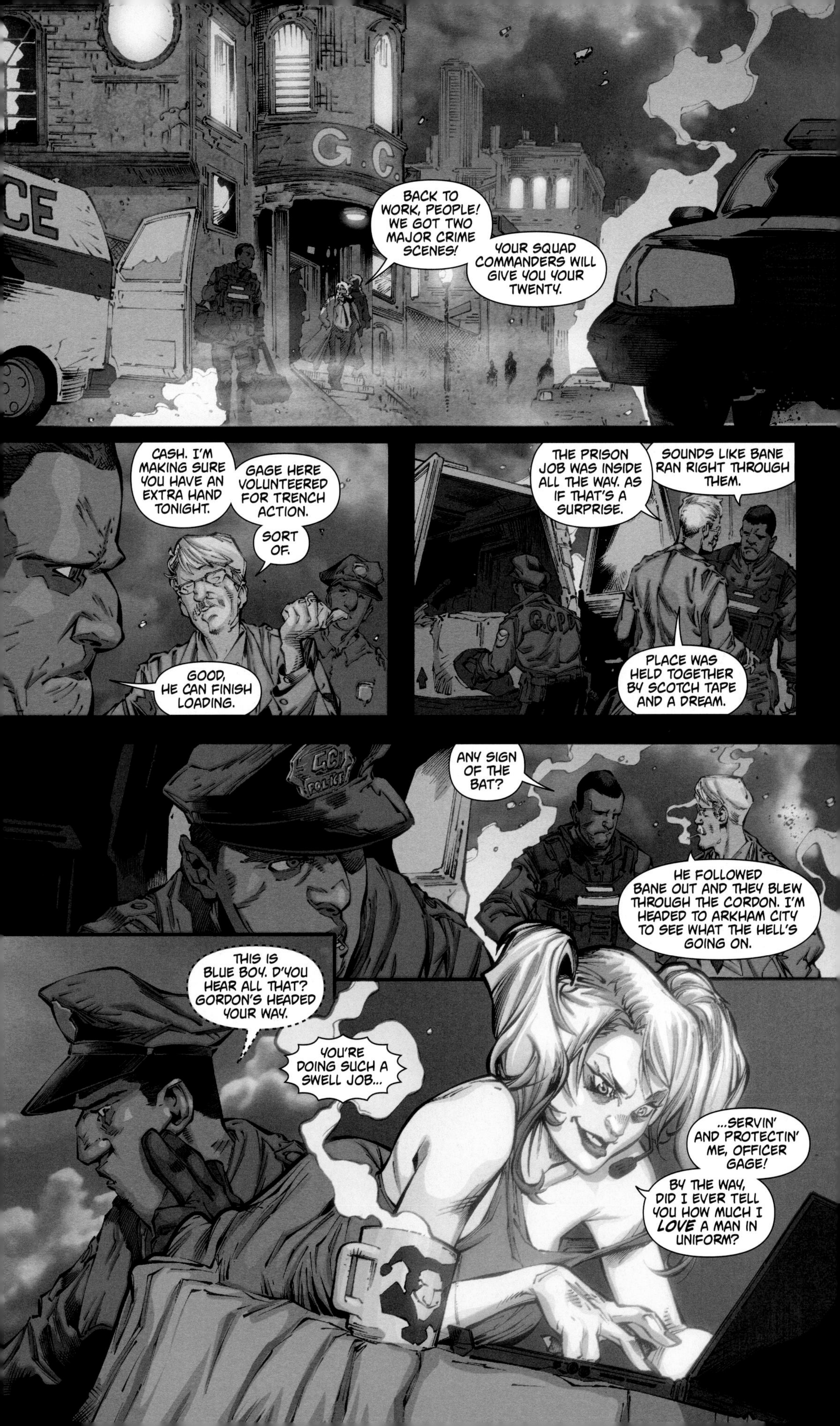

G.C.
BACK TO WORK, PEOPLE! WE GOT TWO MAJOR CRIME SCENES!
YOUR SQUAD COMMANDERS WILL GIVE YOU YOUR TWENTY.
CASH. I'M MAKING SURE YOU HAVE AN EXTRA HAND TONIGHT.
GAGE HERE VOLUNTEERED FOR TRENCH ACTION.
SORT OF.
GOOD, HE CAN FINISH LOADING.
THE PRISON JOB WAS INSIDE ALL THE WAY. AS IF THAT'S A SURPRISE.
SOUNDS LIKE BANE RAN RIGHT THROUGH THEM.
PLACE WAS HELD TOGETHER BY SCOTCH TAPE AND A DREAM.
ANY SIGN OF THE BAT?
HE FOLLOWED BANE OUT AND THEY BLEW THROUGH THE CORDON. I'M HEADED TO ARKHAM CITY TO SEE WHAT THE HELL'S GOING ON.
THIS IS BLUE BOY. D'YOU HEAR ALL THAT? GORDON'S HEADED YOUR WAY.
YOU'RE DOING SUCH A SWELL JOB...
...SERVIN' AND PROTECTIN' ME, OFFICER GAGE!
BY THE WAY, DID I EVER TELL YOU HOW MUCH I *LOVE* A MAN IN UNIFORM?

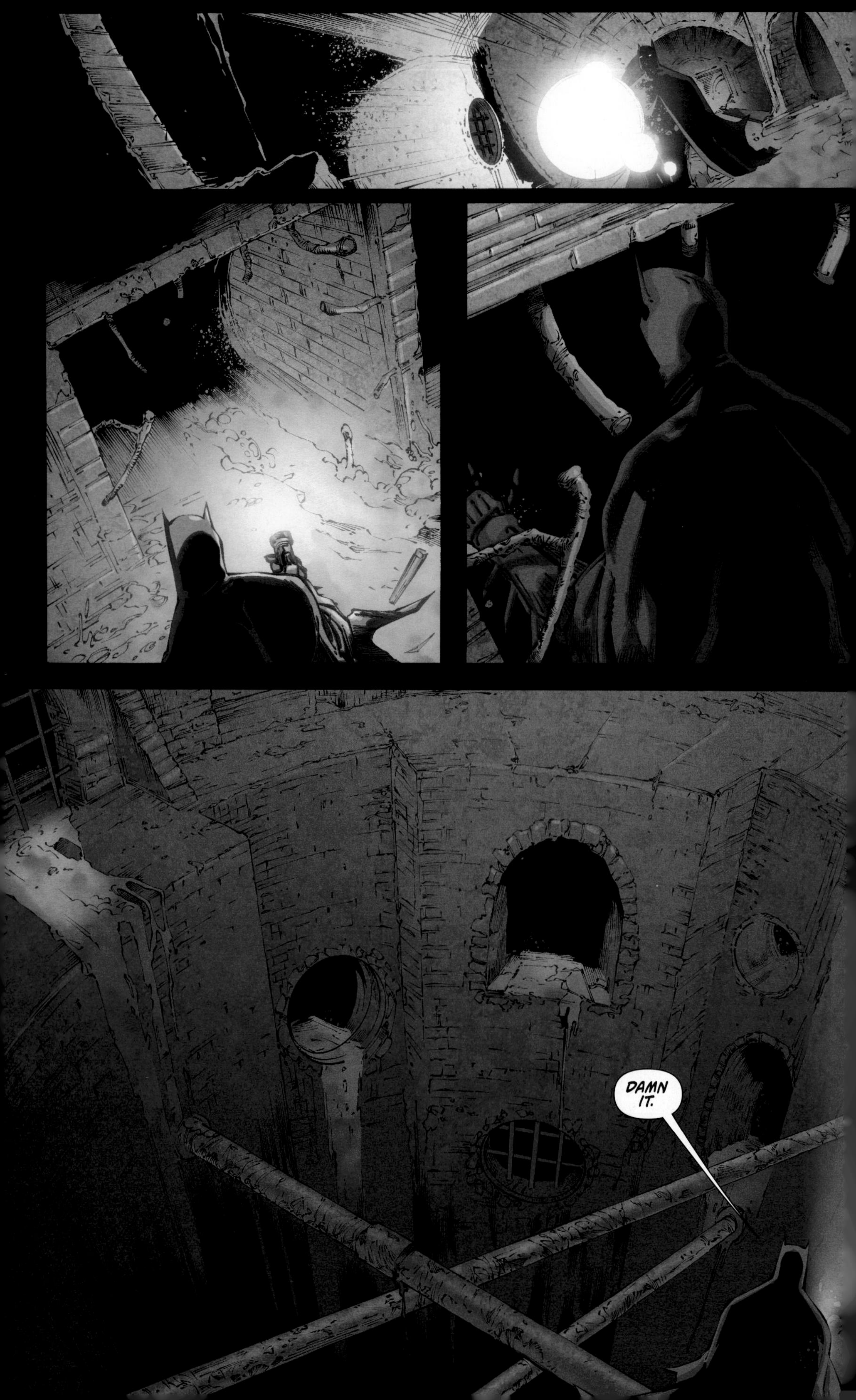
DAMN IT.

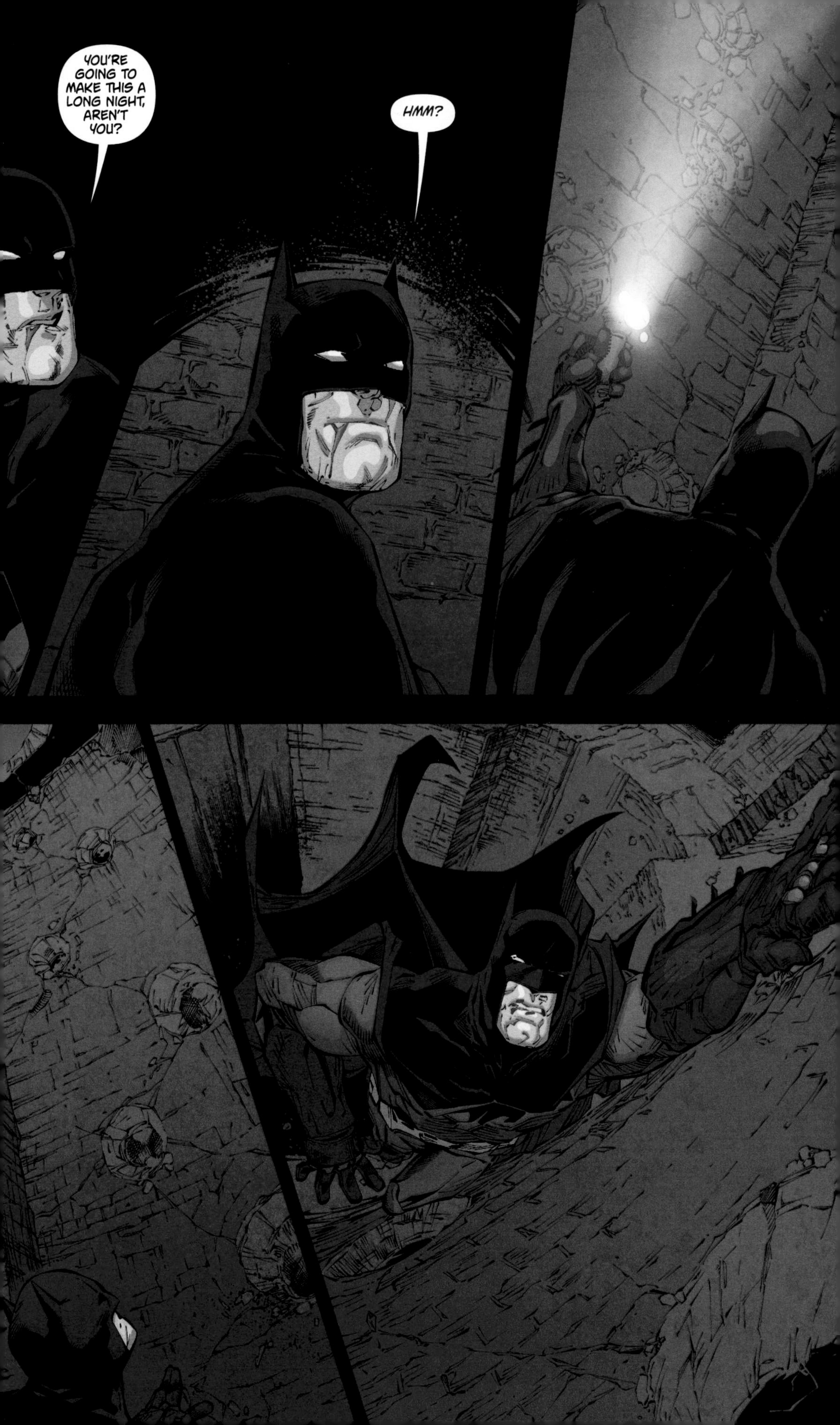
YOU'RE GOING TO MAKE THIS A LONG NIGHT, AREN'T YOU?
HMM?

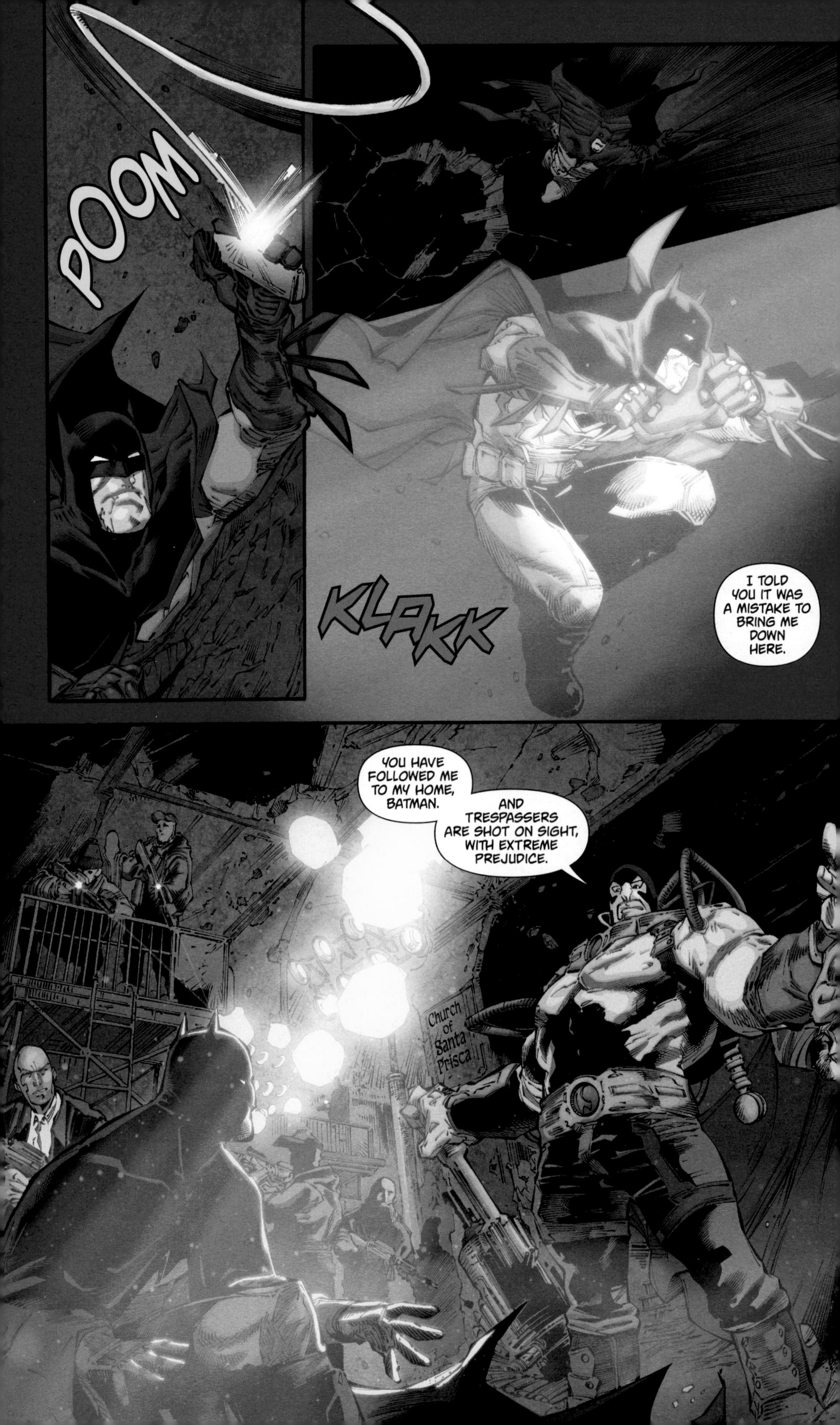
POOM
KLAKK
I TOLD YOU IT WAS A MISTAKE TO BRING ME DOWN HERE.
YOU HAVE FOLLOWED ME TO MY HOME, BATMAN.
AND TRESPASSERS ARE SHOT ON SIGHT, WITH EXTREME PREJUDICE.
Church of Santa Prisca

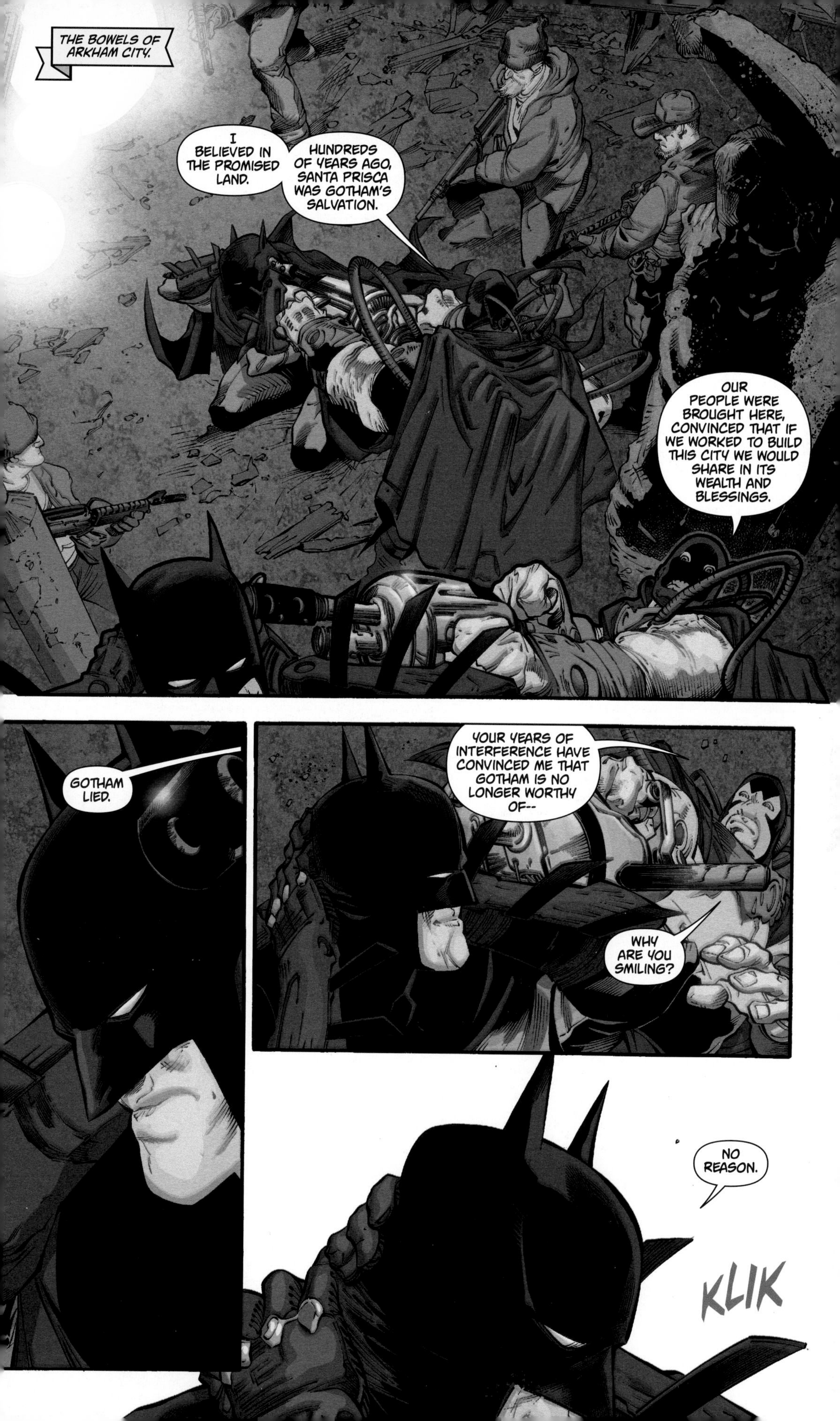
THE BOWELS OF ARKHAM CITY.
I BELIEVED IN THE PROMISED LAND.
HUNDREDS OF YEARS AGO, SANTA PRISCA WAS GOTHAM'S SALVATION.
OUR PEOPLE WERE BROUGHT HERE, CONVINCED THAT IF WE WORKED TO BUILD THIS CITY WE WOULD SHARE IN ITS WEALTH AND BLESSINGS.
GOTHAM LIED.
YOUR YEARS OF INTERFERENCE HAVE CONVINCED ME THAT GOTHAM IS NO LONGER WORTHY OF--
WHY ARE YOU SMILING?
NO REASON.
KLIK

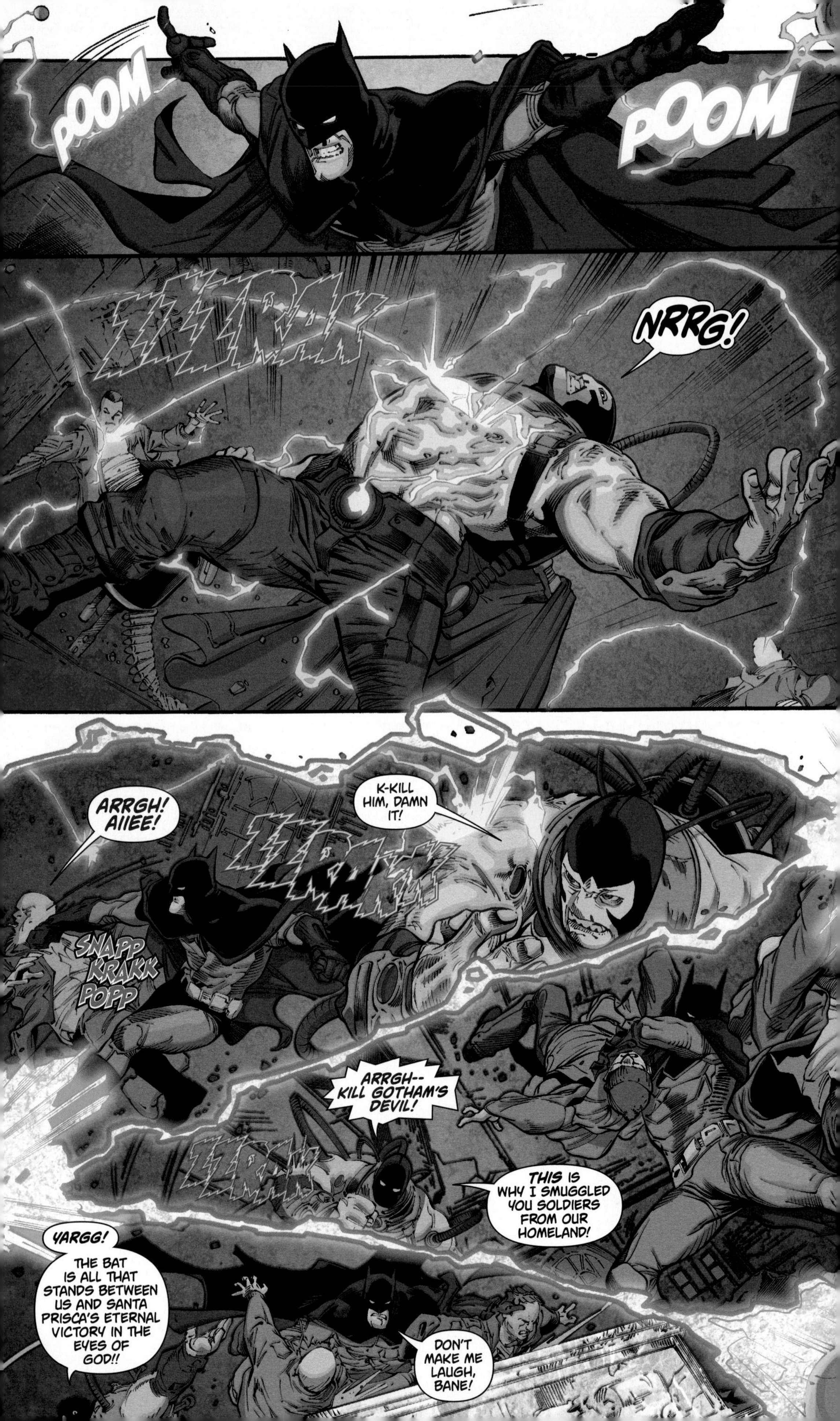
POOM
POOM
NRRG!
ARRGH! AIIEE!
K-KILL HIM, DAMN IT!
SNAPP KRAKK POPP
ARRGH-- KILL GOTHAM'S DEVIL!
THIS IS WHY I SMUGGLED YOU SOLDIERS FROM OUR HOMELAND!
YARGG!
THE BAT IS ALL THAT STANDS BETWEEN US AND SANTA PRISCA'S ETERNAL VICTORY IN THE EYES OF GOD!!
DON'T MAKE ME LAUGH, BANE!

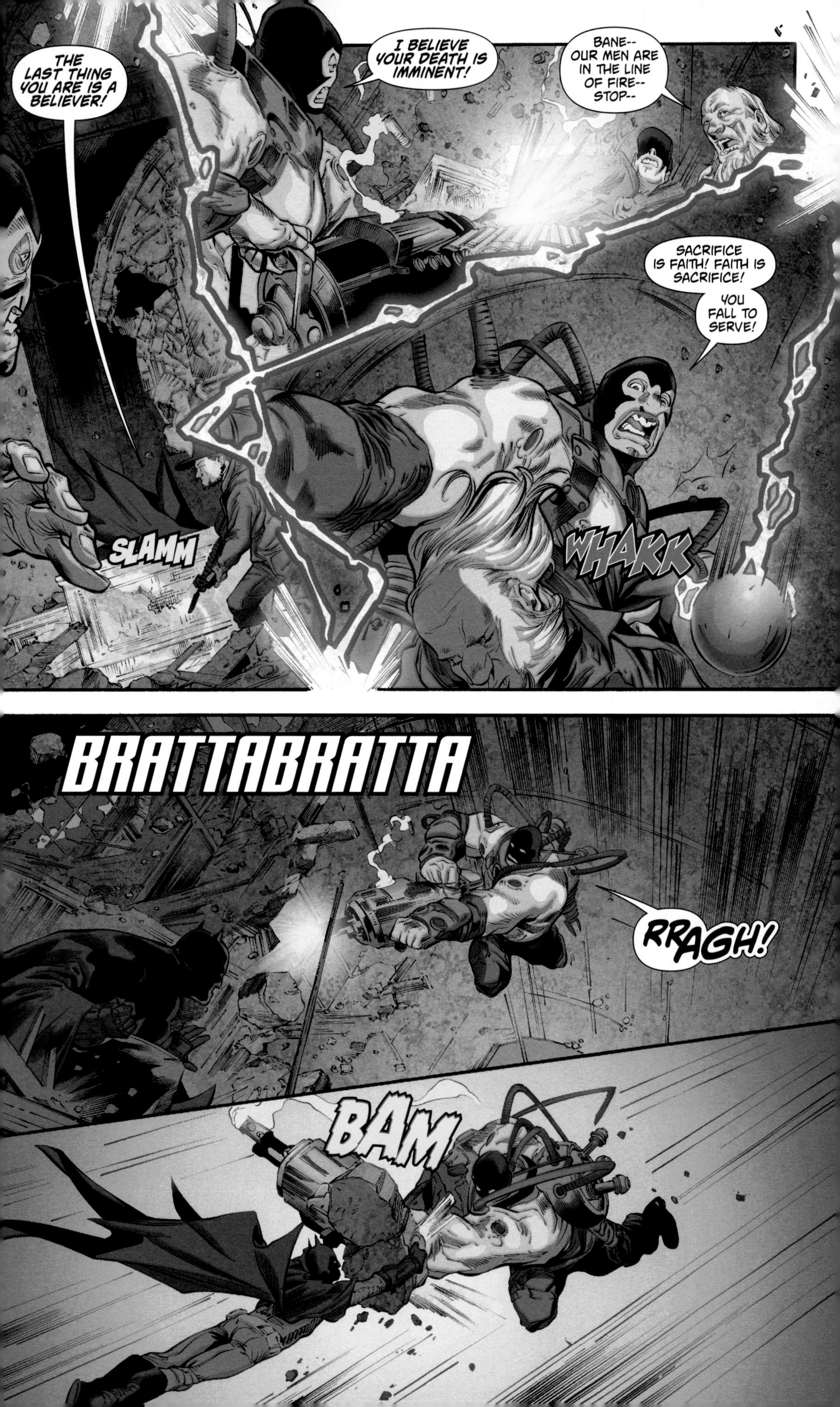
THE LAST THING YOU ARE IS A BELIEVER!
I BELIEVE YOUR DEATH IS IMMINENT!
BANE-- OUR MEN ARE IN THE LINE OF FIRE-- STOP--
SACRIFICE IS FAITH! FAITH IS SACRIFICE!
YOU FALL TO SERVE!
SLAMM
WHAKK
BRATTABRATTA
RRAGH!
BAM

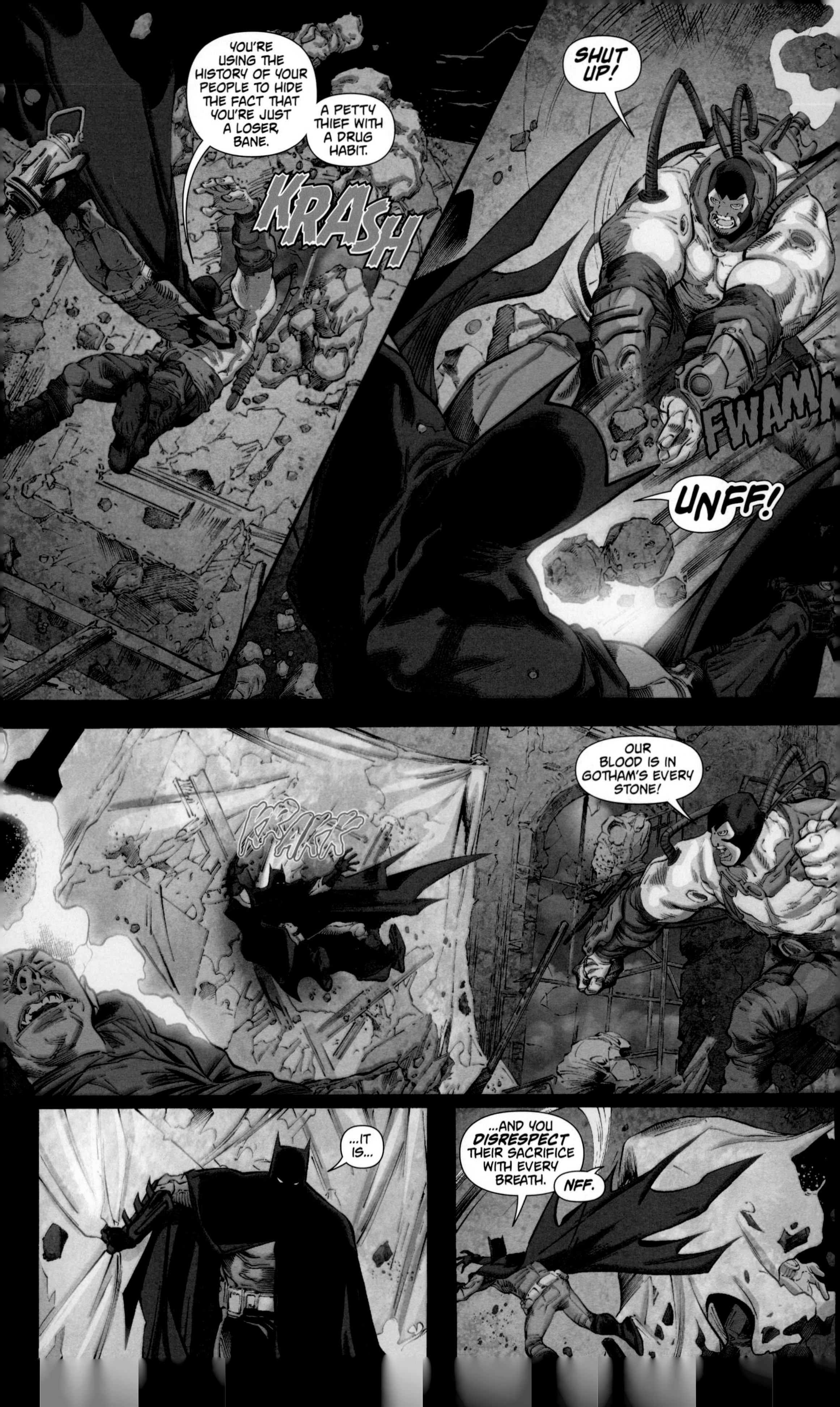
YOU'RE USING THE HISTORY OF YOUR PEOPLE TO HIDE THE FACT THAT YOU'RE JUST A LOSER, BANE.
A PETTY THIEF WITH A DRUG HABIT.
KRASH
SHUT UP!
FWAMM
UNFF!
OUR BLOOD IS IN GOTHAM'S EVERY STONE!
KRAKK
...IT IS...
...AND YOU DISRESPECT THEIR SACRIFICE WITH EVERY BREATH.
NFF.

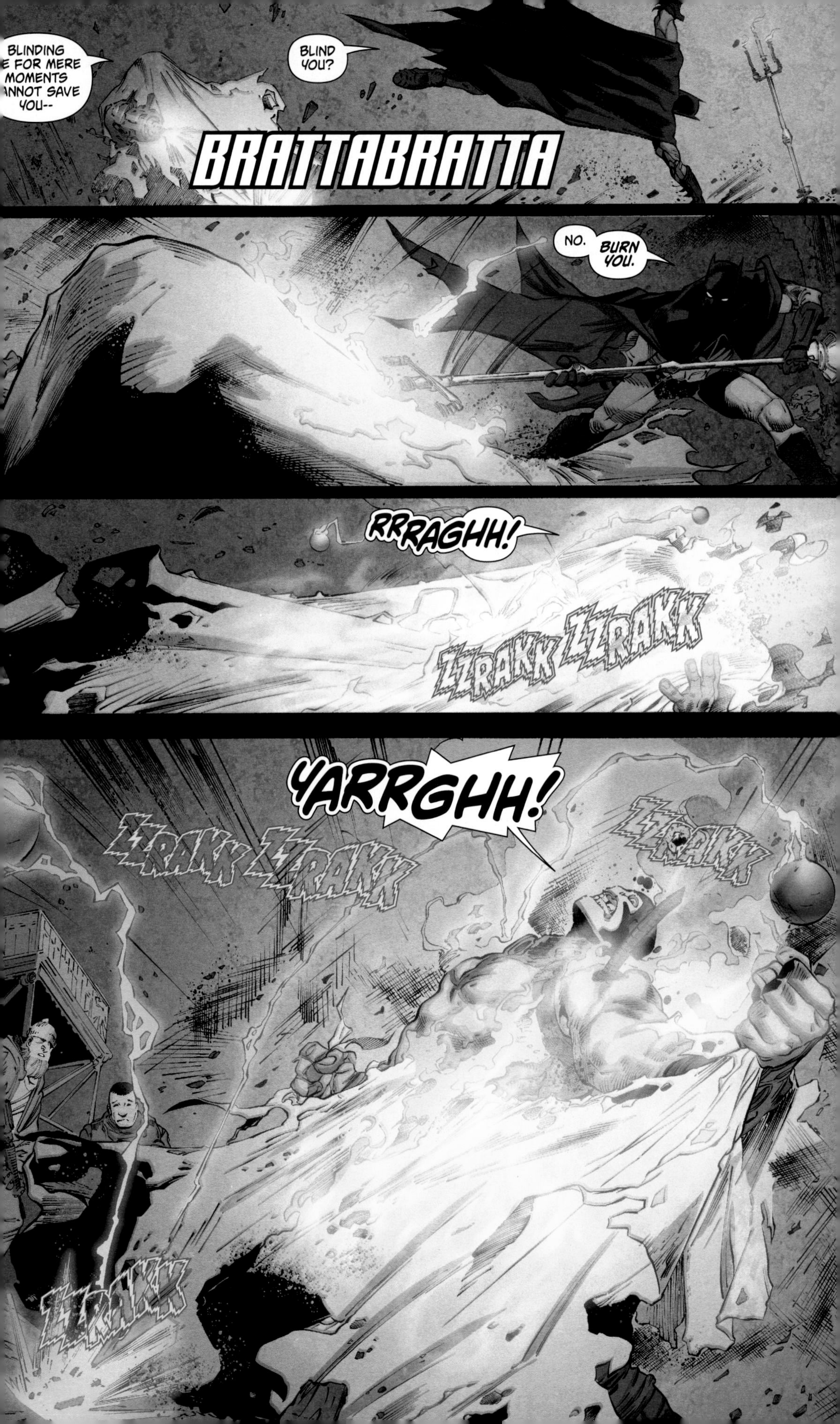

BLINDING
E FOR MERE
MOMENTS
ANNOT SAVE
YOU--
BLIND
YOU?
BRATTABRATTA
NO.
BURN
YOU.
RRRAGHH!
ZZRAKK ZZRAKK
YARRGHH!
ZZRAKK ZZRAKK
ZZRAKK
ZZRAKK

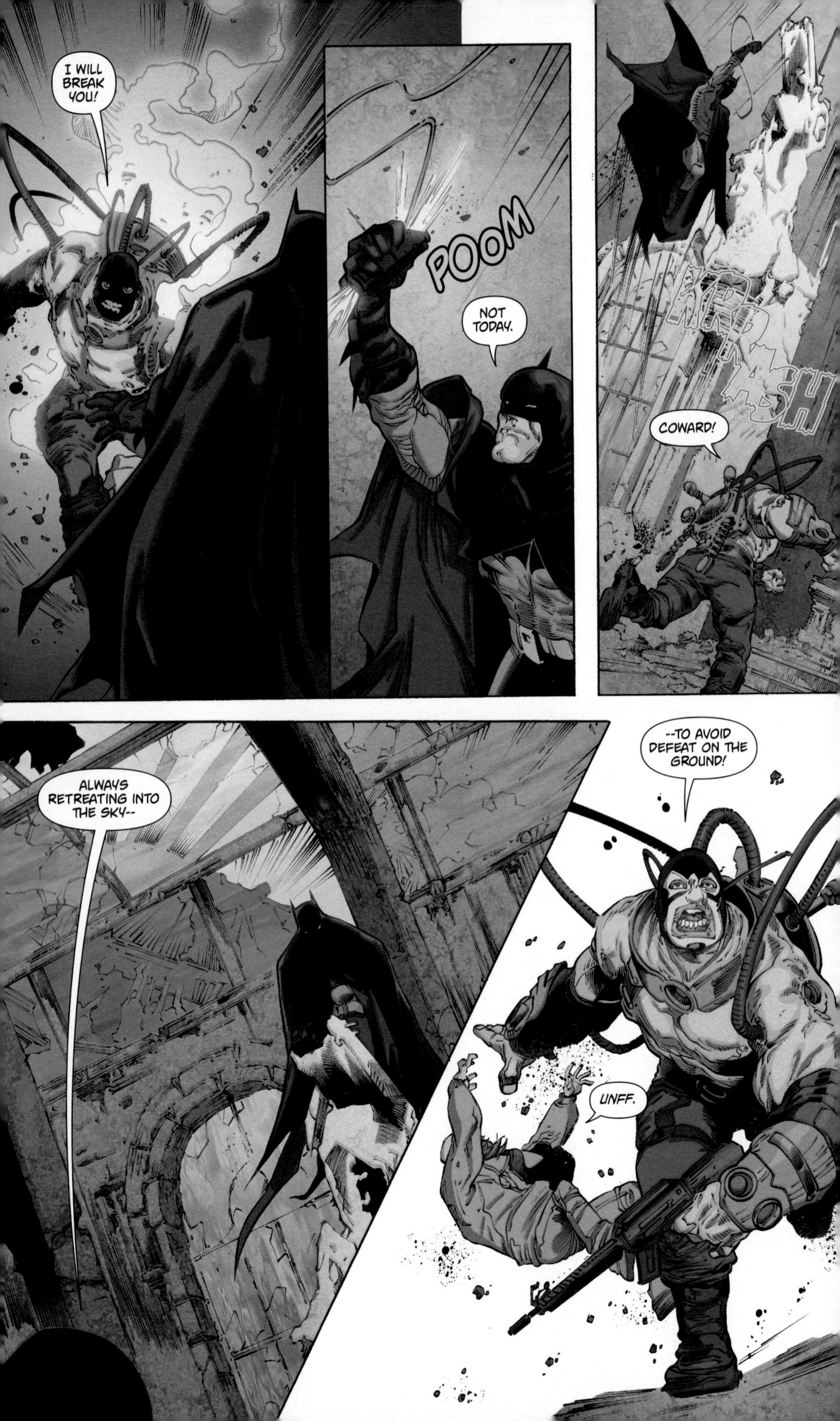
I WILL BREAK YOU!
POOM
NOT TODAY.
COWARD!
ALWAYS RETREATING INTO THE SKY--
--TO AVOID DEFEAT ON THE GROUND!
UNFF.

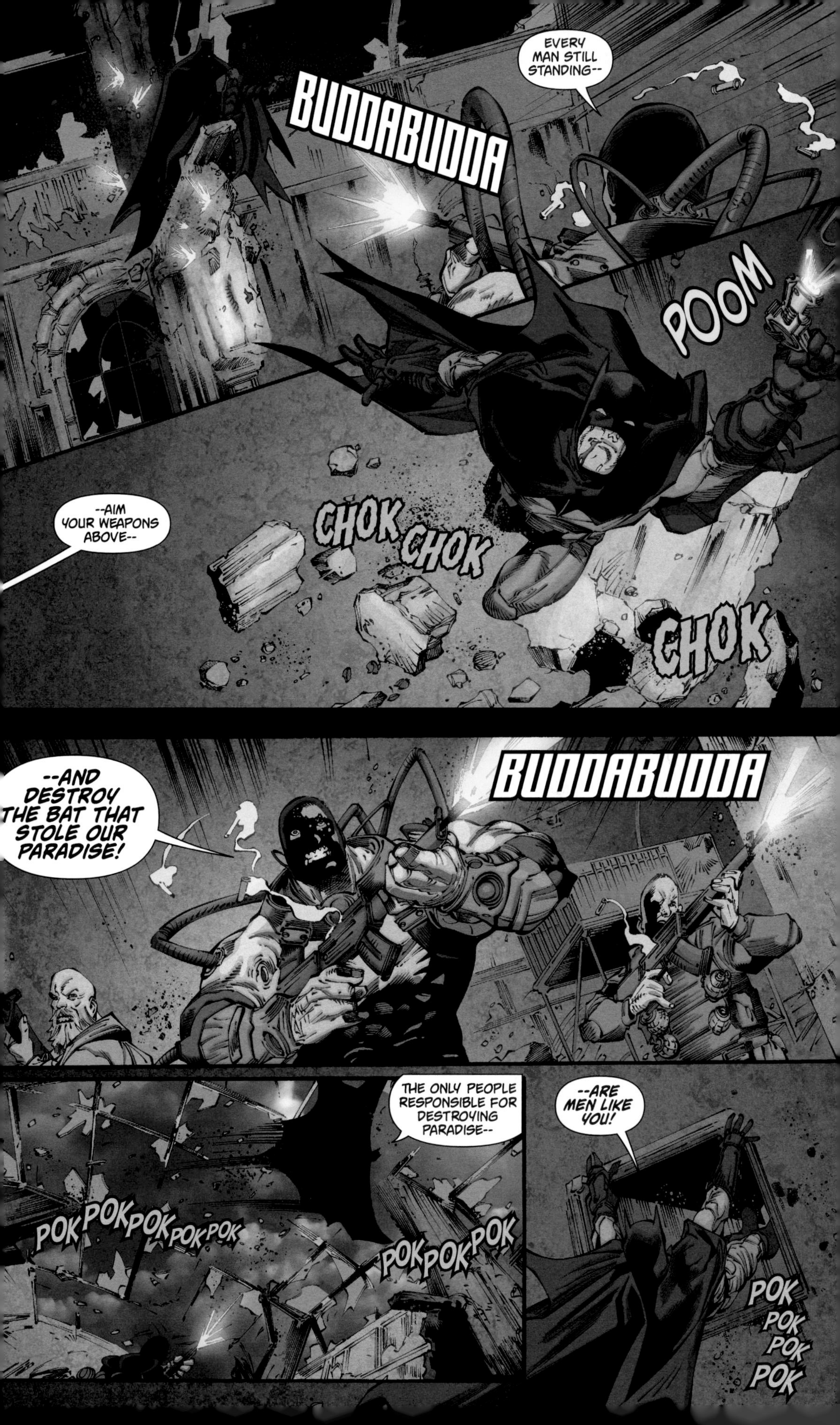

BUDDABUDDA
EVERY MAN STILL STANDING--
POOM
--AIM YOUR WEAPONS ABOVE--
CHOK CHOK
CHOK
--AND DESTROY THE BAT THAT STOLE OUR PARADISE!
BUDDABUDDA
THE ONLY PEOPLE RESPONSIBLE FOR DESTROYING PARADISE--
POKPOKPOKPOKPOK
POKPOKPOK
--ARE MEN LIKE YOU!
POK POK POK POK

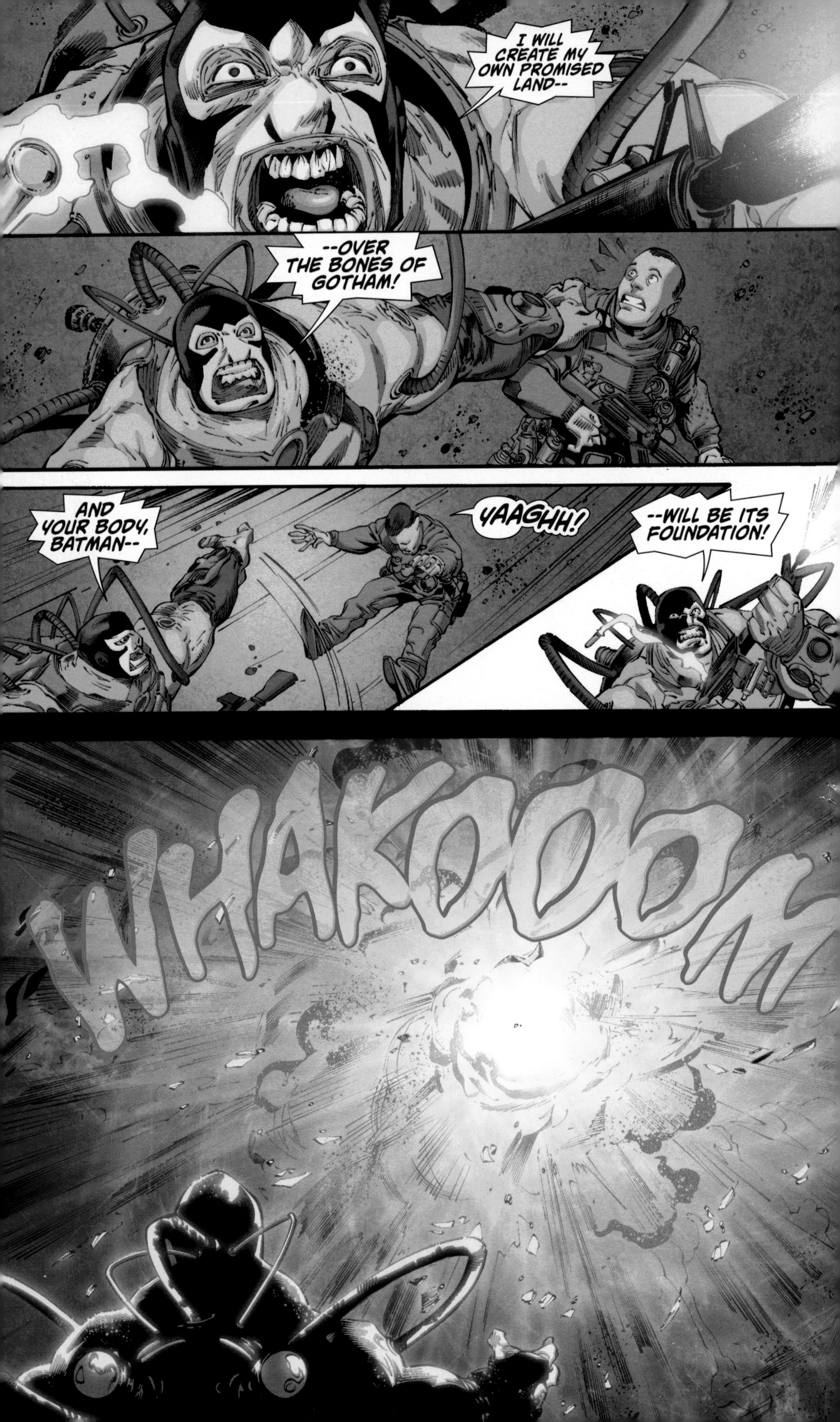
I WILL CREATE MY OWN PROMISED LAND--
--OVER THE BONES OF GOTHAM!
AND YOUR BODY, BATMAN--
YAAGHH!
--WILL BE ITS FOUNDATION!
WHAKOOOM

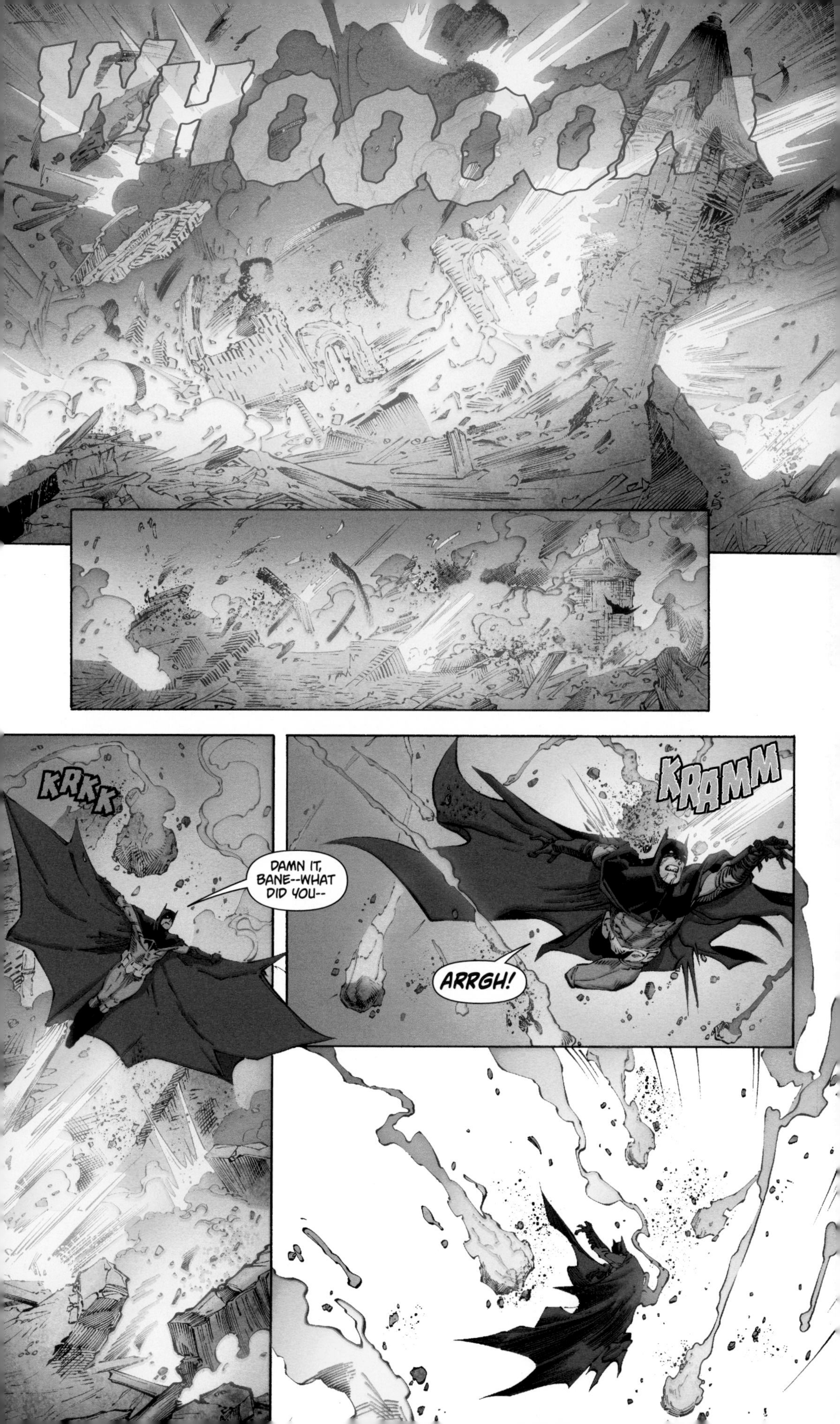
WHOOOOM
KRKK
DAMN IT, BANE--WHAT DID YOU--
KRAMM
ARRGH!

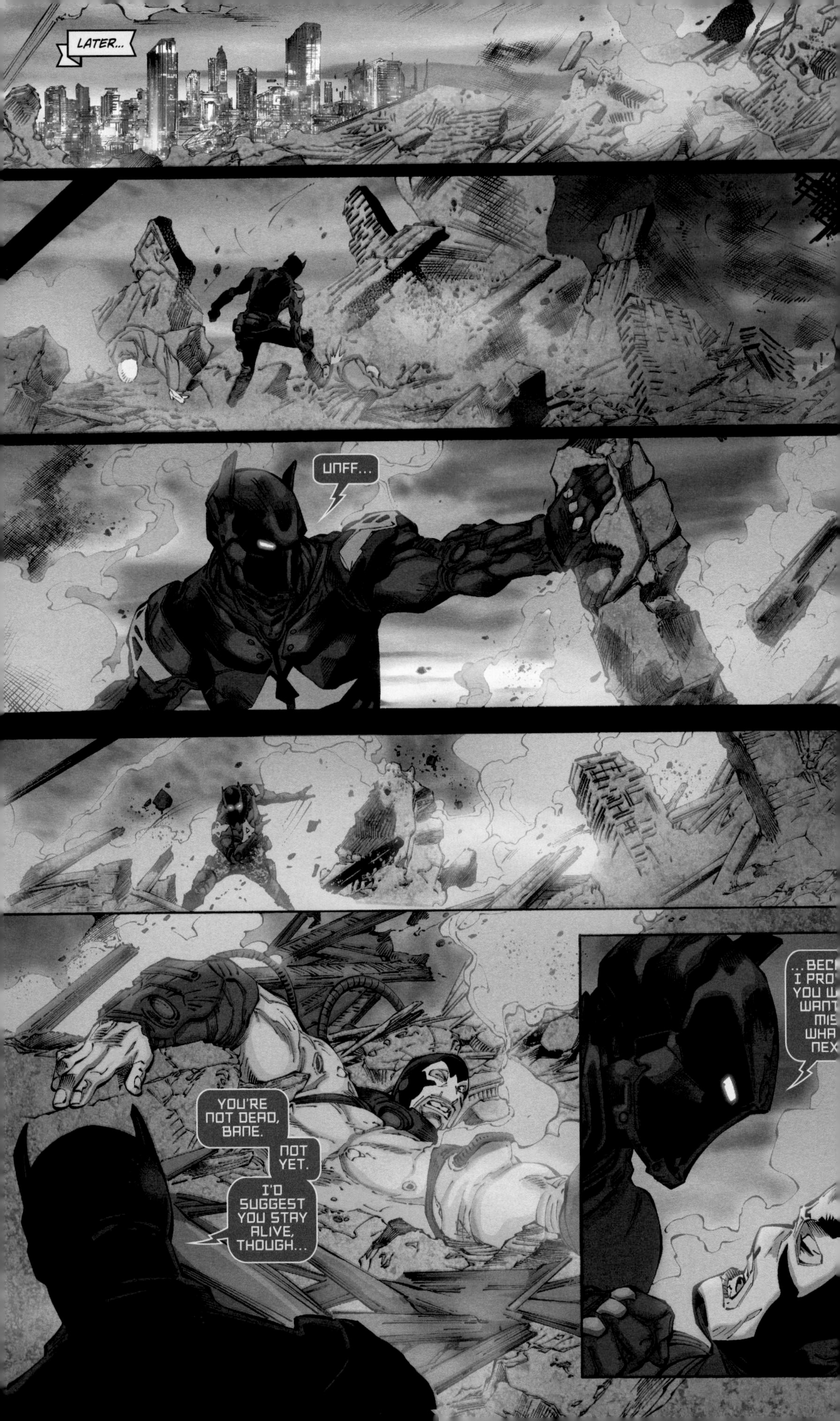
LATER...
UNFF...
YOU'RE NOT DEAD, BANE.
NOT YET.
I'D SUGGEST YOU STAY ALIVE, THOUGH...
...BEC
I PRO
YOU W
WANT
MIS
WHA
NEX

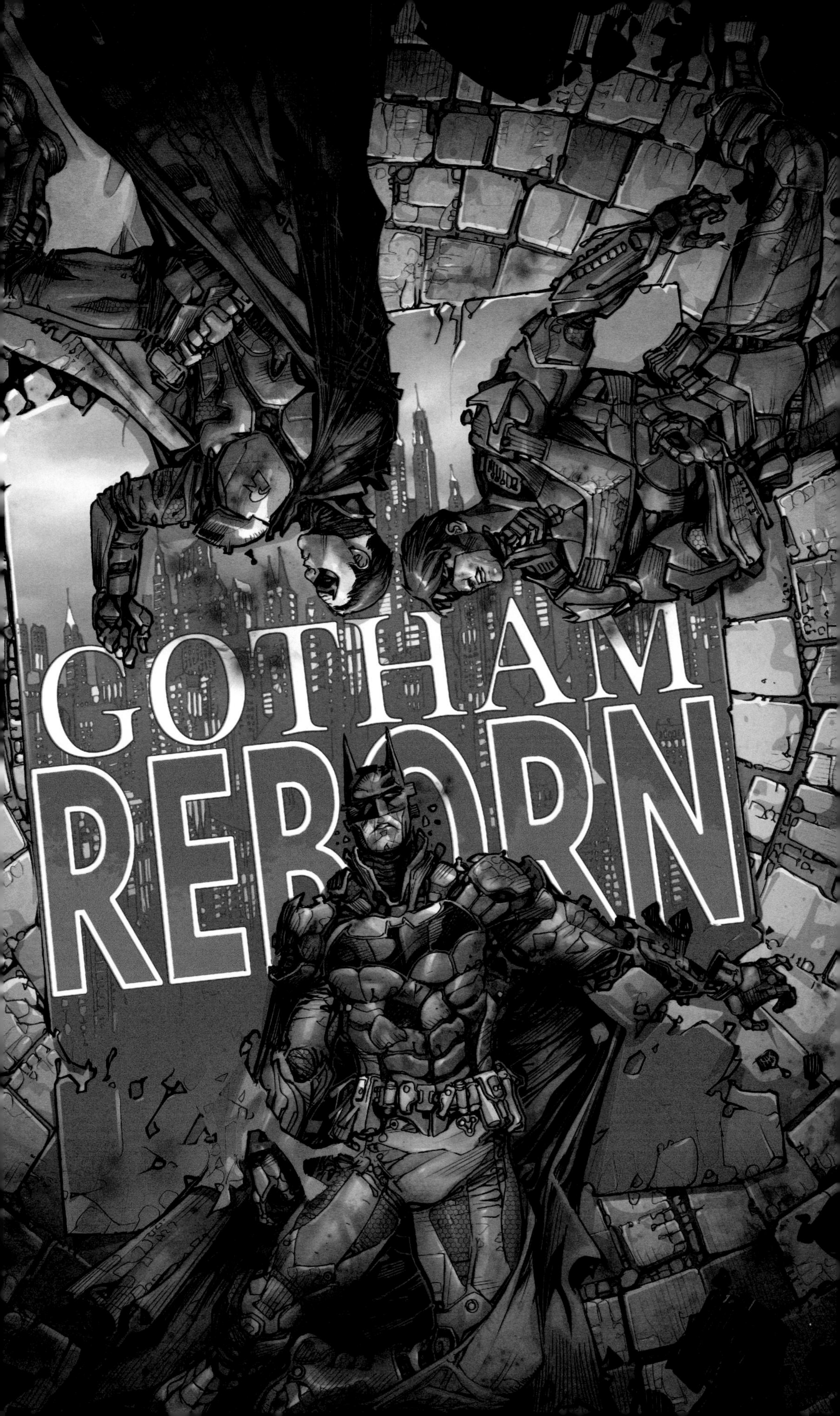
GOTHAM
REBORN

SAFE HOUSE

PETER J. TOMASI story & words · VIKTOR BOGDANOVIC pencils · ART THIBERT inks · JOHN RAUCH color · TRAVIS LANHAM letters · HOWARD PORTER and HI-FI cover

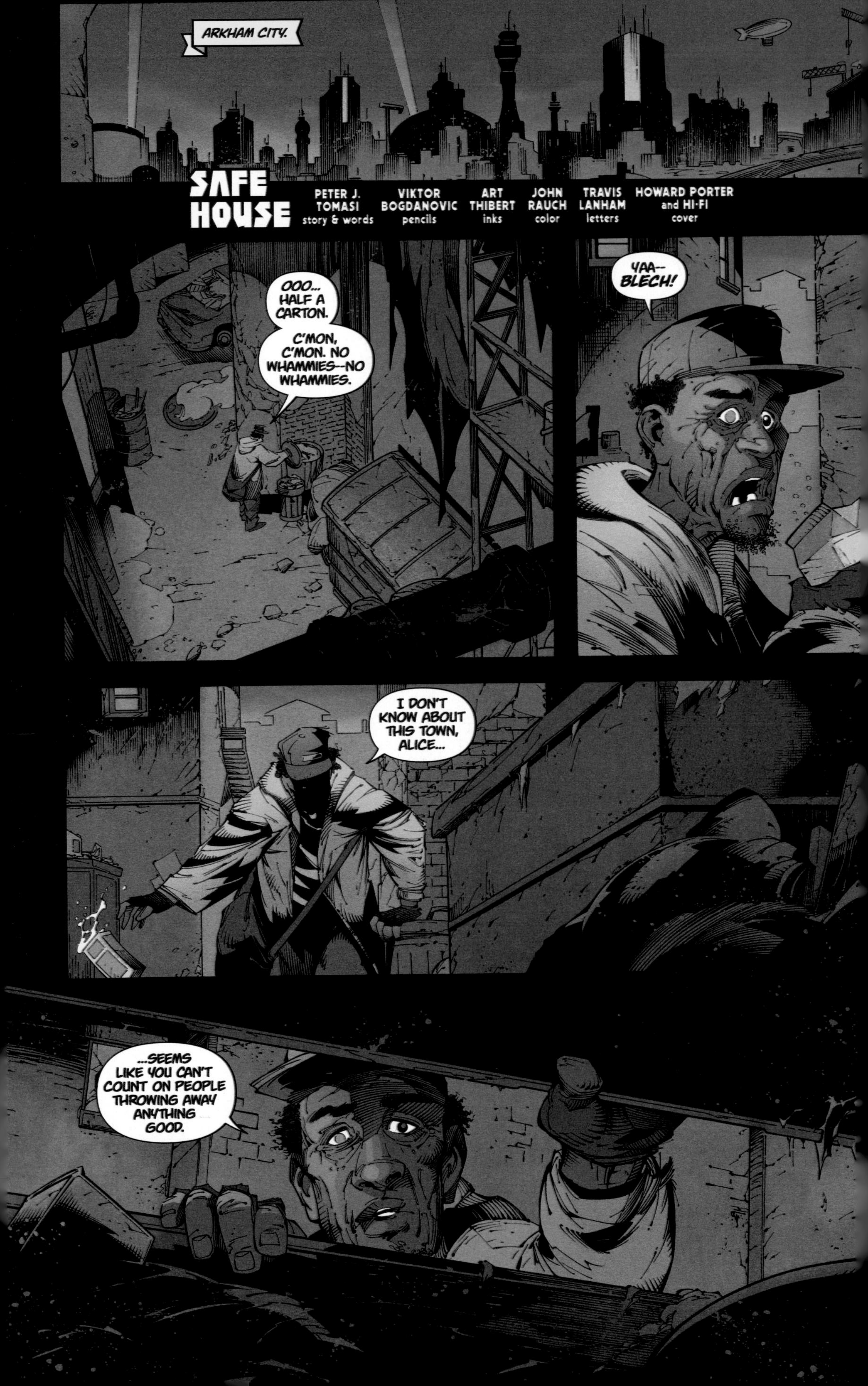
ARKHAM CITY.
OOO... HALF A CARTON.
C'MON, C'MON. NO WHAMMIES--NO WHAMMIES.
YAA-- BLECH!
I DON'T KNOW ABOUT THIS TOWN, ALICE...
...SEEMS LIKE YOU CAN'T COUNT ON PEOPLE THROWING AWAY ANYTHING GOOD.

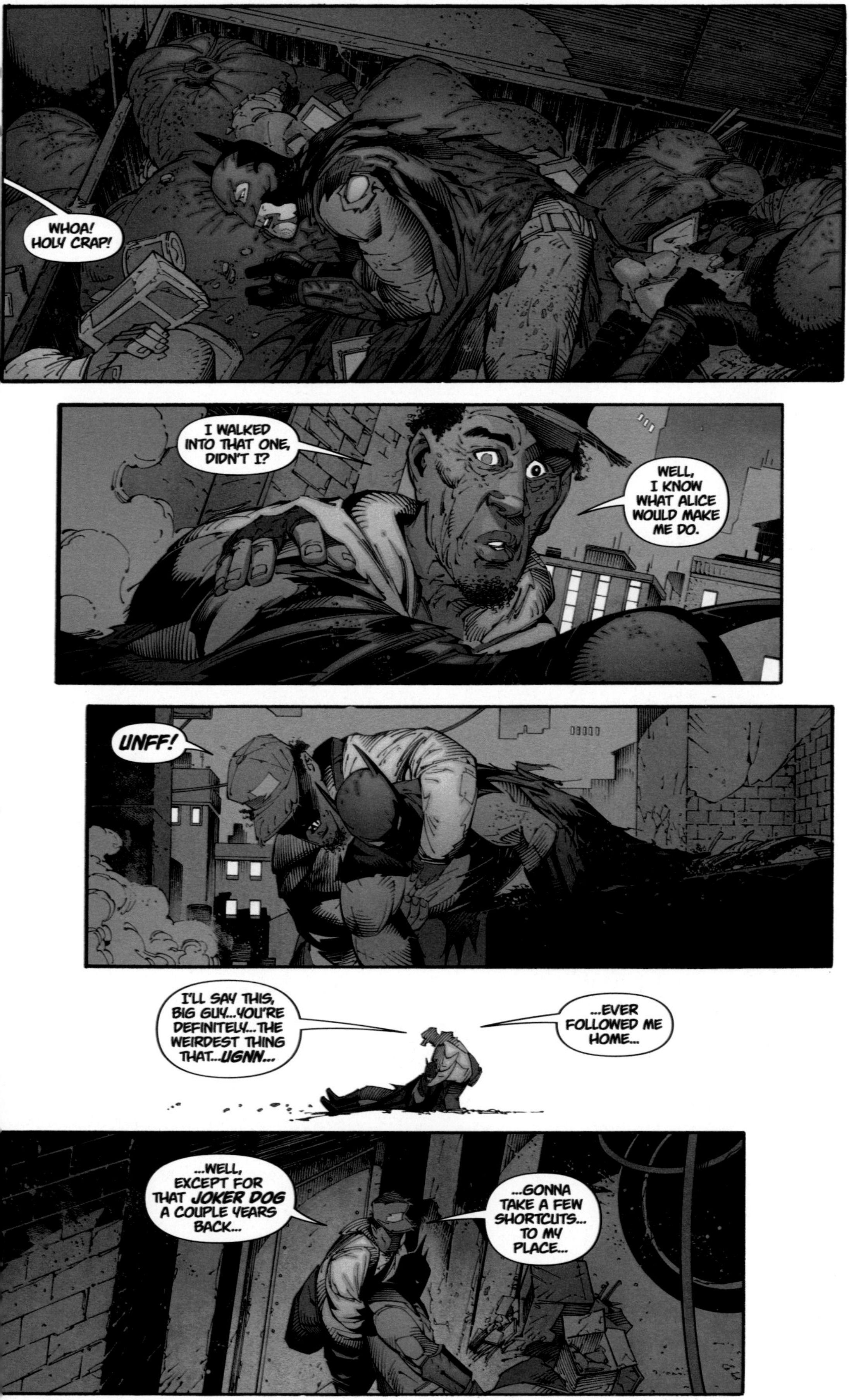
WHOA! HOLY CRAP!
I WALKED INTO THAT ONE, DIDN'T I?
WELL, I KNOW WHAT ALICE WOULD MAKE ME DO.
UNFF!
I'LL SAY THIS, BIG GUY...YOU'RE DEFINITELY...THE WEIRDEST THING THAT...UGNN...
...EVER FOLLOWED ME HOME...
...WELL, EXCEPT FOR THAT JOKER DOG A COUPLE YEARS BACK...
...GONNA TAKE A FEW SHORTCUTS... TO MY PLACE...

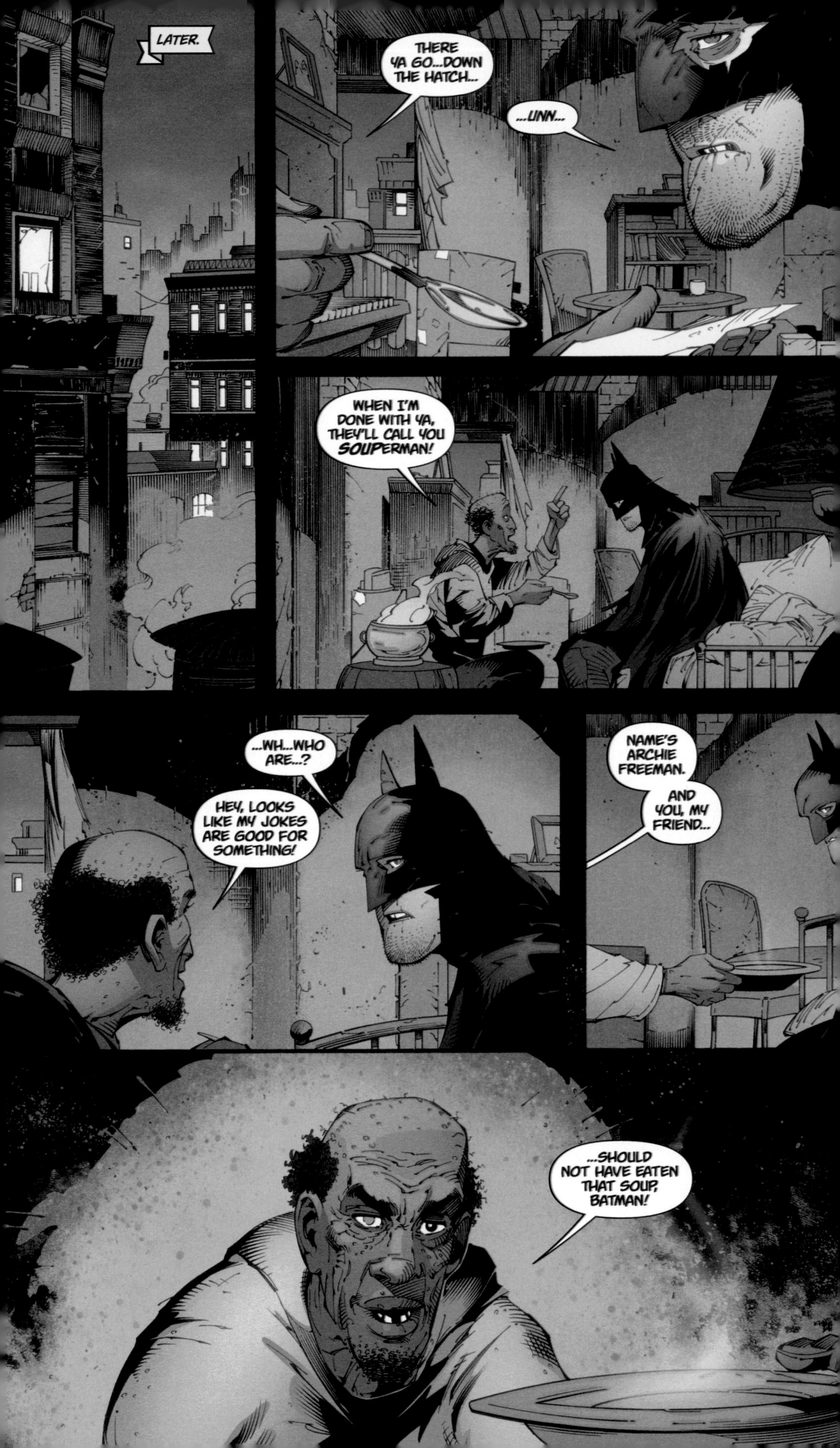

LATER.
THERE YA GO...DOWN THE HATCH...
...UNN...
WHEN I'M DONE WITH YA, THEY'LL CALL YOU SOUPERMAN!
...WH...WHO ARE...?
HEY, LOOKS LIKE MY JOKES ARE GOOD FOR SOMETHING!
NAME'S ARCHIE FREEMAN.
AND YOU, MY FRIEND...
...SHOULD NOT HAVE EATEN THAT SOUP, BATMAN!

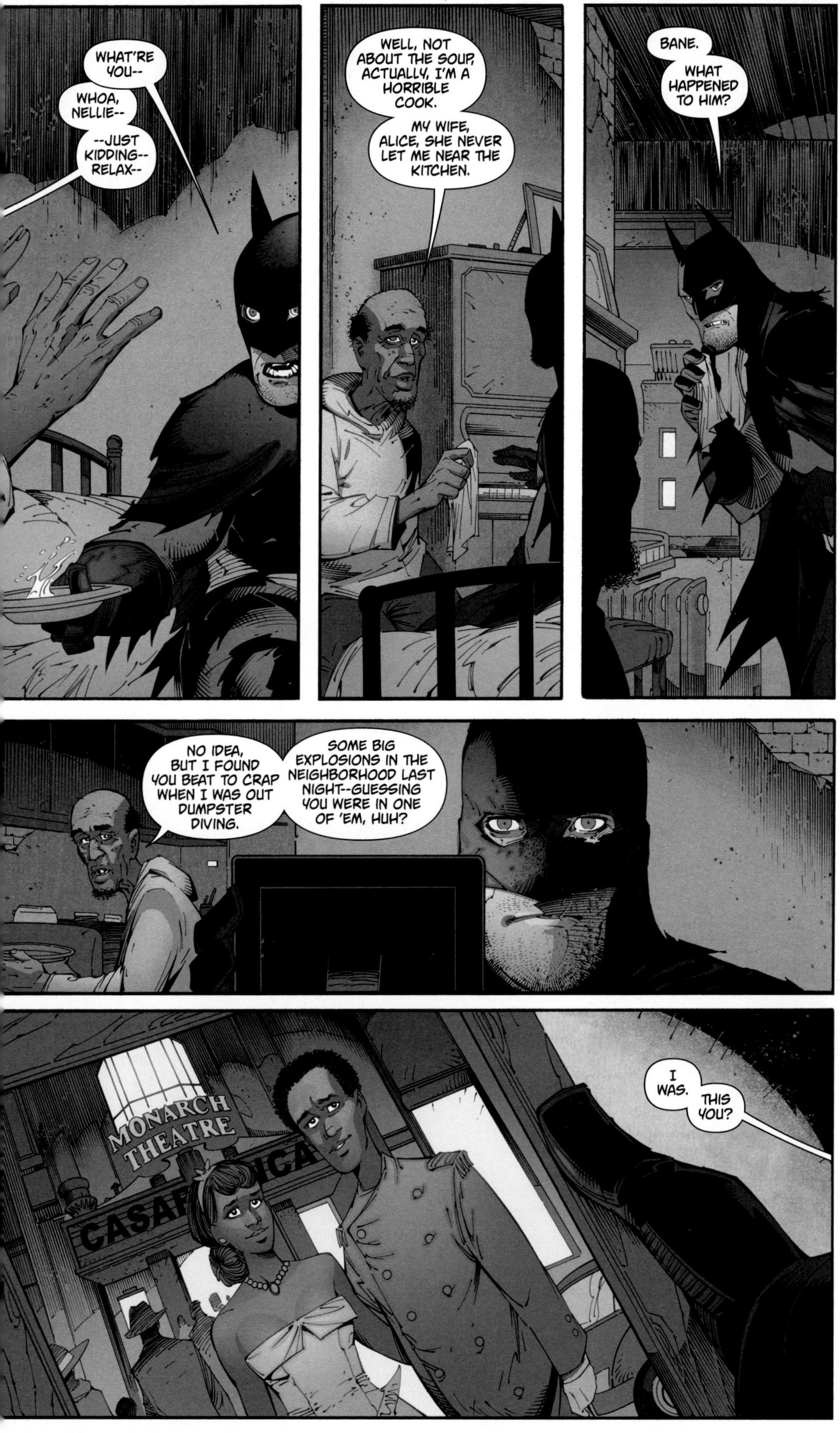
WHAT'RE YOU--
WHOA, NELLIE--
--JUST KIDDING-- RELAX--
WELL, NOT ABOUT THE SOUP, ACTUALLY, I'M A HORRIBLE COOK.
MY WIFE, ALICE, SHE NEVER LET ME NEAR THE KITCHEN.
BANE.
WHAT HAPPENED TO HIM?
NO IDEA, BUT I FOUND YOU BEAT TO CRAP WHEN I WAS OUT DUMPSTER DIVING.
SOME BIG EXPLOSIONS IN THE NEIGHBORHOOD LAST NIGHT--GUESSING YOU WERE IN ONE OF 'EM, HUH?
MONARCH THEATRE
I WAS.
THIS YOU?

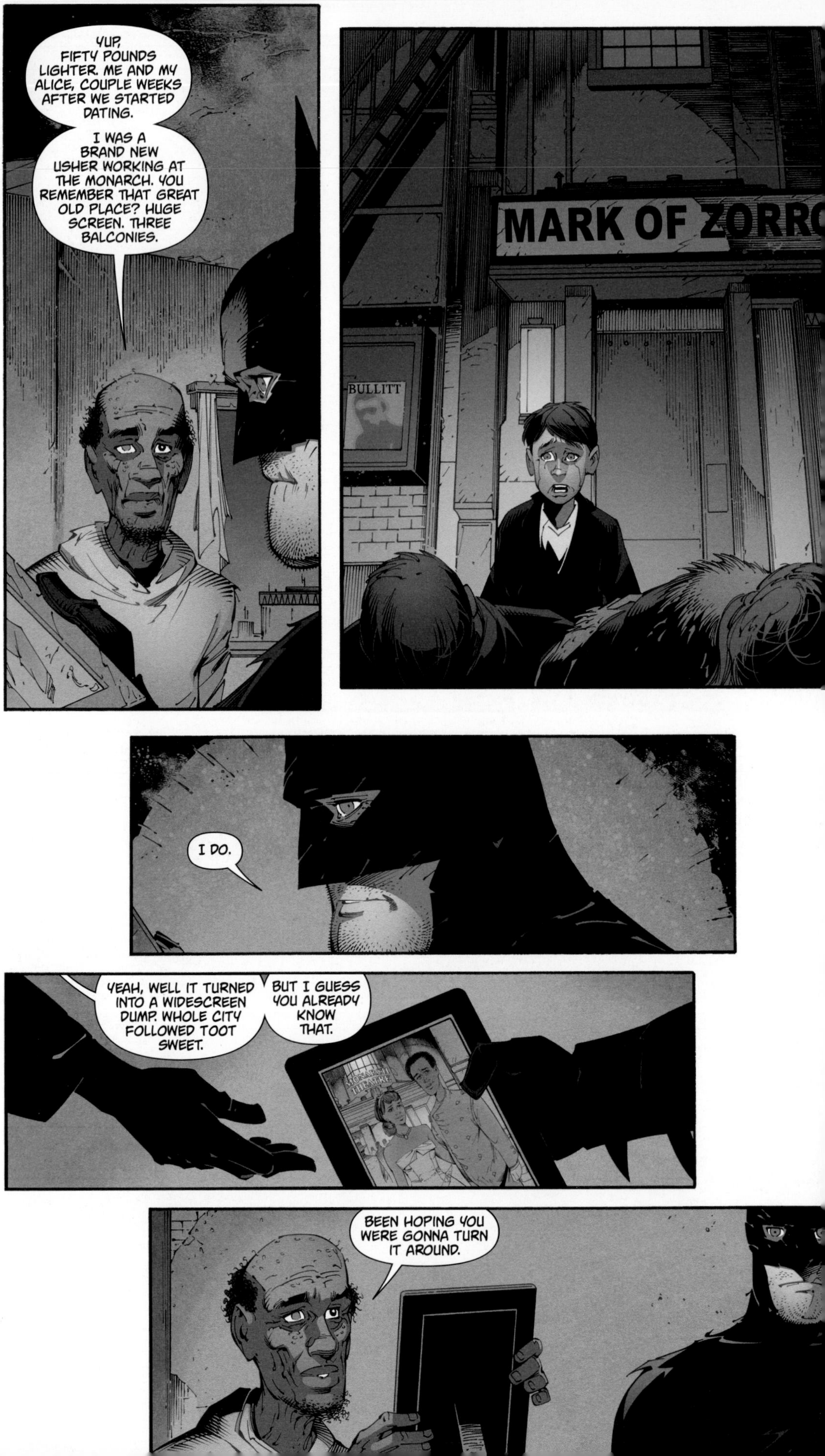
YUP, FIFTY POUNDS LIGHTER. ME AND MY ALICE, COUPLE WEEKS AFTER WE STARTED DATING.
I WAS A BRAND NEW USHER WORKING AT THE MONARCH. YOU REMEMBER THAT GREAT OLD PLACE? HUGE SCREEN. THREE BALCONIES.
MARK OF ZORRO
BULLITT
I DO.
YEAH, WELL IT TURNED INTO A WIDESCREEN DUMP. WHOLE CITY FOLLOWED TOOT SWEET.
BUT I GUESS YOU ALREADY KNOW THAT.
BEEN HOPING YOU WERE GONNA TURN IT AROUND.

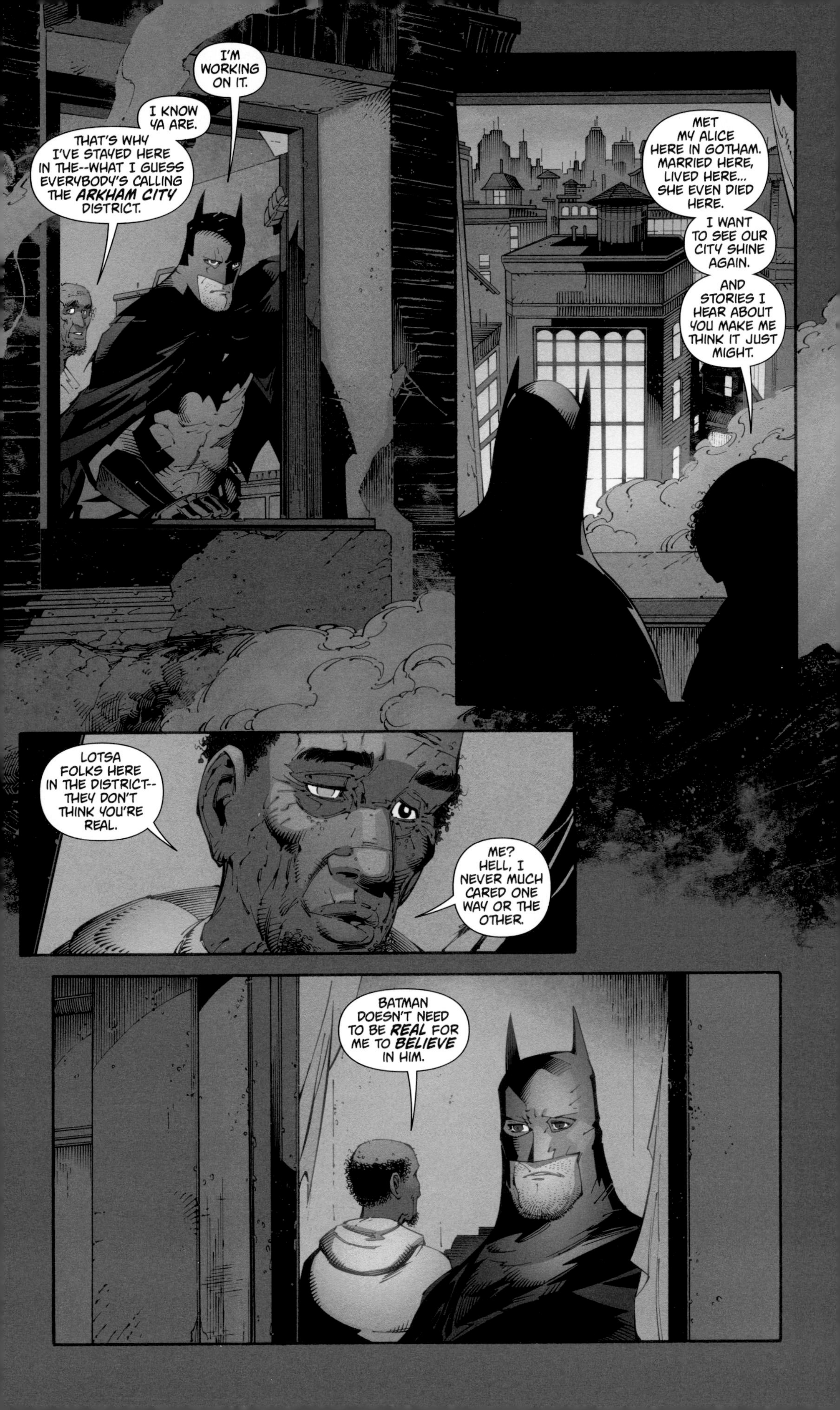
I'M WORKING ON IT.
I KNOW YA ARE.
THAT'S WHY I'VE STAYED HERE IN THE--WHAT I GUESS EVERYBODY'S CALLING THE ARKHAM CITY DISTRICT.
MET MY ALICE HERE IN GOTHAM. MARRIED HERE, LIVED HERE... SHE EVEN DIED HERE.
I WANT TO SEE OUR CITY SHINE AGAIN.
AND STORIES I HEAR ABOUT YOU MAKE ME THINK IT JUST MIGHT.
LOTSA FOLKS HERE IN THE DISTRICT-- THEY DON'T THINK YOU'RE REAL.
ME? HELL, I NEVER MUCH CARED ONE WAY OR THE OTHER.
BATMAN DOESN'T NEED TO BE REAL FOR ME TO BELIEVE IN HIM.

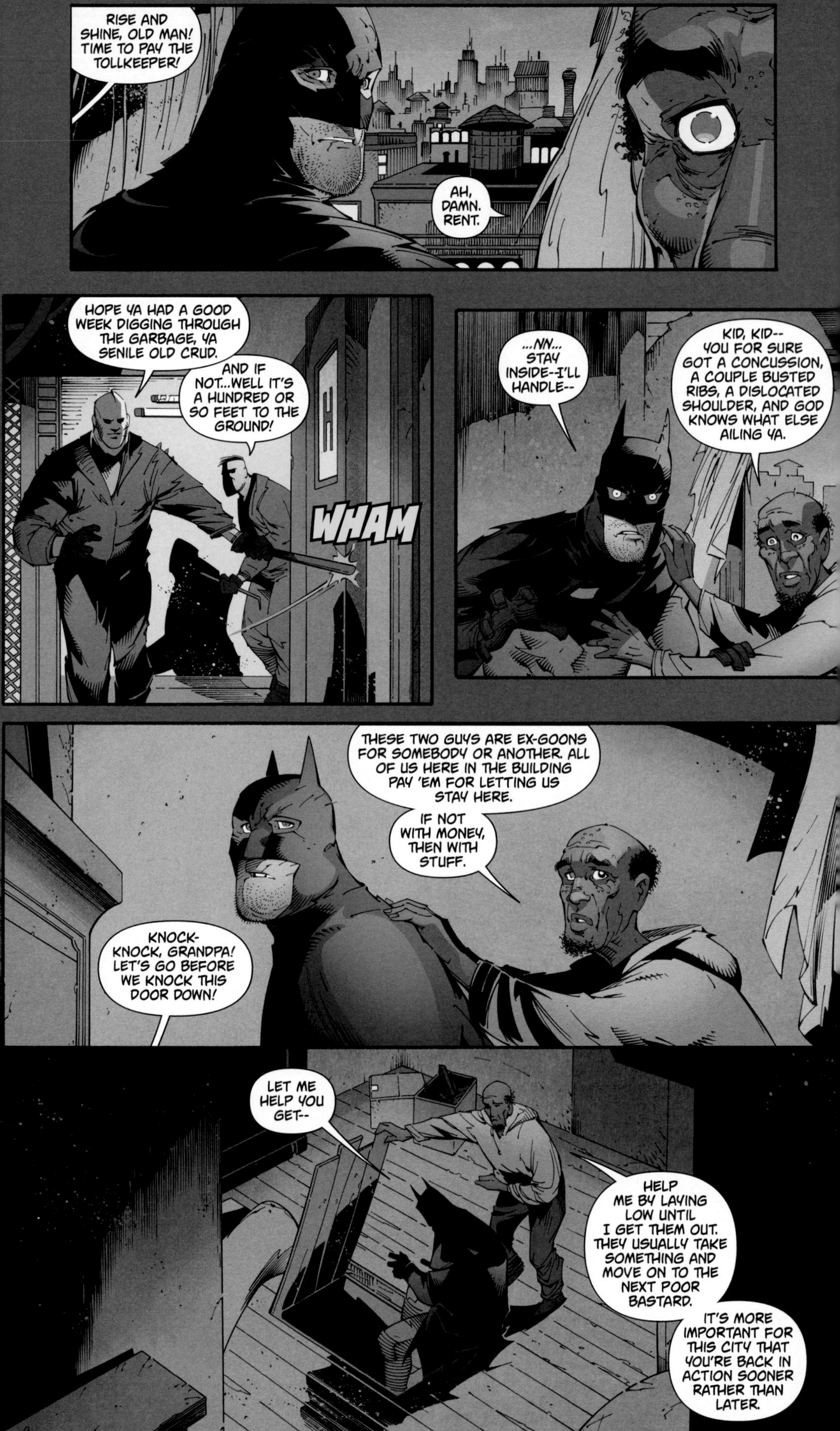
RISE AND SHINE, OLD MAN! TIME TO PAY THE TOLLKEEPER!
AH, DAMN. RENT.
HOPE YA HAD A GOOD WEEK DIGGING THROUGH THE GARBAGE, YA SENILE OLD CRUD.
AND IF NOT...WELL IT'S A HUNDRED OR SO FEET TO THE GROUND!
WHAM
...NN... STAY INSIDE--I'LL HANDLE--
KID, KID-- YOU FOR SURE GOT A CONCUSSION, A COUPLE BUSTED RIBS, A DISLOCATED SHOULDER, AND GOD KNOWS WHAT ELSE AILING YA.
THESE TWO GUYS ARE EX-GOONS FOR SOMEBODY OR ANOTHER. ALL OF US HERE IN THE BUILDING PAY 'EM FOR LETTING US STAY HERE.
IF NOT WITH MONEY, THEN WITH STUFF.
KNOCK-KNOCK, GRANDPA! LET'S GO BEFORE WE KNOCK THIS DOOR DOWN!
LET ME HELP YOU GET--
HELP ME BY LAYING LOW UNTIL I GET THEM OUT. THEY USUALLY TAKE SOMETHING AND MOVE ON TO THE NEXT POOR BASTARD.
IT'S MORE IMPORTANT FOR THIS CITY THAT YOU'RE BACK IN ACTION SOONER RATHER THAN LATER.

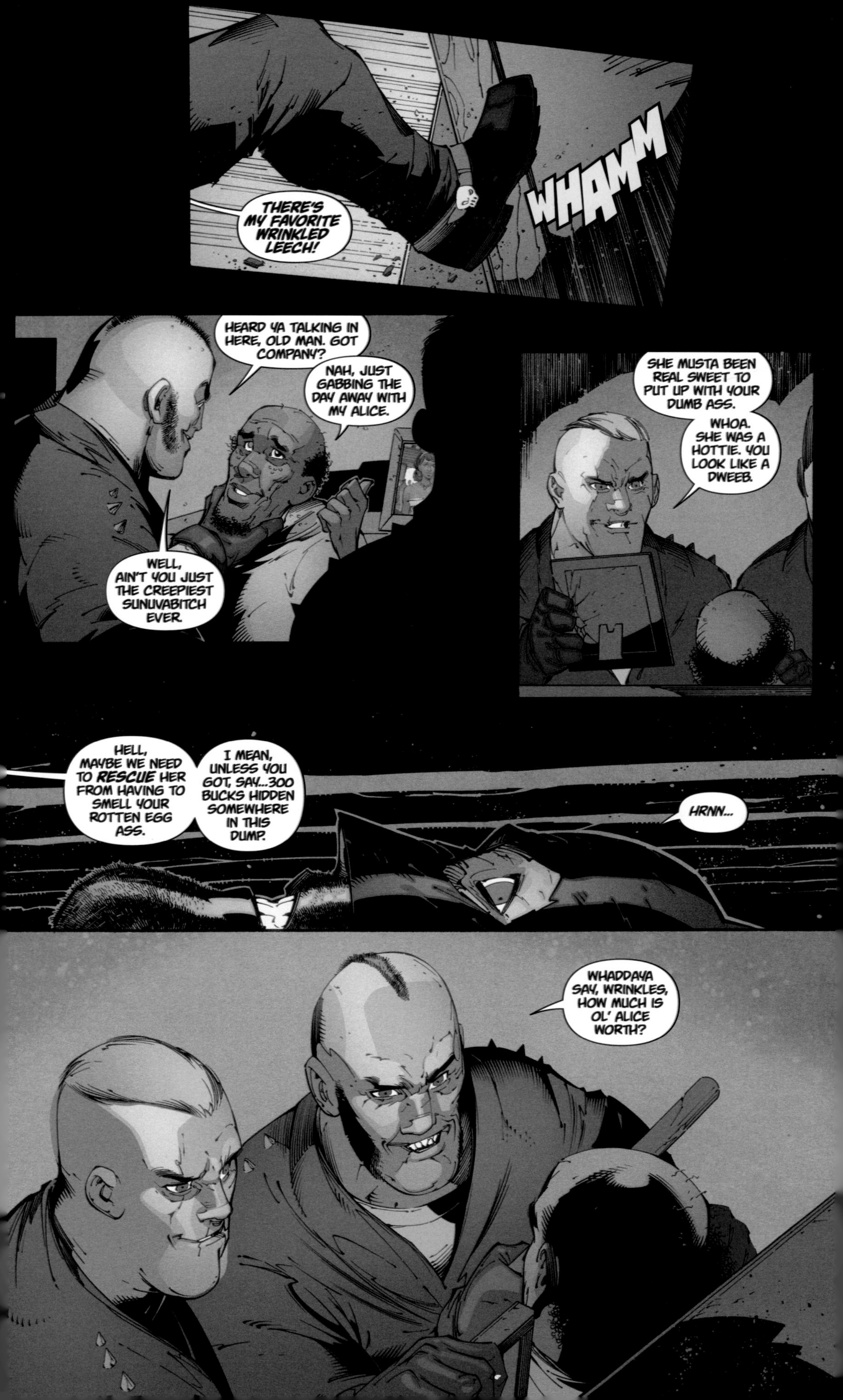
THERE'S MY FAVORITE WRINKLED LEECH!
WHAMM
HEARD YA TALKING IN HERE, OLD MAN. GOT COMPANY?
NAH, JUST GABBING THE DAY AWAY WITH MY ALICE.
WELL, AIN'T YOU JUST THE CREEPIEST SUNUVABITCH EVER.
SHE MUSTA BEEN REAL SWEET TO PUT UP WITH YOUR DUMB ASS.
WHOA. SHE WAS A HOTTIE. YOU LOOK LIKE A DWEEB.
HELL, MAYBE WE NEED TO *RESCUE* HER FROM HAVING TO SMELL YOUR ROTTEN EGG ASS.
I MEAN, UNLESS YOU GOT, SAY...300 BUCKS HIDDEN SOMEWHERE IN THIS DUMP.
HRNN...
WHADDAYA SAY, WRINKLES, HOW MUCH IS OL' ALICE WORTH?

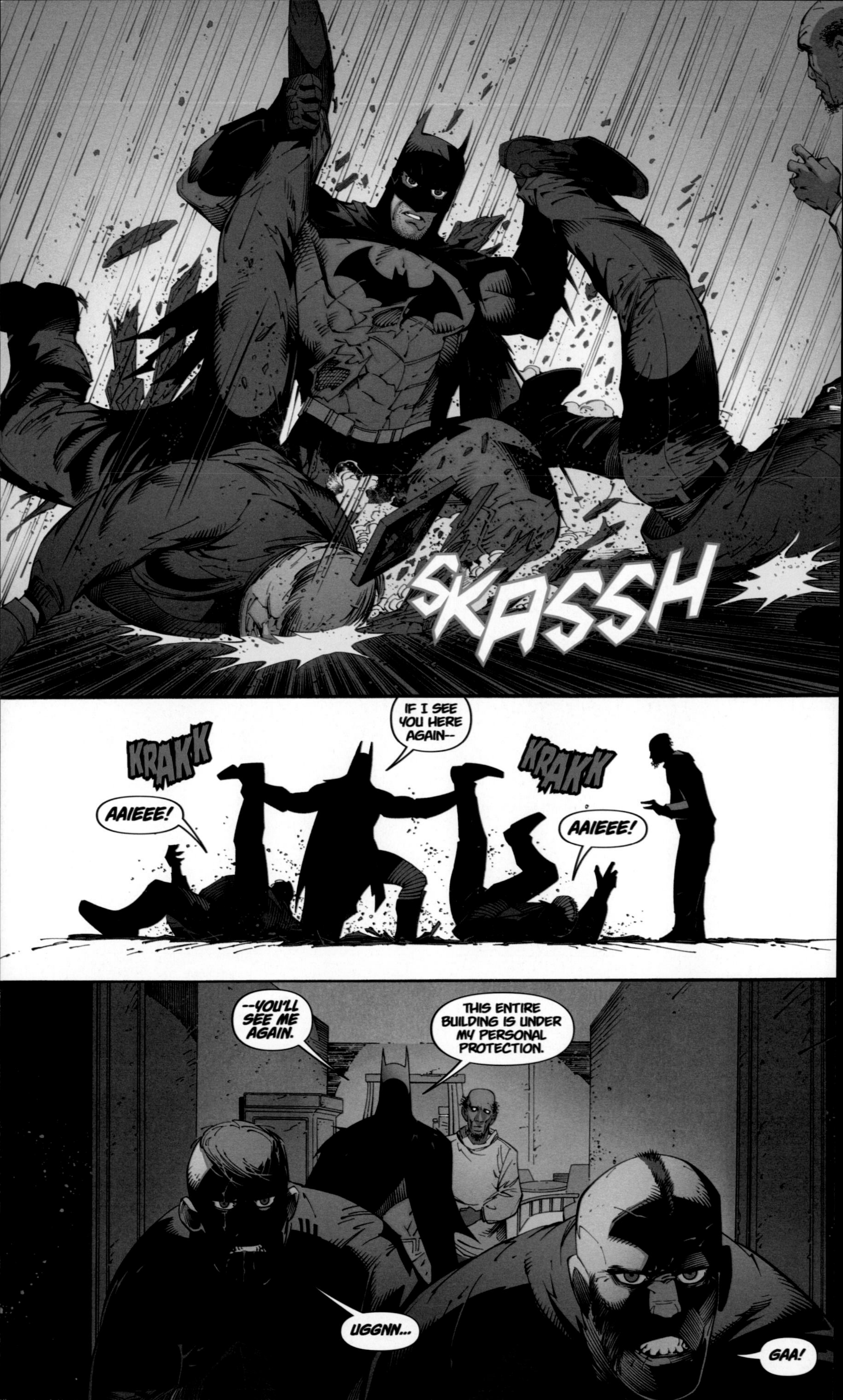
SKASSH
KRAKK
IF I SEE YOU HERE AGAIN--
KRAKK
AAIEEE!
AAIEEE!
--YOU'LL SEE ME AGAIN.
THIS ENTIRE BUILDING IS UNDER MY PERSONAL PROTECTION.
UGGNN...
GAA!

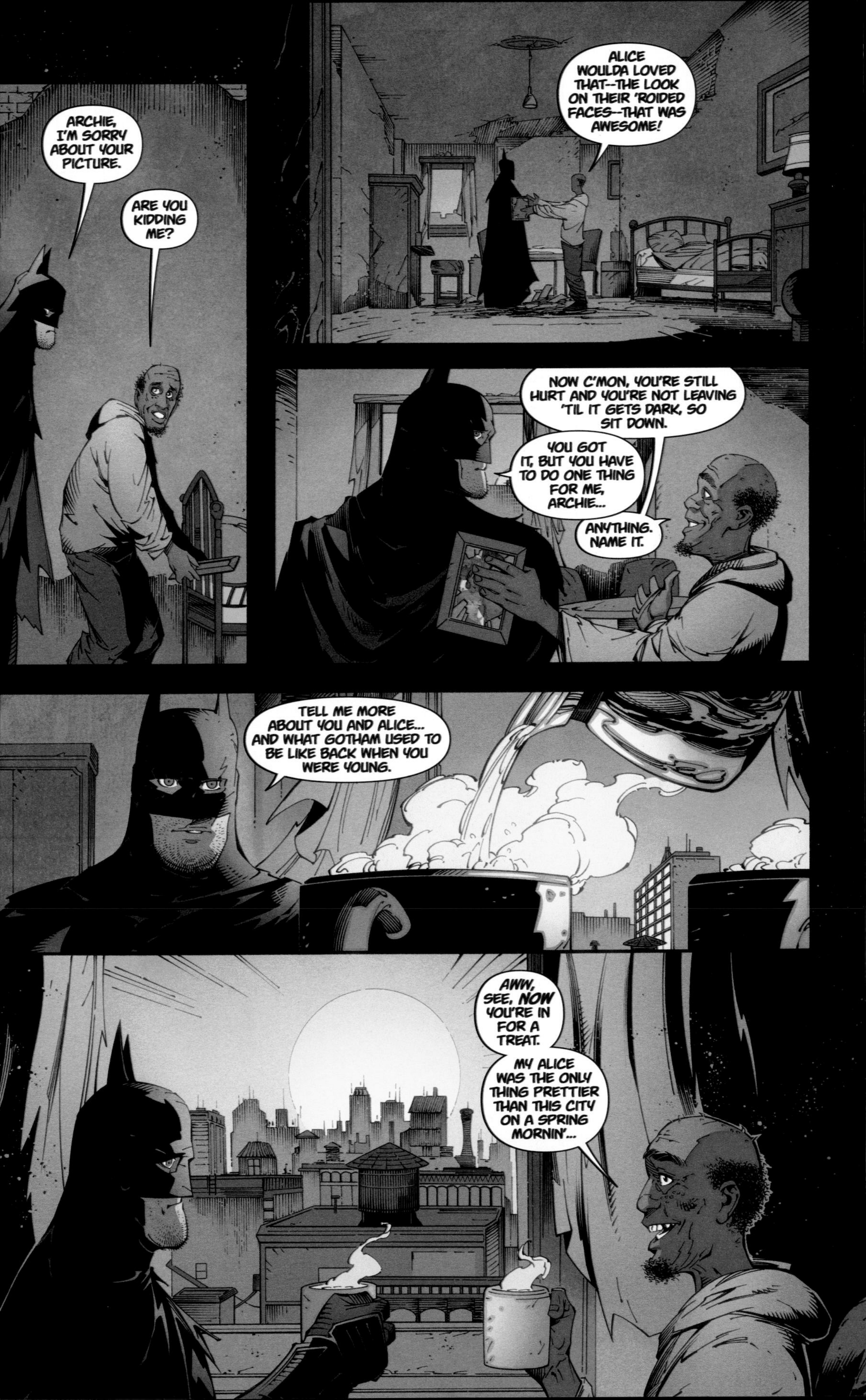

ARCHIE, I'M SORRY ABOUT YOUR PICTURE.
ARE YOU KIDDING ME?
ALICE WOULDA LOVED THAT--THE LOOK ON THEIR 'ROIDED FACES--THAT WAS AWESOME!
NOW C'MON, YOU'RE STILL HURT AND YOU'RE NOT LEAVING 'TIL IT GETS DARK, SO SIT DOWN.
YOU GOT IT, BUT YOU HAVE TO DO ONE THING FOR ME, ARCHIE...
ANYTHING. NAME IT.
TELL ME MORE ABOUT YOU AND ALICE... AND WHAT GOTHAM USED TO BE LIKE BACK WHEN YOU WERE YOUNG.
AWW, SEE, NOW YOU'RE IN FOR A TREAT.
MY ALICE WAS THE ONLY THING PRETTIER THAN THIS CITY ON A SPRING MORNIN'...

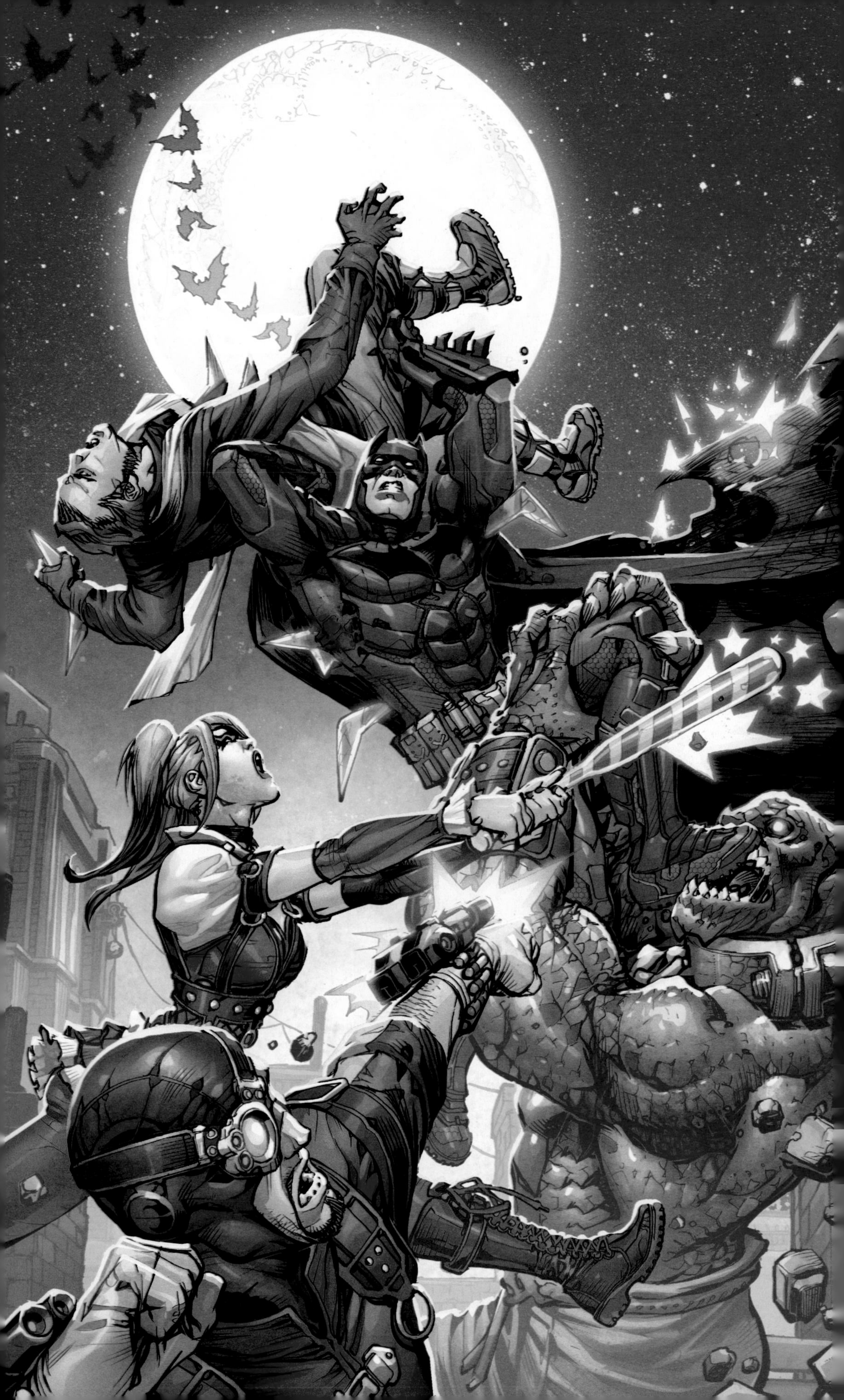

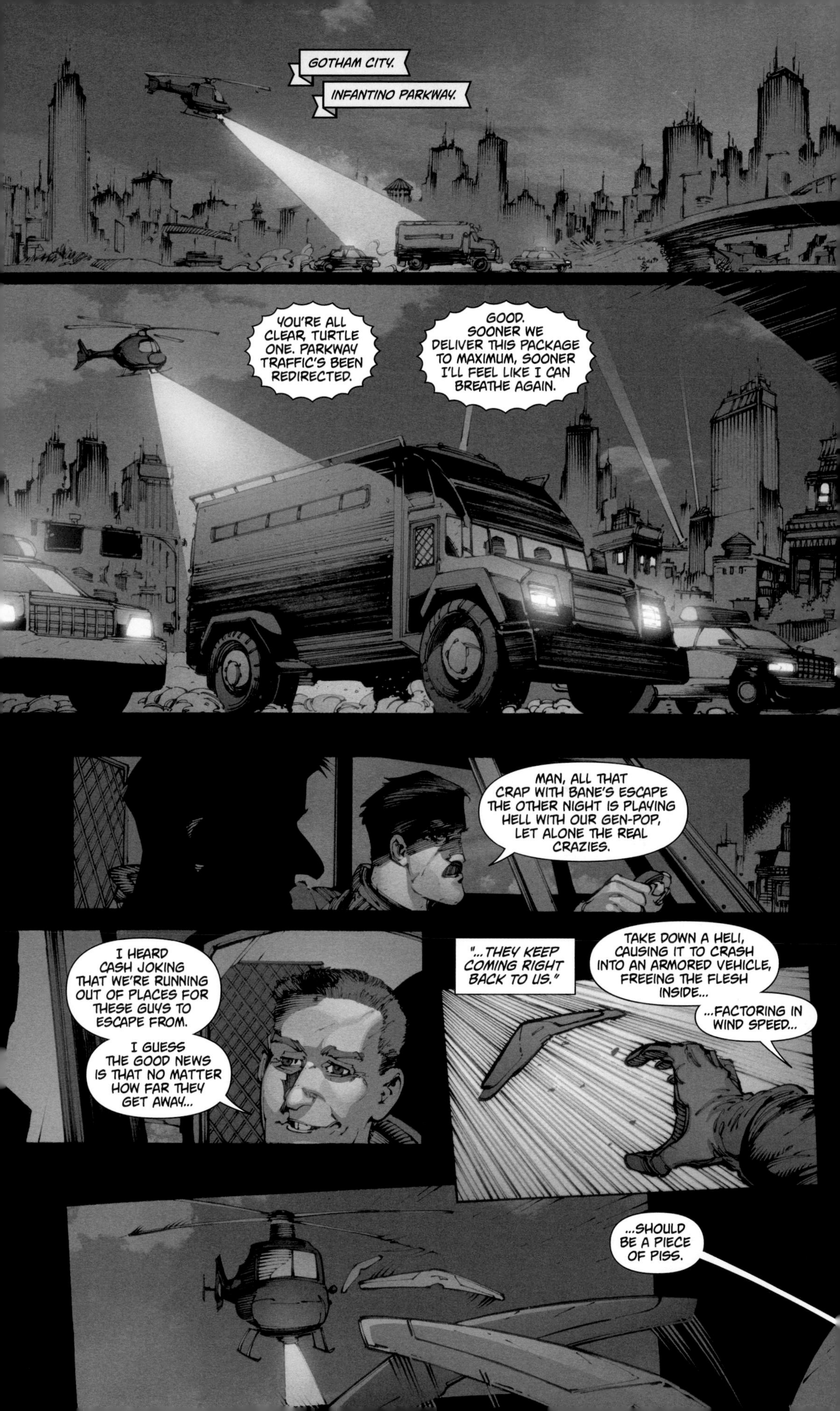
GOTHAM CITY.
INFANTINO PARKWAY.
YOU'RE ALL CLEAR, TURTLE ONE. PARKWAY TRAFFIC'S BEEN REDIRECTED.
GOOD. SOONER WE DELIVER THIS PACKAGE TO MAXIMUM, SOONER I'LL FEEL LIKE I CAN BREATHE AGAIN.
MAN, ALL THAT CRAP WITH BANE'S ESCAPE THE OTHER NIGHT IS PLAYING HELL WITH OUR GEN-POP, LET ALONE THE REAL CRAZIES.
I HEARD CASH JOKING THAT WE'RE RUNNING OUT OF PLACES FOR THESE GUYS TO ESCAPE FROM.
I GUESS THE GOOD NEWS IS THAT NO MATTER HOW FAR THEY GET AWAY...
"...THEY KEEP COMING RIGHT BACK TO US."
TAKE DOWN A HELI, CAUSING IT TO CRASH INTO AN ARMORED VEHICLE, FREEING THE FLESH INSIDE...
...FACTORING IN WIND SPEED...
...SHOULD BE A PIECE OF PISS.

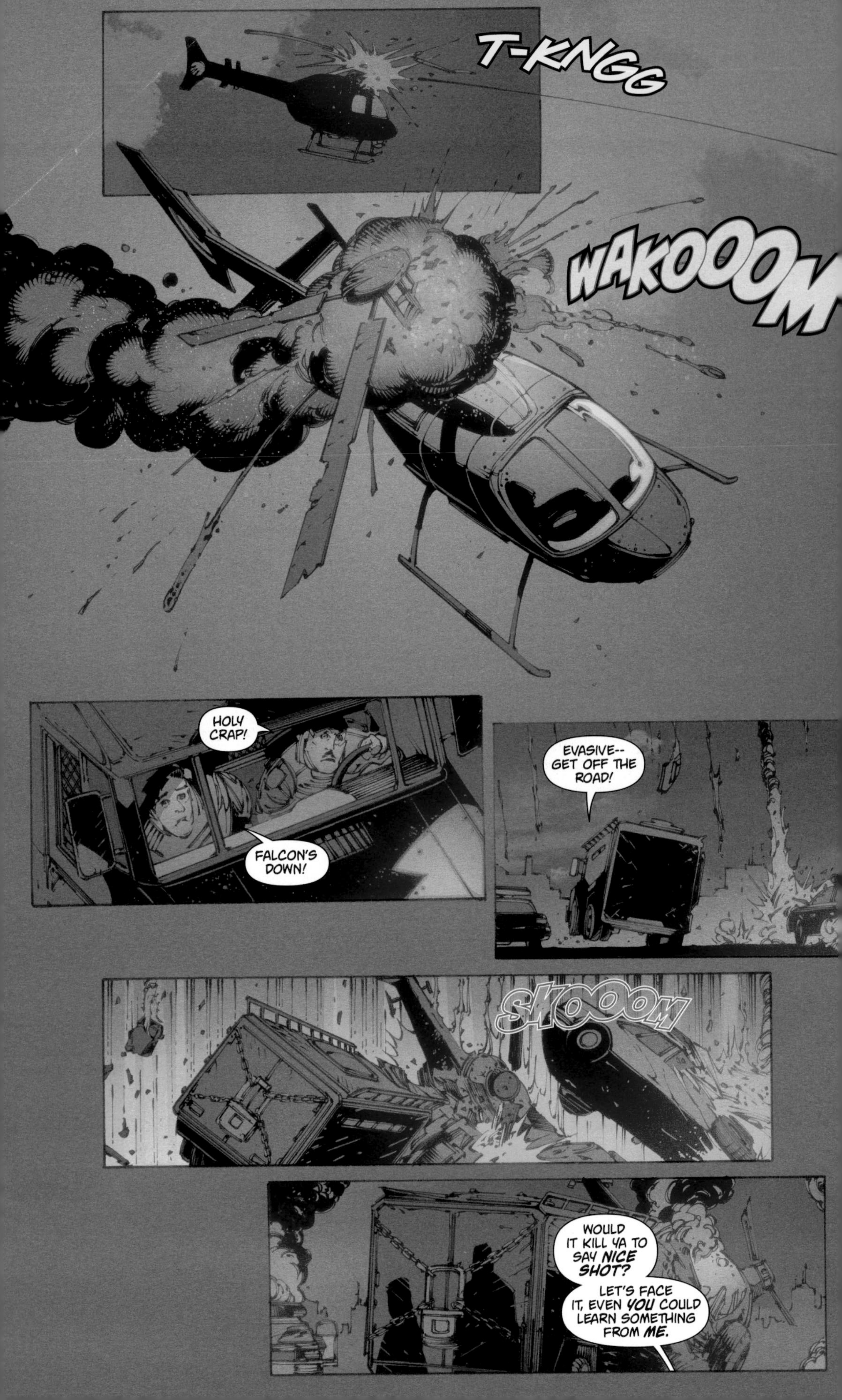

T-KNGG
WAKOOOM
HOLY CRAP!
FALCON'S DOWN!
EVASIVE-- GET OFF THE ROAD!
SKOOOM
WOULD IT KILL YA TO SAY NICE SHOT?
LET'S FACE IT, EVEN YOU COULD LEARN SOMETHING FROM ME.

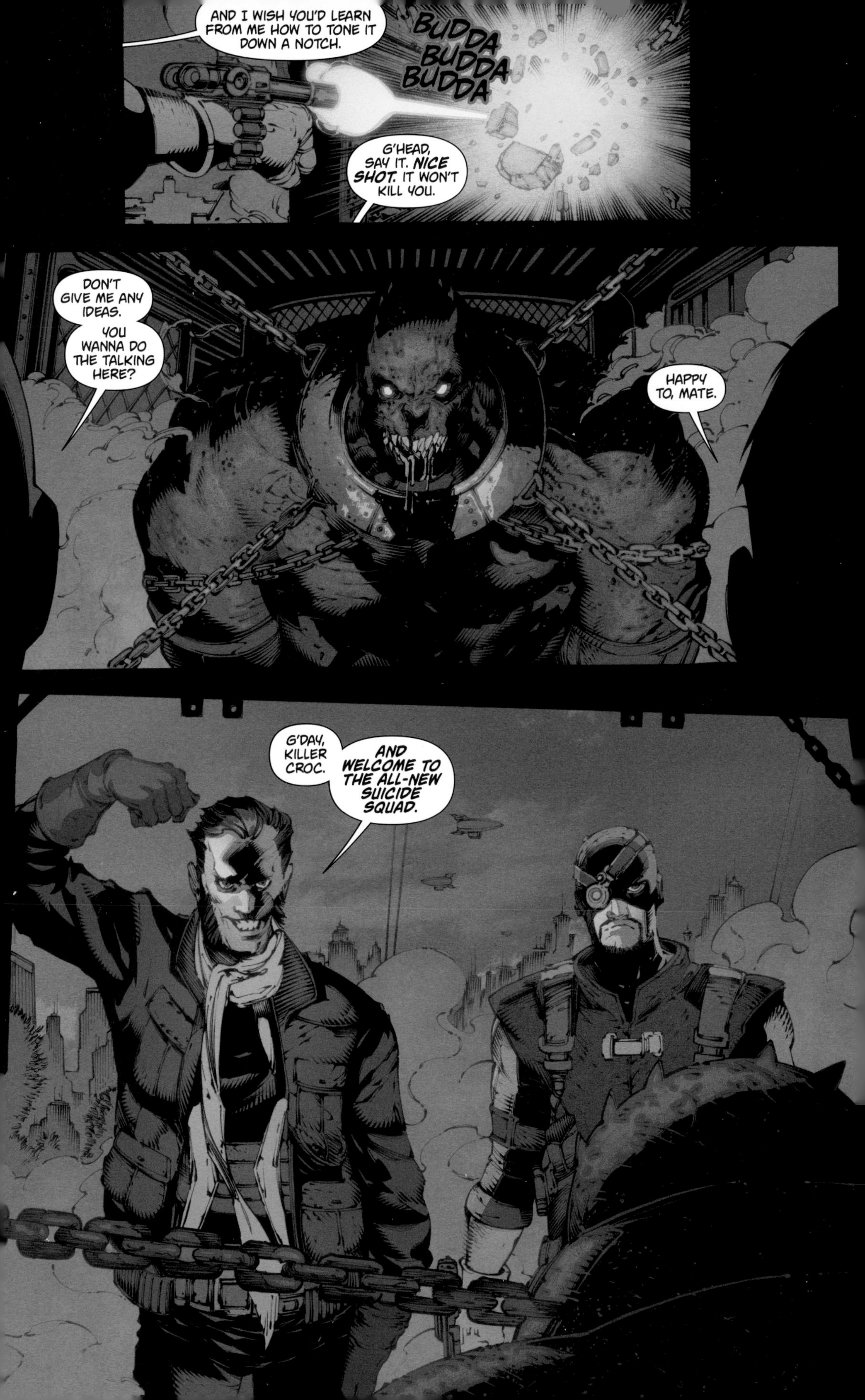
AND I WISH YOU'D LEARN FROM ME HOW TO TONE IT DOWN A NOTCH.
BUDDA BUDDA BUDDA
G'HEAD, SAY IT. NICE SHOT. IT WON'T KILL YOU.
DON'T GIVE ME ANY IDEAS.
YOU WANNA DO THE TALKING HERE?
HAPPY TO, MATE.
G'DAY, KILLER CROC.
AND WELCOME TO THE ALL-NEW SUICIDE SQUAD.

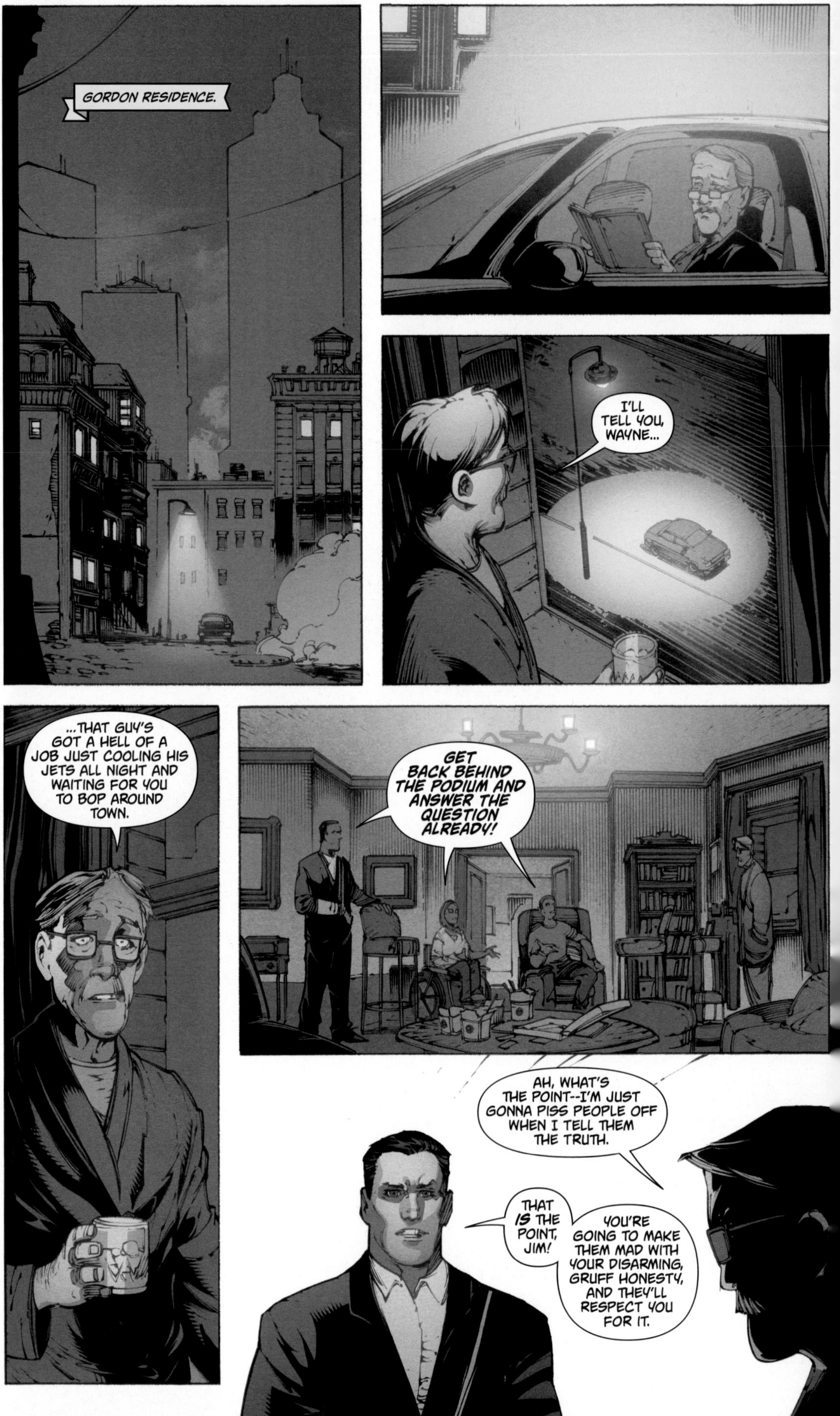

GORDON RESIDENCE.
I'LL TELL YOU, WAYNE...
...THAT GUY'S GOT A HELL OF A JOB JUST COOLING HIS JETS ALL NIGHT AND WAITING FOR YOU TO BOP AROUND TOWN.
GET BACK BEHIND THE PODIUM AND ANSWER THE QUESTION ALREADY!
AH, WHAT'S THE POINT--I'M JUST GONNA PISS PEOPLE OFF WHEN I TELL THEM THE TRUTH.
THAT IS THE POINT, JIM!
YOU'RE GOING TO MAKE THEM MAD WITH YOUR DISARMING, GRUFF HONESTY, AND THEY'LL RESPECT YOU FOR IT.

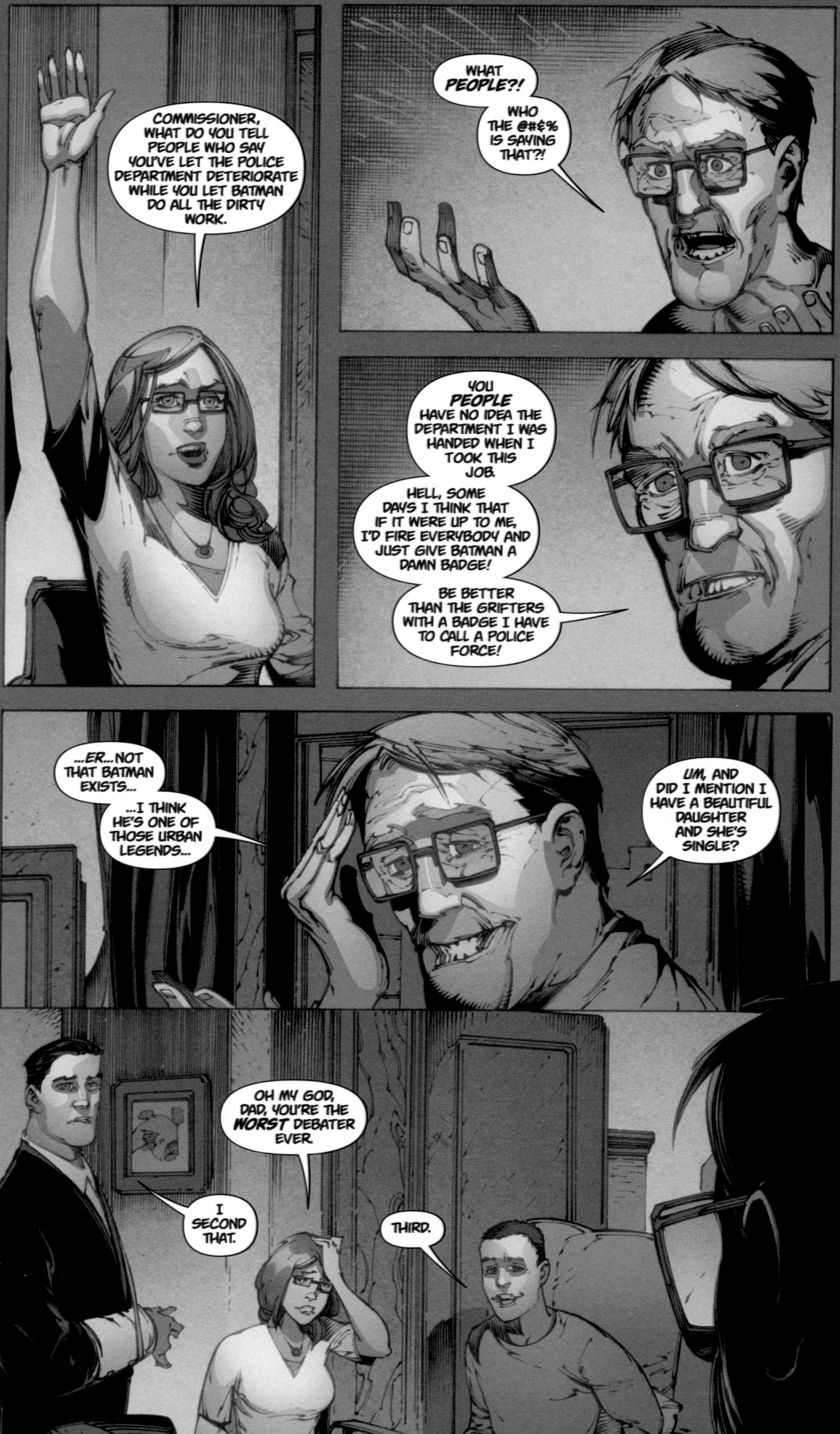
COMMISSIONER, WHAT DO YOU TELL PEOPLE WHO SAY YOU'VE LET THE POLICE DEPARTMENT DETERIORATE WHILE YOU LET BATMAN DO ALL THE DIRTY WORK.
WHAT PEOPLE?!
WHO THE @#&% IS SAYING THAT?!
YOU PEOPLE HAVE NO IDEA THE DEPARTMENT I WAS HANDED WHEN I TOOK THIS JOB.
HELL, SOME DAYS I THINK THAT IF IT WERE UP TO ME, I'D FIRE EVERYBODY AND JUST GIVE BATMAN A DAMN BADGE!
BE BETTER THAN THE GRIFTERS WITH A BADGE I HAVE TO CALL A POLICE FORCE!
...ER...NOT THAT BATMAN EXISTS...
...I THINK HE'S ONE OF THOSE URBAN LEGENDS...
UM, AND DID I MENTION I HAVE A BEAUTIFUL DAUGHTER AND SHE'S SINGLE?
OH MY GOD, DAD, YOU'RE THE WORST DEBATER EVER.
I SECOND THAT.
THIRD.

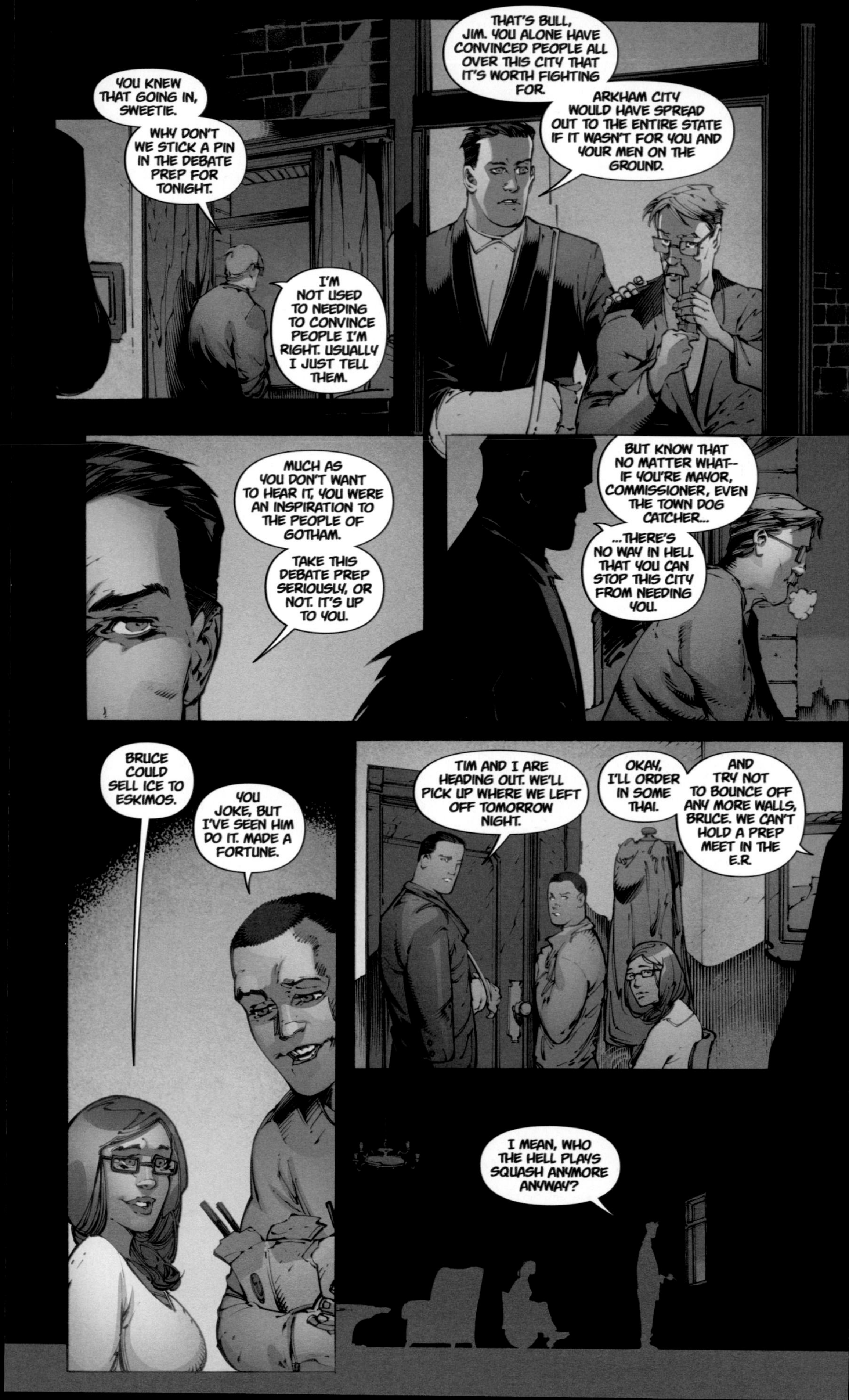
YOU KNEW THAT GOING IN, SWEETIE.
WHY DON'T WE STICK A PIN IN THE DEBATE PREP FOR TONIGHT.
I'M NOT USED TO NEEDING TO CONVINCE PEOPLE I'M RIGHT. USUALLY I JUST TELL THEM.
THAT'S BULL, JIM. YOU ALONE HAVE CONVINCED PEOPLE ALL OVER THIS CITY THAT IT'S WORTH FIGHTING FOR.
ARKHAM CITY WOULD HAVE SPREAD OUT TO THE ENTIRE STATE IF IT WASN'T FOR YOU AND YOUR MEN ON THE GROUND.
MUCH AS YOU DON'T WANT TO HEAR IT, YOU WERE AN INSPIRATION TO THE PEOPLE OF GOTHAM.
TAKE THIS DEBATE PREP SERIOUSLY, OR NOT. IT'S UP TO YOU.
BUT KNOW THAT NO MATTER WHAT-- IF YOU'RE MAYOR, COMMISSIONER, EVEN THE TOWN DOG CATCHER...
...THERE'S NO WAY IN HELL THAT YOU CAN STOP THIS CITY FROM NEEDING YOU.
BRUCE COULD SELL ICE TO ESKIMOS.
YOU JOKE, BUT I'VE SEEN HIM DO IT. MADE A FORTUNE.
TIM AND I ARE HEADING OUT. WE'LL PICK UP WHERE WE LEFT OFF TOMORROW NIGHT.
OKAY, I'LL ORDER IN SOME THAI.
AND TRY NOT TO BOUNCE OFF ANY MORE WALLS, BRUCE. WE CAN'T HOLD A PREP MEET IN THE E.R.
I MEAN, WHO THE HELL PLAYS SQUASH ANYMORE ANYWAY?

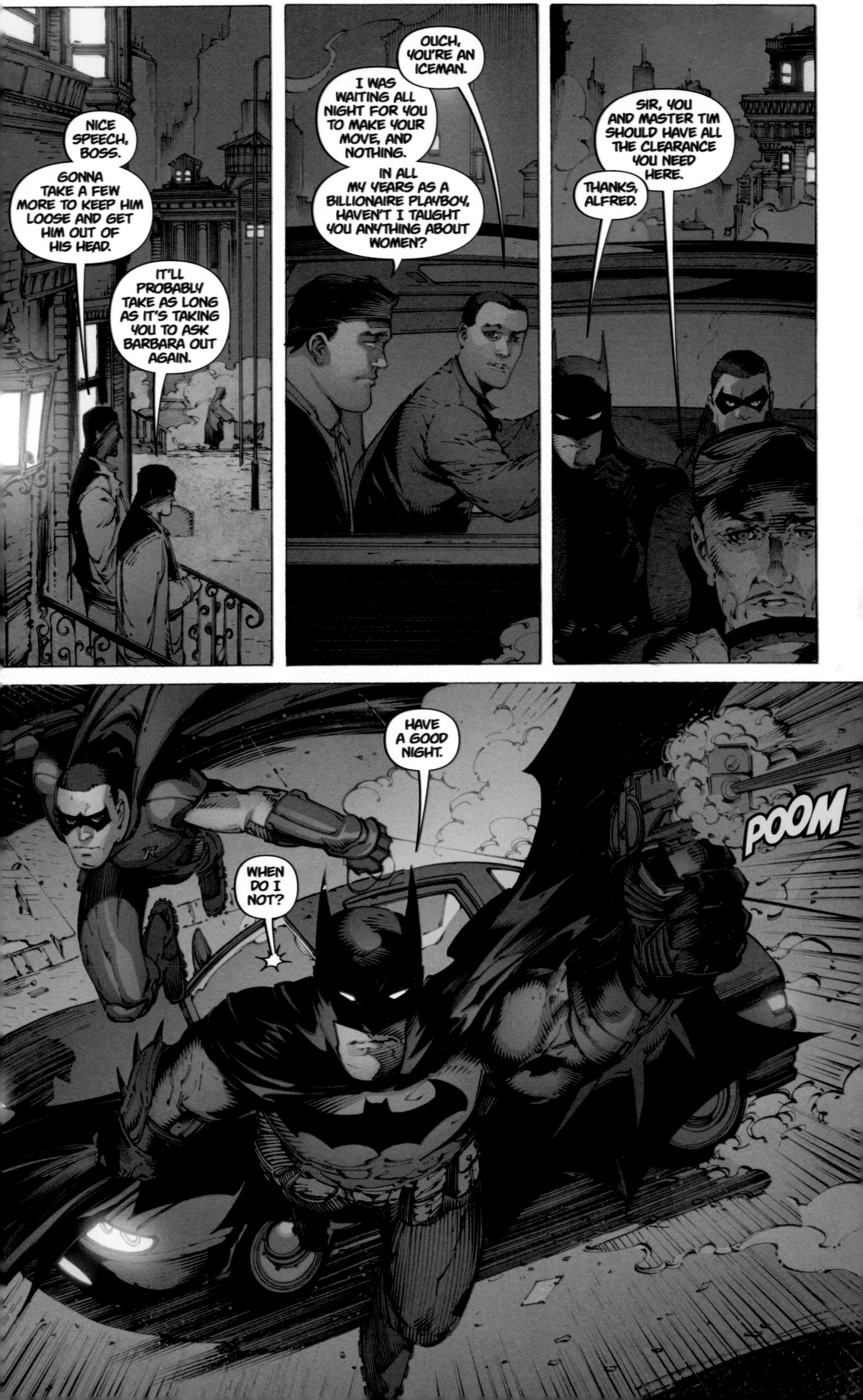
NICE SPEECH, BOSS.
GONNA TAKE A FEW MORE TO KEEP HIM LOOSE AND GET HIM OUT OF HIS HEAD.
IT'LL PROBABLY TAKE AS LONG AS IT'S TAKING YOU TO ASK BARBARA OUT AGAIN.
OUCH, YOU'RE AN ICEMAN.
I WAS WAITING ALL NIGHT FOR YOU TO MAKE YOUR MOVE, AND NOTHING.
IN ALL MY YEARS AS A BILLIONAIRE PLAYBOY, HAVEN'T I TAUGHT YOU ANYTHING ABOUT WOMEN?
SIR, YOU AND MASTER TIM SHOULD HAVE ALL THE CLEARANCE YOU NEED HERE.
THANKS, ALFRED.
HAVE A GOOD NIGHT.
WHEN DO I NOT?
POOM

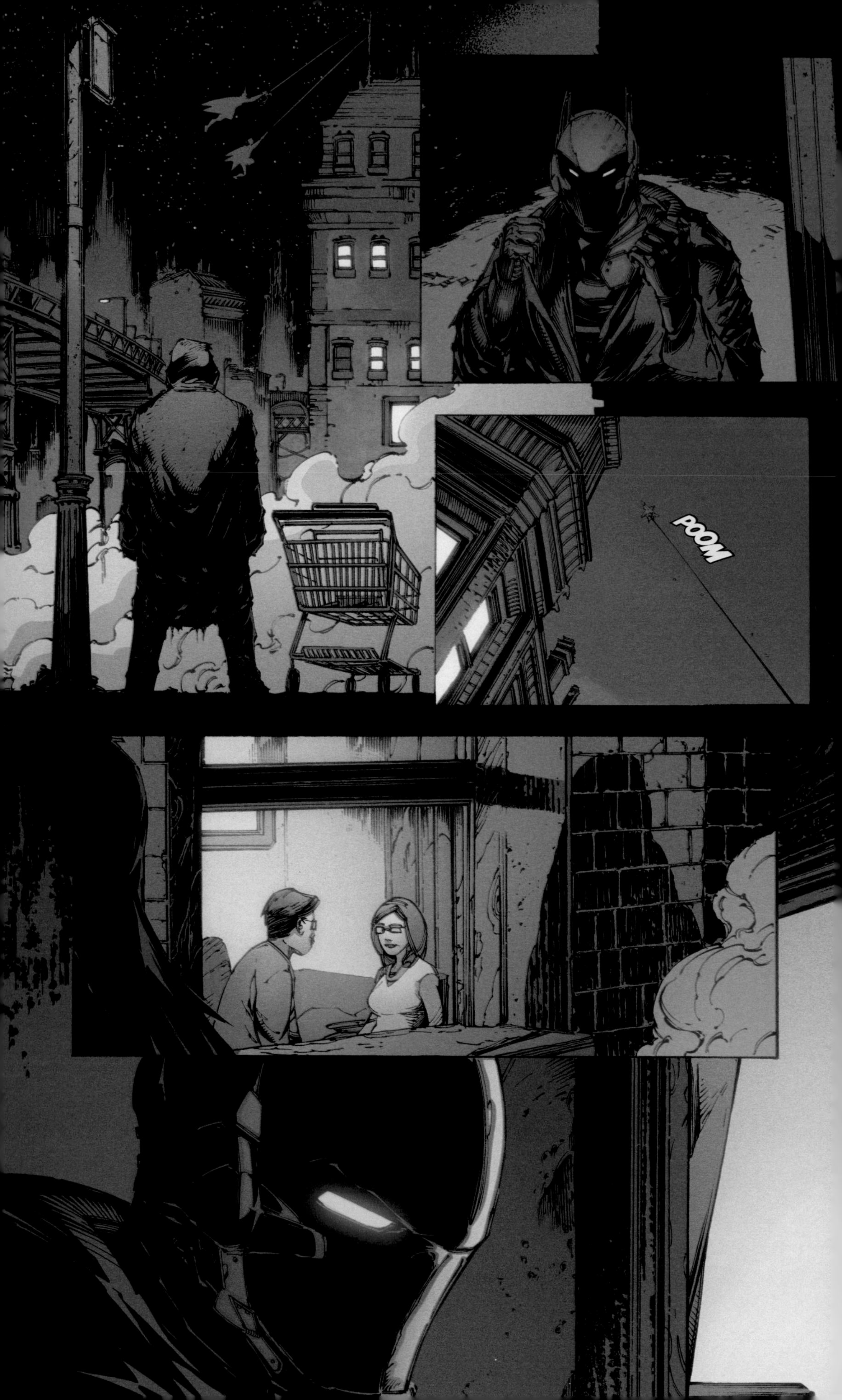
POOM

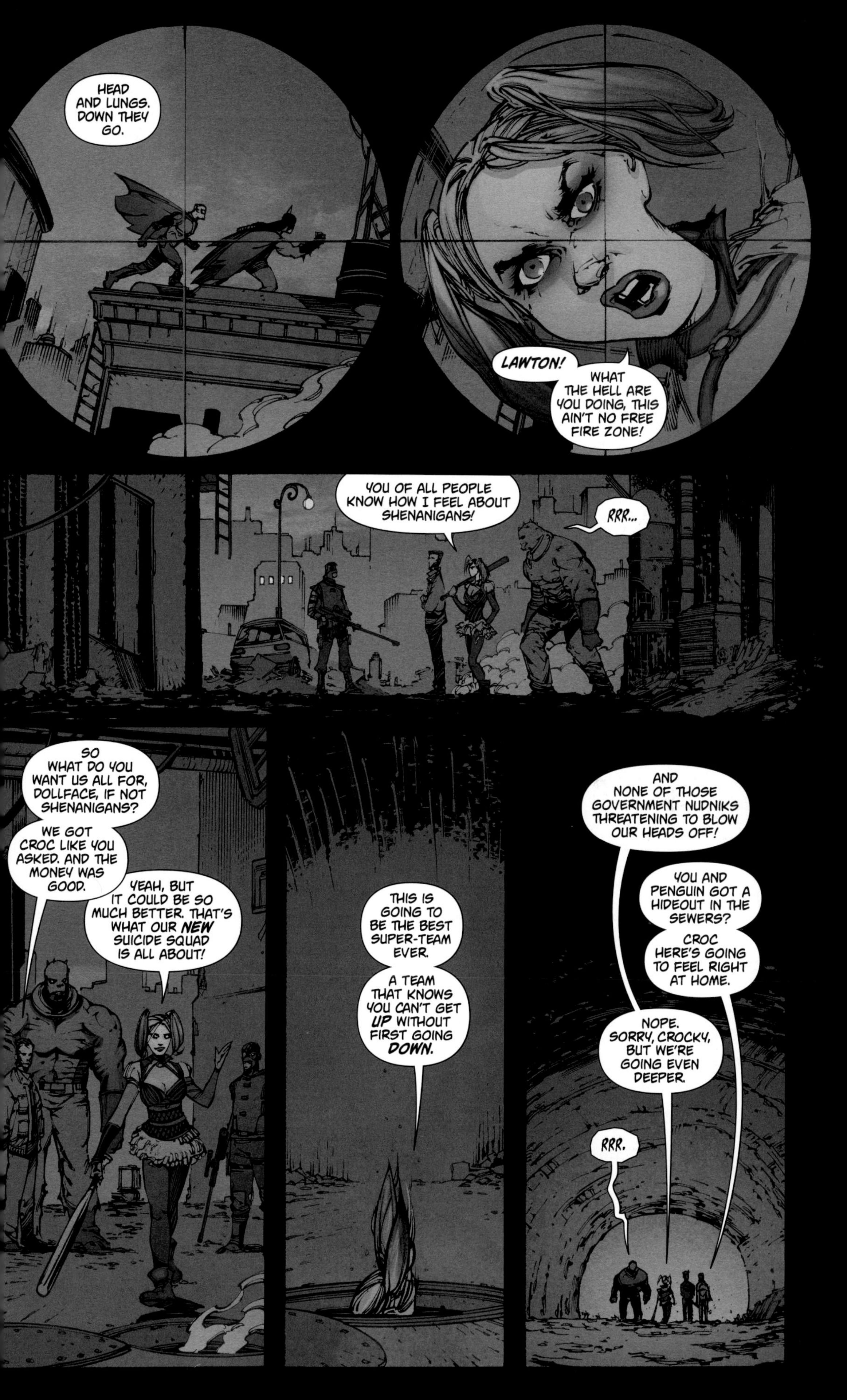
HEAD AND LUNGS. DOWN THEY GO.
LAWTON!
WHAT THE HELL ARE YOU DOING, THIS AIN'T NO FREE FIRE ZONE!
YOU OF ALL PEOPLE KNOW HOW I FEEL ABOUT SHENANIGANS!
RRR...
SO WHAT DO YOU WANT US ALL FOR, DOLLFACE, IF NOT SHENANIGANS?
WE GOT CROC LIKE YOU ASKED. AND THE MONEY WAS GOOD.
YEAH, BUT IT COULD BE SO MUCH BETTER. THAT'S WHAT OUR NEW SUICIDE SQUAD IS ALL ABOUT!
THIS IS GOING TO BE THE BEST SUPER-TEAM EVER.
A TEAM THAT KNOWS YOU CAN'T GET UP WITHOUT FIRST GOING DOWN.
AND NONE OF THOSE GOVERNMENT NUDNIKS THREATENING TO BLOW OUR HEADS OFF!
YOU AND PENGUIN GOT A HIDEOUT IN THE SEWERS?
CROC HERE'S GOING TO FEEL RIGHT AT HOME.
NOPE. SORRY, CROCKY, BUT WE'RE GOING EVEN DEEPER.
RRR.

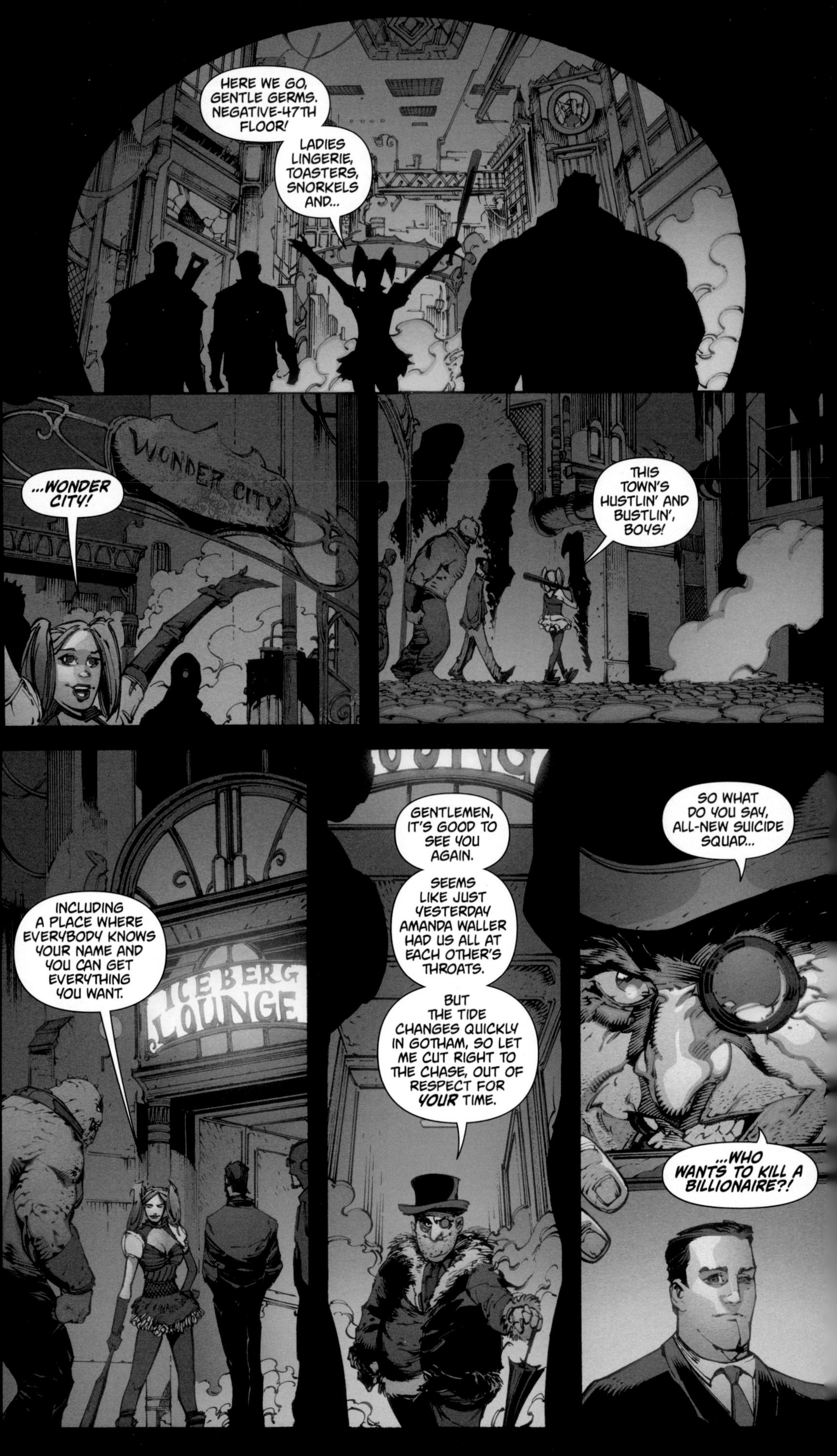
HERE WE GO, GENTLE GERMS. NEGATIVE-47TH FLOOR!
LADIES LINGERIE, TOASTERS, SNORKELS AND...
...WONDER CITY!
WONDER CITY
THIS TOWN'S HUSTLIN' AND BUSTLIN', BOYS!
INCLUDING A PLACE WHERE EVERYBODY KNOWS YOUR NAME AND YOU CAN GET EVERYTHING YOU WANT.
ICEBERG LOUNGE
GENTLEMEN, IT'S GOOD TO SEE YOU AGAIN.
SEEMS LIKE JUST YESTERDAY AMANDA WALLER HAD US ALL AT EACH OTHER'S THROATS.
BUT THE TIDE CHANGES QUICKLY IN GOTHAM, SO LET ME CUT RIGHT TO THE CHASE, OUT OF RESPECT FOR YOUR TIME.
SO WHAT DO YOU SAY, ALL-NEW SUICIDE SQUAD...
...WHO WANTS TO KILL A BILLIONAIRE?!

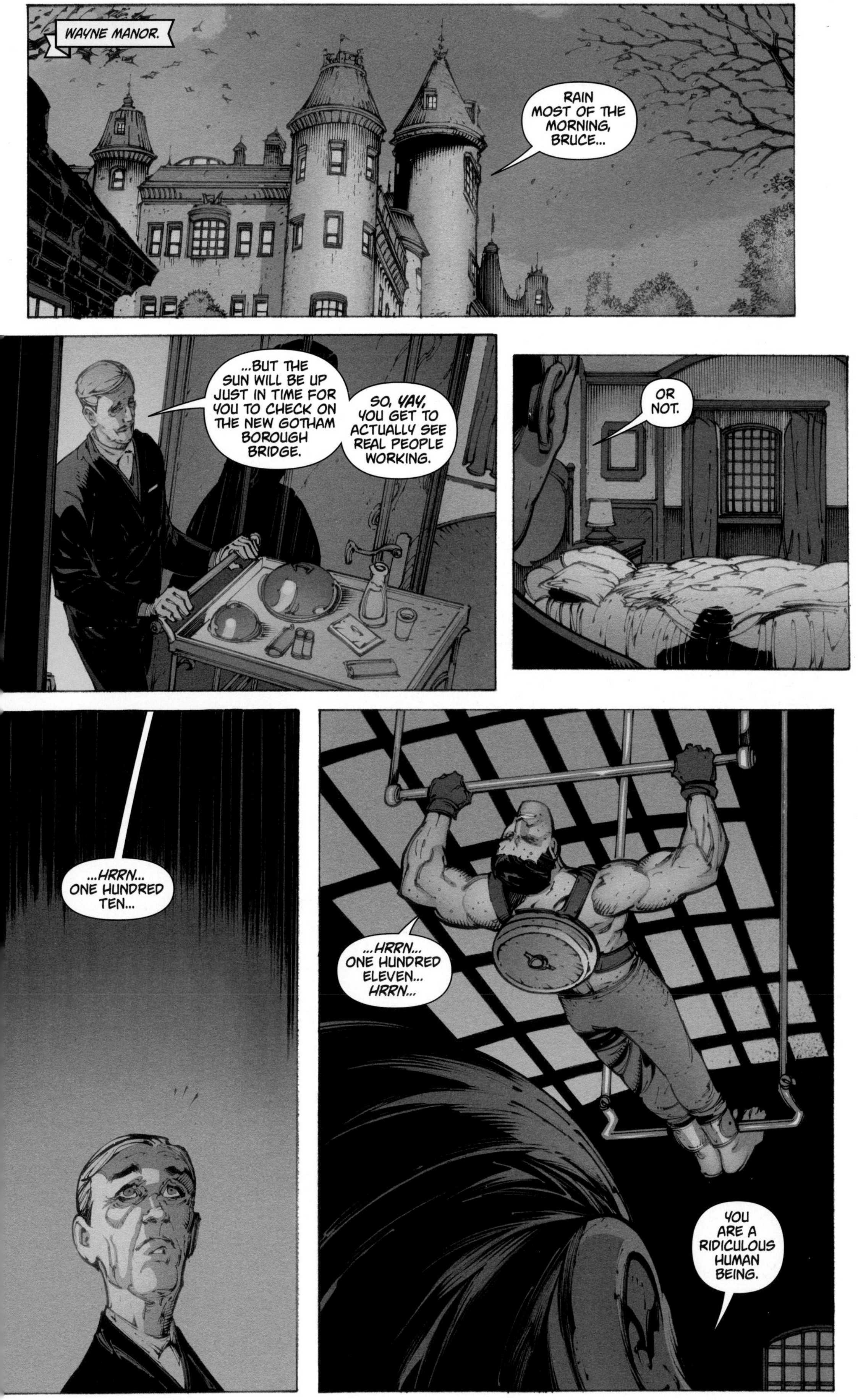
WAYNE MANOR.
RAIN MOST OF THE MORNING, BRUCE...
...BUT THE SUN WILL BE UP JUST IN TIME FOR YOU TO CHECK ON THE NEW GOTHAM BOROUGH BRIDGE.
SO, YAY, YOU GET TO ACTUALLY SEE REAL PEOPLE WORKING.
OR NOT.
...HRRN... ONE HUNDRED TEN...
...HRRN... ONE HUNDRED ELEVEN... HRRN...
YOU ARE A RIDICULOUS HUMAN BEING.

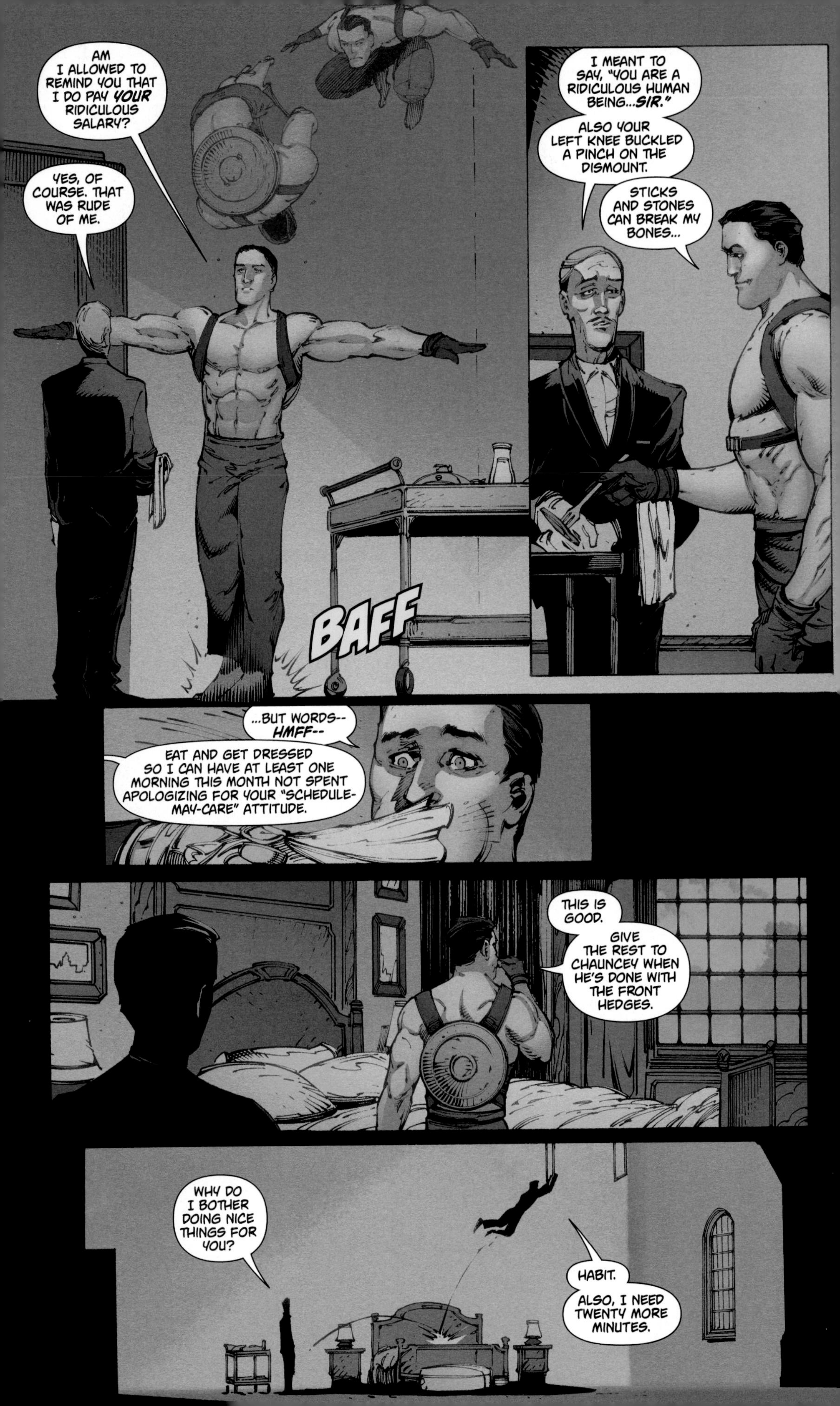
AM I ALLOWED TO REMIND YOU THAT I DO PAY ***YOUR*** RIDICULOUS SALARY?
YES, OF COURSE. THAT WAS RUDE OF ME.
I MEANT TO SAY, "YOU ARE A RIDICULOUS HUMAN BEING...***SIR.***"
ALSO YOUR LEFT KNEE BUCKLED A PINCH ON THE DISMOUNT.
STICKS AND STONES CAN BREAK MY BONES...
BAFF
...BUT WORDS-- ***HMFF--***
EAT AND GET DRESSED SO I CAN HAVE AT LEAST ONE MORNING THIS MONTH NOT SPENT APOLOGIZING FOR YOUR "SCHEDULE-MAY-CARE" ATTITUDE.
THIS IS GOOD.
GIVE THE REST TO CHAUNCEY WHEN HE'S DONE WITH THE FRONT HEDGES.
WHY DO I BOTHER DOING NICE THINGS FOR YOU?
HABIT.
ALSO, I NEED TWENTY MORE MINUTES.

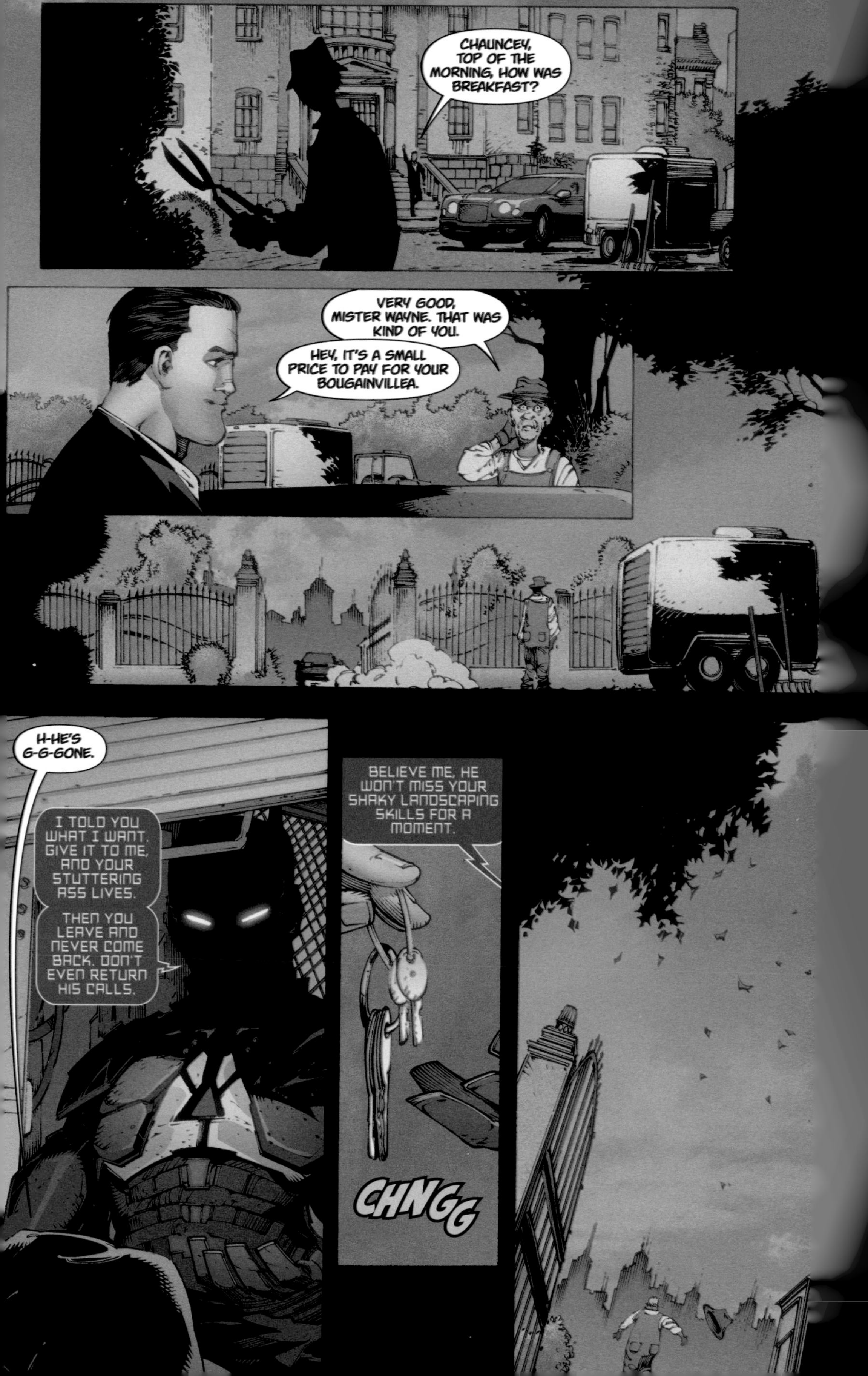
CHAUNCEY, TOP OF THE MORNING, HOW WAS BREAKFAST?
VERY GOOD, MISTER WAYNE. THAT WAS KIND OF YOU.
HEY, IT'S A SMALL PRICE TO PAY FOR YOUR BOUGAINVILLEA.
H-HE'S G-G-GONE.
I TOLD YOU WHAT I WANT. GIVE IT TO ME, AND YOUR STUTTERING ASS LIVES.
THEN YOU LEAVE AND NEVER COME BACK. DON'T EVEN RETURN HIS CALLS.
BELIEVE ME, HE WON'T MISS YOUR SHAKY LANDSCAPING SKILLS FOR A MOMENT.
CHNGG

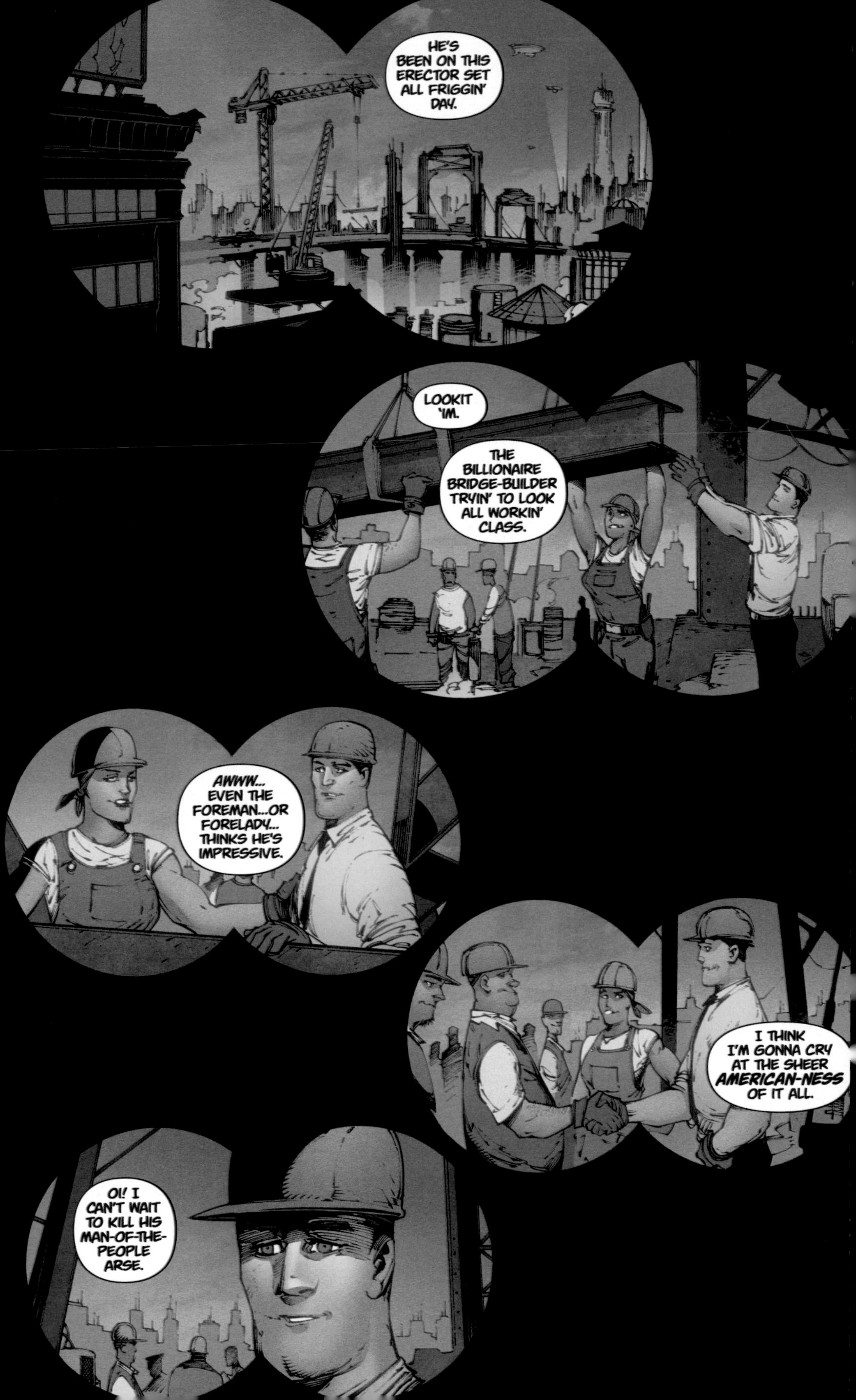
HE'S BEEN ON THIS ERECTOR SET ALL FRIGGIN' DAY.
LOOKIT 'IM.
THE BILLIONAIRE BRIDGE-BUILDER TRYIN' TO LOOK ALL WORKIN' CLASS.
AWWW... EVEN THE FOREMAN...OR FORELADY... THINKS HE'S IMPRESSIVE.
I THINK I'M GONNA CRY AT THE SHEER AMERICAN-NESS OF IT ALL.
OI! I CAN'T WAIT TO KILL HIS MAN-OF-THE-PEOPLE ARSE.

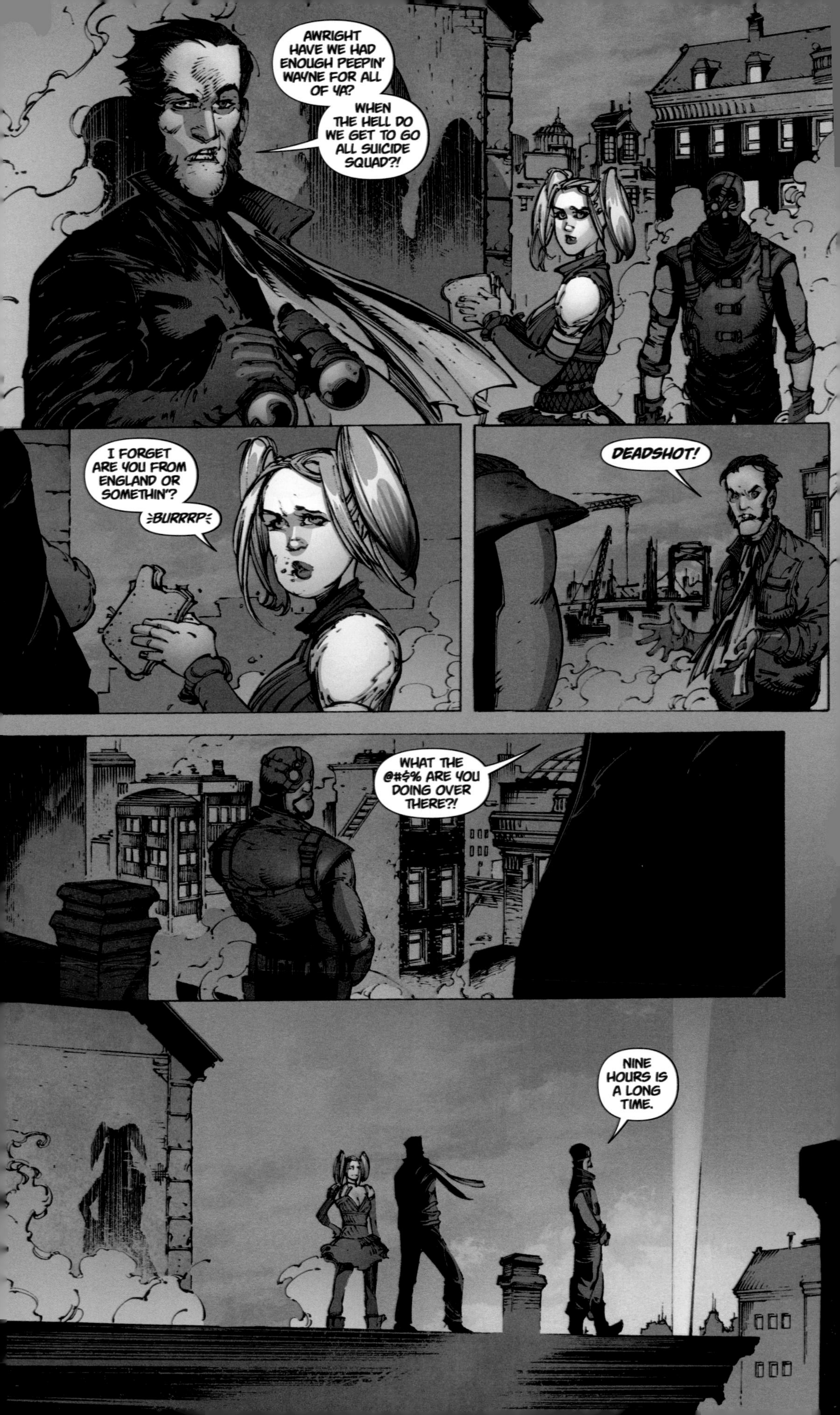
AWRIGHT HAVE WE HAD ENOUGH PEEPIN' WAYNE FOR ALL OF YA?
WHEN THE HELL DO WE GET TO GO ALL SUICIDE SQUAD?!
I FORGET ARE YOU FROM ENGLAND OR SOMETHIN'?
BURRRP
DEADSHOT!
WHAT THE @#$% ARE YOU DOING OVER THERE?!
NINE HOURS IS A LONG TIME.

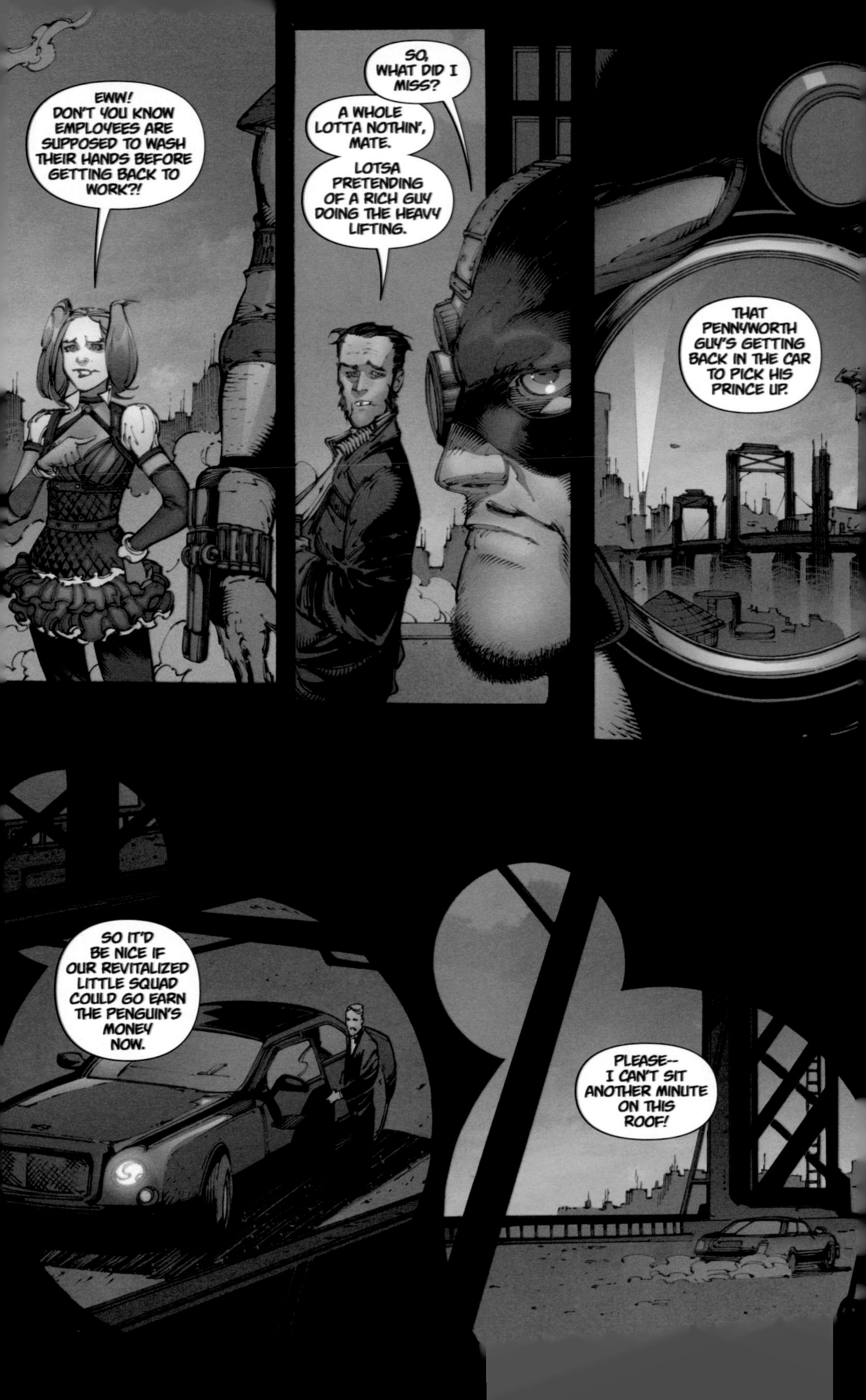
EWW! DON'T YOU KNOW EMPLOYEES ARE SUPPOSED TO WASH THEIR HANDS BEFORE GETTING BACK TO WORK?!
SO, WHAT DID I MISS?
A WHOLE LOTTA NOTHIN', MATE.
LOTSA PRETENDING OF A RICH GUY DOING THE HEAVY LIFTING.
THAT PENNYWORTH GUY'S GETTING BACK IN THE CAR TO PICK HIS PRINCE UP.
SO IT'D BE NICE IF OUR REVITALIZED LITTLE SQUAD COULD GO EARN THE PENGUIN'S MONEY NOW.
PLEASE-- I CAN'T SIT ANOTHER MINUTE ON THIS ROOF!

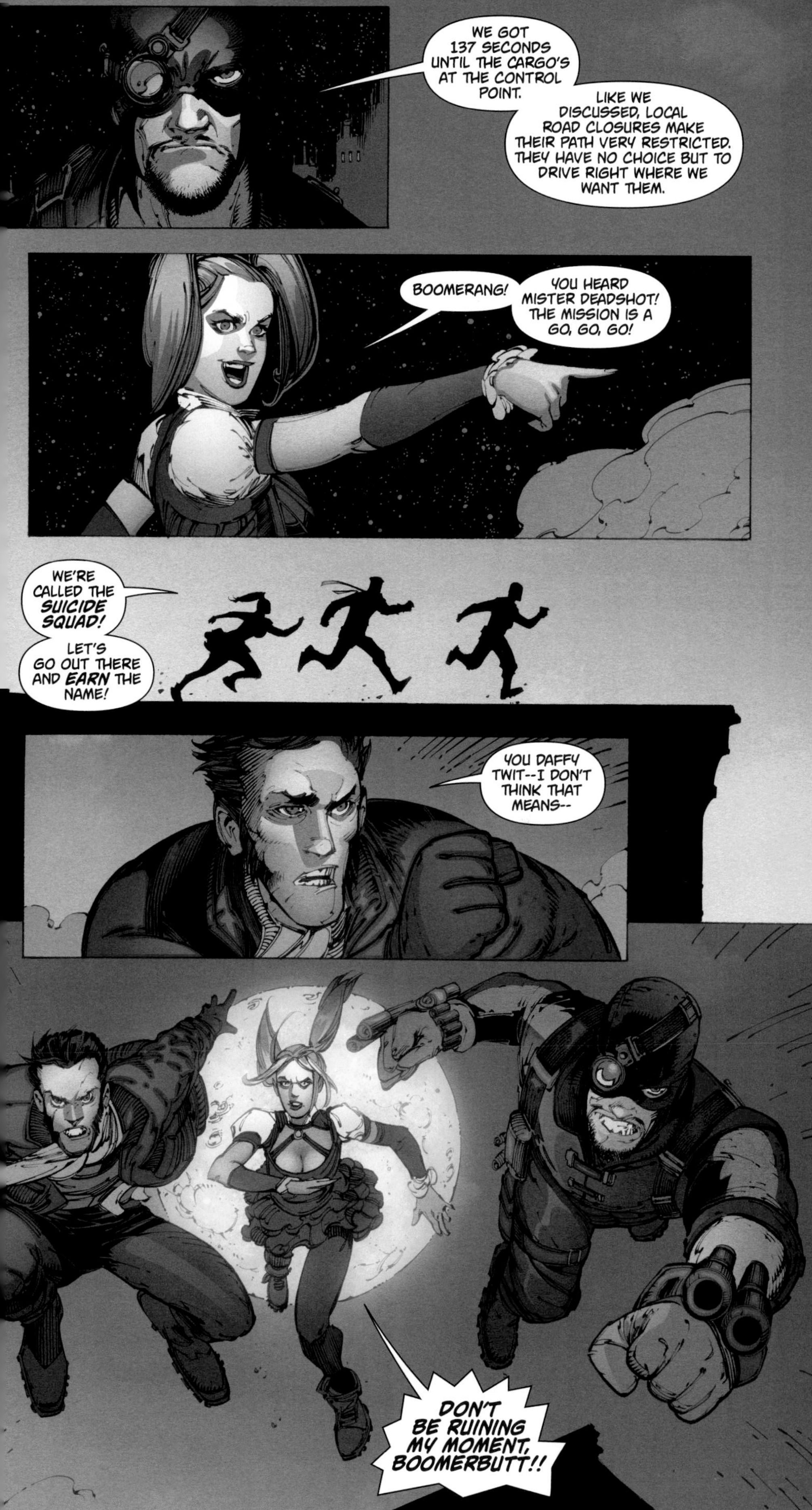
WE GOT 137 SECONDS UNTIL THE CARGO'S AT THE CONTROL POINT.
LIKE WE DISCUSSED, LOCAL ROAD CLOSURES MAKE THEIR PATH VERY RESTRICTED. THEY HAVE NO CHOICE BUT TO DRIVE RIGHT WHERE WE WANT THEM.
BOOMERANG!
YOU HEARD MISTER DEADSHOT! THE MISSION IS A GO, GO, GO!
WE'RE CALLED THE ***SUICIDE SQUAD!***
LET'S GO OUT THERE AND ***EARN*** THE NAME!
YOU DAFFY TWIT--I DON'T THINK THAT MEANS--
DON'T BE RUINING MY MOMENT, BOOMERBUTT!!

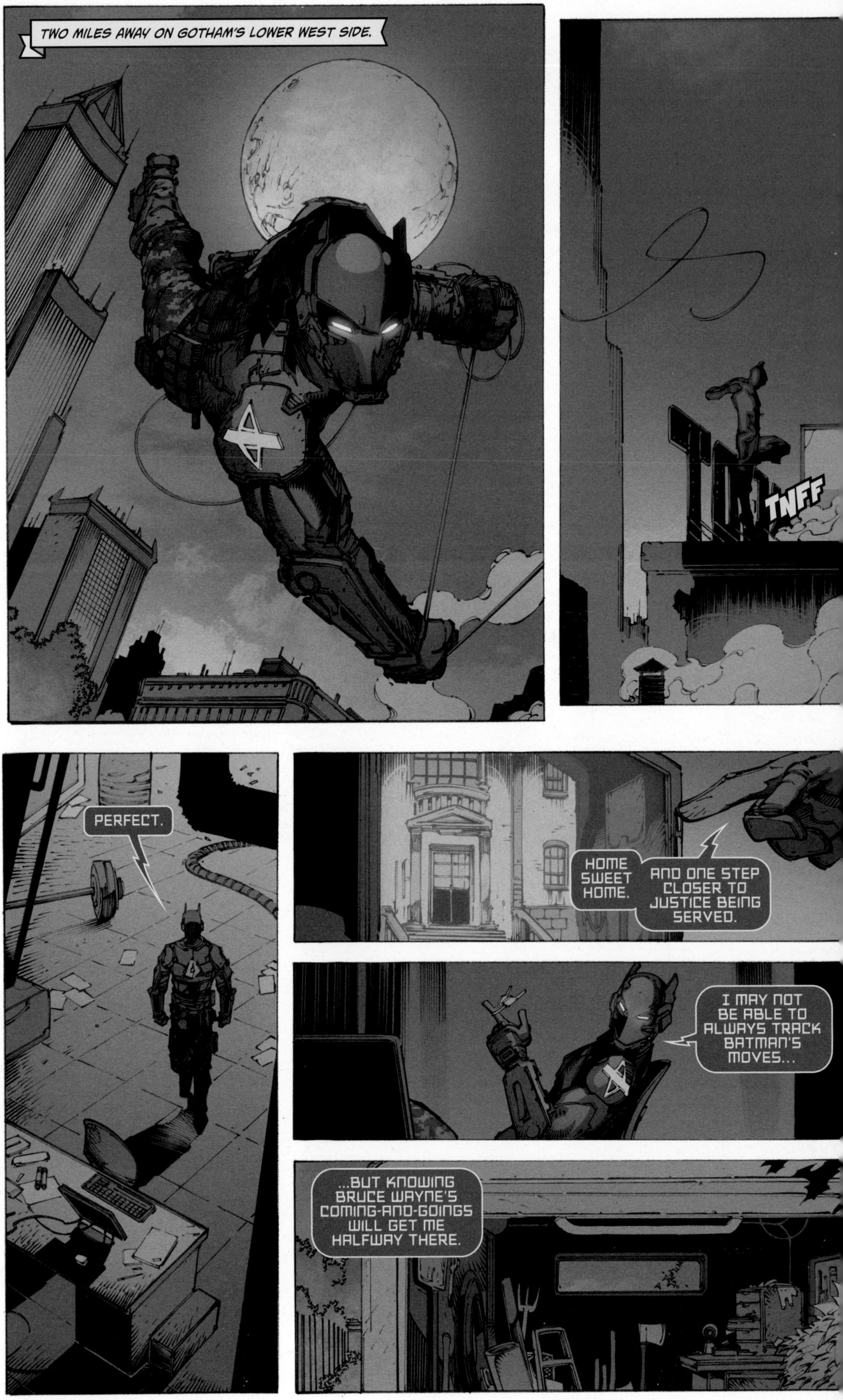
TWO MILES AWAY ON GOTHAM'S LOWER WEST SIDE.
TNFF
PERFECT.
HOME SWEET HOME.
AND ONE STEP CLOSER TO JUSTICE BEING SERVED.
I MAY NOT BE ABLE TO ALWAYS TRACK BATMAN'S MOVES...
...BUT KNOWING BRUCE WAYNE'S COMING-AND-GOINGS WILL GET ME HALFWAY THERE.

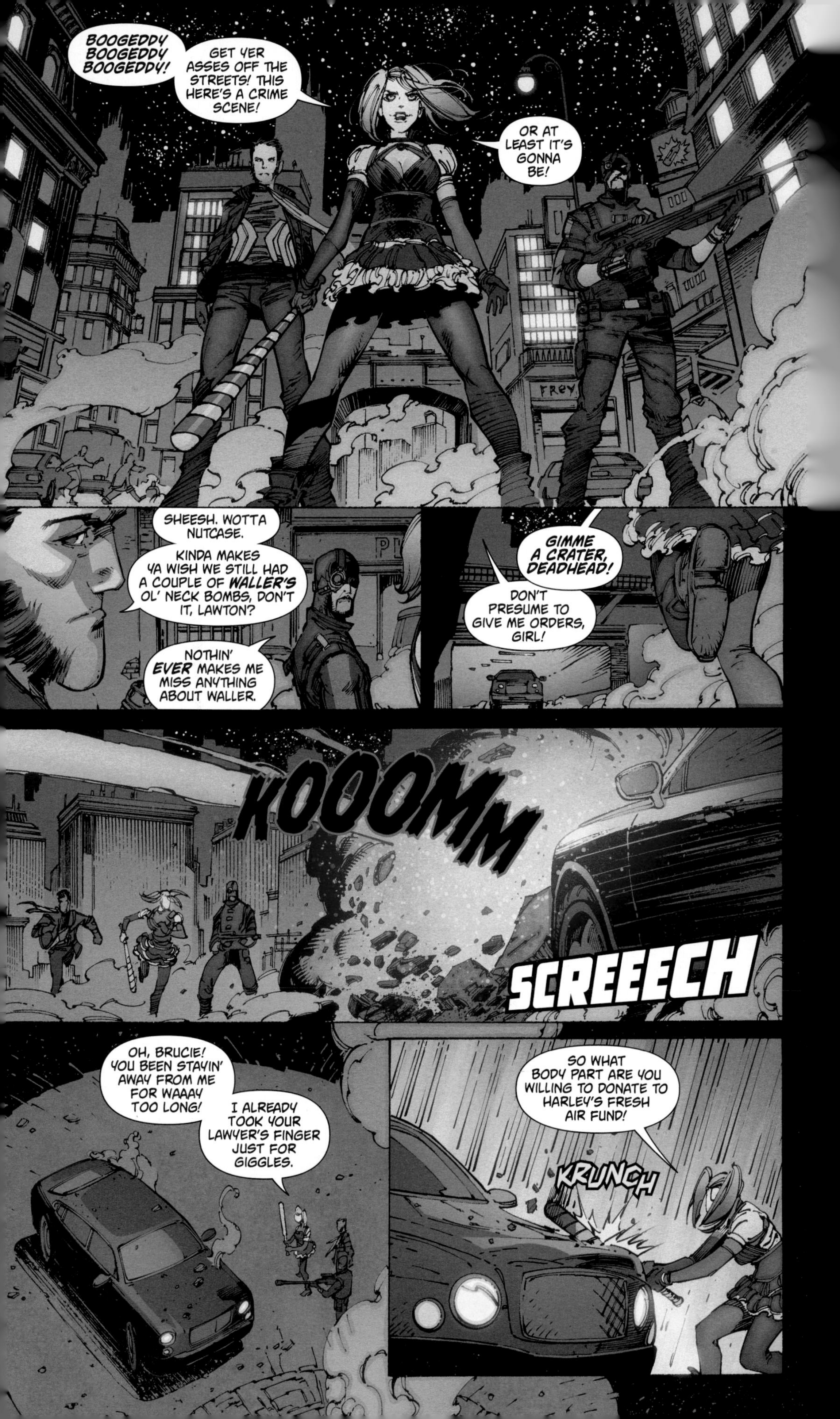
BOOGEDDY BOOGEDDY BOOGEDDY!
GET YER ASSES OFF THE STREETS! THIS HERE'S A CRIME SCENE!
OR AT LEAST IT'S GONNA BE!
FREY
SHEESH. WOTTA NUTCASE.
KINDA MAKES YA WISH WE STILL HAD A COUPLE OF WALLER'S OL' NECK BOMBS, DON'T IT, LAWTON?
NOTHIN' EVER MAKES ME MISS ANYTHING ABOUT WALLER.
GIMME A CRATER, DEADHEAD!
DON'T PRESUME TO GIVE ME ORDERS, GIRL!
KOOOMM
SCREEECH
OH, BRUCIE! YOU BEEN STAYIN' AWAY FROM ME FOR WAAAY TOO LONG!
I ALREADY TOOK YOUR LAWYER'S FINGER JUST FOR GIGGLES.
SO WHAT BODY PART ARE YOU WILLING TO DONATE TO HARLEY'S FRESH AIR FUND!
KRUNCH

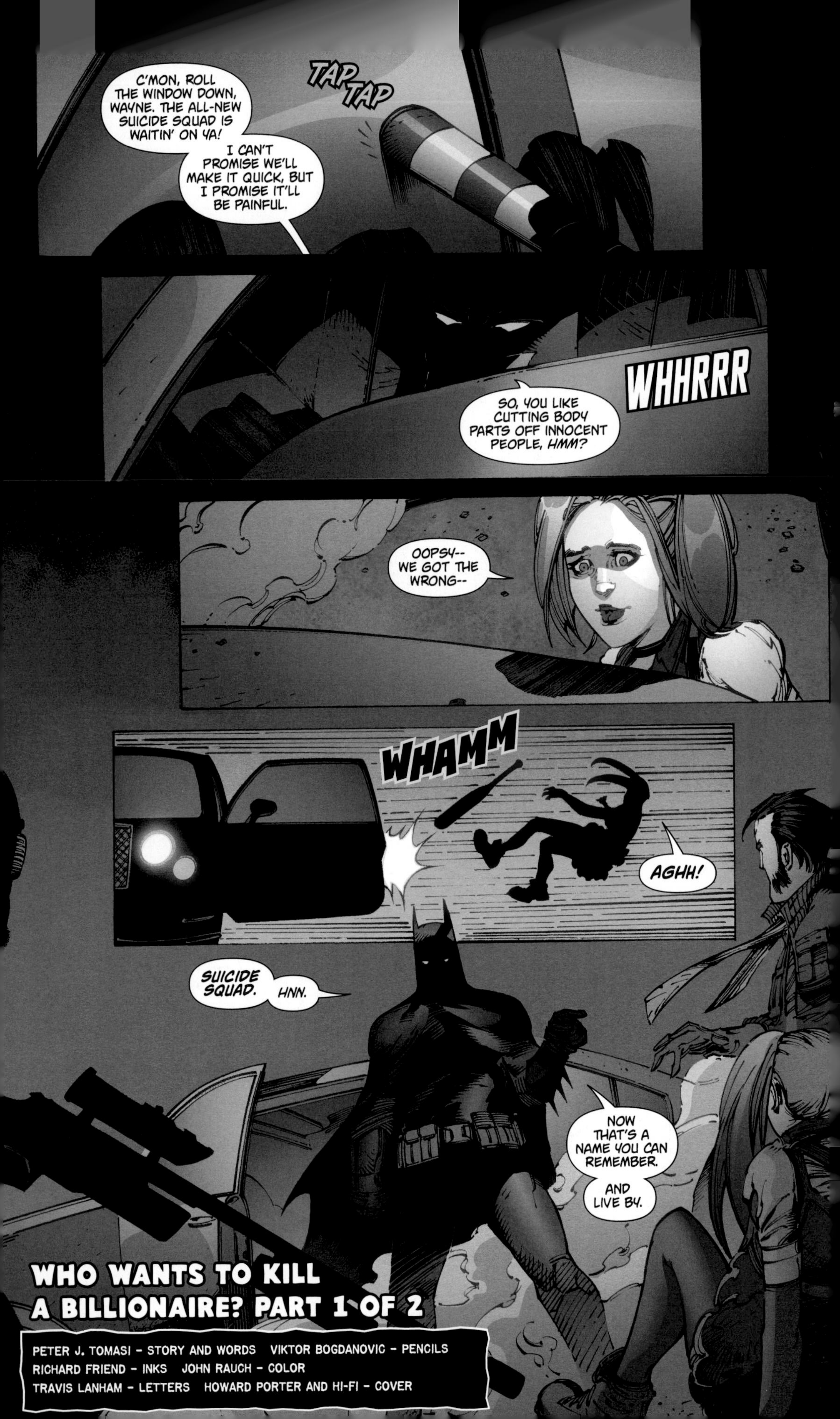
C'MON, ROLL THE WINDOW DOWN, WAYNE. THE ALL-NEW SUICIDE SQUAD IS WAITIN' ON YA!
TAP TAP
I CAN'T PROMISE WE'LL MAKE IT QUICK, BUT I PROMISE IT'LL BE PAINFUL.
WHHRRR
SO, YOU LIKE CUTTING BODY PARTS OFF INNOCENT PEOPLE, HMM?
OOPSY-- WE GOT THE WRONG--
WHAMM
AGHH!
SUICIDE SQUAD.
HNN.
NOW THAT'S A NAME YOU CAN REMEMBER.
AND LIVE BY.

WHO WANTS TO KILL A BILLIONAIRE? PART 1 OF 2

PETER J. TOMASI - STORY AND WORDS VIKTOR BOGDANOVIC - PENCILS
RICHARD FRIEND - INKS JOHN RAUCH - COLOR
TRAVIS LANHAM - LETTERS HOWARD PORTER AND HI-FI - COVER

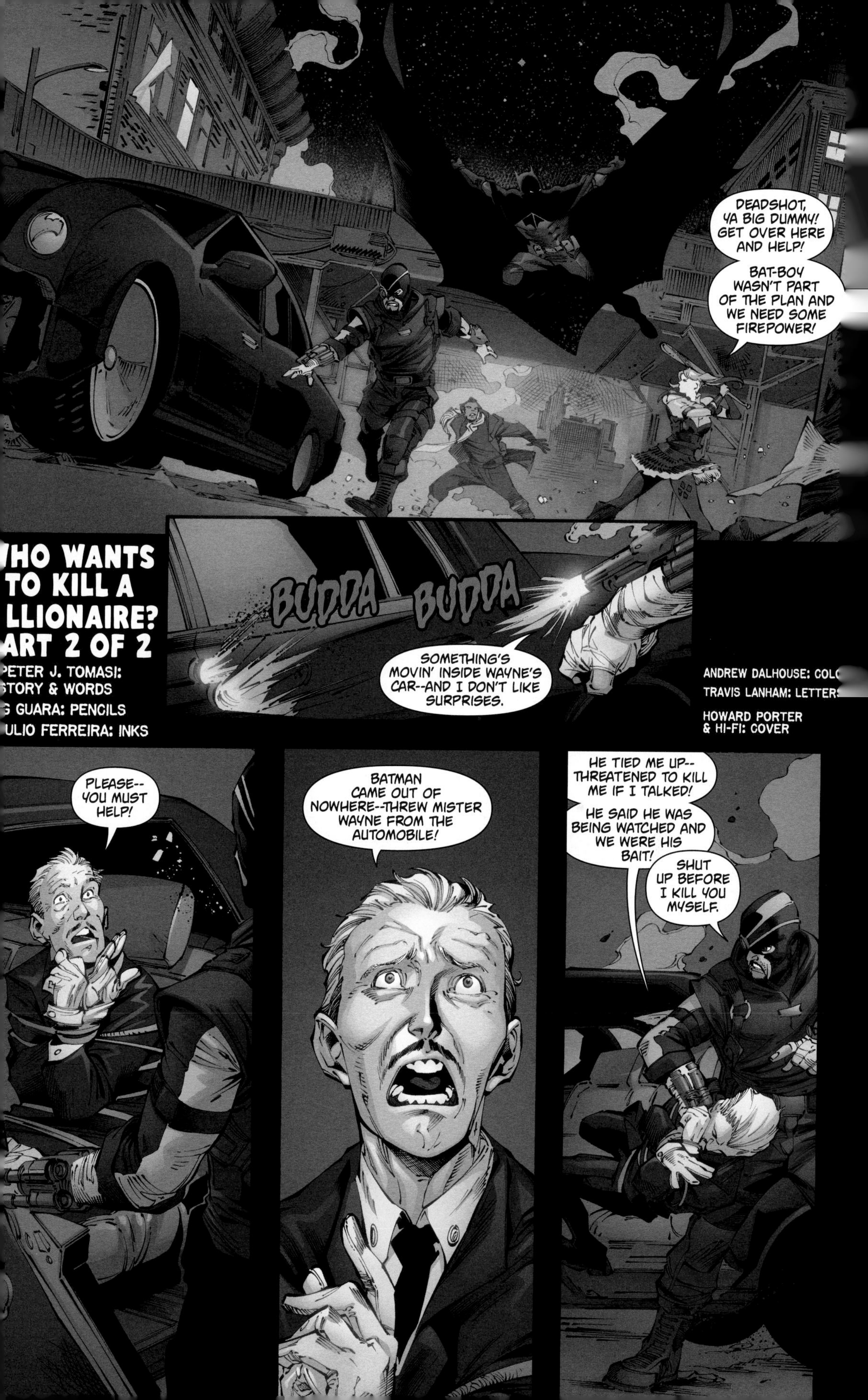

DEADSHOT, YA BIG DUMMY! GET OVER HERE AND HELP!
BAT-BOY WASN'T PART OF THE PLAN AND WE NEED SOME FIREPOWER!
HO WANTS TO KILL A LLIONAIRE? ART 2 OF 2
PETER J. TOMASI: STORY & WORDS
GUARA: PENCILS
ULIO FERREIRA: INKS
BUDDA BUDDA
SOMETHING'S MOVIN' INSIDE WAYNE'S CAR--AND I DON'T LIKE SURPRISES.
ANDREW DALHOUSE: COLO
TRAVIS LANHAM: LETTER
HOWARD PORTER & HI-FI: COVER
PLEASE-- YOU MUST HELP!
BATMAN CAME OUT OF NOWHERE--THREW MISTER WAYNE FROM THE AUTOMOBILE!
HE TIED ME UP-- THREATENED TO KILL ME IF I TALKED!
HE SAID HE WAS BEING WATCHED AND WE WERE HIS BAIT!
SHUT UP BEFORE I KILL YOU MYSELF.

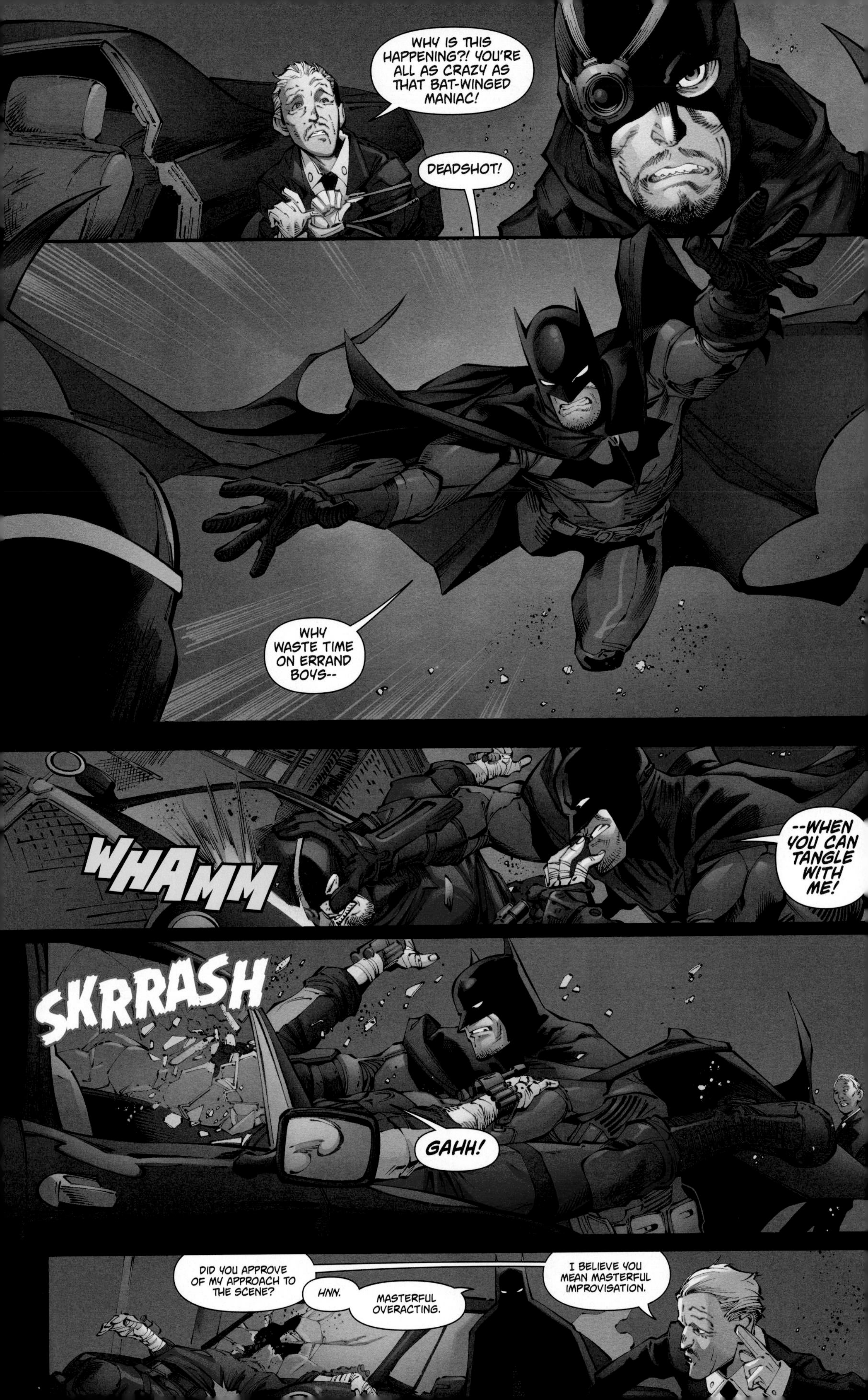
WHY IS THIS HAPPENING?! YOU'RE ALL AS CRAZY AS THAT BAT-WINGED MANIAC!
DEADSHOT!
WHY WASTE TIME ON ERRAND BOYS--
WHAMM
--WHEN YOU CAN TANGLE WITH ME!
SKRRASH
GAHH!
DID YOU APPROVE OF MY APPROACH TO THE SCENE?
HNN.
MASTERFUL OVERACTING.
I BELIEVE YOU MEAN MASTERFUL IMPROVISATION.

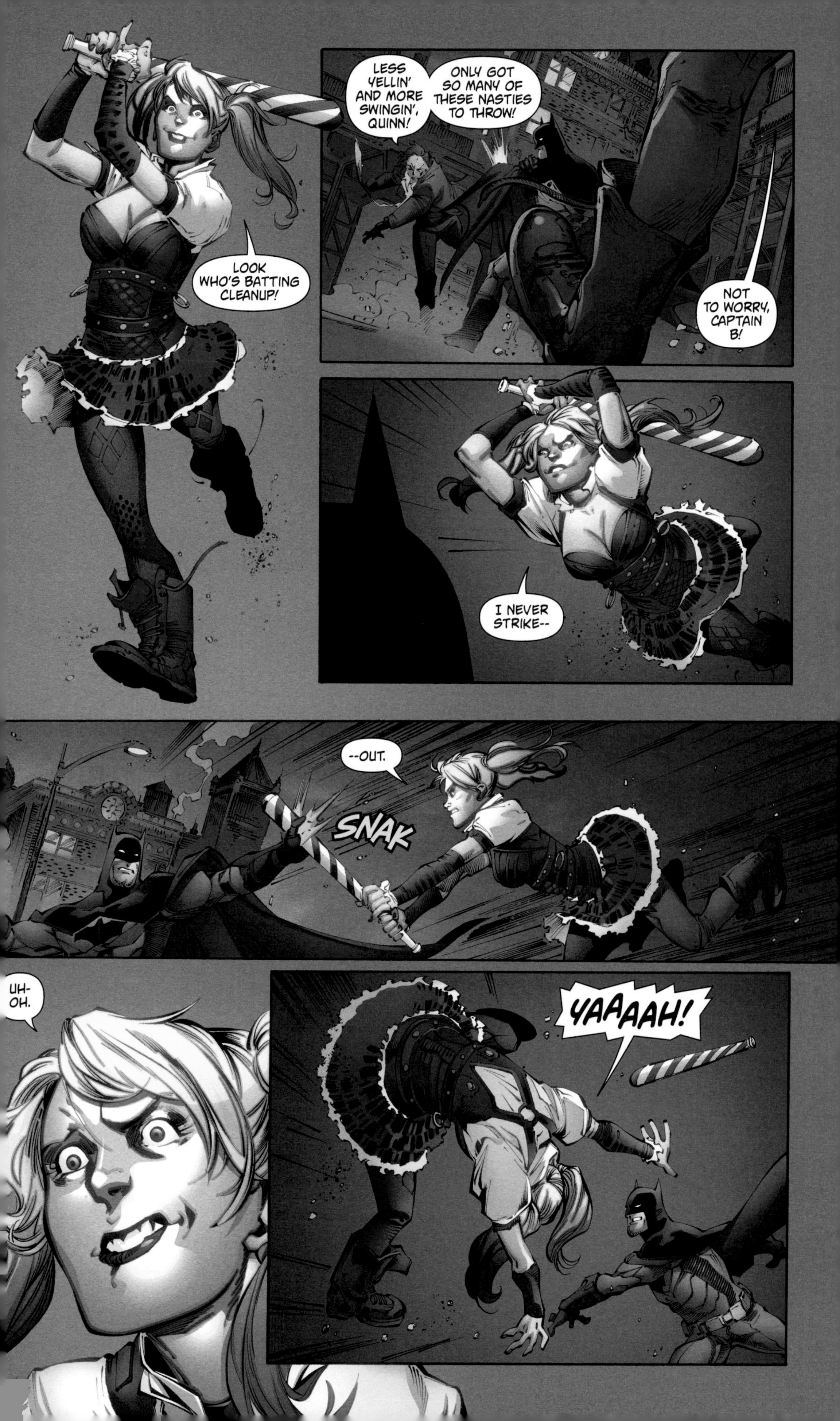
LESS YELLIN' AND MORE SWINGIN', QUINN!
ONLY GOT SO MANY OF THESE NASTIES TO THROW!
LOOK WHO'S BATTING CLEANUP!
NOT TO WORRY, CAPTAIN B!
I NEVER STRIKE--
--OUT.
SNAK
UH-OH.
YAAAAH!

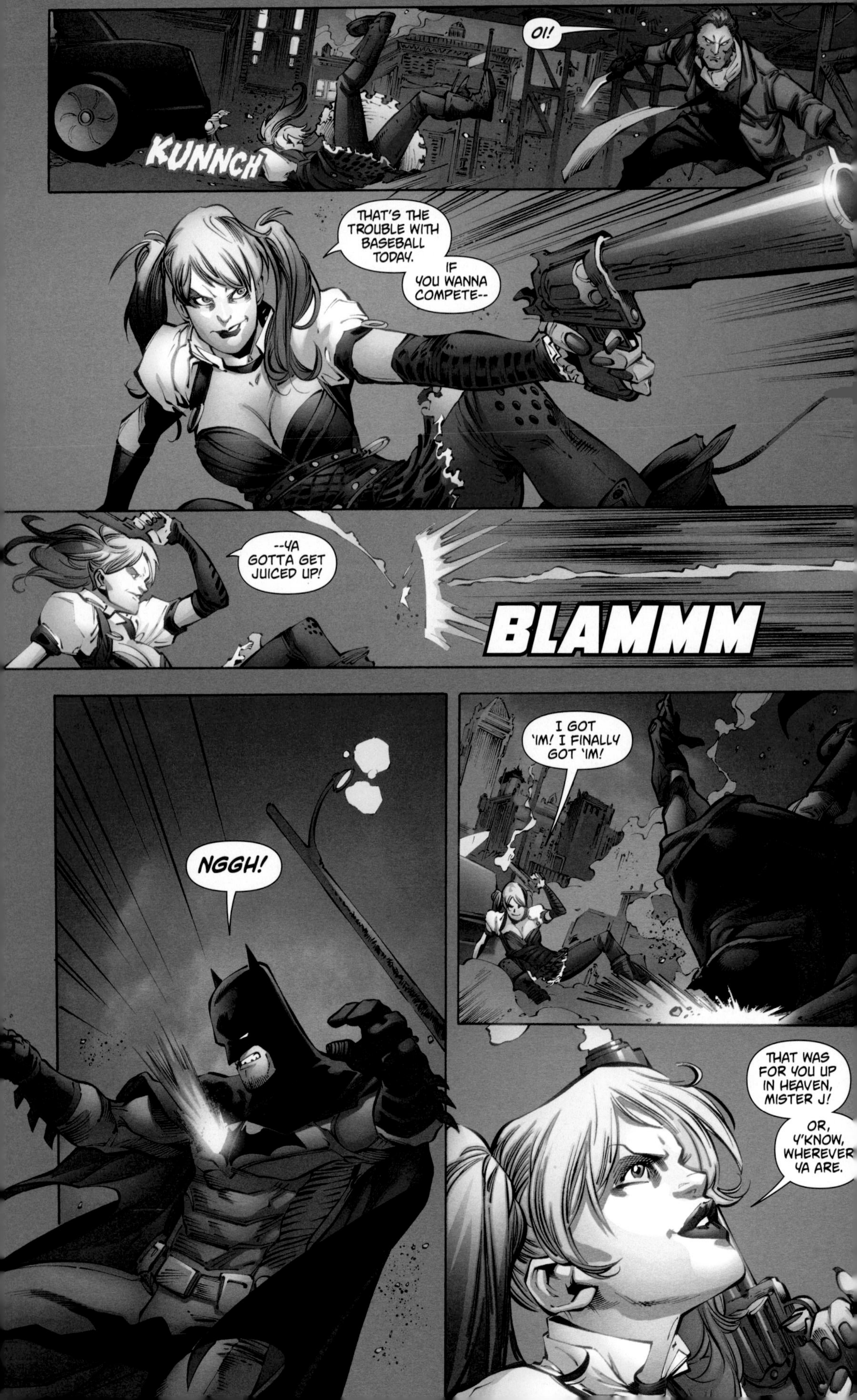
KUNNCH
OI!
THAT'S THE TROUBLE WITH BASEBALL TODAY.
IF YOU WANNA COMPETE--
--YA GOTTA GET JUICED UP!
BLAMMM
NGGH!
I GOT 'IM! I FINALLY GOT 'IM!
THAT WAS FOR YOU UP IN HEAVEN, MISTER J!
OR, Y'KNOW, WHEREVER YA ARE.

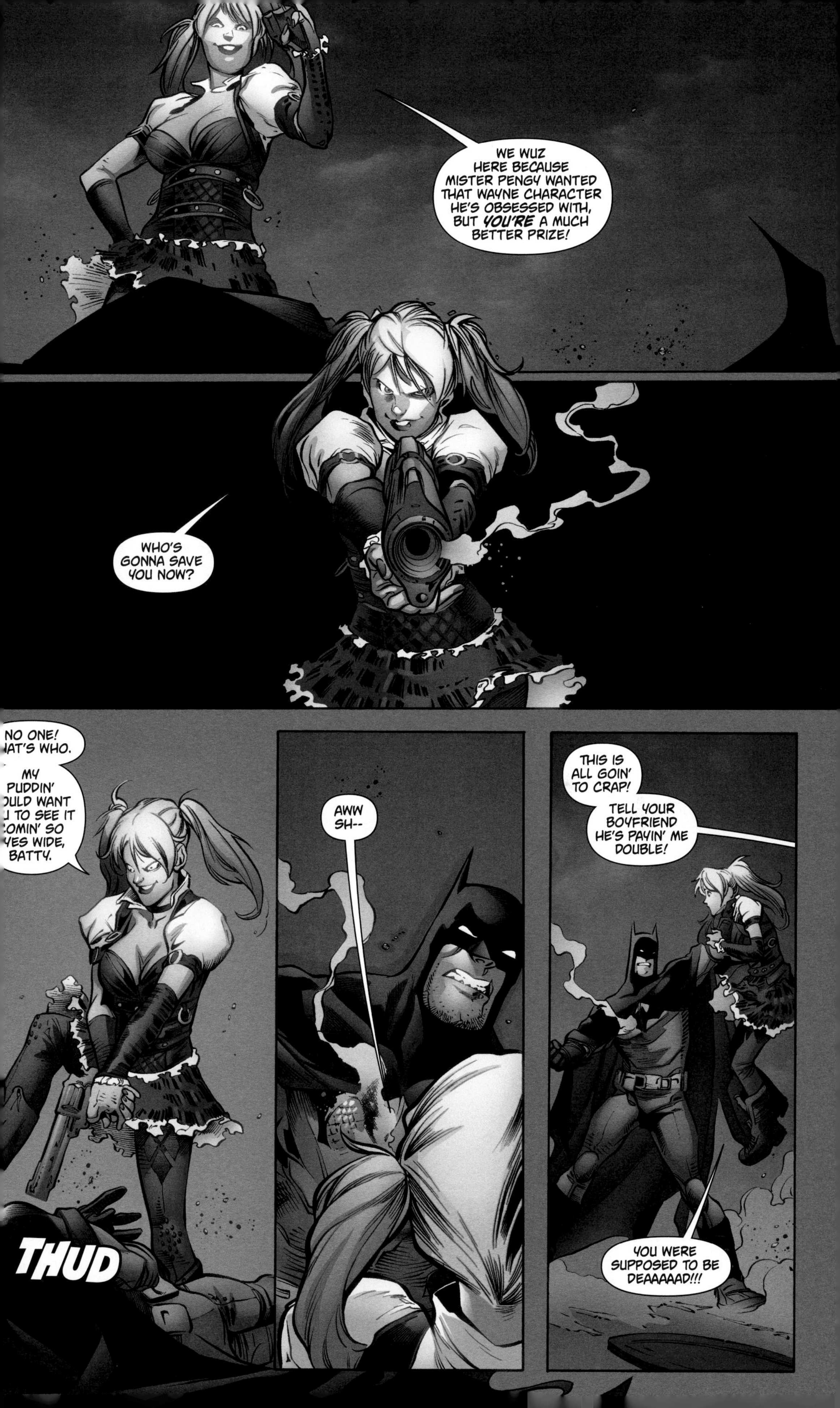
WE WUZ HERE BECAUSE MISTER PENGY WANTED THAT WAYNE CHARACTER HE'S OBSESSED WITH, BUT *YOU'RE* A MUCH BETTER PRIZE!
WHO'S GONNA SAVE YOU NOW?
NO ONE! IAT'S WHO.
MY PUDDIN' OULD WANT I TO SEE IT COMIN' SO YES WIDE, BATTY.
THUD
AWW SH--
THIS IS ALL GOIN' TO CRAP!
TELL YOUR BOYFRIEND HE'S PAYIN' ME DOUBLE!
YOU WERE SUPPOSED TO BE DEAAAAAD!!!

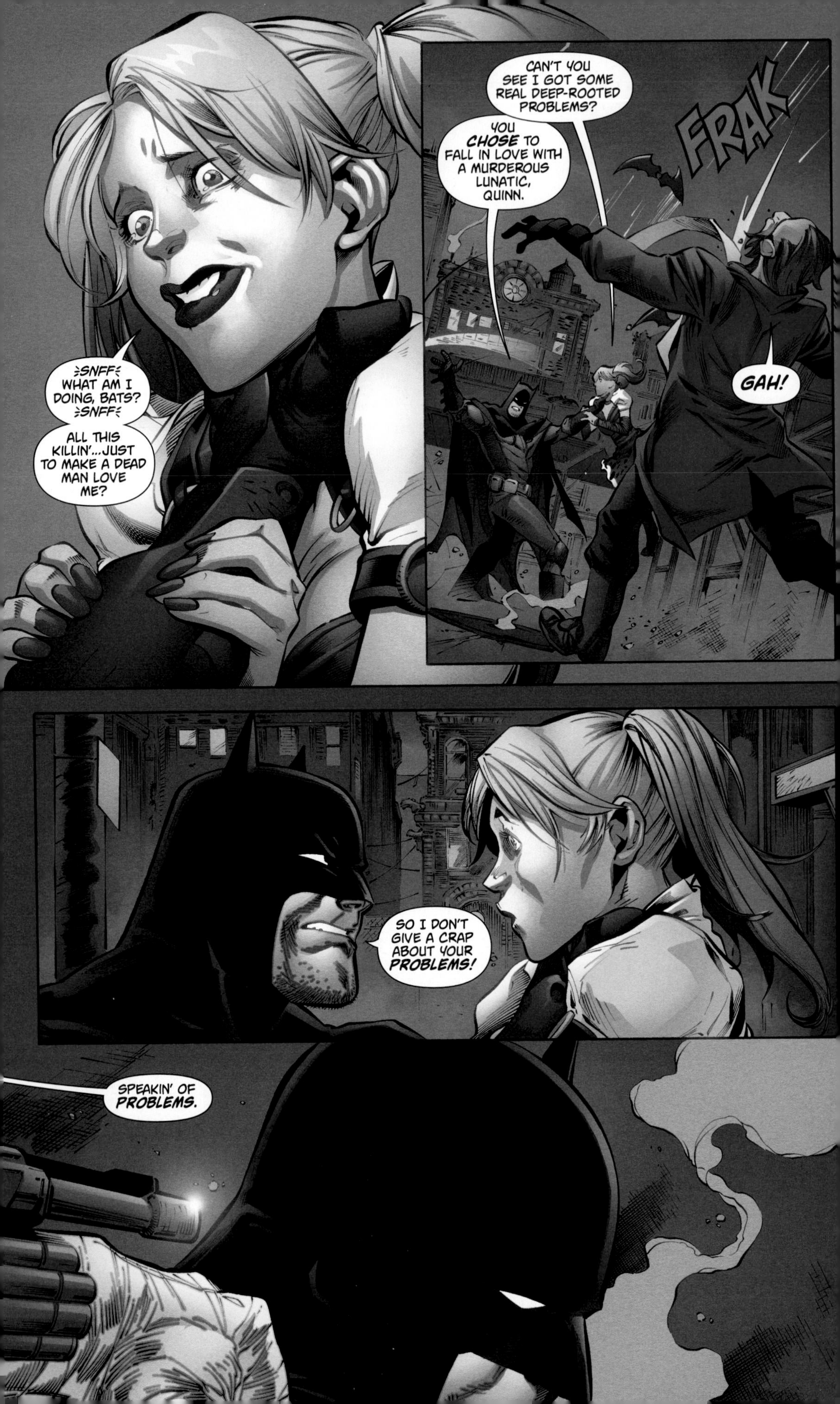
≷SNFF≶ WHAT AM I DOING, BATS? ≷SNFF≶
ALL THIS KILLIN'...JUST TO MAKE A DEAD MAN LOVE ME?
CAN'T YOU SEE I GOT SOME REAL DEEP-ROOTED PROBLEMS?
YOU CHOSE TO FALL IN LOVE WITH A MURDEROUS LUNATIC, QUINN.
FRAK
GAH!
SO I DON'T GIVE A CRAP ABOUT YOUR PROBLEMS!
SPEAKIN' OF PROBLEMS.

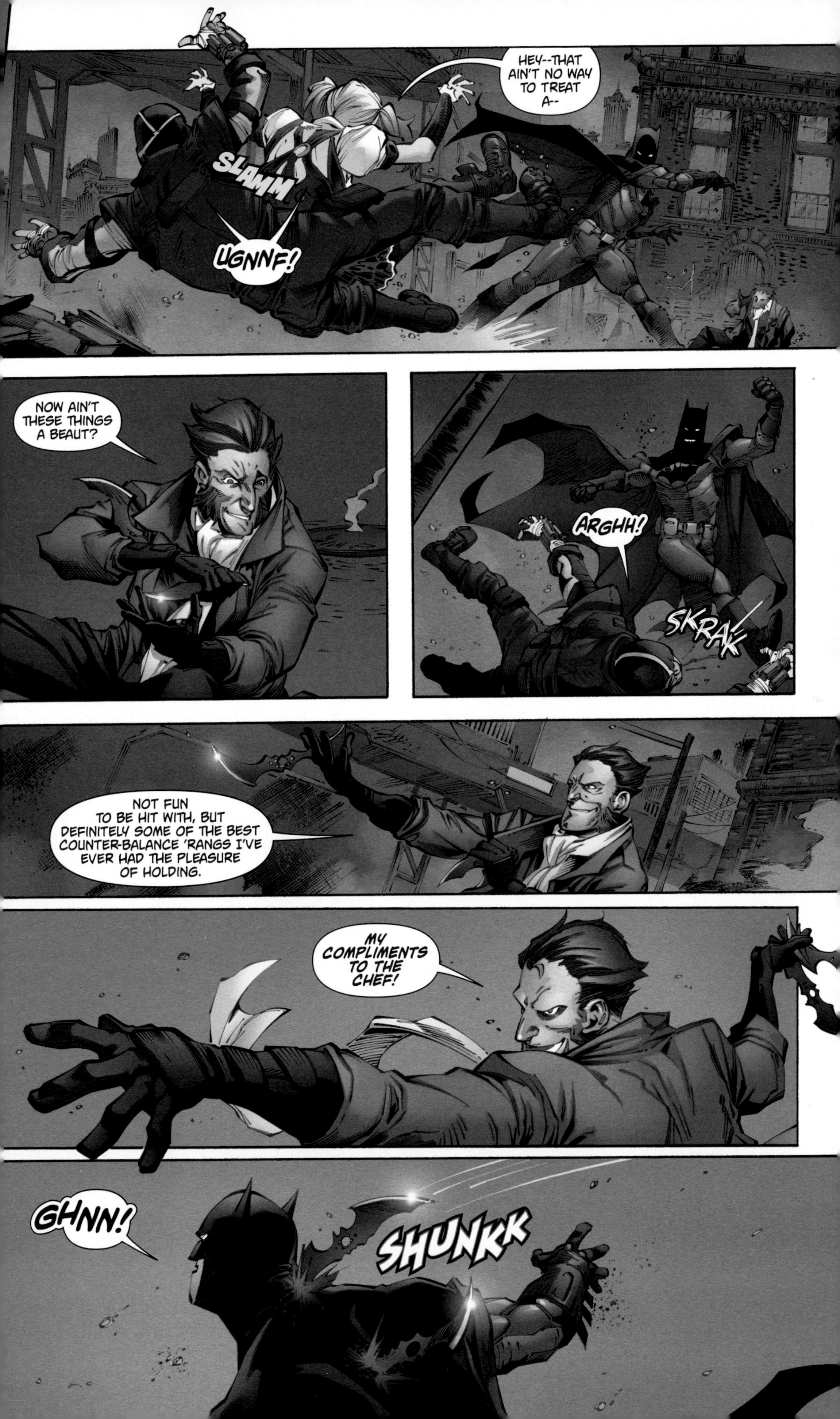
HEY--THAT AIN'T NO WAY TO TREAT A--
SLAMM
UGNNF!
NOW AIN'T THESE THINGS A BEAUT?
ARGHH!
SKRAK
NOT FUN TO BE HIT WITH, BUT DEFINITELY SOME OF THE BEST COUNTER-BALANCE 'RANGS I'VE EVER HAD THE PLEASURE OF HOLDING.
MY COMPLIMENTS TO THE CHEF!
GHNN!
SHUNKK

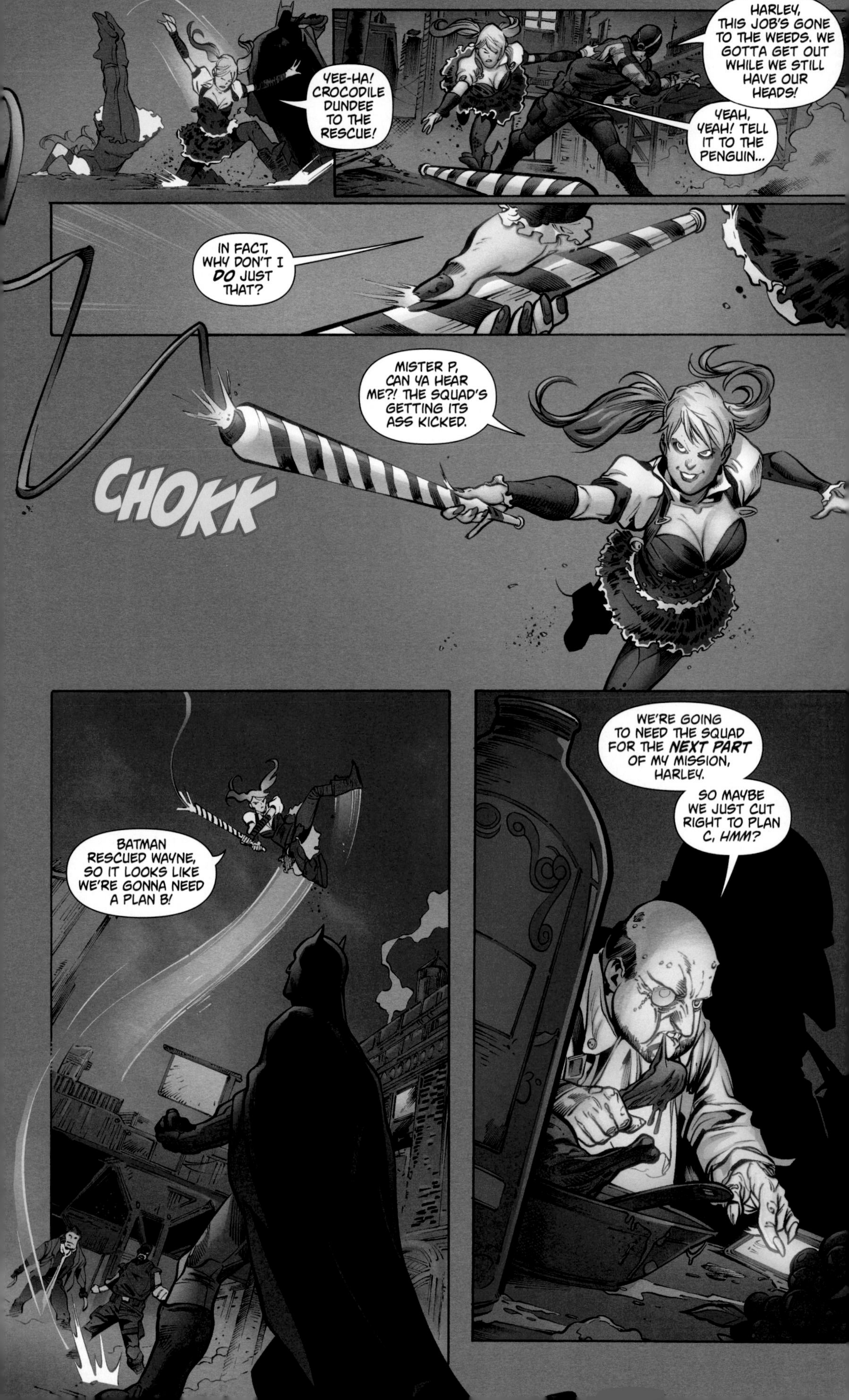
YEE-HA! CROCODILE DUNDEE TO THE RESCUE!
HARLEY, THIS JOB'S GONE TO THE WEEDS. WE GOTTA GET OUT WHILE WE STILL HAVE OUR HEADS!
YEAH, YEAH! TELL IT TO THE PENGUIN...
IN FACT, WHY DON'T I DO JUST THAT?
MISTER P, CAN YA HEAR ME?! THE SQUAD'S GETTING ITS ASS KICKED.
CHOKK
BATMAN RESCUED WAYNE, SO IT LOOKS LIKE WE'RE GONNA NEED A PLAN B!
WE'RE GOING TO NEED THE SQUAD FOR THE NEXT PART OF MY MISSION, HARLEY.
SO MAYBE WE JUST CUT RIGHT TO PLAN C, HMM?

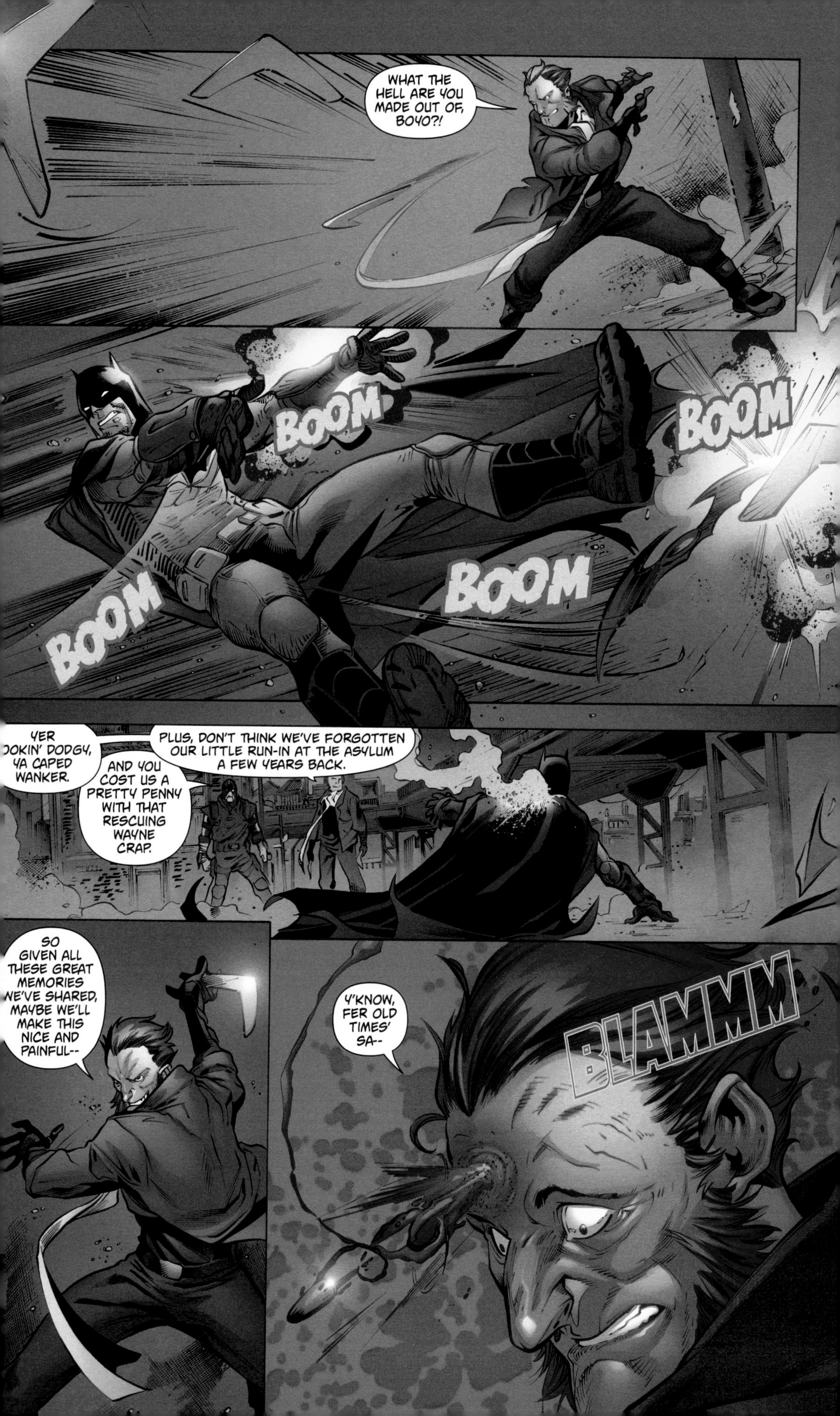
WHAT THE HELL ARE YOU MADE OUT OF, BOYO?!
BOOM
BOOM
BOOM
BOOM
YER LOOKIN' DODGY, YA CAPED WANKER.
AND YOU COST US A PRETTY PENNY WITH THAT RESCUING WAYNE CRAP.
PLUS, DON'T THINK WE'VE FORGOTTEN OUR LITTLE RUN-IN AT THE ASYLUM A FEW YEARS BACK.
SO GIVEN ALL THESE GREAT MEMORIES WE'VE SHARED, MAYBE WE'LL MAKE THIS NICE AND PAINFUL--
Y'KNOW, FER OLD TIMES' SA--
BLAMMM

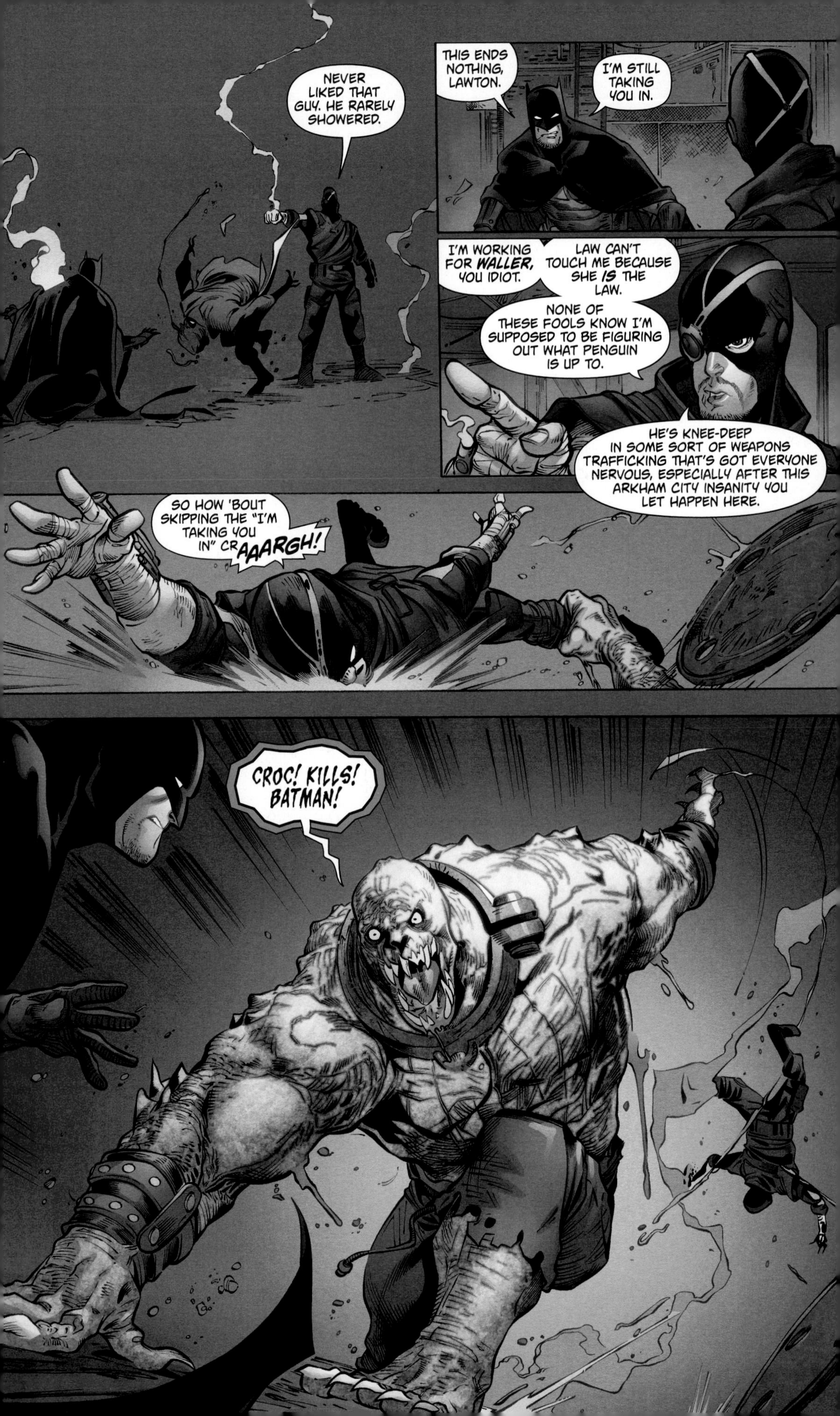
NEVER LIKED THAT GUY. HE RARELY SHOWERED.
THIS ENDS NOTHING, LAWTON.
I'M STILL TAKING YOU IN.
I'M WORKING FOR WALLER, YOU IDIOT.
LAW CAN'T TOUCH ME BECAUSE SHE IS THE LAW.
NONE OF THESE FOOLS KNOW I'M SUPPOSED TO BE FIGURING OUT WHAT PENGUIN IS UP TO.
HE'S KNEE-DEEP IN SOME SORT OF WEAPONS TRAFFICKING THAT'S GOT EVERYONE NERVOUS, ESPECIALLY AFTER THIS ARKHAM CITY INSANITY YOU LET HAPPEN HERE.
SO HOW 'BOUT SKIPPING THE "I'M TAKING YOU IN" CRAAARGH!
CROC! KILLS! BATMAN!

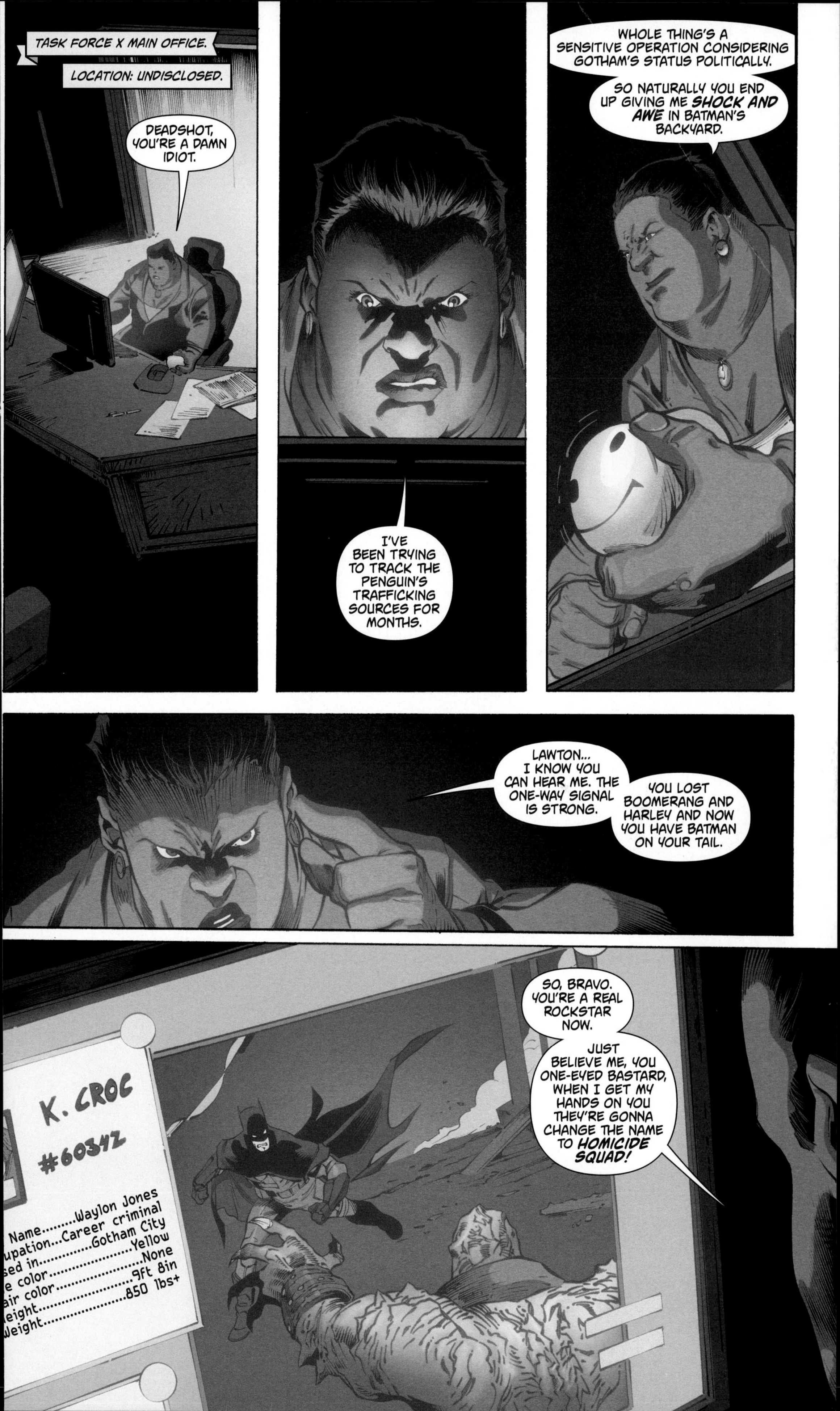
TASK FORCE X MAIN OFFICE.
LOCATION: UNDISCLOSED.
DEADSHOT, YOU'RE A DAMN IDIOT.
I'VE BEEN TRYING TO TRACK THE PENGUIN'S TRAFFICKING SOURCES FOR MONTHS.
WHOLE THING'S A SENSITIVE OPERATION CONSIDERING GOTHAM'S STATUS POLITICALLY.
SO NATURALLY YOU END UP GIVING ME SHOCK AND AWE IN BATMAN'S BACKYARD.
LAWTON... I KNOW YOU CAN HEAR ME. THE ONE-WAY SIGNAL IS STRONG.
YOU LOST BOOMERANG AND HARLEY AND NOW YOU HAVE BATMAN ON YOUR TAIL.
K. CROC
#60342
Name.........Waylon Jones
upation...Career criminal
sed in..............Gotham City
e color......................Yellow
air color........................None
eight..........................9ft 8in
Weight.....................850 lbs+
SO, BRAVO. YOU'RE A REAL ROCKSTAR NOW.
JUST BELIEVE ME, YOU ONE-EYED BASTARD, WHEN I GET MY HANDS ON YOU THEY'RE GONNA CHANGE THE NAME TO HOMICIDE SQUAD!

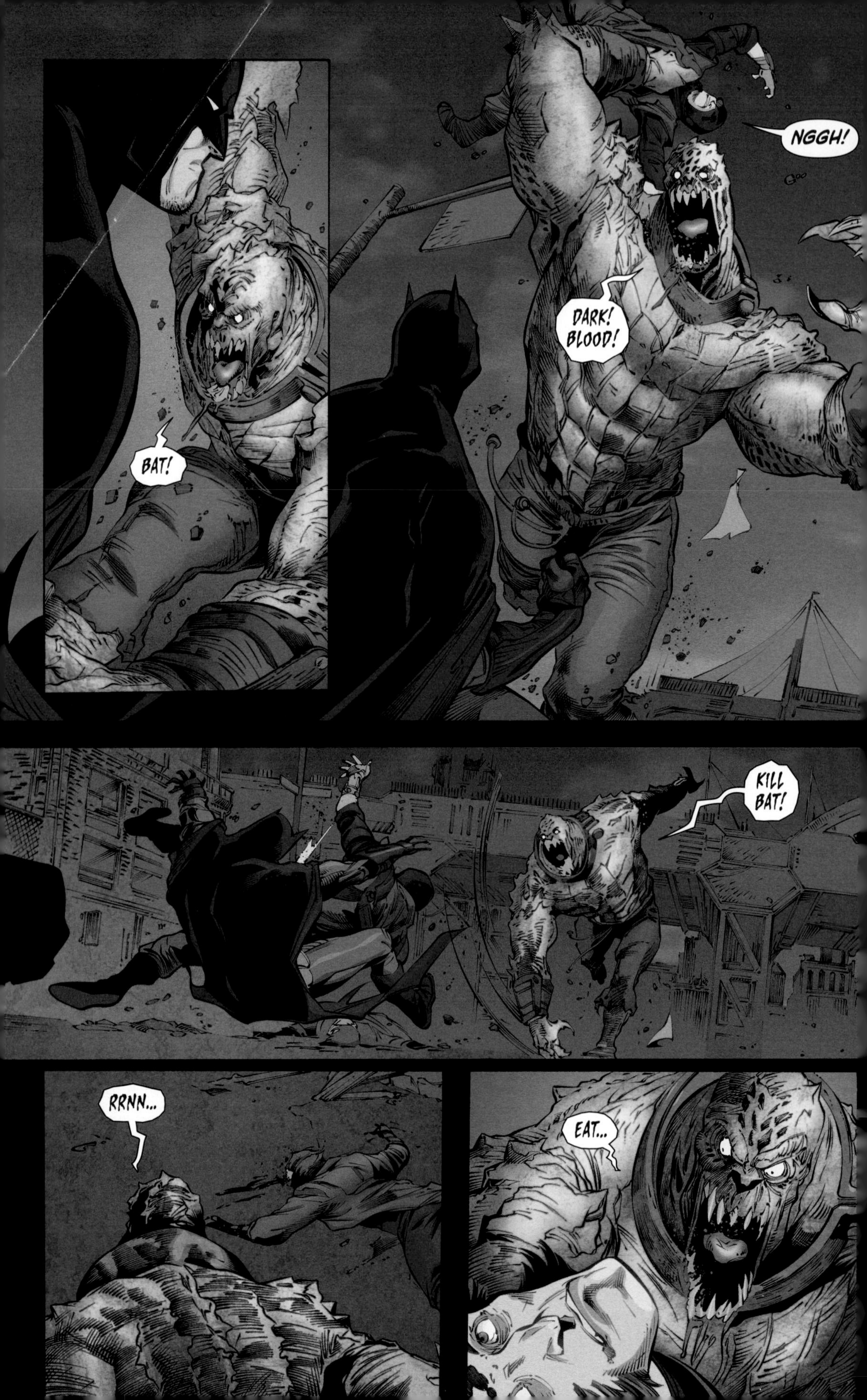
BAT!
NGGH!
DARK! BLOOD!
KILL BAT!
RRNN...
EAT...

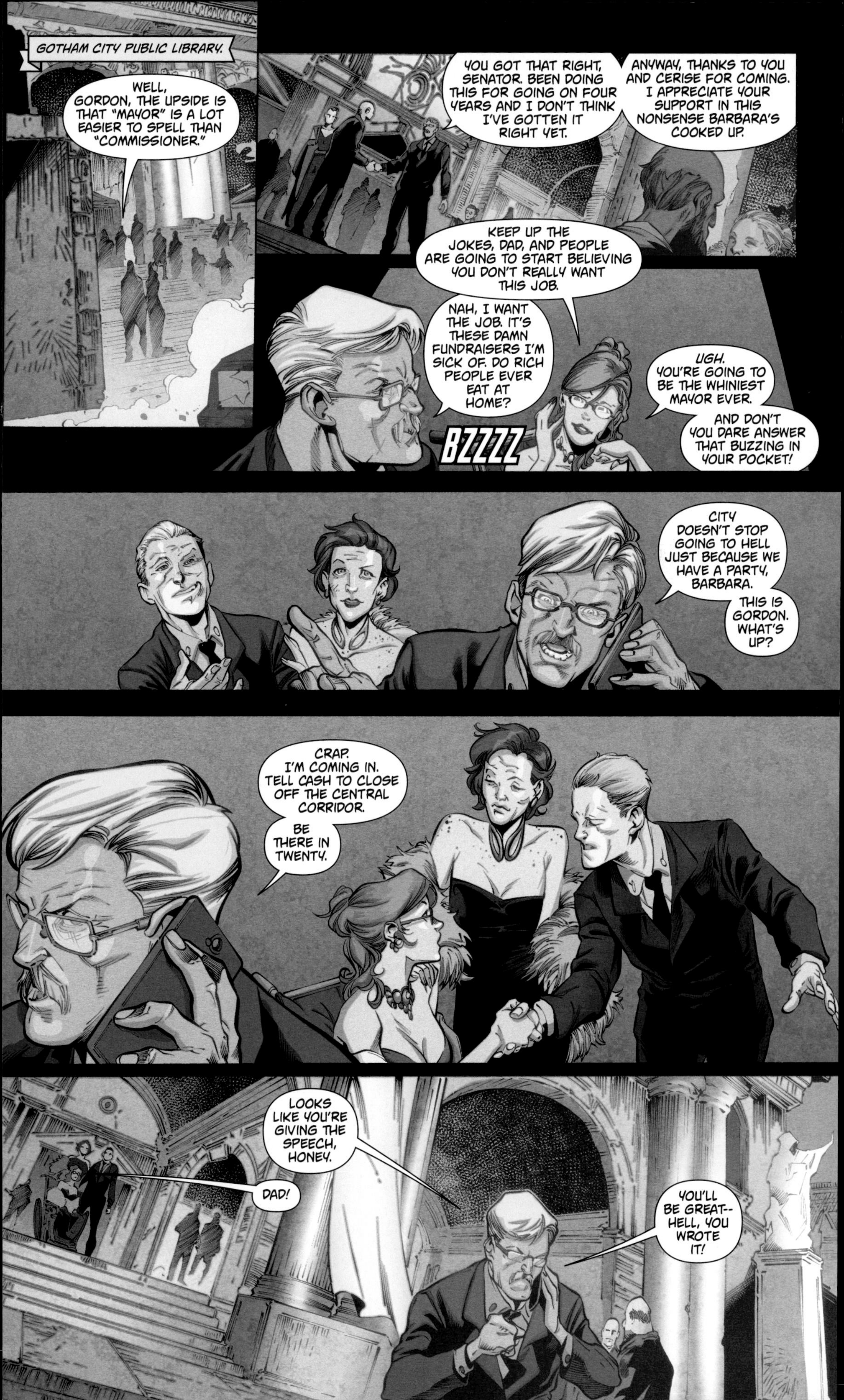
GOTHAM CITY PUBLIC LIBRARY.
WELL, GORDON, THE UPSIDE IS THAT "MAYOR" IS A LOT EASIER TO SPELL THAN "COMMISSIONER."
YOU GOT THAT RIGHT, SENATOR. BEEN DOING THIS FOR GOING ON FOUR YEARS AND I DON'T THINK I'VE GOTTEN IT RIGHT YET.
ANYWAY, THANKS TO YOU AND CERISE FOR COMING. I APPRECIATE YOUR SUPPORT IN THIS NONSENSE BARBARA'S COOKED UP.
KEEP UP THE JOKES, DAD, AND PEOPLE ARE GOING TO START BELIEVING YOU DON'T REALLY WANT THIS JOB.
NAH, I WANT THE JOB. IT'S THESE DAMN FUNDRAISERS I'M SICK OF. DO RICH PEOPLE EVER EAT AT HOME?
BZZZZ
UGH. YOU'RE GOING TO BE THE WHINIEST MAYOR EVER.
AND DON'T YOU DARE ANSWER THAT BUZZING IN YOUR POCKET!
CITY DOESN'T STOP GOING TO HELL JUST BECAUSE WE HAVE A PARTY, BARBARA.
THIS IS GORDON. WHAT'S UP?
CRAP. I'M COMING IN. TELL CASH TO CLOSE OFF THE CENTRAL CORRIDOR.
BE THERE IN TWENTY.
LOOKS LIKE YOU'RE GIVING THE SPEECH, HONEY.
DAD!
YOU'LL BE GREAT-- HELL, YOU WROTE IT!

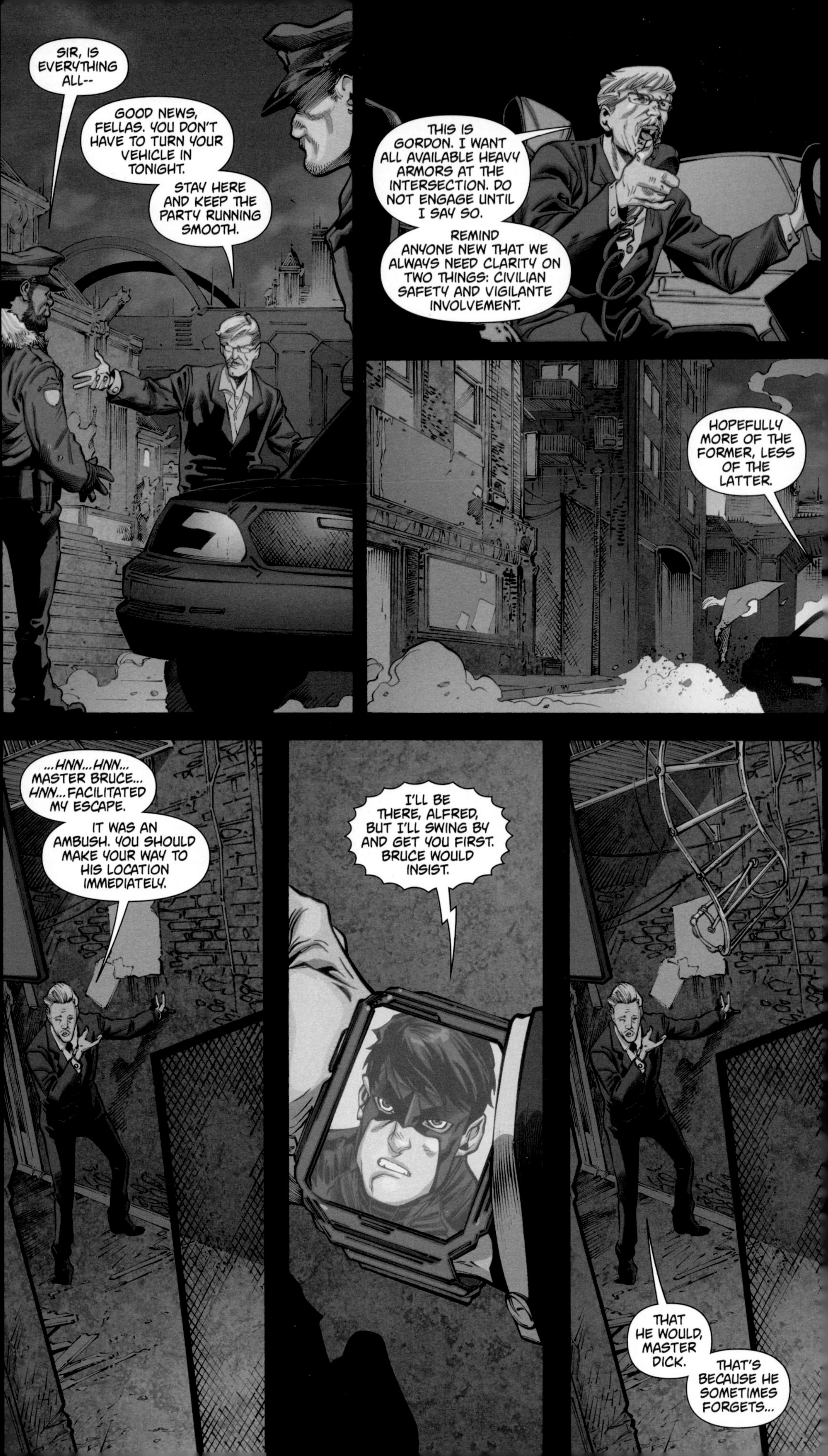
SIR, IS EVERYTHING ALL--
GOOD NEWS, FELLAS. YOU DON'T HAVE TO TURN YOUR VEHICLE IN TONIGHT.
STAY HERE AND KEEP THE PARTY RUNNING SMOOTH.
THIS IS GORDON. I WANT ALL AVAILABLE HEAVY ARMORS AT THE INTERSECTION. DO NOT ENGAGE UNTIL I SAY SO.
REMIND ANYONE NEW THAT WE ALWAYS NEED CLARITY ON TWO THINGS: CIVILIAN SAFETY AND VIGILANTE INVOLVEMENT.
HOPEFULLY MORE OF THE FORMER, LESS OF THE LATTER.
...HNN...HNN... MASTER BRUCE... HNN...FACILITATED MY ESCAPE.
IT WAS AN AMBUSH. YOU SHOULD MAKE YOUR WAY TO HIS LOCATION IMMEDIATELY.
I'LL BE THERE, ALFRED, BUT I'LL SWING BY AND GET YOU FIRST. BRUCE WOULD INSIST.
THAT HE WOULD, MASTER DICK.
THAT'S BECAUSE HE SOMETIMES FORGETS...

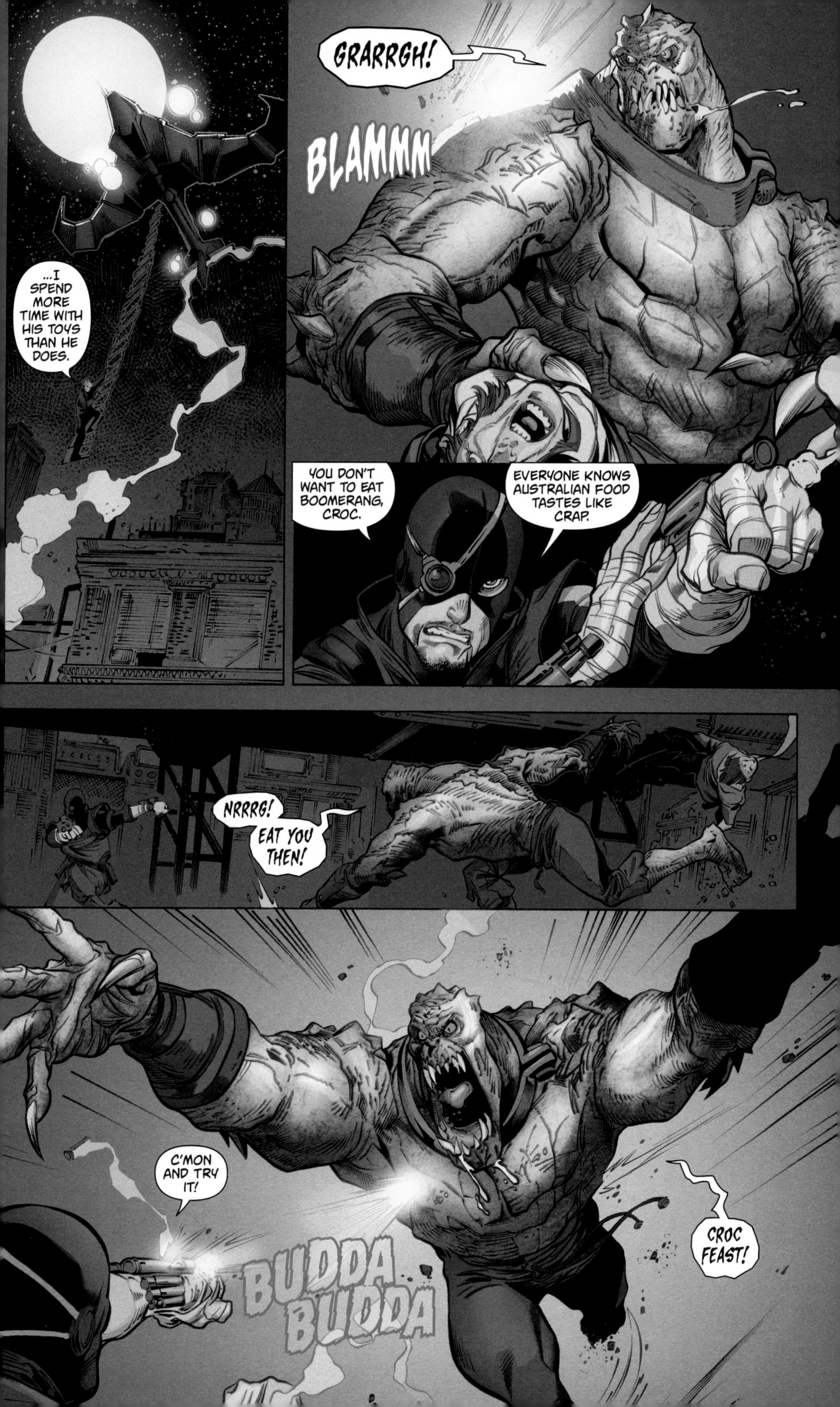
...I SPEND MORE TIME WITH HIS TOYS THAN HE DOES.
GRARRGH!
BLAMMM
YOU DON'T WANT TO EAT BOOMERANG, CROC.
EVERYONE KNOWS AUSTRALIAN FOOD TASTES LIKE CRAP.
NRRRG!
EAT YOU THEN!
C'MON AND TRY IT!
CROC FEAST!
BUDDA BUDDA

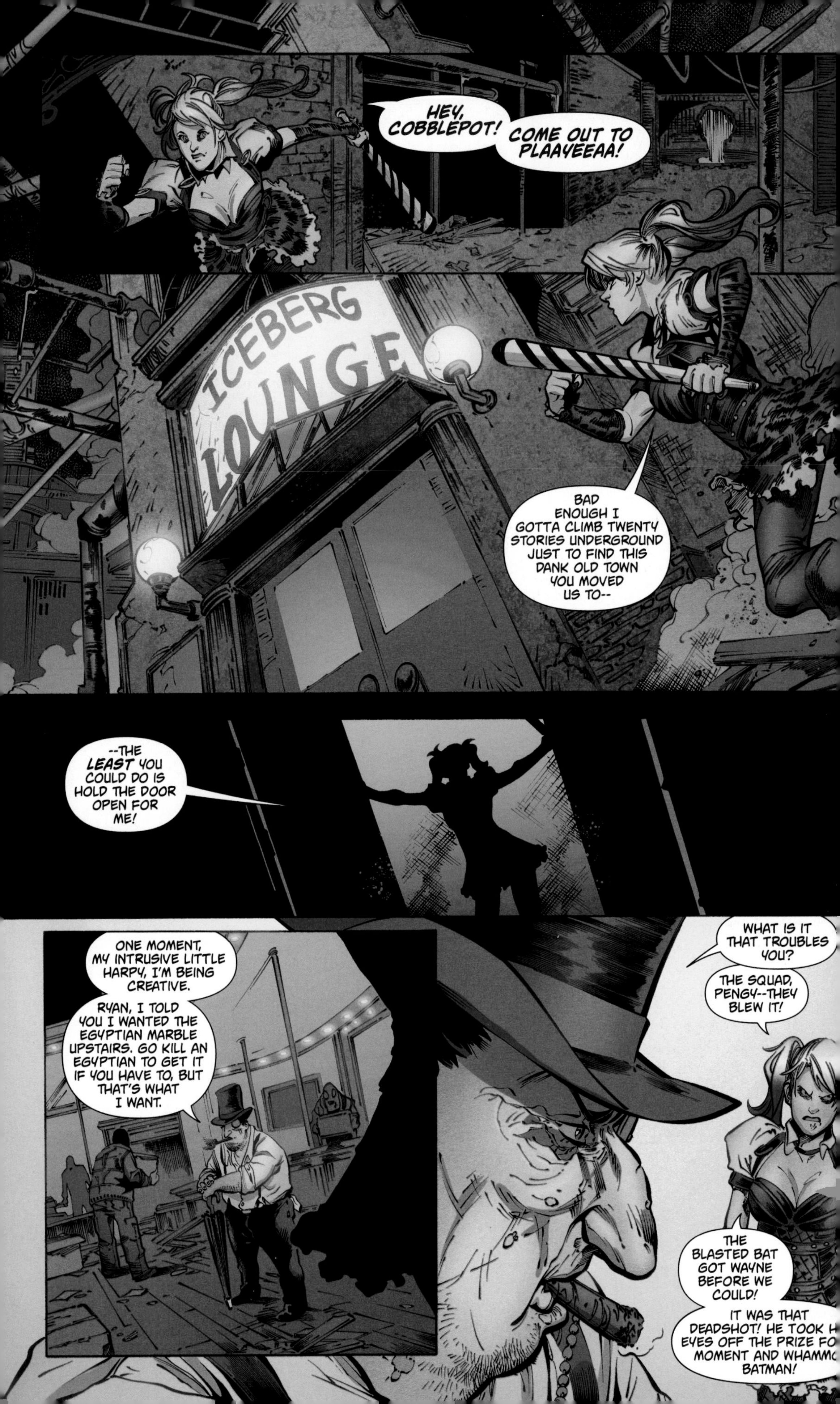
HEY, COBBLEPOT!
COME OUT TO PLAAYEEAA!
BAD ENOUGH I GOTTA CLIMB TWENTY STORIES UNDERGROUND JUST TO FIND THIS DANK OLD TOWN YOU MOVED US TO--
--THE LEAST YOU COULD DO IS HOLD THE DOOR OPEN FOR ME!
ONE MOMENT, MY INTRUSIVE LITTLE HARPY, I'M BEING CREATIVE.
RYAN, I TOLD YOU I WANTED THE EGYPTIAN MARBLE UPSTAIRS. GO KILL AN EGYPTIAN TO GET IT IF YOU HAVE TO, BUT THAT'S WHAT I WANT.
WHAT IS IT THAT TROUBLES YOU?
THE SQUAD, PENGY--THEY BLEW IT!
THE BLASTED BAT GOT WAYNE BEFORE WE COULD!
ICEBERG LOUNGE

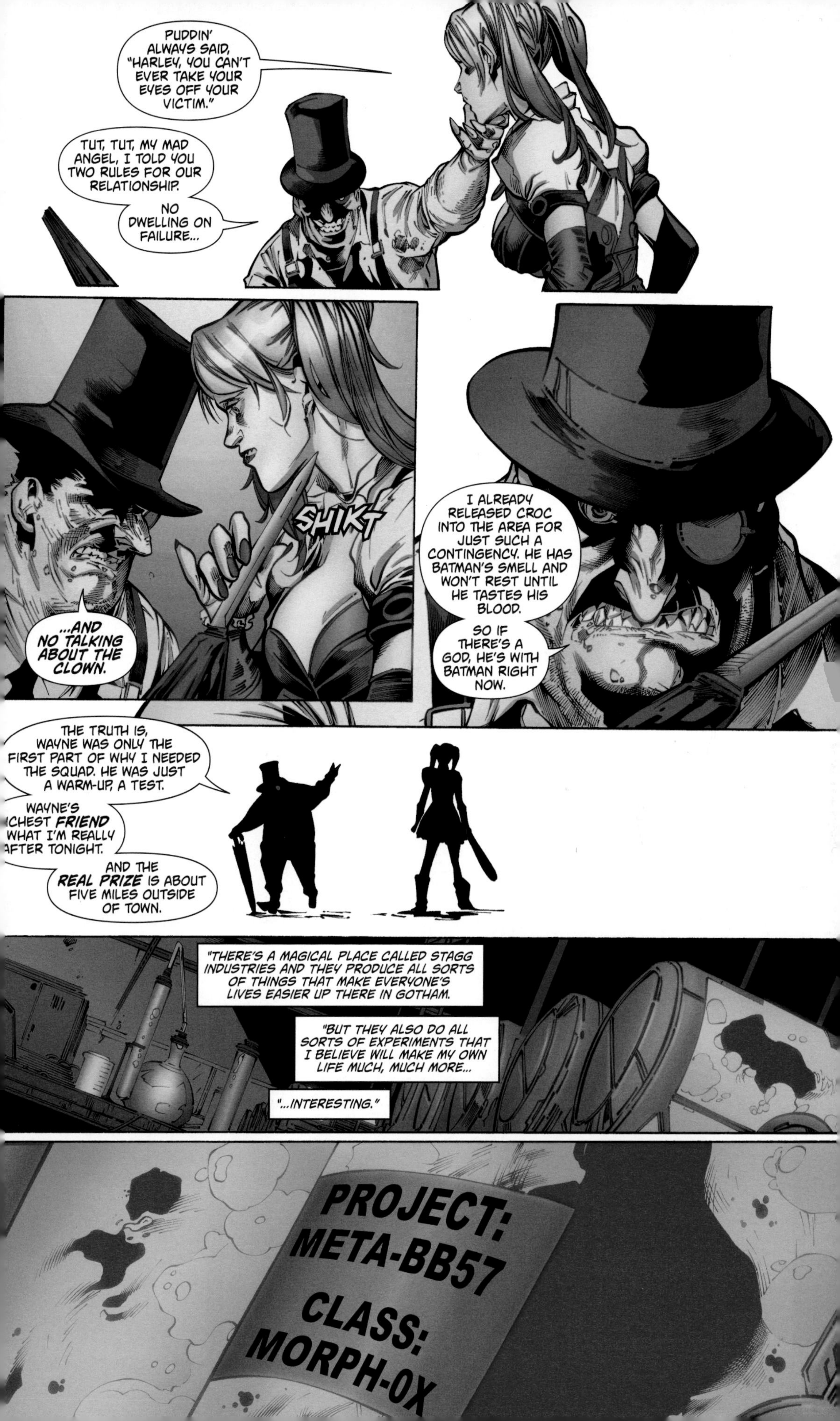

PUDDIN' ALWAYS SAID, "HARLEY, YOU CAN'T EVER TAKE YOUR EYES OFF YOUR VICTIM."
TUT, TUT, MY MAD ANGEL, I TOLD YOU TWO RULES FOR OUR RELATIONSHIP.
NO DWELLING ON FAILURE...
SHIKT
...AND NO TALKING ABOUT THE CLOWN.
I ALREADY RELEASED CROC INTO THE AREA FOR JUST SUCH A CONTINGENCY. HE HAS BATMAN'S SMELL AND WON'T REST UNTIL HE TASTES HIS BLOOD.
SO IF THERE'S A GOD, HE'S WITH BATMAN RIGHT NOW.
THE TRUTH IS, WAYNE WAS ONLY THE FIRST PART OF WHY I NEEDED THE SQUAD. HE WAS JUST A WARM-UP, A TEST.
WAYNE'S ICHEST FRIEND WHAT I'M REALLY AFTER TONIGHT.
AND THE REAL PRIZE IS ABOUT FIVE MILES OUTSIDE OF TOWN.
"THERE'S A MAGICAL PLACE CALLED STAGG INDUSTRIES AND THEY PRODUCE ALL SORTS OF THINGS THAT MAKE EVERYONE'S LIVES EASIER UP THERE IN GOTHAM.
"BUT THEY ALSO DO ALL SORTS OF EXPERIMENTS THAT I BELIEVE WILL MAKE MY OWN LIFE MUCH, MUCH MORE...
"...INTERESTING."
PROJECT: META-BB57
CLASS: MORPH-0X

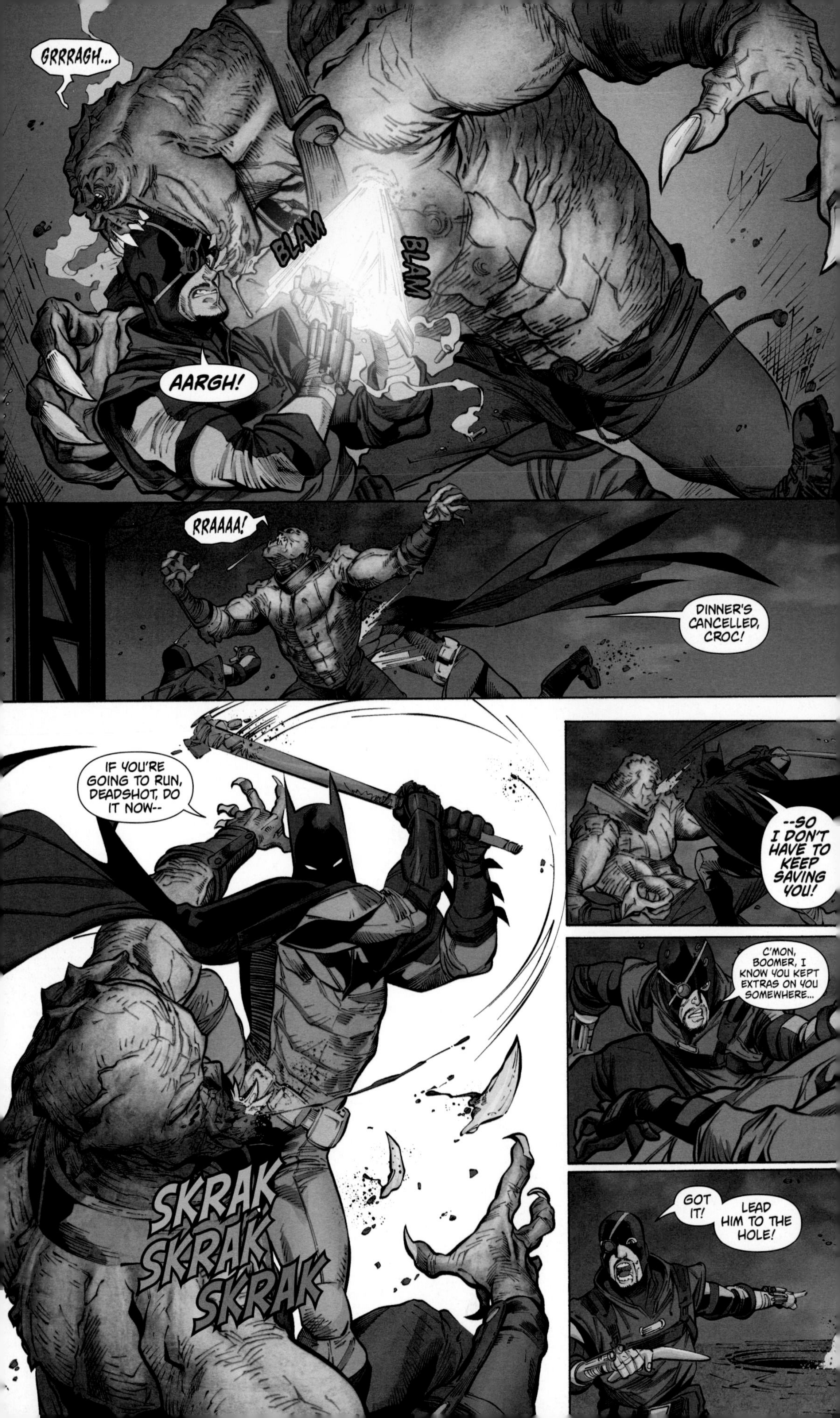
GRRRAGH...
BLAM
BLAM
AARGH!
RRAAAA!
DINNER'S CANCELLED, CROC!
IF YOU'RE GOING TO RUN, DEADSHOT, DO IT NOW--
--SO I DON'T HAVE TO KEEP SAVING YOU!
SKRAK SKRAK SKRAK
C'MON, BOOMER, I KNOW YOU KEPT EXTRAS ON YOU SOMEWHERE...
GOT IT!
LEAD HIM TO THE HOLE!

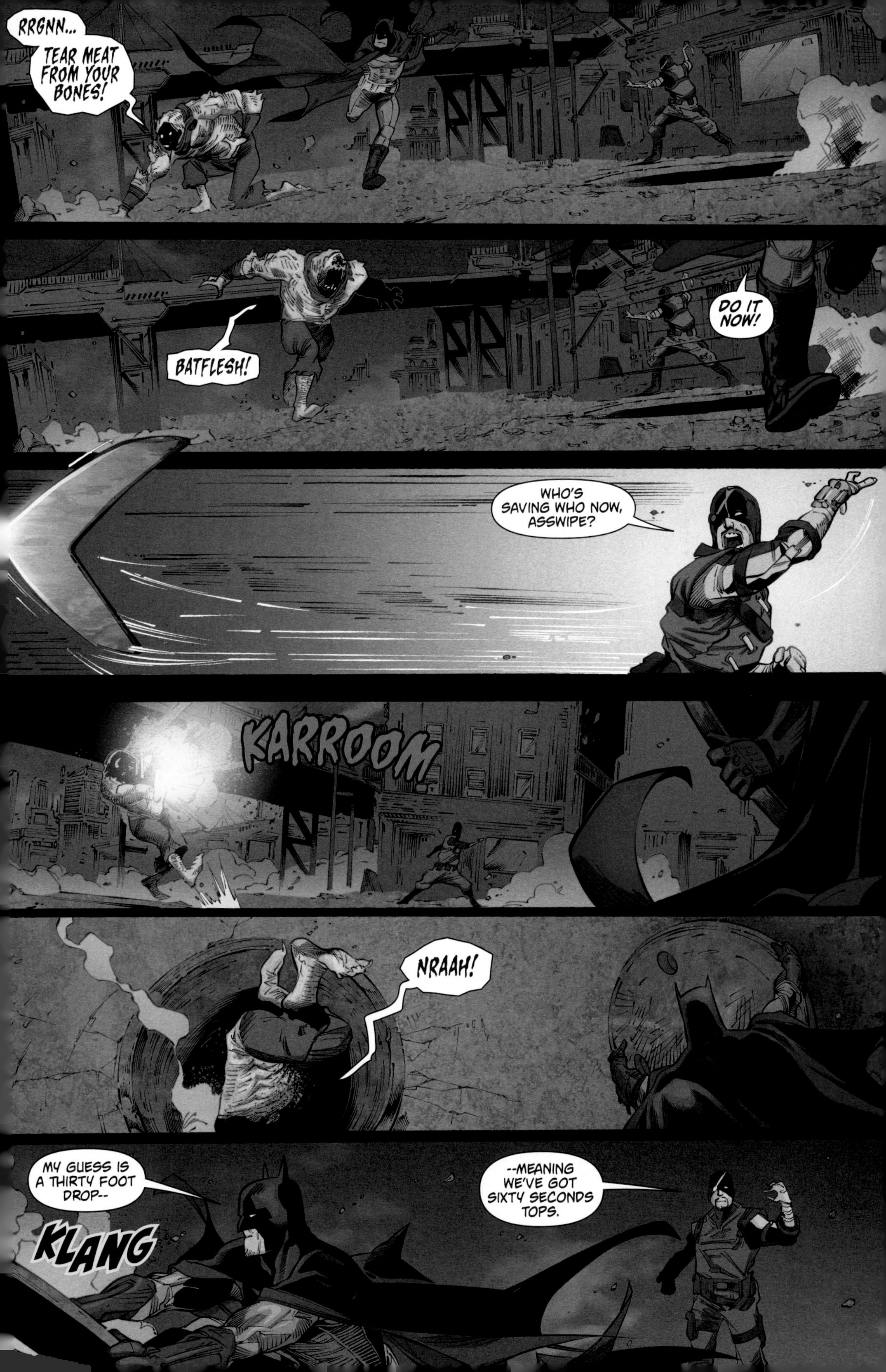
RRGNN...
TEAR MEAT FROM YOUR BONES!
BATFLESH!
DO IT NOW!
WHO'S SAVING WHO NOW, ASSWIPE?
KARROOM
NRAAH!
MY GUESS IS A THIRTY FOOT DROP--
KLANG
--MEANING WE'VE GOT SIXTY SECONDS TOPS.

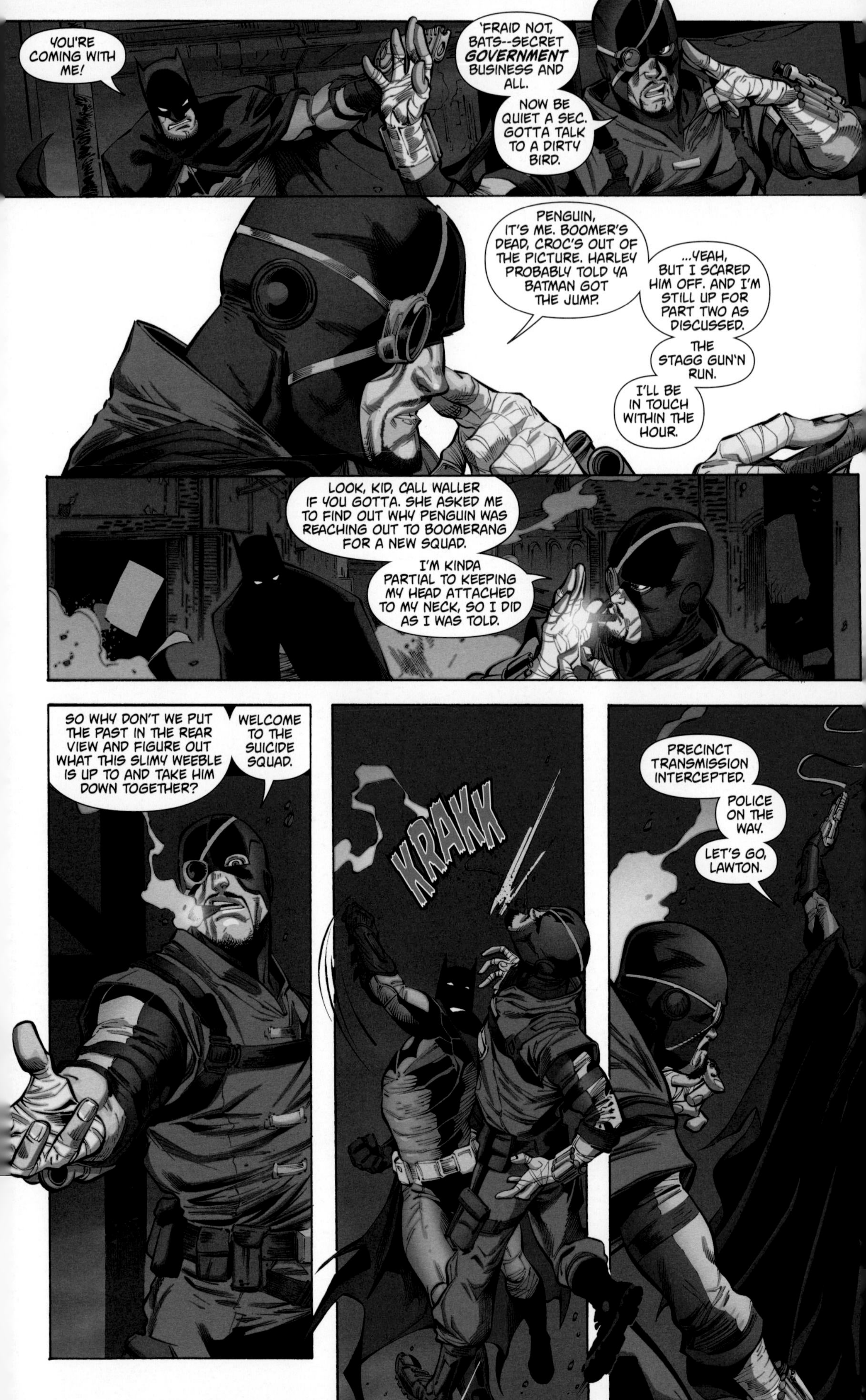
YOU'RE COMING WITH ME!
'FRAID NOT, BATS--SECRET GOVERNMENT BUSINESS AND ALL.
NOW BE QUIET A SEC. GOTTA TALK TO A DIRTY BIRD.
PENGUIN, IT'S ME. BOOMER'S DEAD, CROC'S OUT OF THE PICTURE. HARLEY PROBABLY TOLD YA BATMAN GOT THE JUMP.
...YEAH, BUT I SCARED HIM OFF. AND I'M STILL UP FOR PART TWO AS DISCUSSED.
THE STAGG GUN'N RUN.
I'LL BE IN TOUCH WITHIN THE HOUR.
LOOK, KID, CALL WALLER IF YOU GOTTA. SHE ASKED ME TO FIND OUT WHY PENGUIN WAS REACHING OUT TO BOOMERANG FOR A NEW SQUAD.
I'M KINDA PARTIAL TO KEEPING MY HEAD ATTACHED TO MY NECK, SO I DID AS I WAS TOLD.
SO WHY DON'T WE PUT THE PAST IN THE REAR VIEW AND FIGURE OUT WHAT THIS SLIMY WEEBLE IS UP TO AND TAKE HIM DOWN TOGETHER?
WELCOME TO THE SUICIDE SQUAD.
KRAKK
PRECINCT TRANSMISSION INTERCEPTED.
POLICE ON THE WAY.
LET'S GO, LAWTON.

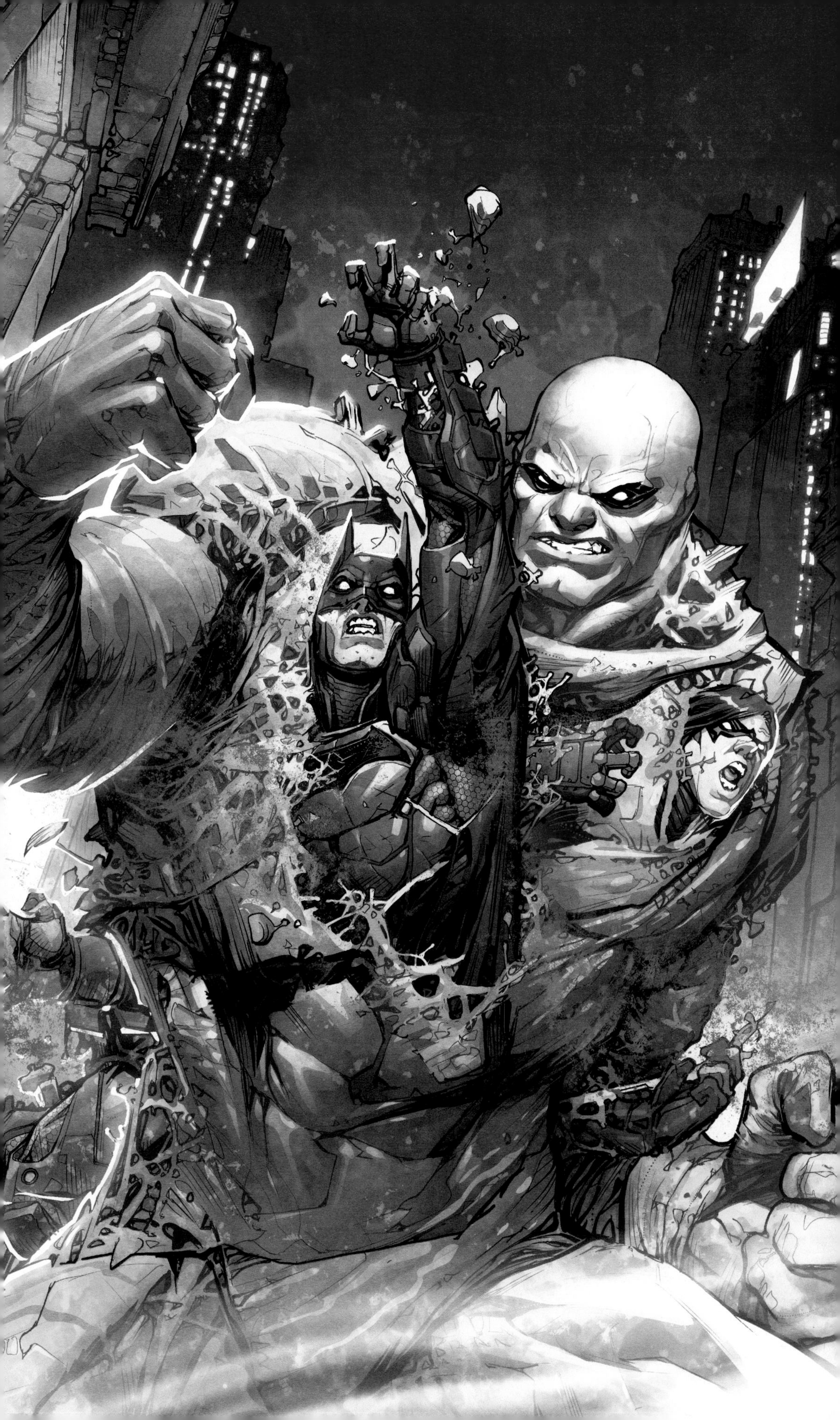

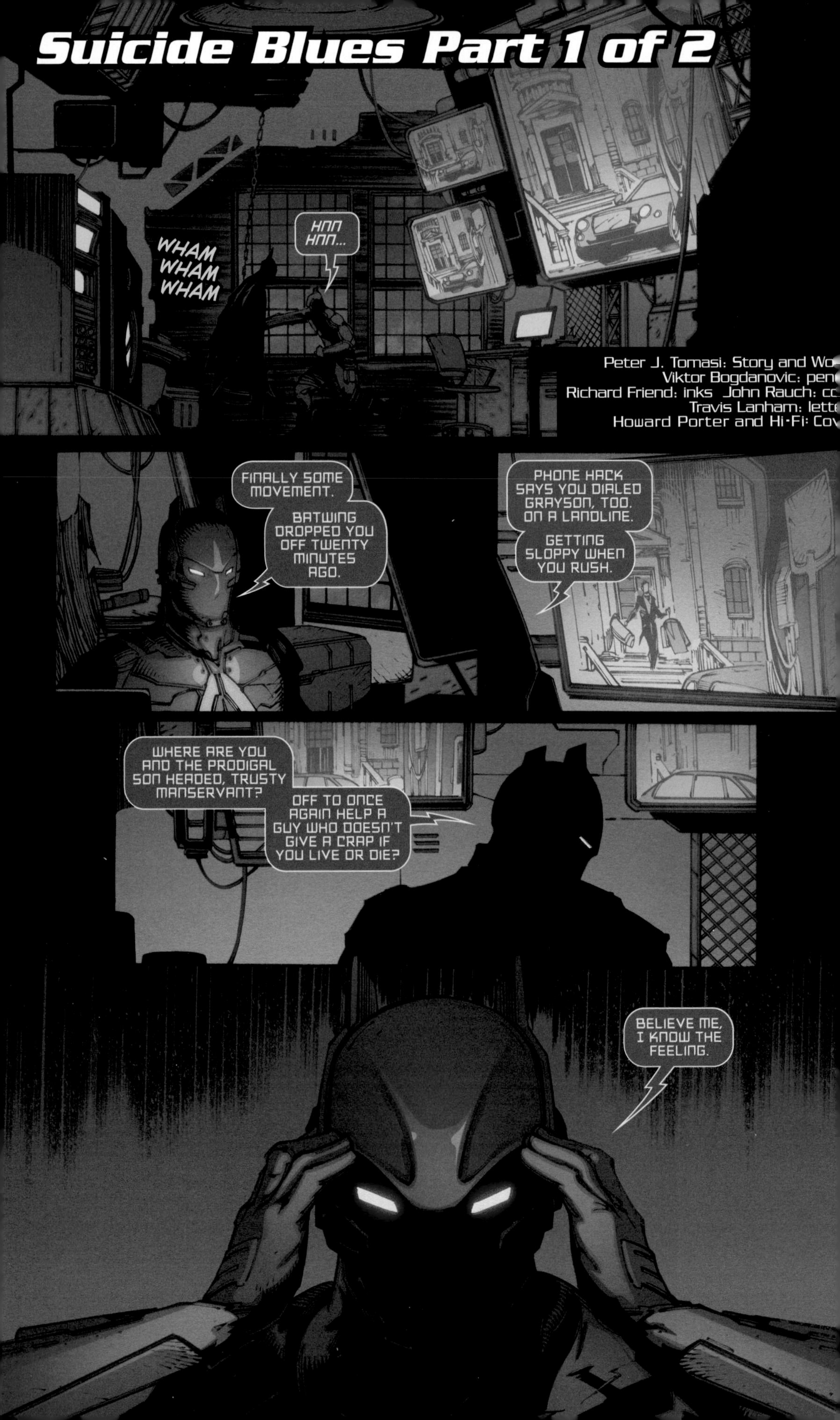

Suicide Blues Part 1 of 2
WHAM WHAM WHAM
HNN HNN...
Peter J. Tomasi: Story and Wo
Viktor Bogdanovic: pen
Richard Friend: inks John Rauch: co
Travis Lanham: lette
Howard Porter and Hi-Fi: Cov
FINALLY SOME MOVEMENT.
BATWING DROPPED YOU OFF TWENTY MINUTES AGO.
PHONE HACK SAYS YOU DIALED GRAYSON, TOO. ON A LANDLINE.
GETTING SLOPPY WHEN YOU RUSH.
WHERE ARE YOU AND THE PRODIGAL SON HEADED, TRUSTY MANSERVANT?
OFF TO ONCE AGAIN HELP A GUY WHO DOESN'T GIVE A CRAP IF YOU LIVE OR DIE?
BELIEVE ME, I KNOW THE FEELING.

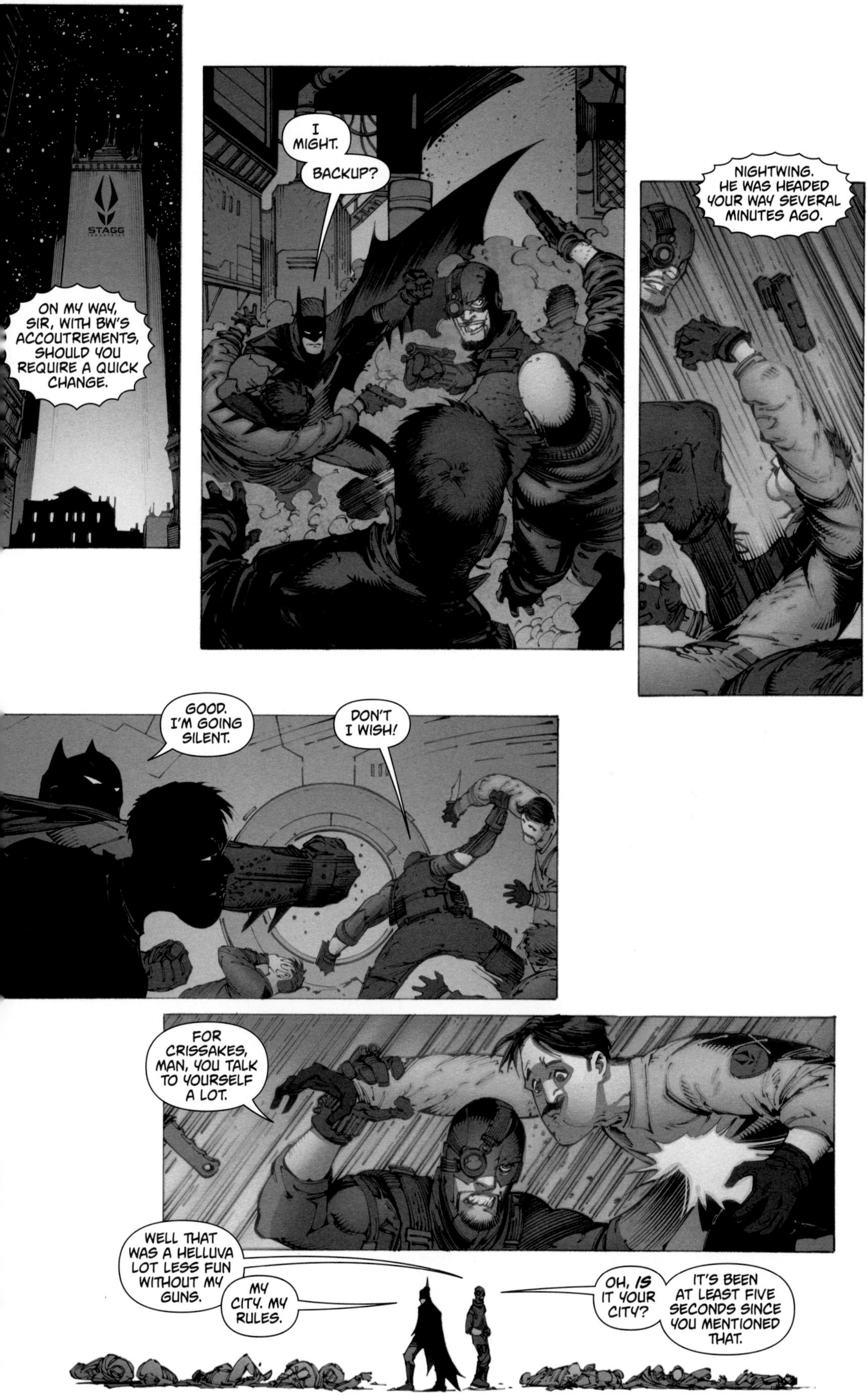
ON MY WAY, SIR, WITH BW'S ACCOUTREMENTS, SHOULD YOU REQUIRE A QUICK CHANGE.
I MIGHT.
BACKUP?
NIGHTWING. HE WAS HEADED YOUR WAY SEVERAL MINUTES AGO.
GOOD. I'M GOING SILENT.
DON'T I WISH!
FOR CRISSAKES, MAN, YOU TALK TO YOURSELF A LOT.
WELL THAT WAS A HELLUVA LOT LESS FUN WITHOUT MY GUNS.
MY CITY. MY RULES.
OH, IS IT YOUR CITY?
IT'S BEEN AT LEAST FIVE SECONDS SINCE YOU MENTIONED THAT.

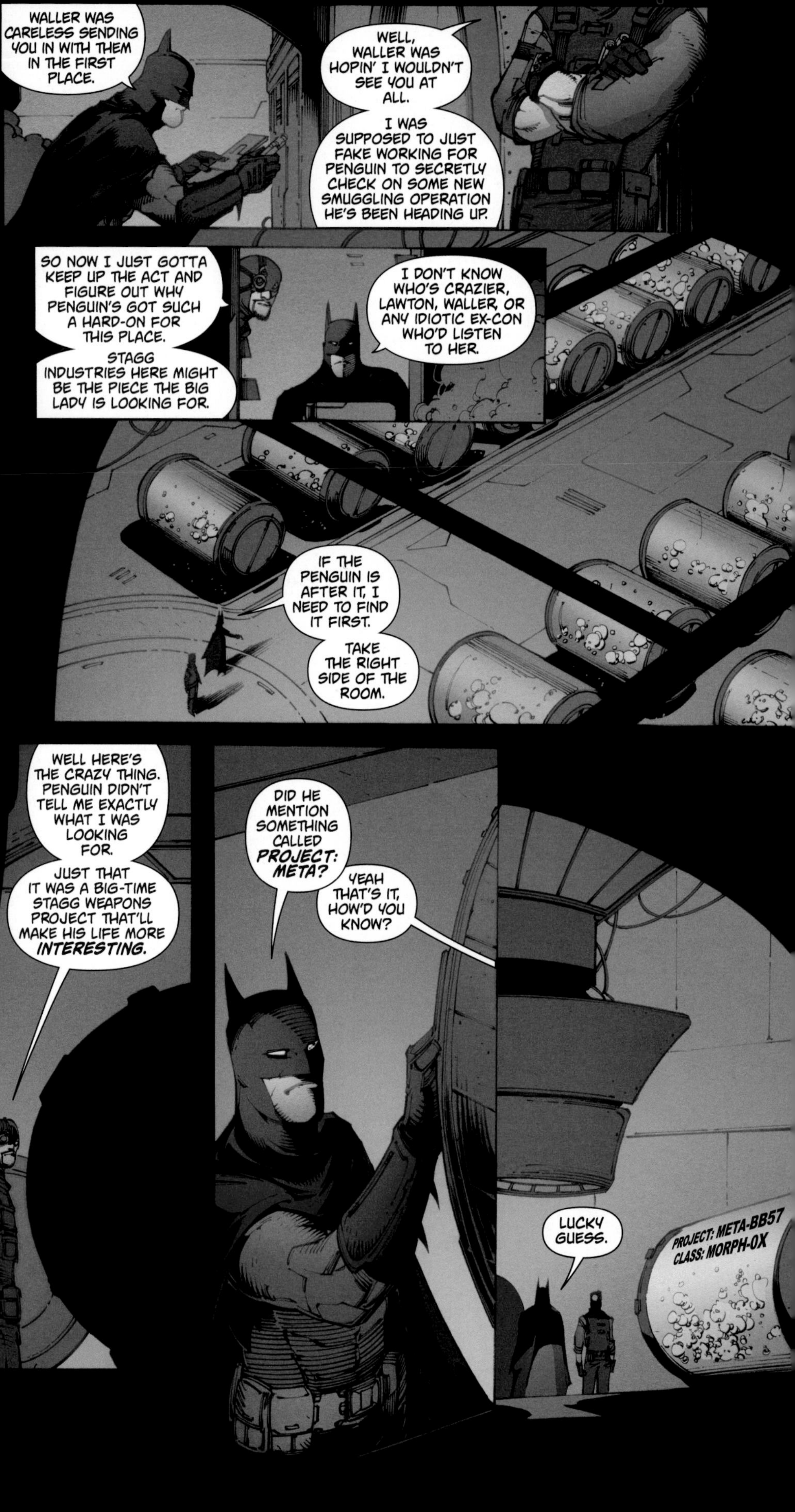
WALLER WAS CARELESS SENDING YOU IN WITH THEM IN THE FIRST PLACE.
WELL, WALLER WAS HOPIN' I WOULDN'T SEE YOU AT ALL.
I WAS SUPPOSED TO JUST FAKE WORKING FOR PENGUIN TO SECRETLY CHECK ON SOME NEW SMUGGLING OPERATION HE'S BEEN HEADING UP.
SO NOW I JUST GOTTA KEEP UP THE ACT AND FIGURE OUT WHY PENGUIN'S GOT SUCH A HARD-ON FOR THIS PLACE.
STAGG INDUSTRIES HERE MIGHT BE THE PIECE THE BIG LADY IS LOOKING FOR.
I DON'T KNOW WHO'S CRAZIER, LAWTON, WALLER, OR ANY IDIOTIC EX-CON WHO'D LISTEN TO HER.
IF THE PENGUIN IS AFTER IT, I NEED TO FIND IT FIRST.
TAKE THE RIGHT SIDE OF THE ROOM.
WELL HERE'S THE CRAZY THING. PENGUIN DIDN'T TELL ME EXACTLY WHAT I WAS LOOKING FOR.
JUST THAT IT WAS A BIG-TIME STAGG WEAPONS PROJECT THAT'LL MAKE HIS LIFE MORE INTERESTING.
DID HE MENTION SOMETHING CALLED PROJECT: META?
YEAH THAT'S IT, HOW'D YOU KNOW?
LUCKY GUESS.
PROJECT: META-BB57
CLASS: MORPH-OX

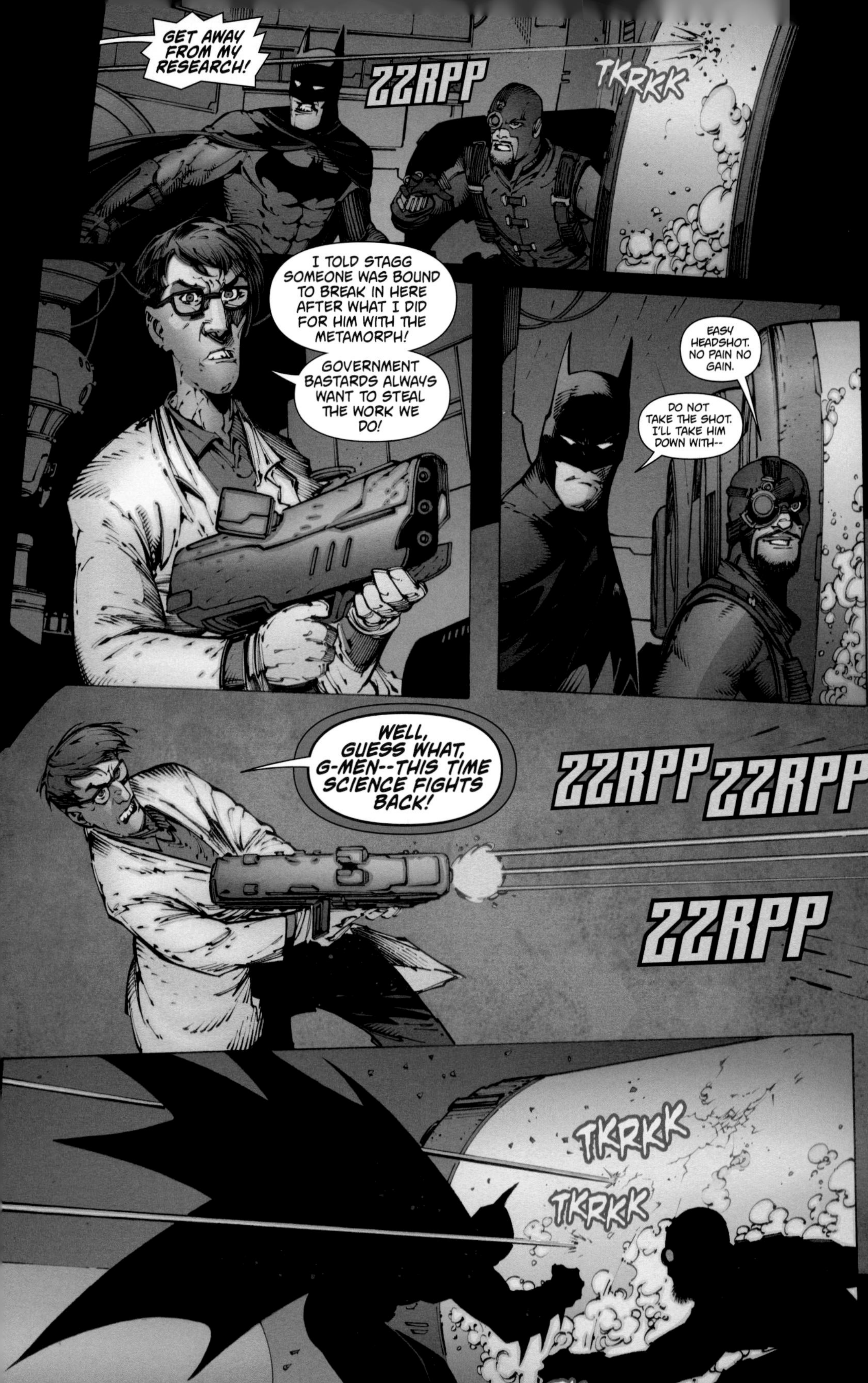
GET AWAY FROM MY RESEARCH!
ZZRPP
TKRKK
I TOLD STAGG SOMEONE WAS BOUND TO BREAK IN HERE AFTER WHAT I DID FOR HIM WITH THE METAMORPH!
GOVERNMENT BASTARDS ALWAYS WANT TO STEAL THE WORK WE DO!
EASY HEADSHOT. NO PAIN NO GAIN.
DO NOT TAKE THE SHOT. I'LL TAKE HIM DOWN WITH--
WELL, GUESS WHAT, G-MEN--THIS TIME SCIENCE FIGHTS BACK!
ZZRPP ZZRPP
ZZRPP
TKRKK
TKRKK
TKRKK

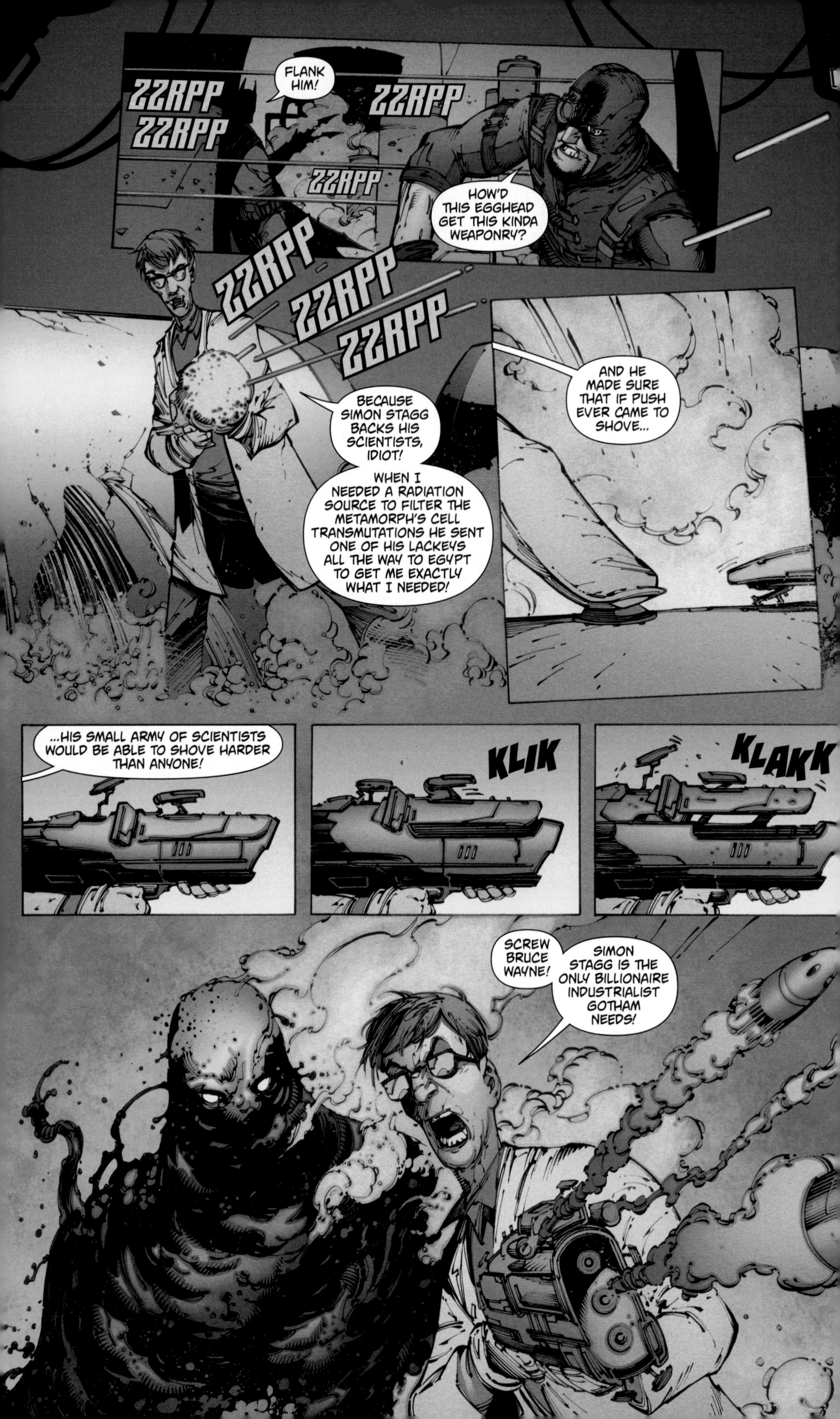
ZZRPP
ZZRPP
FLANK HIM!
ZZRPP
ZZRPP
HOW'D THIS EGGHEAD GET THIS KINDA WEAPONRY?
ZZRPP
ZZRPP
ZZRPP
BECAUSE SIMON STAGG BACKS HIS SCIENTISTS, IDIOT!
WHEN I NEEDED A RADIATION SOURCE TO FILTER THE METAMORPH'S CELL TRANSMUTATIONS HE SENT ONE OF HIS LACKEYS ALL THE WAY TO EGYPT TO GET ME EXACTLY WHAT I NEEDED!
AND HE MADE SURE THAT IF PUSH EVER CAME TO SHOVE...
...HIS SMALL ARMY OF SCIENTISTS WOULD BE ABLE TO SHOVE HARDER THAN ANYONE!
KLIK
KLAKK
SCREW BRUCE WAYNE!
SIMON STAGG IS THE ONLY BILLIONAIRE INDUSTRIALIST GOTHAM NEEDS!

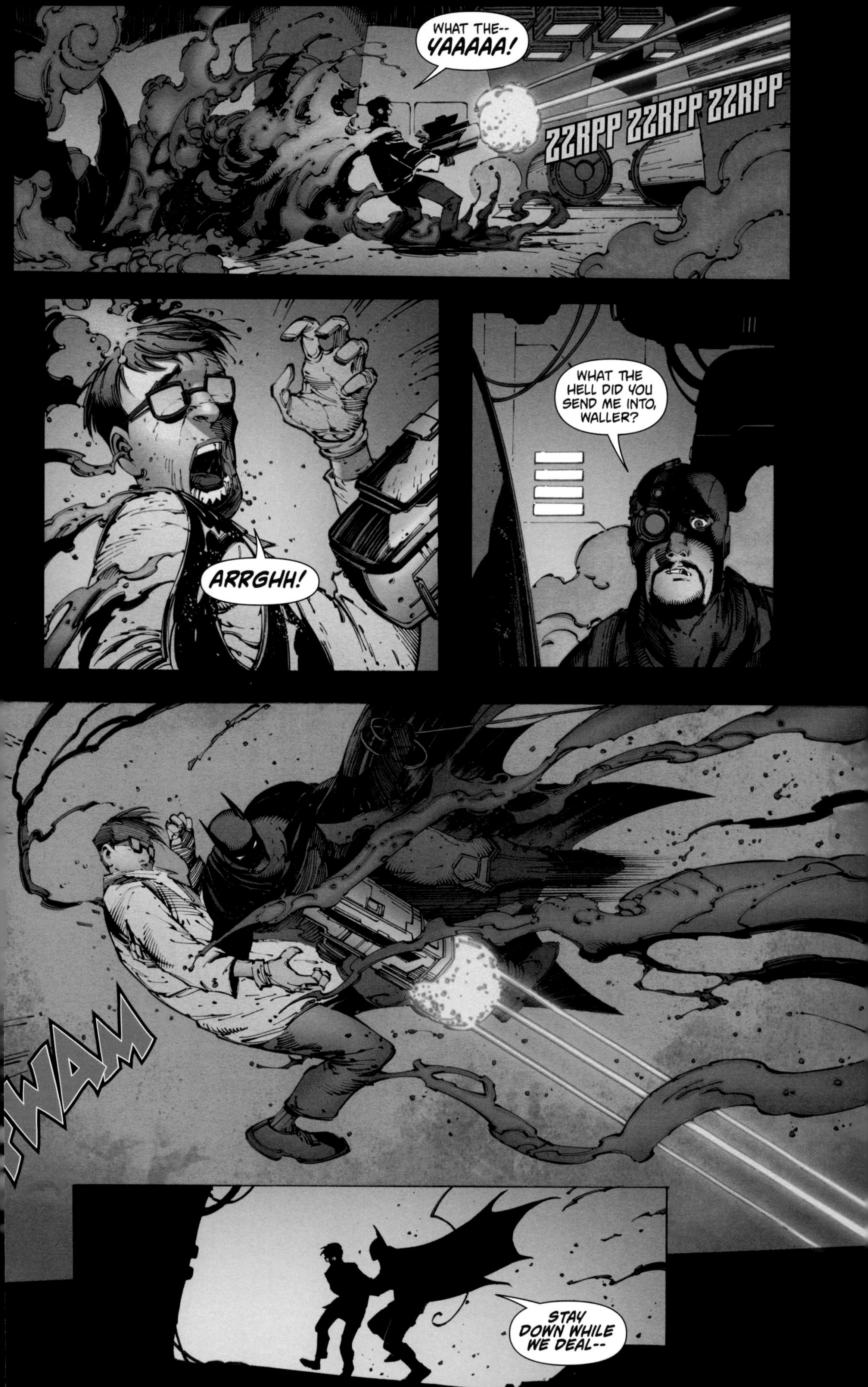
WHAT THE--
YAAAAA!
ZZRPP ZZRPP ZZRPP
ARRGHH!
WHAT THE HELL DID YOU SEND ME INTO, WALLER?
WAM
STAY DOWN WHILE WE DEAL--

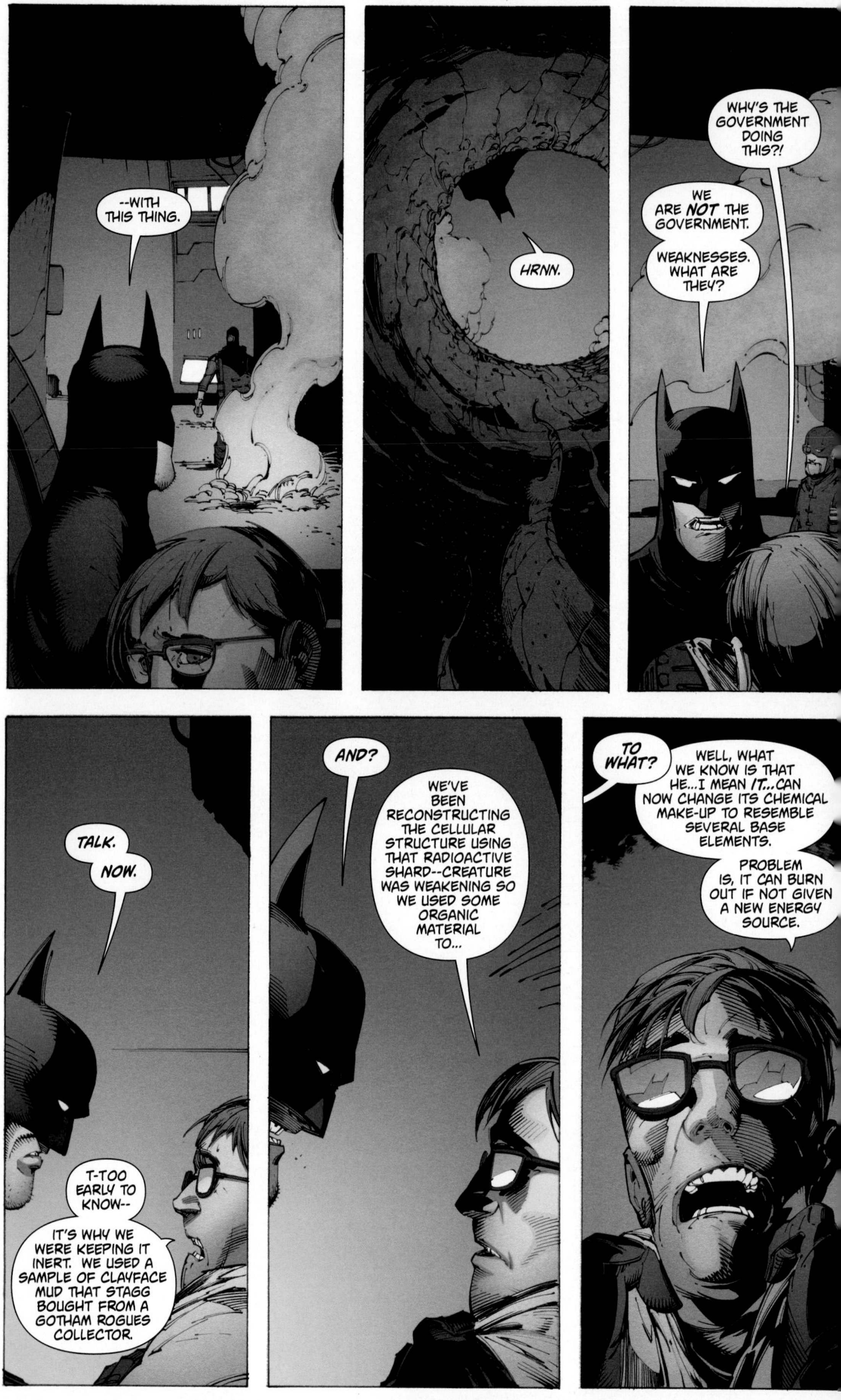
--WITH THIS THING.
HRNN.
WHY'S THE GOVERNMENT DOING THIS?!
WE ARE *NOT* THE GOVERNMENT.
WEAKNESSES. WHAT ARE THEY?
TALK.
NOW.
T-TOO EARLY TO KNOW--
IT'S WHY WE WERE KEEPING IT INERT. WE USED A SAMPLE OF CLAYFACE MUD THAT STAGG BOUGHT FROM A GOTHAM ROGUES COLLECTOR.
AND?
WE'VE BEEN RECONSTRUCTING THE CELLULAR STRUCTURE USING THAT RADIOACTIVE SHARD--CREATURE WAS WEAKENING SO WE USED SOME ORGANIC MATERIAL TO...
TO WHAT?
WELL, WHAT WE KNOW IS THAT HE...I MEAN *IT*...CAN NOW CHANGE ITS CHEMICAL MAKE-UP TO RESEMBLE SEVERAL BASE ELEMENTS.
PROBLEM IS, IT CAN BURN OUT IF NOT GIVEN A NEW ENERGY SOURCE.

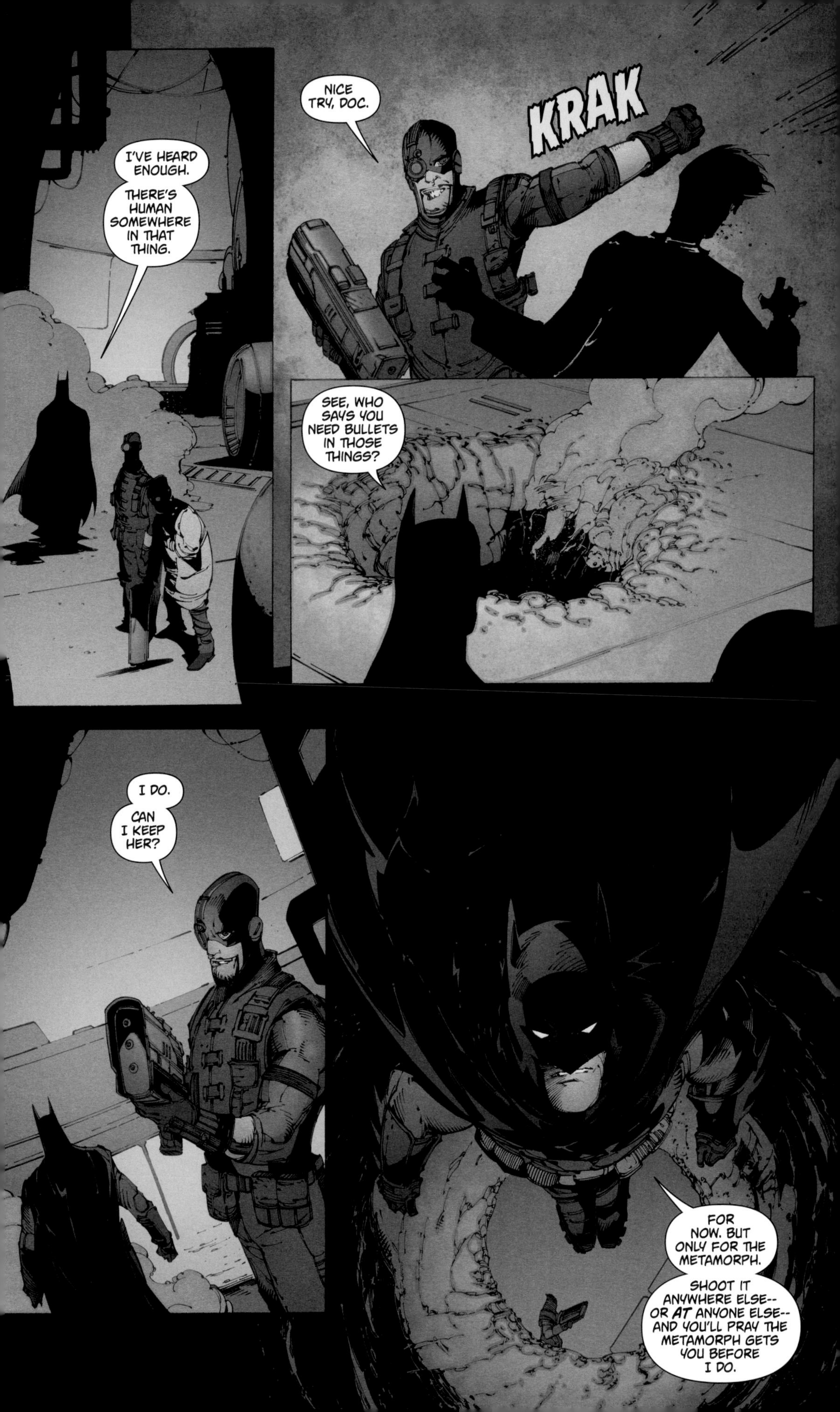
I'VE HEARD ENOUGH.
THERE'S HUMAN SOMEWHERE IN THAT THING.
NICE TRY, DOC.
KRAK
SEE, WHO SAYS YOU NEED BULLETS IN THOSE THINGS?
I DO.
CAN I KEEP HER?
FOR NOW. BUT ONLY FOR THE METAMORPH.
SHOOT IT ANYWHERE ELSE-- OR *AT* ANYONE ELSE-- AND YOU'LL PRAY THE METAMORPH GETS YOU BEFORE I DO.

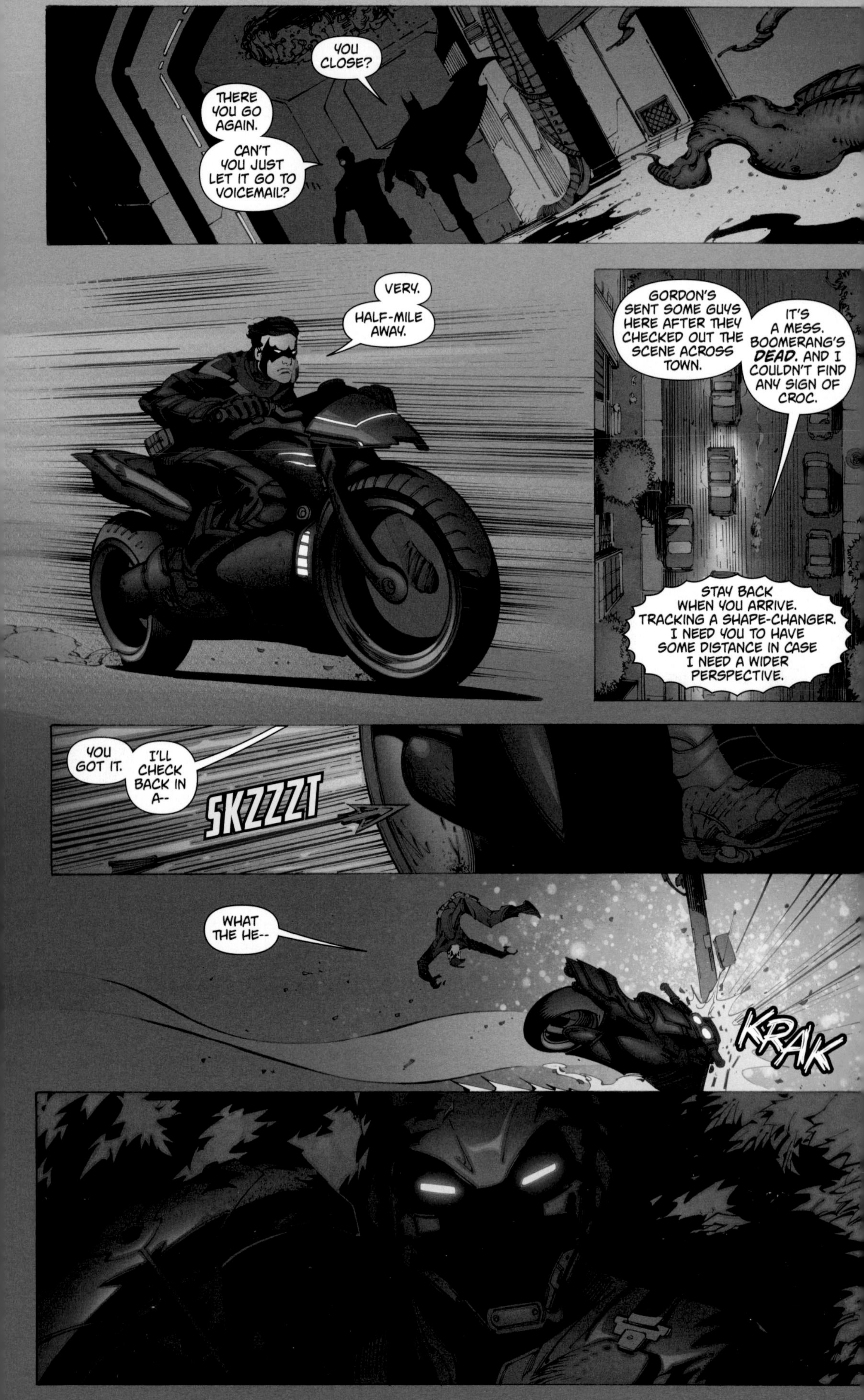
YOU CLOSE?
THERE YOU GO AGAIN.
CAN'T YOU JUST LET IT GO TO VOICEMAIL?
VERY.
HALF-MILE AWAY.
GORDON'S SENT SOME GUYS HERE AFTER THEY CHECKED OUT THE SCENE ACROSS TOWN.
IT'S A MESS. BOOMERANG'S DEAD. AND I COULDN'T FIND ANY SIGN OF CROC.
STAY BACK WHEN YOU ARRIVE. TRACKING A SHAPE-CHANGER. I NEED YOU TO HAVE SOME DISTANCE IN CASE I NEED A WIDER PERSPECTIVE.
YOU GOT IT.
I'LL CHECK BACK IN A--
SKZZZT
WHAT THE HE--
KRAK

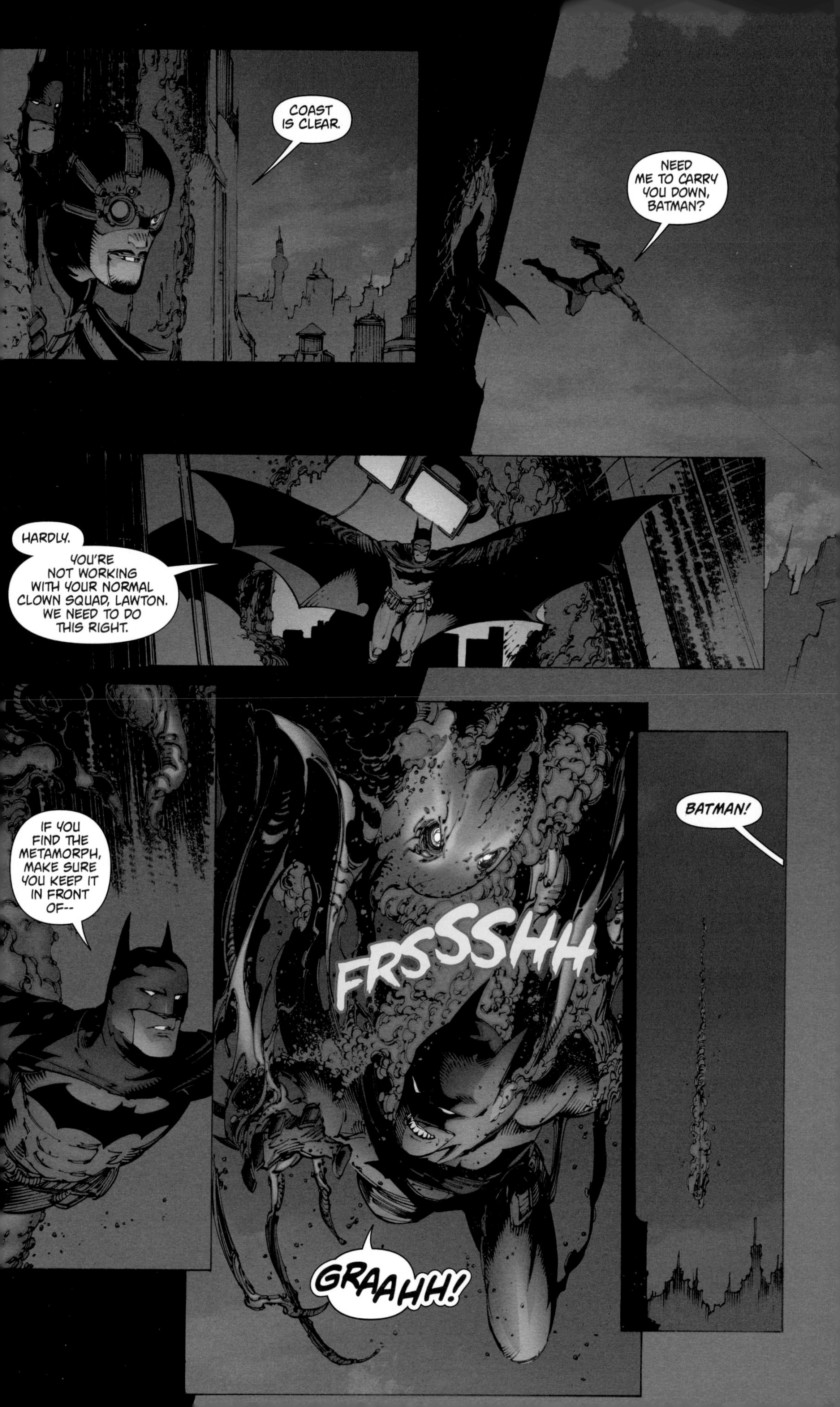
COAST IS CLEAR.
NEED ME TO CARRY YOU DOWN, BATMAN?
HARDLY.
YOU'RE NOT WORKING WITH YOUR NORMAL CLOWN SQUAD, LAWTON. WE NEED TO DO THIS RIGHT.
IF YOU FIND THE METAMORPH, MAKE SURE YOU KEEP IT IN FRONT OF--
FRSSSHH
GRAAHH!
BATMAN!

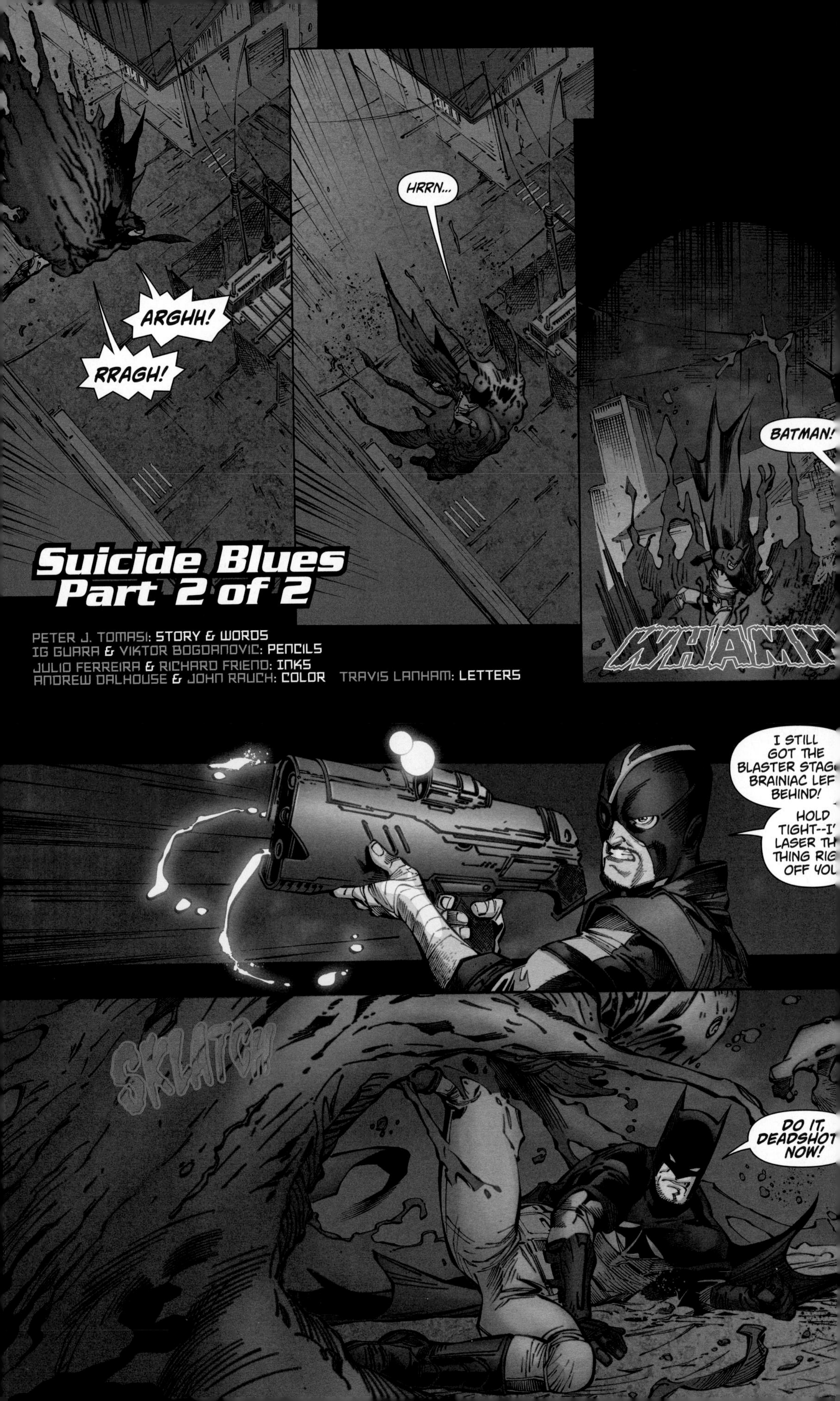

ARGHH!
RRAGH!
HRRN...
BATMAN!
KHAMX
Suicide Blues Part 2 of 2
PETER J. TOMASI: STORY & WORDS
IG GUARA & VIKTOR BOGDANOVIC: PENCILS
JULIO FERREIRA & RICHARD FRIEND: INKS
ANDREW DALHOUSE & JOHN RAUCH: COLOR
TRAVIS LANHAM: LETTERS
SKLATCH!
DO IT, DEADSHOT NOW!

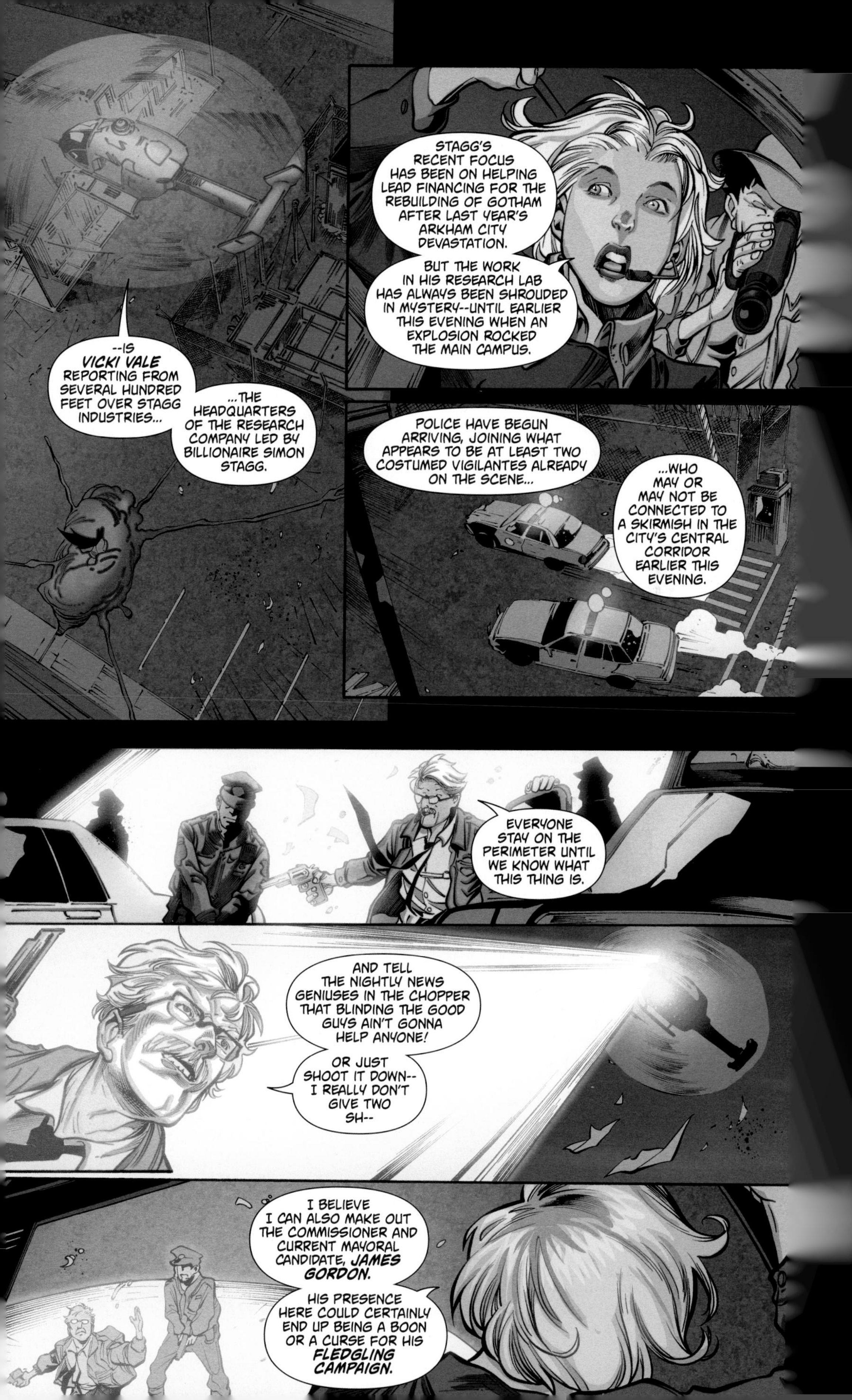
--IS VICKI VALE REPORTING FROM SEVERAL HUNDRED FEET OVER STAGG INDUSTRIES...
...THE HEADQUARTERS OF THE RESEARCH COMPANY LED BY BILLIONAIRE SIMON STAGG.
STAGG'S RECENT FOCUS HAS BEEN ON HELPING LEAD FINANCING FOR THE REBUILDING OF GOTHAM AFTER LAST YEAR'S ARKHAM CITY DEVASTATION.
BUT THE WORK IN HIS RESEARCH LAB HAS ALWAYS BEEN SHROUDED IN MYSTERY--UNTIL EARLIER THIS EVENING WHEN AN EXPLOSION ROCKED THE MAIN CAMPUS.
POLICE HAVE BEGUN ARRIVING, JOINING WHAT APPEARS TO BE AT LEAST TWO COSTUMED VIGILANTES ALREADY ON THE SCENE...
...WHO MAY OR MAY NOT BE CONNECTED TO A SKIRMISH IN THE CITY'S CENTRAL CORRIDOR EARLIER THIS EVENING.
EVERYONE STAY ON THE PERIMETER UNTIL WE KNOW WHAT THIS THING IS.
AND TELL THE NIGHTLY NEWS GENIUSES IN THE CHOPPER THAT BLINDING THE GOOD GUYS AIN'T GONNA HELP ANYONE!
OR JUST SHOOT IT DOWN-- I REALLY DON'T GIVE TWO SH--
I BELIEVE I CAN ALSO MAKE OUT THE COMMISSIONER AND CURRENT MAYORAL CANDIDATE, JAMES GORDON.
HIS PRESENCE HERE COULD CERTAINLY END UP BEING A BOON OR A CURSE FOR HIS FLEDGLING CAMPAIGN.

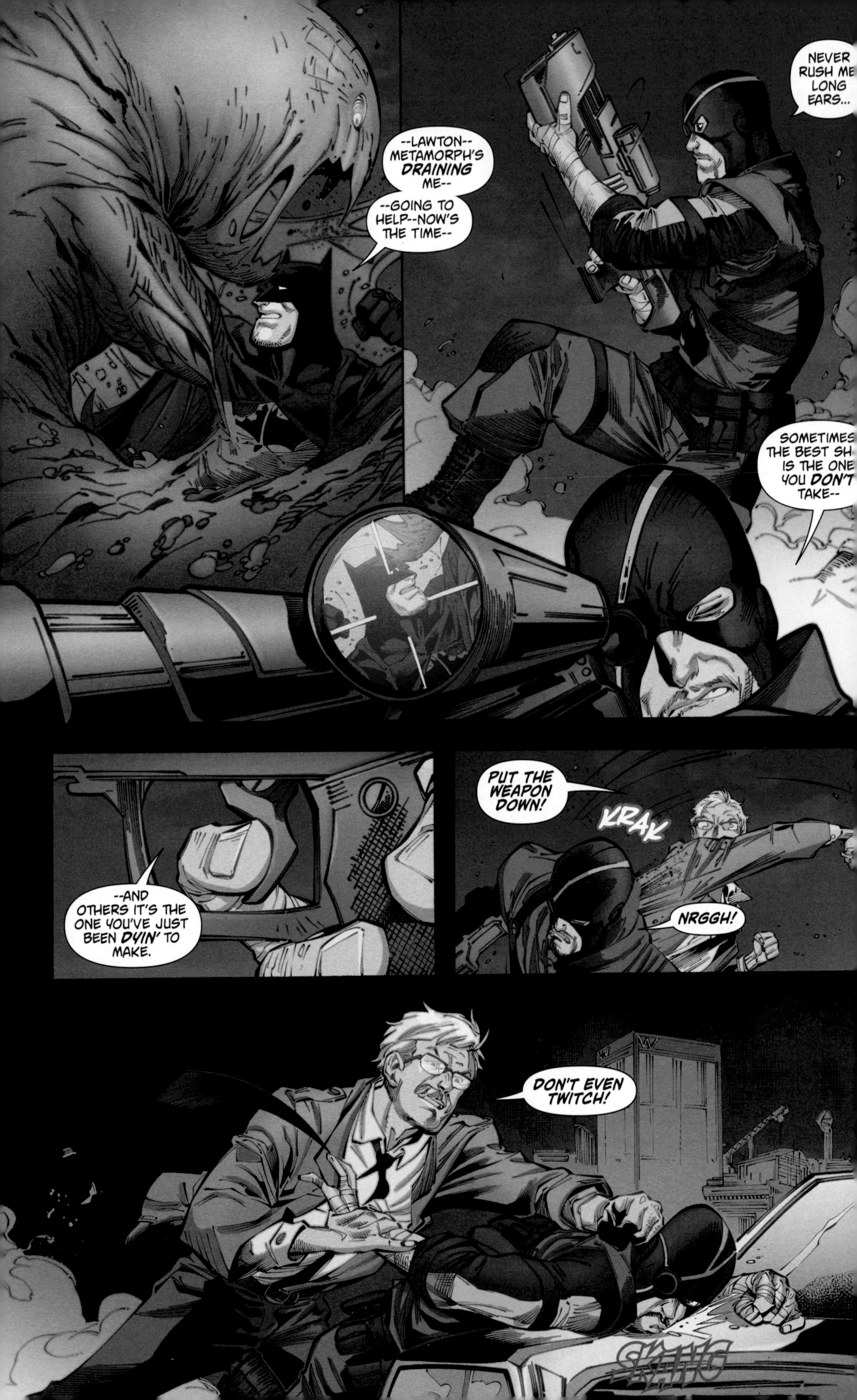
--LAWTON-- METAMORPH'S DRAINING ME--
--GOING TO HELP--NOW'S THE TIME--
NEVER RUSH ME LONG EARS...
SOMETIMES THE BEST SH IS THE ONE YOU DON'T TAKE--
--AND OTHERS IT'S THE ONE YOU'VE JUST BEEN DYIN' TO MAKE.
PUT THE WEAPON DOWN!
KRAK
NRGGH!
DON'T EVEN TWITCH!

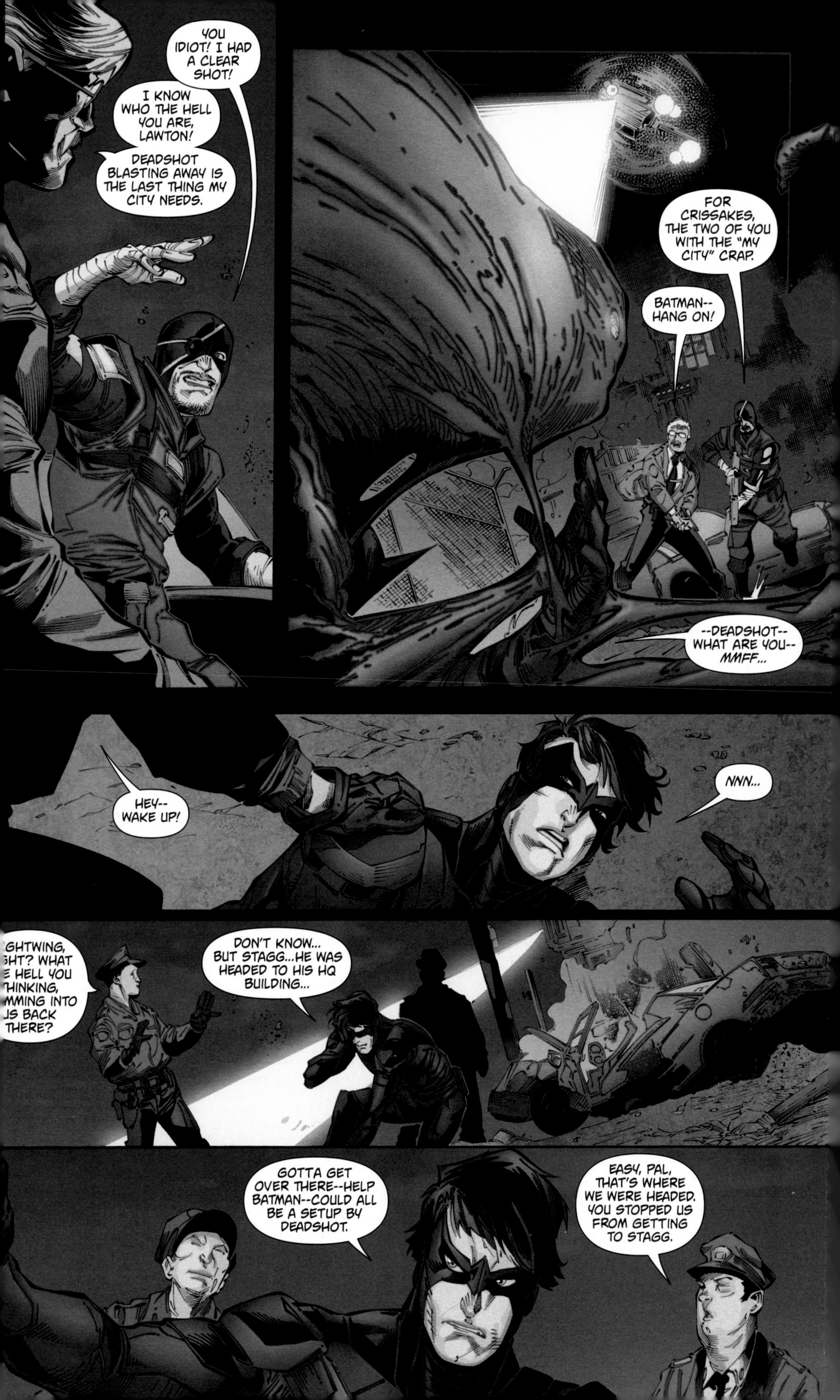

YOU IDIOT! I HAD A CLEAR SHOT!
I KNOW WHO THE HELL YOU ARE, LAWTON!
DEADSHOT BLASTING AWAY IS THE LAST THING MY CITY NEEDS.
FOR CRISSAKES, THE TWO OF YOU WITH THE "MY CITY" CRAP.
BATMAN-- HANG ON!
--DEADSHOT-- WHAT ARE YOU-- MMFF...
HEY-- WAKE UP!
NNN...
GHTWING, GHT? WHAT E HELL YOU THINKING, MMING INTO US BACK THERE?
DON'T KNOW... BUT STAGG...HE WAS HEADED TO HIS HQ BUILDING...
GOTTA GET OVER THERE--HELP BATMAN--COULD ALL BE A SETUP BY DEADSHOT.
EASY, PAL, THAT'S WHERE WE WERE HEADED. YOU STOPPED US FROM GETTING TO STAGG.

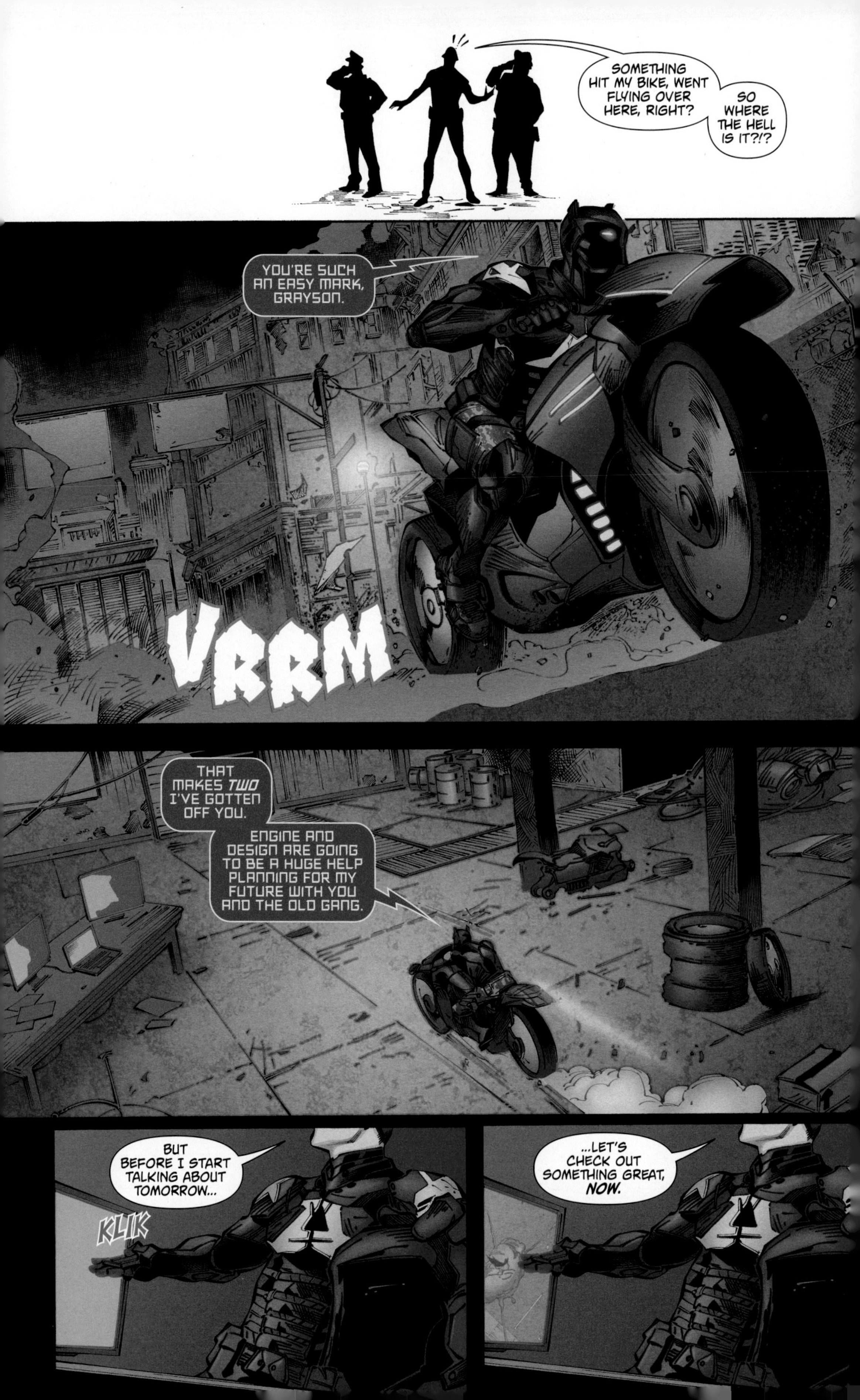
SOMETHING HIT MY BIKE, WENT FLYING OVER HERE, RIGHT?
SO WHERE THE HELL IS IT?!?
YOU'RE SUCH AN EASY MARK, GRAYSON.
VRRM
THAT MAKES *TWO* I'VE GOTTEN OFF YOU.
ENGINE AND DESIGN ARE GOING TO BE A HUGE HELP PLANNING FOR MY FUTURE WITH YOU AND THE OLD GANG.
BUT BEFORE I START TALKING ABOUT TOMORROW...
KLIK
...LET'S CHECK OUT SOMETHING GREAT, **NOW.**

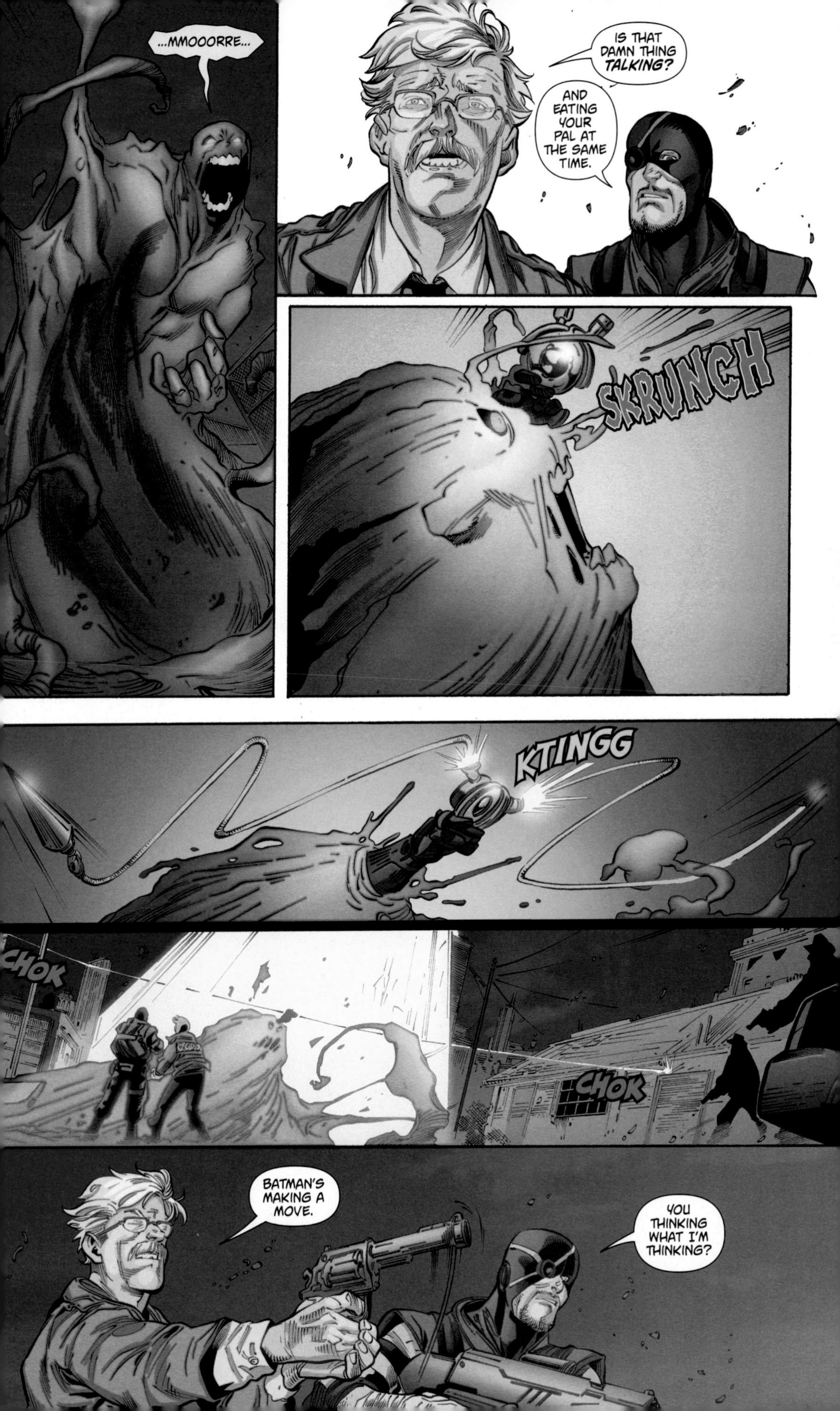
...MMOOORRE...
IS THAT DAMN THING TALKING?
AND EATING YOUR PAL AT THE SAME TIME.
SKRUNCH
KTINGG
CHOK
CHOK
BATMAN'S MAKING A MOVE.
YOU THINKING WHAT I'M THINKING?

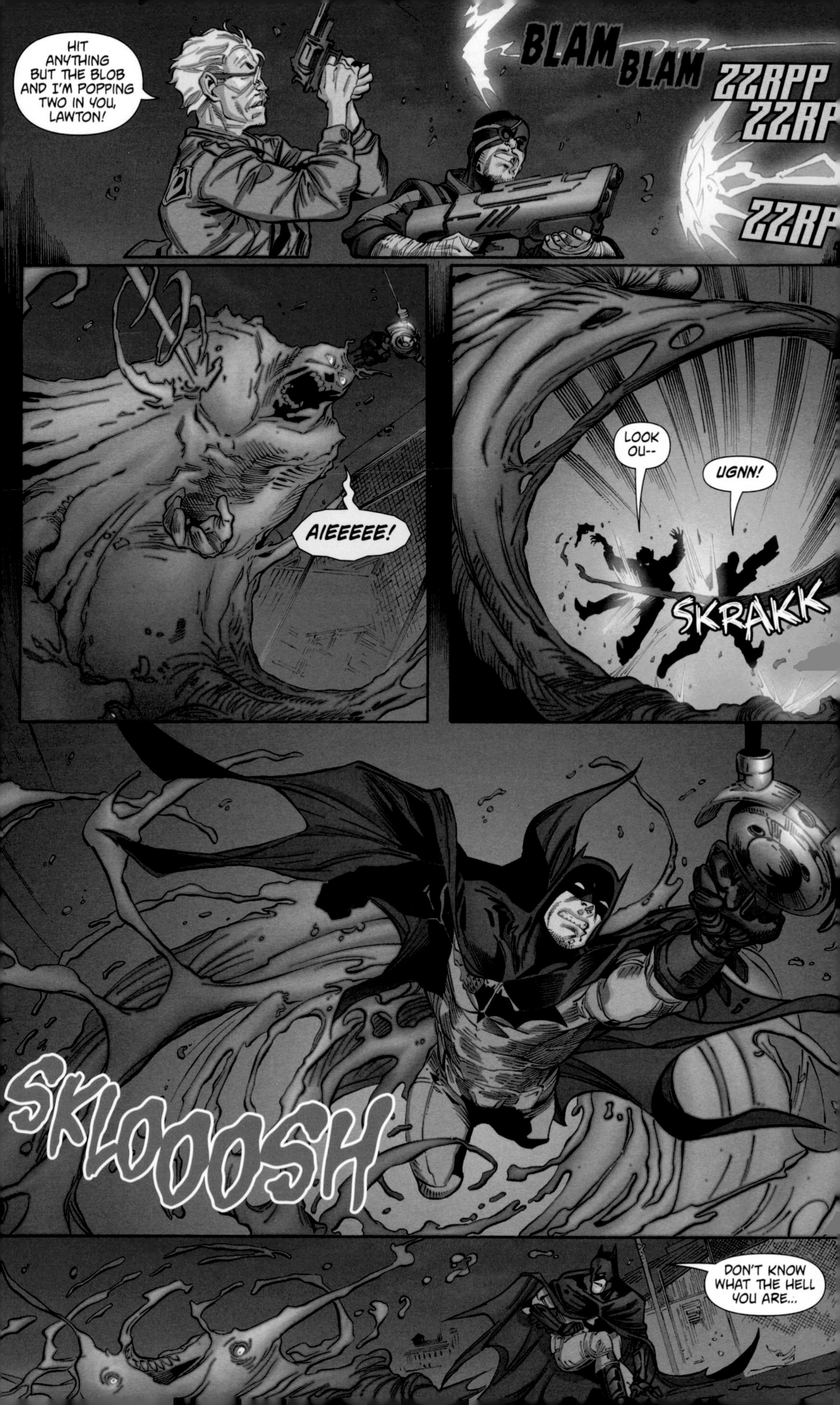
HIT ANYTHING BUT THE BLOB AND I'M POPPING TWO IN YOU, LAWTON!
BLAM BLAM
ZZRPP ZZRP
ZZRP
AIEEEEE!
LOOK OU--
UGNN!
SKRAKK
SKLOOOSH
DON'T KNOW WHAT THE HELL YOU ARE...

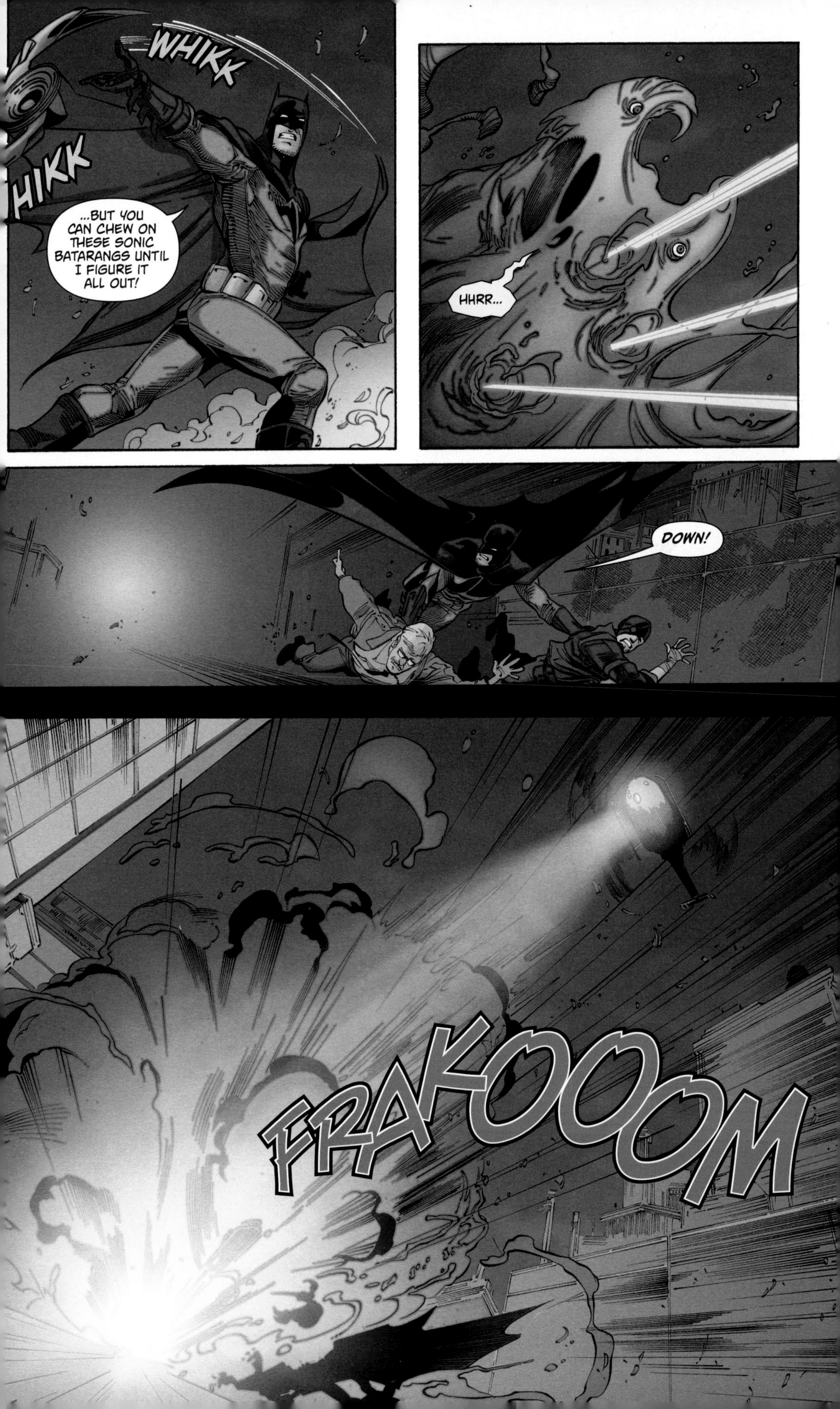
WHIKK
HIKK
...BUT YOU CAN CHEW ON THESE SONIC BATARANGS UNTIL I FIGURE IT ALL OUT!
HHRR...
DOWN!
FRAKOOOM

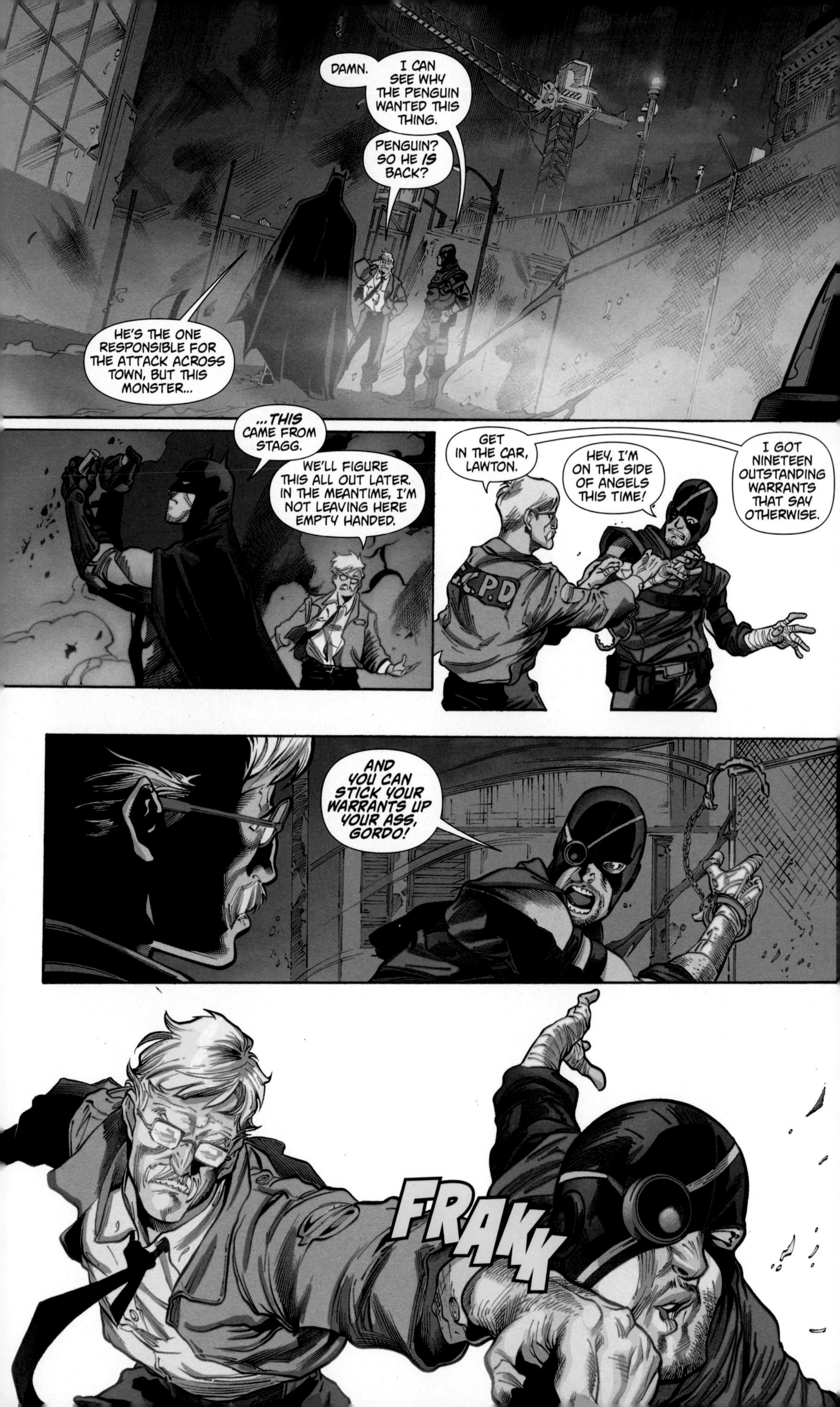
DAMN.
I CAN SEE WHY THE PENGUIN WANTED THIS THING.
PENGUIN? SO HE *IS* BACK?
HE'S THE ONE RESPONSIBLE FOR THE ATTACK ACROSS TOWN, BUT THIS MONSTER...
...*THIS* CAME FROM STAGG.
WE'LL FIGURE THIS ALL OUT LATER. IN THE MEANTIME, I'M NOT LEAVING HERE EMPTY HANDED.
GET IN THE CAR, LAWTON.
HEY, I'M ON THE SIDE OF ANGELS THIS TIME!
I GOT NINETEEN OUTSTANDING WARRANTS THAT SAY OTHERWISE.
AND YOU CAN STICK YOUR WARRANTS UP YOUR ASS, GORDO!
FRAKK

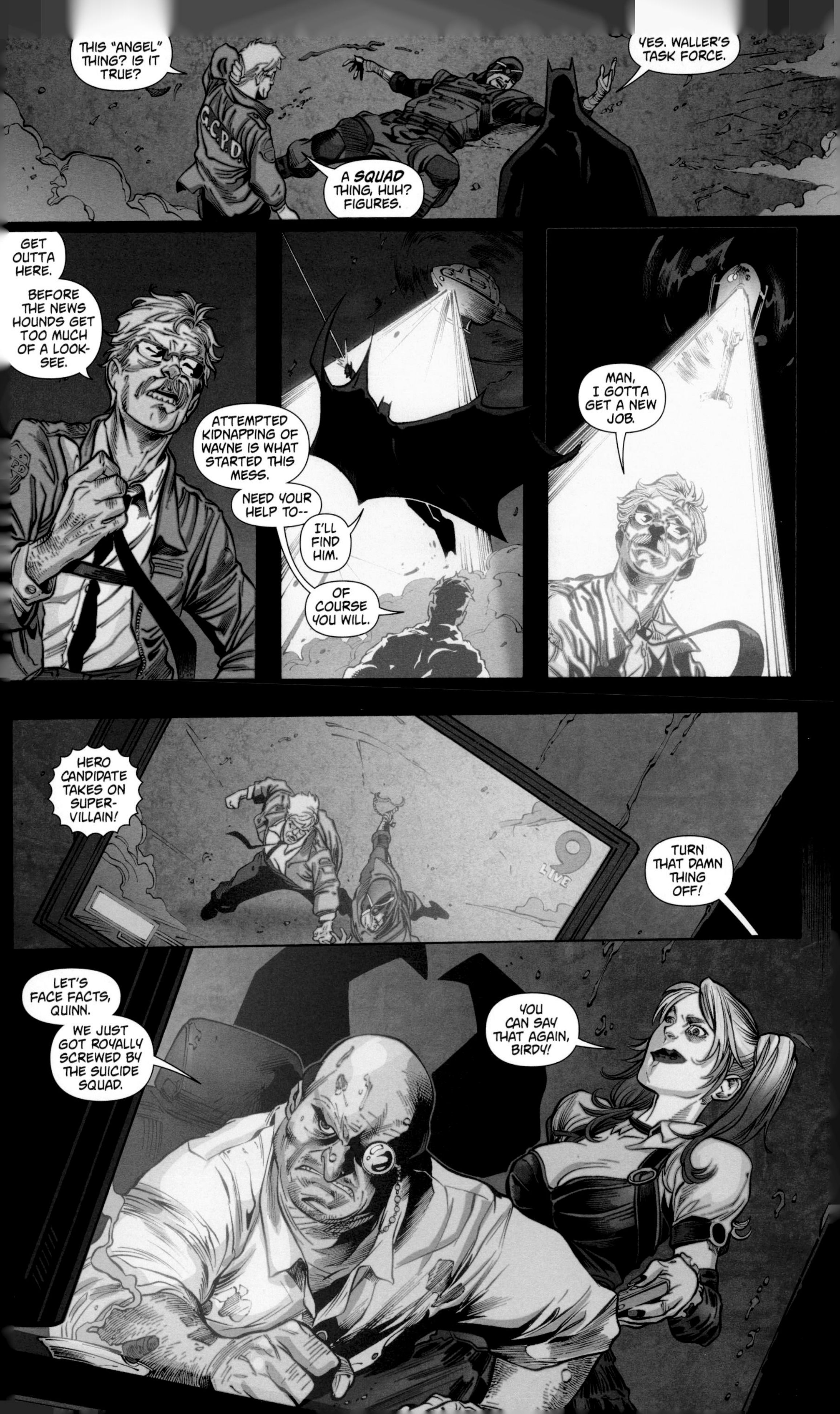
THIS "ANGEL" THING? IS IT TRUE?
YES. WALLER'S TASK FORCE.
A SQUAD THING, HUH? FIGURES.
GET OUTTA HERE.
BEFORE THE NEWS HOUNDS GET TOO MUCH OF A LOOK-SEE.
ATTEMPTED KIDNAPPING OF WAYNE IS WHAT STARTED THIS MESS.
NEED YOUR HELP TO--
I'LL FIND HIM.
OF COURSE YOU WILL.
MAN, I GOTTA GET A NEW JOB.
HERO CANDIDATE TAKES ON SUPER-VILLAIN!
TURN THAT DAMN THING OFF!
LET'S FACE FACTS, QUINN.
WE JUST GOT ROYALLY SCREWED BY THE SUICIDE SQUAD.
YOU CAN SAY THAT AGAIN, BIRDY!

CUTE MASK, DEADSHOT.

BUT WE'RE MUCH MORE INTERESTED IN TALKING TO *FLOYD LAWTON* RIGHT NOW.

EXPLAIN TO ME AND THE COMMISSIONER WHAT THE HELL THE *SUICIDE SQUAD* WA DOING OPERATING WITHIN GOTHAM CITY LIMITS.

WE'VE CHECKED WITH D.C. NO ONE KNOWS ABOL ANY ACTIVE SQUAD OPERATIONS.

WALLER'S COMIN'.

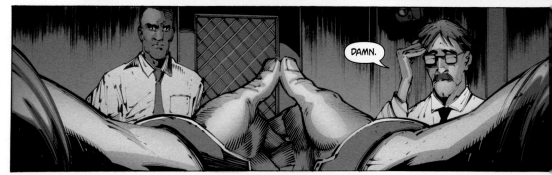

DAMN.

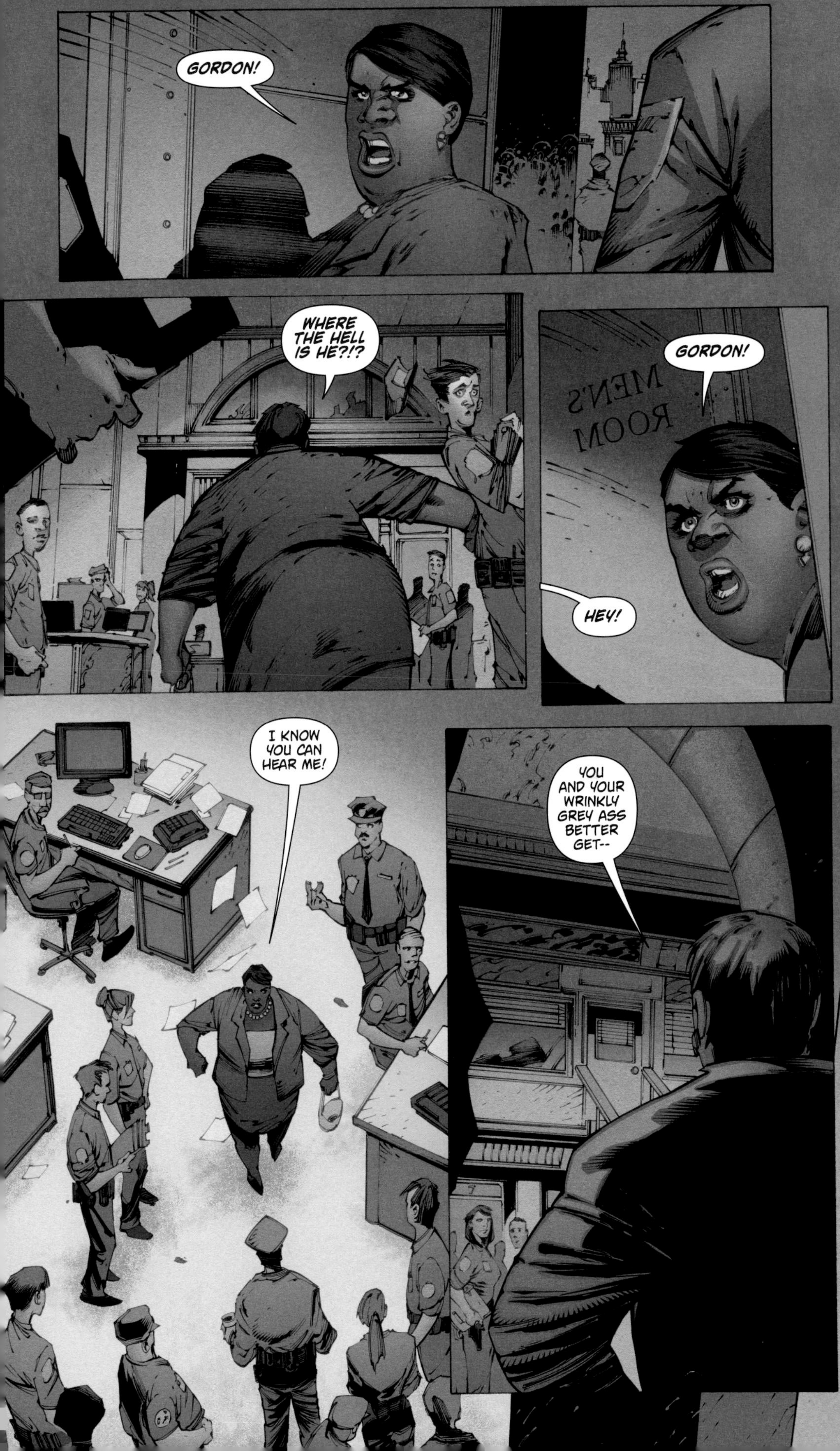
GORDON!
WHERE THE HELL IS HE?!?
GORDON!
MEN'S ROOM
HEY!
I KNOW YOU CAN HEAR ME!
YOU AND YOUR WRINKLY GREY ASS BETTER GET--

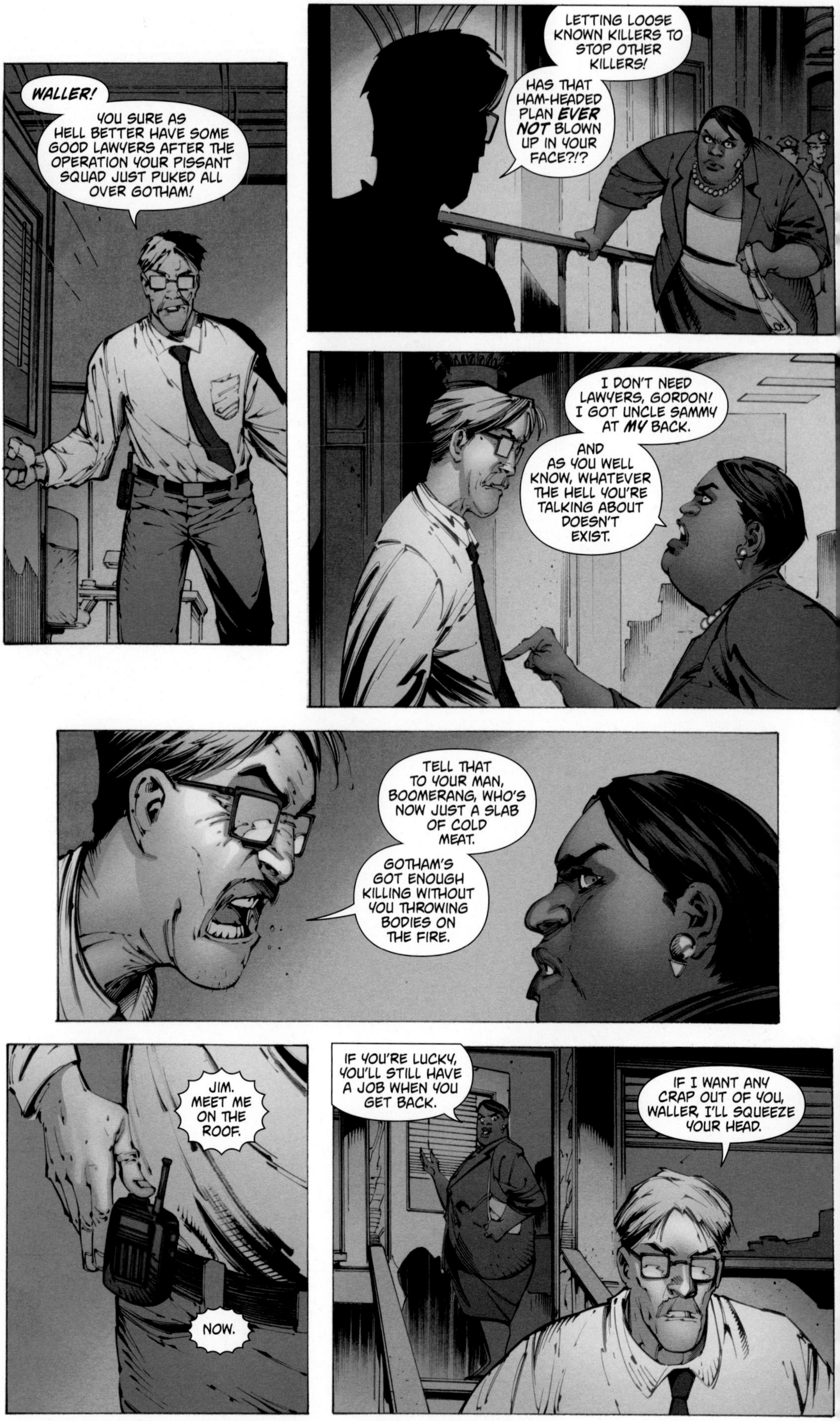
WALLER!
YOU SURE AS HELL BETTER HAVE SOME GOOD LAWYERS AFTER THE OPERATION YOUR PISSANT SQUAD JUST PUKED ALL OVER GOTHAM!
LETTING LOOSE KNOWN KILLERS TO STOP OTHER KILLERS!
HAS THAT HAM-HEADED PLAN EVER NOT BLOWN UP IN YOUR FACE?!?
I DON'T NEED LAWYERS, GORDON! I GOT UNCLE SAMMY AT MY BACK.
AND AS YOU WELL KNOW, WHATEVER THE HELL YOU'RE TALKING ABOUT DOESN'T EXIST.
TELL THAT TO YOUR MAN, BOOMERANG, WHO'S NOW JUST A SLAB OF COLD MEAT.
GOTHAM'S GOT ENOUGH KILLING WITHOUT YOU THROWING BODIES ON THE FIRE.
JIM. MEET ME ON THE ROOF.
NOW.
IF YOU'RE LUCKY, YOU'LL STILL HAVE A JOB WHEN YOU GET BACK.
IF I WANT ANY CRAP OUT OF YOU, WALLER, I'LL SQUEEZE YOUR HEAD.

BATMAN!

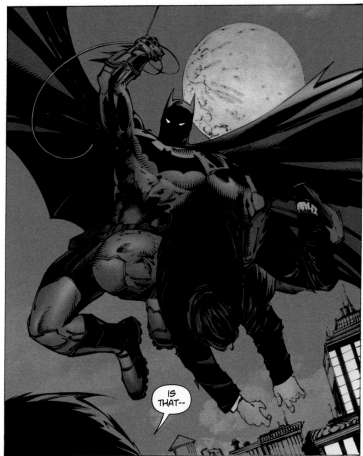

IS THAT--

JIM?

BRUCE, WHERE HAVE YOU BEEN?

BATMAN... HE...THREW ME OUT OF THE CAR... SAID THERE WAS AN ATTACK IMMINENT.

I WAS SO CONFUSED--I JUST STAYED HIDDEN UNTIL HE CAME BACK FOR ME.

WELL THAT WAS VERY NICE OF YOU...

...BATMAN.

HNN.

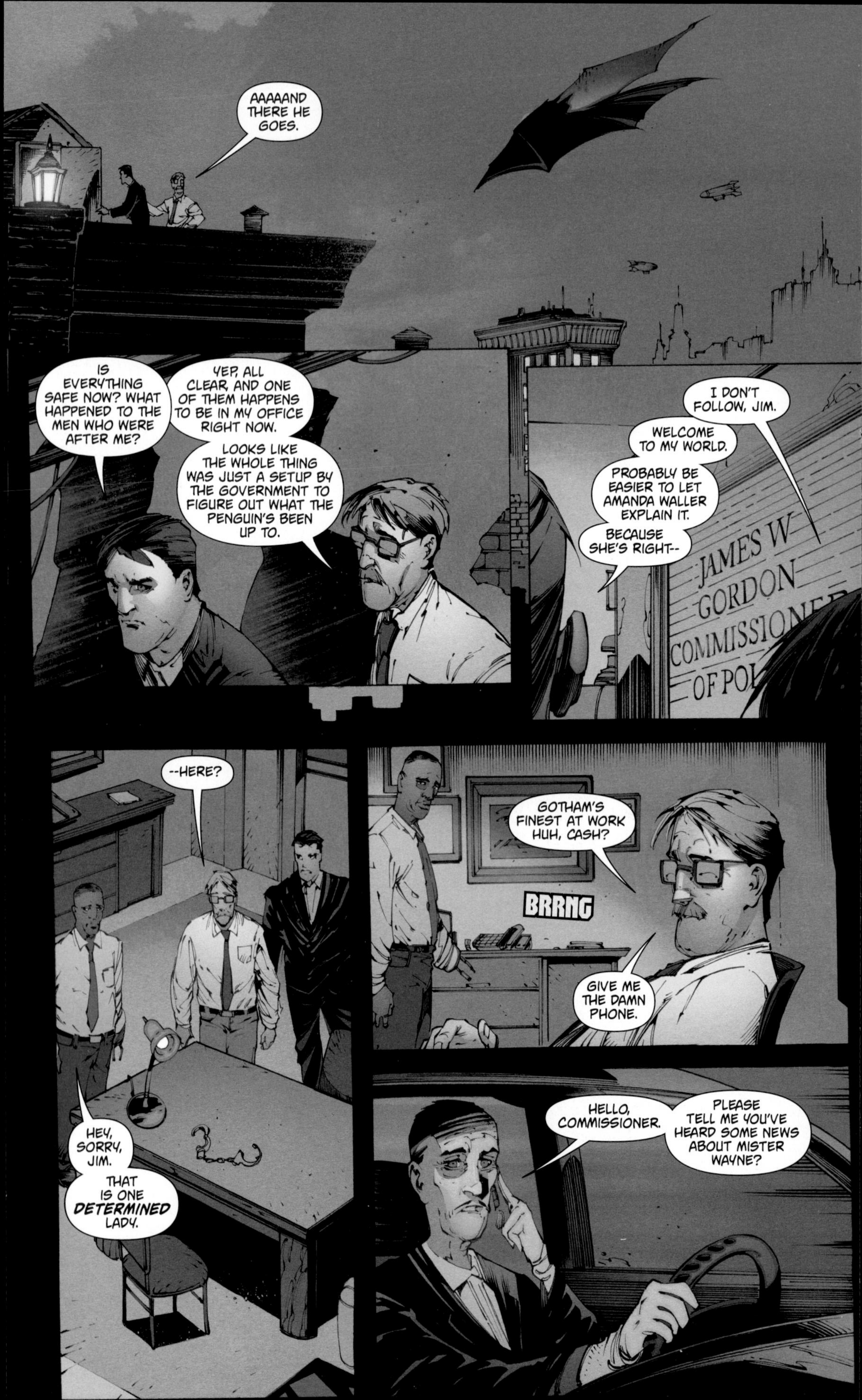
AAAAAND THERE HE GOES.
IS EVERYTHING SAFE NOW? WHAT HAPPENED TO THE MEN WHO WERE AFTER ME?
YEP, ALL CLEAR, AND ONE OF THEM HAPPENS TO BE IN MY OFFICE RIGHT NOW.
LOOKS LIKE THE WHOLE THING WAS JUST A SETUP BY THE GOVERNMENT TO FIGURE OUT WHAT THE PENGUIN'S BEEN UP TO.
I DON'T FOLLOW, JIM.
WELCOME TO MY WORLD.
PROBABLY BE EASIER TO LET AMANDA WALLER EXPLAIN IT.
BECAUSE SHE'S RIGHT--
JAMES W GORDON COMMISSIONER OF POL
--HERE?
HEY, SORRY, JIM.
THAT IS ONE DETERMINED LADY.
GOTHAM'S FINEST AT WORK HUH, CASH?
BRRNG
GIVE ME THE DAMN PHONE.
HELLO, COMMISSIONER.
PLEASE TELL ME YOU'VE HEARD SOME NEWS ABOUT MISTER WAYNE?

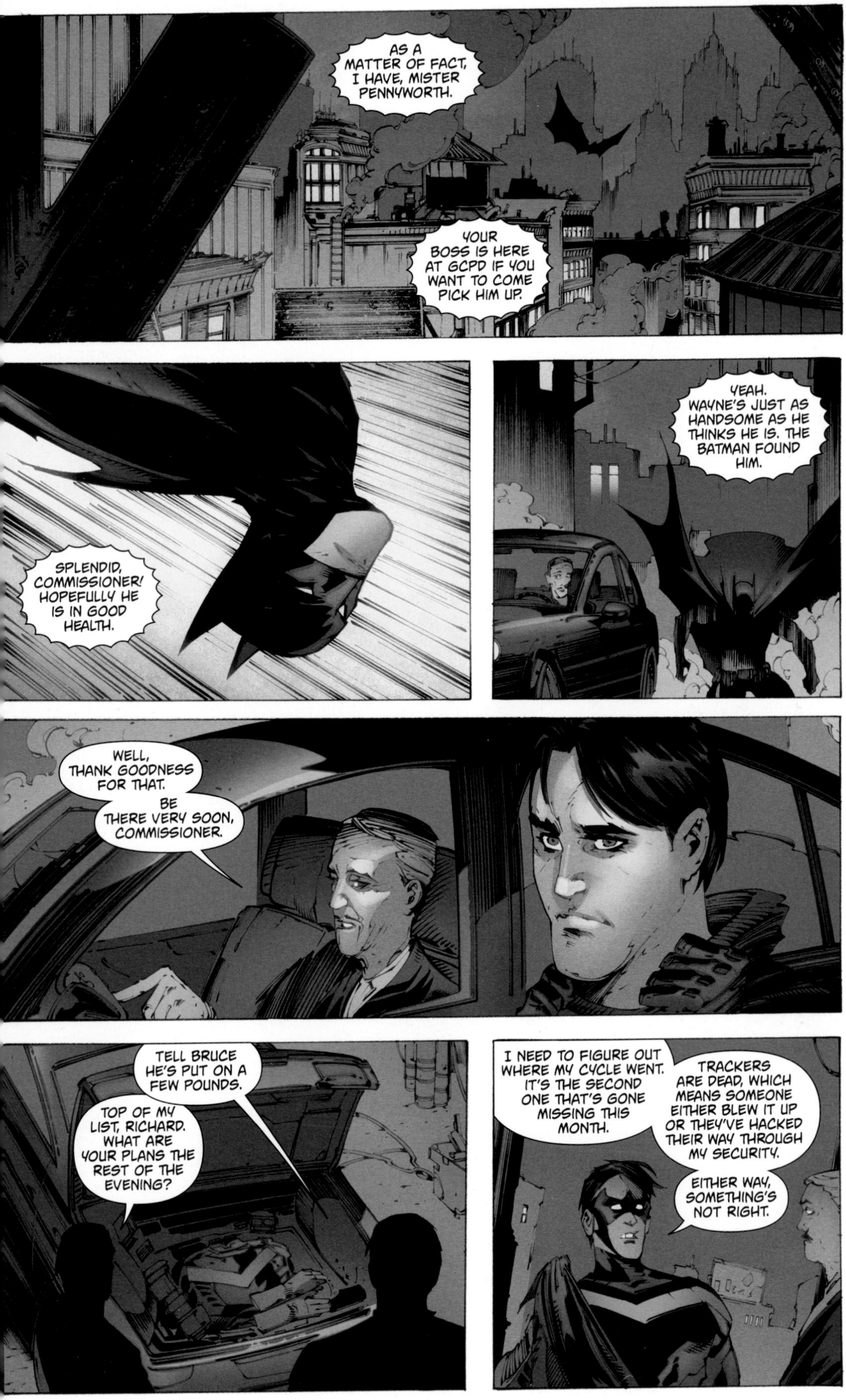
AS A MATTER OF FACT, I HAVE, MISTER PENNYWORTH.
YOUR BOSS IS HERE AT GCPD IF YOU WANT TO COME PICK HIM UP.
SPLENDID, COMMISSIONER! HOPEFULLY HE IS IN GOOD HEALTH.
YEAH. WAYNE'S JUST AS HANDSOME AS HE THINKS HE IS. THE BATMAN FOUND HIM.
WELL, THANK GOODNESS FOR THAT.
BE THERE VERY SOON, COMMISSIONER.
TELL BRUCE HE'S PUT ON A FEW POUNDS.
TOP OF MY LIST, RICHARD. WHAT ARE YOUR PLANS THE REST OF THE EVENING?
I NEED TO FIGURE OUT WHERE MY CYCLE WENT. IT'S THE SECOND ONE THAT'S GONE MISSING THIS MONTH.
TRACKERS ARE DEAD, WHICH MEANS SOMEONE EITHER BLEW IT UP OR THEY'VE HACKED THEIR WAY THROUGH MY SECURITY.
EITHER WAY, SOMETHING'S NOT RIGHT.

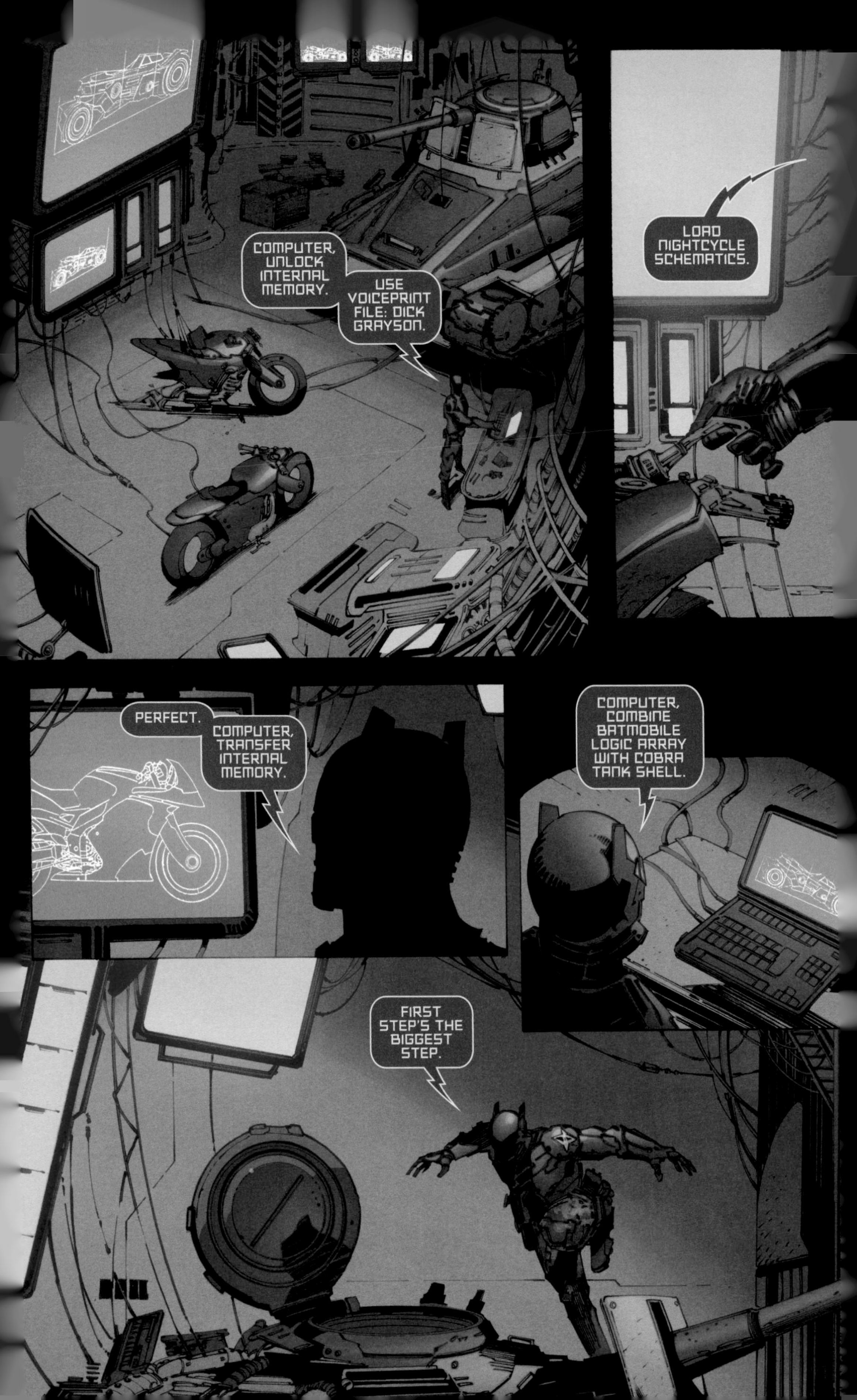
COMPUTER, UNLOCK INTERNAL MEMORY.
USE VOICEPRINT FILE: DICK GRAYSON.
LOAD NIGHTCYCLE SCHEMATICS.
PERFECT.
COMPUTER, TRANSFER INTERNAL MEMORY.
COMPUTER, COMBINE BATMOBILE LOGIC ARRAY WITH COBRA TANK SHELL.
FIRST STEP'S THE BIGGEST STEP.

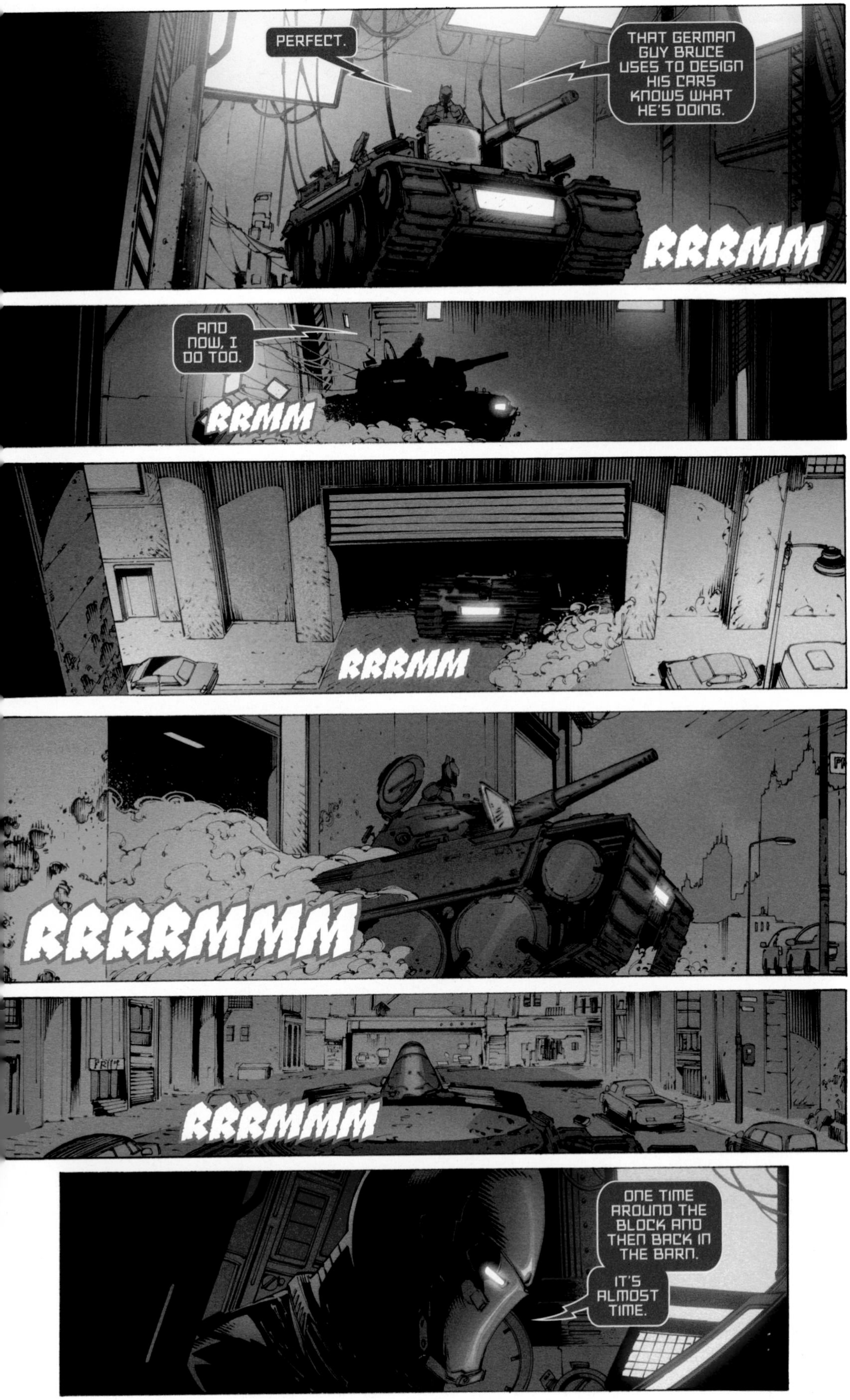
PERFECT.
THAT GERMAN GUY BRUCE USES TO DESIGN HIS CARS KNOWS WHAT HE'S DOING.
RRRMM
AND NOW, I DO TOO.
RRMM
RRRMM
RRRRMMM
RRRMMM
ONE TIME AROUND THE BLOCK AND THEN BACK IN THE BARN.
IT'S ALMOST TIME.

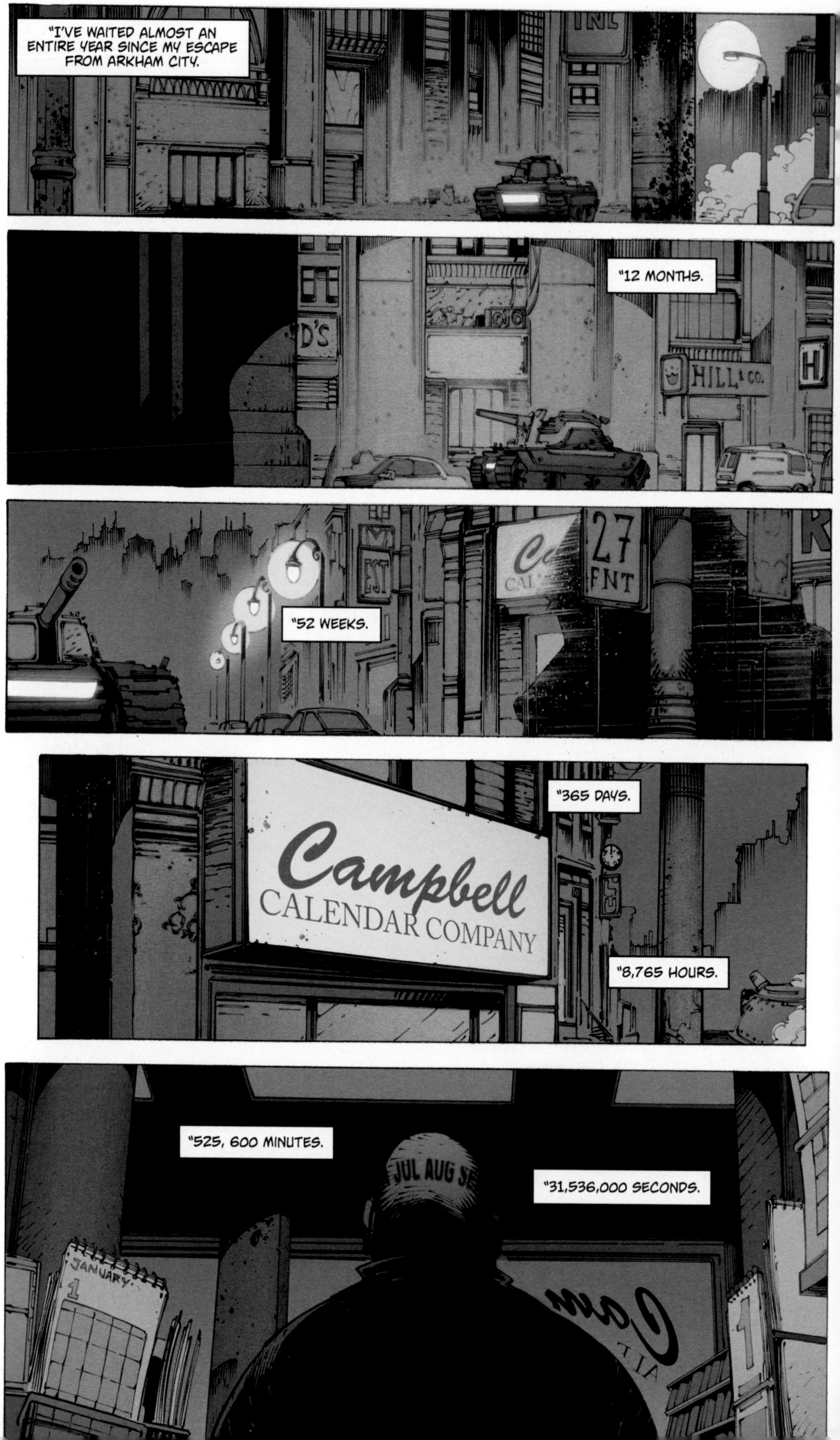
"I'VE WAITED ALMOST AN ENTIRE YEAR SINCE MY ESCAPE FROM ARKHAM CITY.
"12 MONTHS.
D'S
HILL & CO.
"52 WEEKS.
27 FNT
"365 DAYS.
Campbell
CALENDAR COMPANY
"8,765 HOURS.
"525, 600 MINUTES.
JUL AUG SE
"31,536,000 SECONDS.
JANUARY
1

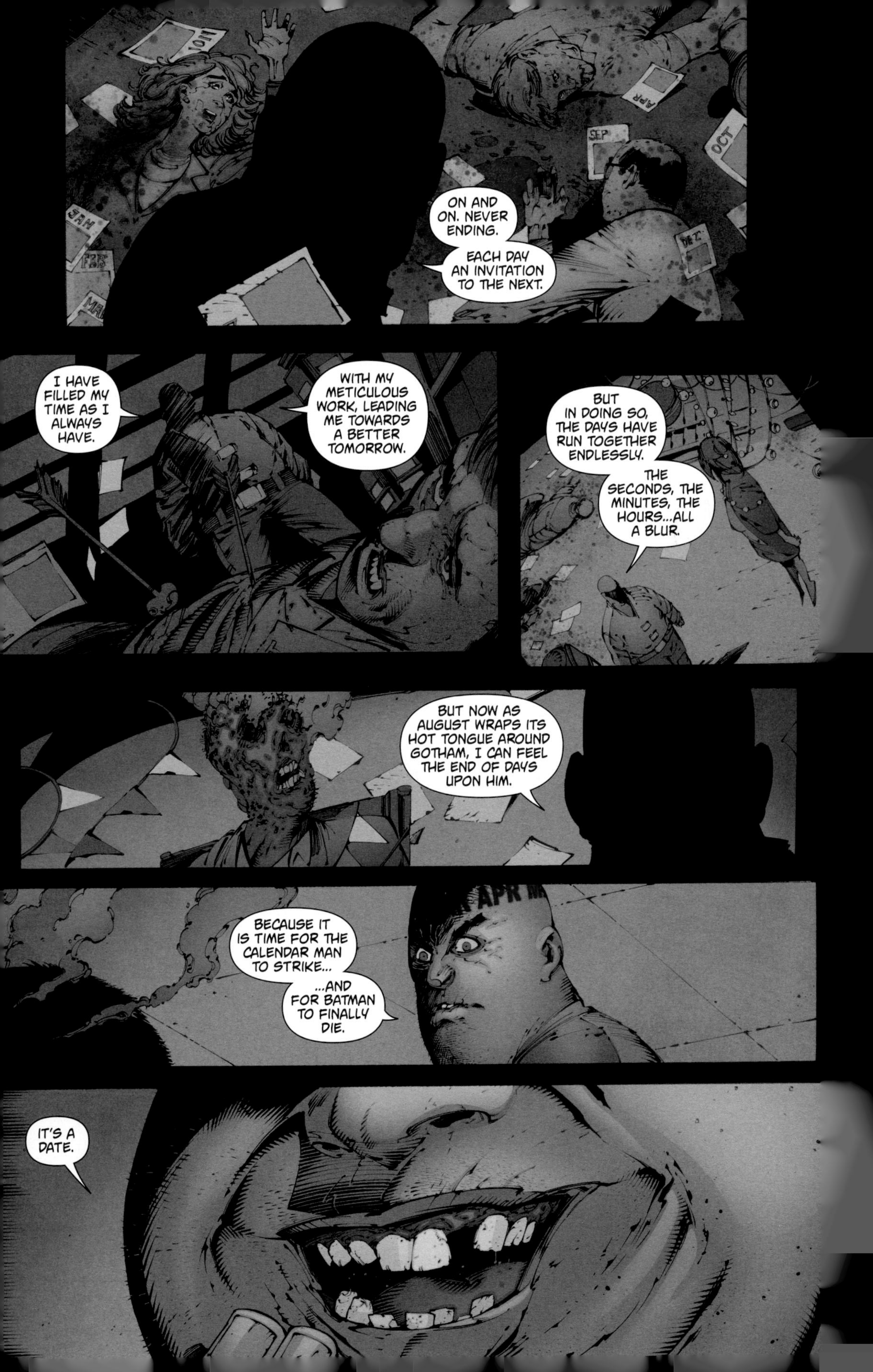
ON AND ON. NEVER ENDING.
EACH DAY AN INVITATION TO THE NEXT.
I HAVE FILLED MY TIME AS I ALWAYS HAVE.
WITH MY METICULOUS WORK, LEADING ME TOWARDS A BETTER TOMORROW.
BUT IN DOING SO, THE DAYS HAVE RUN TOGETHER ENDLESSLY.
THE SECONDS, THE MINUTES, THE HOURS...ALL A BLUR.
BUT NOW AS AUGUST WRAPS ITS HOT TONGUE AROUND GOTHAM, I CAN FEEL THE END OF DAYS UPON HIM.
BECAUSE IT IS TIME FOR THE CALENDAR MAN TO STRIKE...
...AND FOR BATMAN TO FINALLY DIE.
IT'S A DATE.

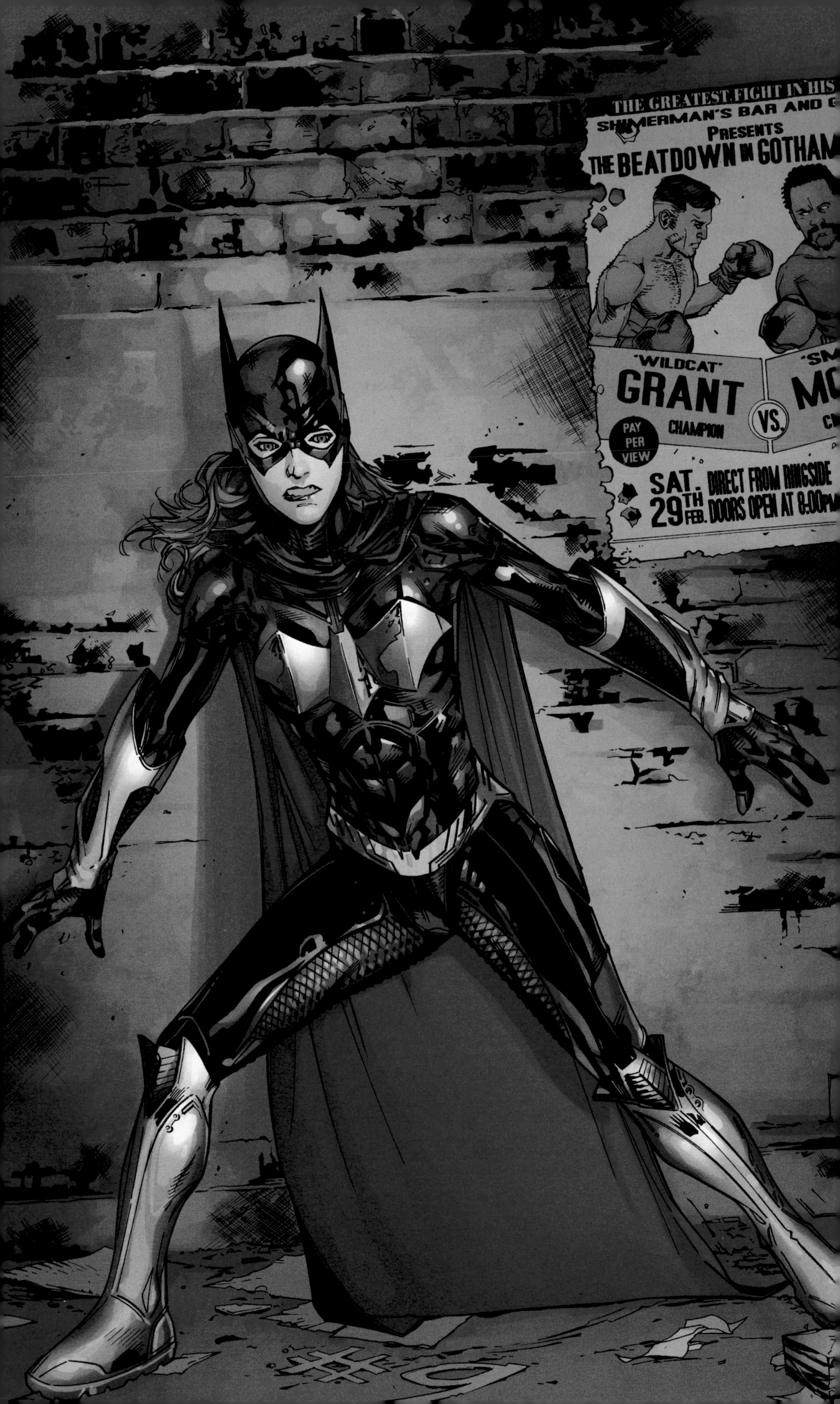

THE GREATEST FIGHT IN HIS
SHIMERMAN'S BAR AND G
PRESENTS
THE BEATDOWN IN GOTHAM
"WILDCAT"
GRANT
CHAMPION
PAY PER VIEW
VS.
SAT. 29TH FEB.
DIRECT FROM RINGSIDE
DOORS OPEN AT 8:00PM

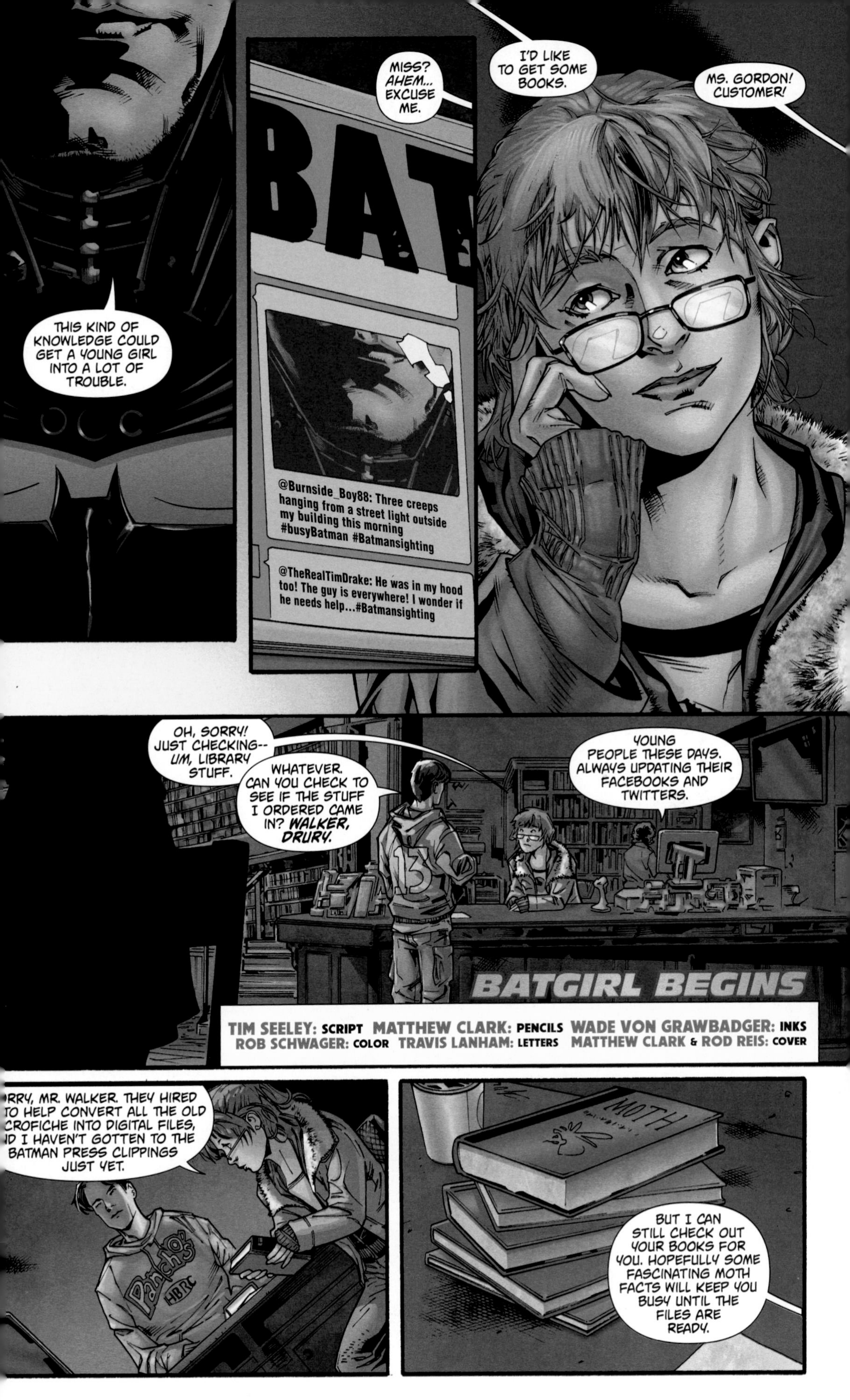

THIS KIND OF KNOWLEDGE COULD GET A YOUNG GIRL INTO A LOT OF TROUBLE.
MISS? AHEM... EXCUSE ME.
BAT
@Burnside_Boy88: Three creeps hanging from a street light outside my building this morning #busyBatman #Batmansighting
@TheRealTimDrake: He was in my hood too! The guy is everywhere! I wonder if he needs help...#Batmansighting
I'D LIKE TO GET SOME BOOKS.
MS. GORDON! CUSTOMER!
OH, SORRY! JUST CHECKING-- UM, LIBRARY STUFF.
WHATEVER. CAN YOU CHECK TO SEE IF THE STUFF I ORDERED CAME IN? WALKER, DRURY.
YOUNG PEOPLE THESE DAYS. ALWAYS UPDATING THEIR FACEBOOKS AND TWITTERS.
13
BATGIRL BEGINS
TIM SEELEY: SCRIPT MATTHEW CLARK: PENCILS WADE VON GRAWBADGER: INKS
ROB SCHWAGER: COLOR TRAVIS LANHAM: LETTERS MATTHEW CLARK & ROD REIS: COVER
RRY, MR. WALKER. THEY HIRED TO HELP CONVERT ALL THE OLD CROFICHE INTO DIGITAL FILES, ID I HAVEN'T GOTTEN TO THE BATMAN PRESS CLIPPINGS JUST YET.
Panchos HBRC
MOTH
BUT I CAN STILL CHECK OUT YOUR BOOKS FOR YOU. HOPEFULLY SOME FASCINATING MOTH FACTS WILL KEEP YOU BUSY UNTIL THE FILES ARE READY.

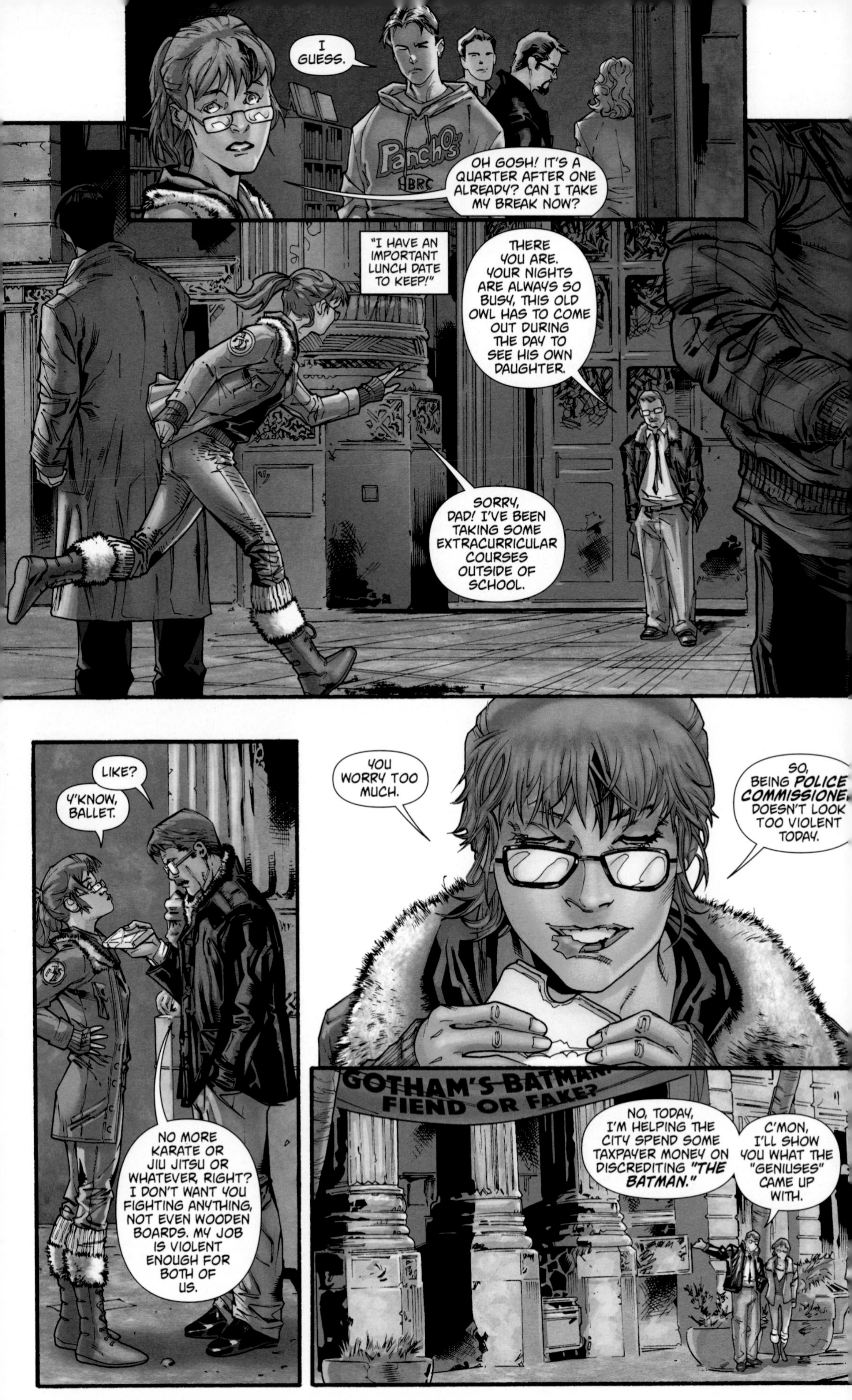
I GUESS.
OH GOSH! IT'S A QUARTER AFTER ONE ALREADY? CAN I TAKE MY BREAK NOW?
"I HAVE AN IMPORTANT LUNCH DATE TO KEEP!"
THERE YOU ARE. YOUR NIGHTS ARE ALWAYS SO BUSY, THIS OLD OWL HAS TO COME OUT DURING THE DAY TO SEE HIS OWN DAUGHTER.
SORRY, DAD! I'VE BEEN TAKING SOME EXTRACURRICULAR COURSES OUTSIDE OF SCHOOL.
LIKE?
Y'KNOW, BALLET.
NO MORE KARATE OR JIU JITSU OR WHATEVER, RIGHT? I DON'T WANT YOU FIGHTING ANYTHING, NOT EVEN WOODEN BOARDS. MY JOB IS VIOLENT ENOUGH FOR BOTH OF US.
YOU WORRY TOO MUCH.
SO, BEING POLICE COMMISSIONE DOESN'T LOOK TOO VIOLENT TODAY.
GOTHAM'S BATMAN FIEND OR FAKE?
NO, TODAY, I'M HELPING THE CITY SPEND SOME TAXPAYER MONEY ON DISCREDITING "THE BATMAN."
C'MON, I'LL SHOW YOU WHAT THE "GENIUSES" CAME UP WITH.

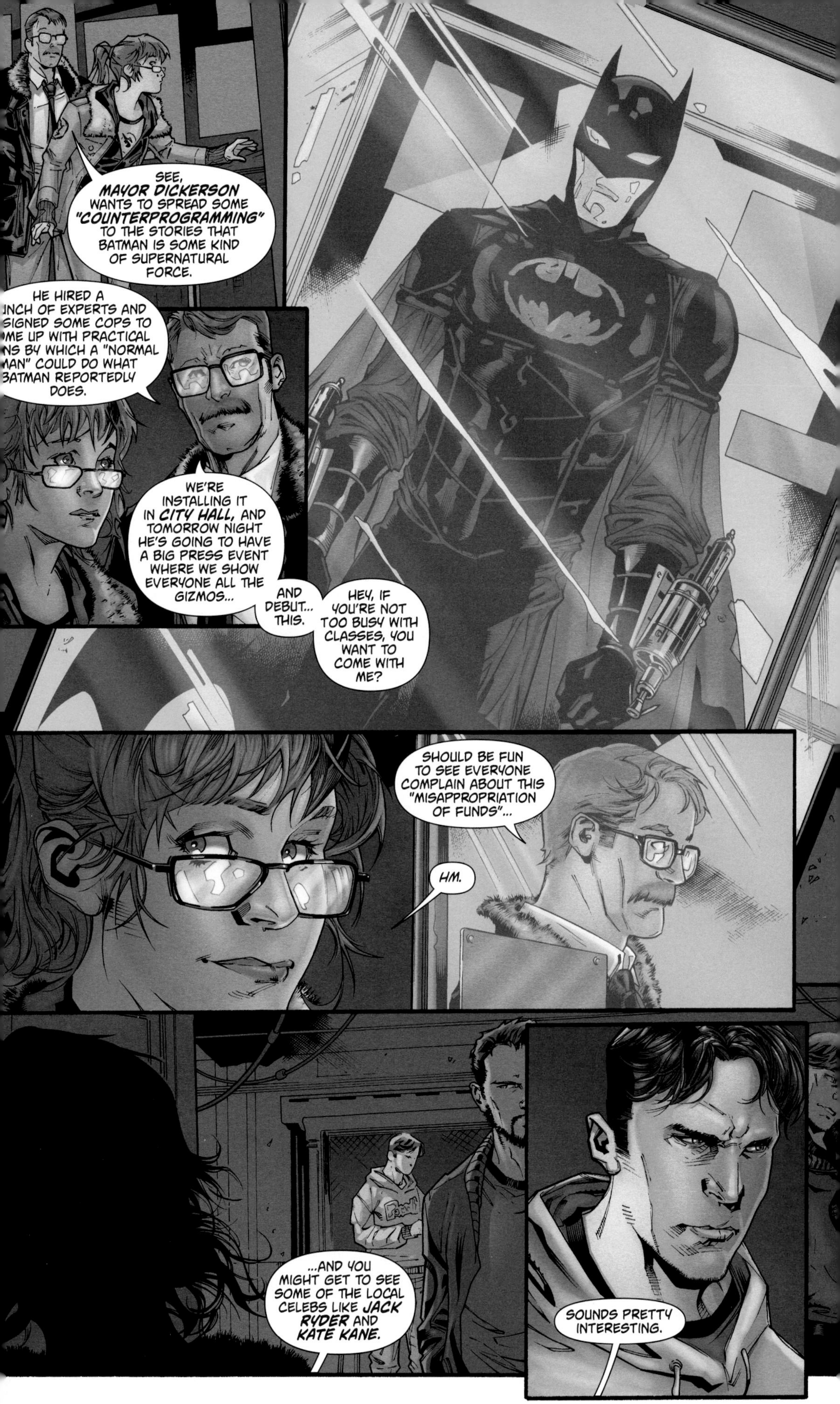

SEE, MAYOR DICKERSON WANTS TO SPREAD SOME "COUNTERPROGRAMMING" TO THE STORIES THAT BATMAN IS SOME KIND OF SUPERNATURAL FORCE.
HE HIRED A UNCH OF EXPERTS AND SIGNED SOME COPS TO ME UP WITH PRACTICAL NS BY WHICH A "NORMAL MAN" COULD DO WHAT BATMAN REPORTEDLY DOES.
WE'RE INSTALLING IT IN CITY HALL, AND TOMORROW NIGHT HE'S GOING TO HAVE A BIG PRESS EVENT WHERE WE SHOW EVERYONE ALL THE GIZMOS...
AND DEBUT... THIS.
HEY, IF YOU'RE NOT TOO BUSY WITH CLASSES, YOU WANT TO COME WITH ME?
SHOULD BE FUN TO SEE EVERYONE COMPLAIN ABOUT THIS "MISAPPROPRIATION OF FUNDS"...
HM.
...AND YOU MIGHT GET TO SEE SOME OF THE LOCAL CELEBS LIKE JACK RYDER AND KATE KANE.
SOUNDS PRETTY INTERESTING.

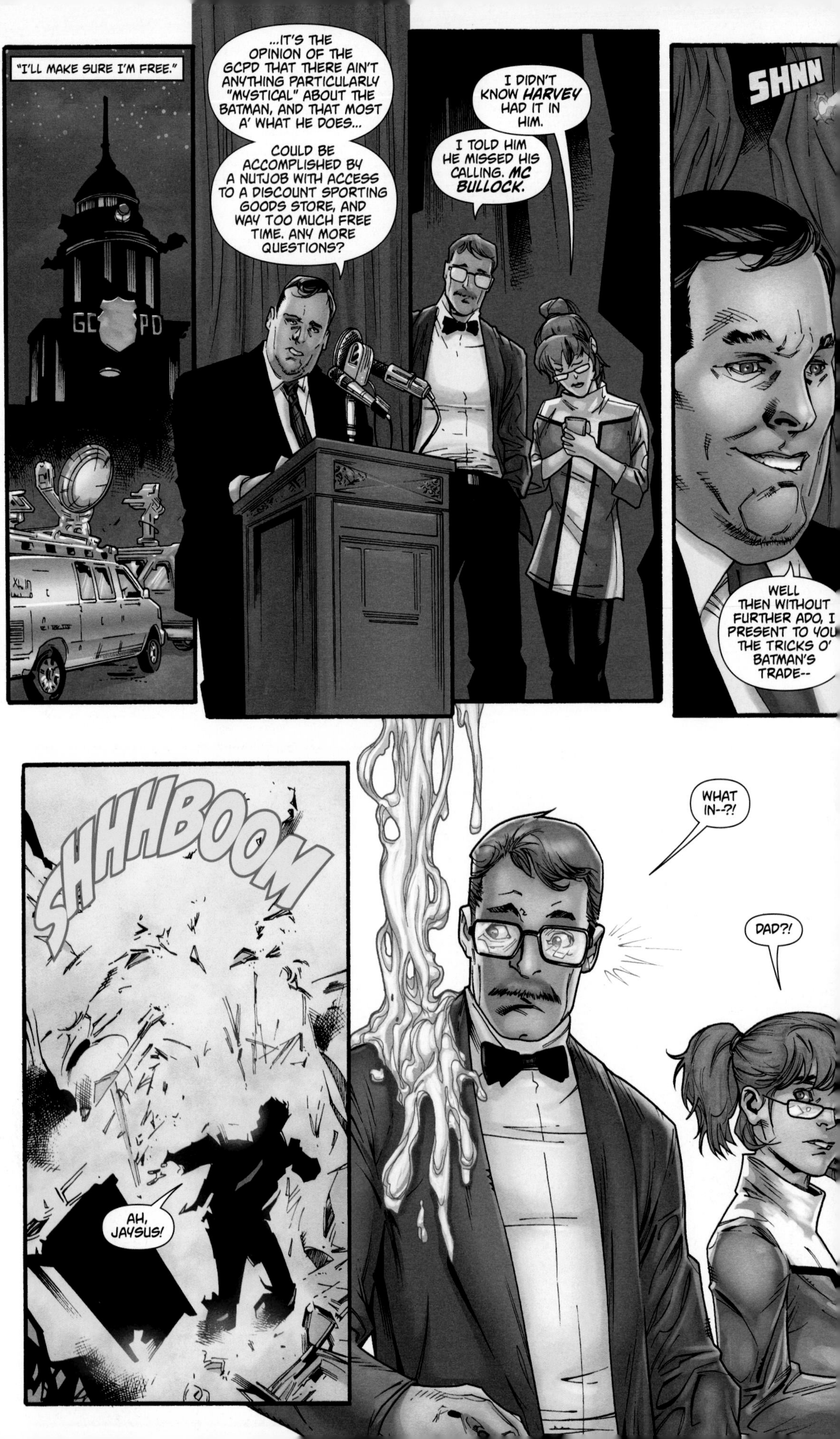
"I'LL MAKE SURE I'M FREE."
GC PD
...IT'S THE OPINION OF THE GCPD THAT THERE AIN'T ANYTHING PARTICULARLY "MYSTICAL" ABOUT THE BATMAN, AND THAT MOST A' WHAT HE DOES...
COULD BE ACCOMPLISHED BY A NUTJOB WITH ACCESS TO A DISCOUNT SPORTING GOODS STORE, AND WAY TOO MUCH FREE TIME. ANY MORE QUESTIONS?
I DIDN'T KNOW HARVEY HAD IT IN HIM.
I TOLD HIM HE MISSED HIS CALLING. MC BULLOCK.
SHNN
WELL THEN WITHOUT FURTHER ADO, I PRESENT TO YOU THE TRICKS O' BATMAN'S TRADE--
SHHHBOOM
AH, JAYSUS!
WHAT IN--?!
DAD?!

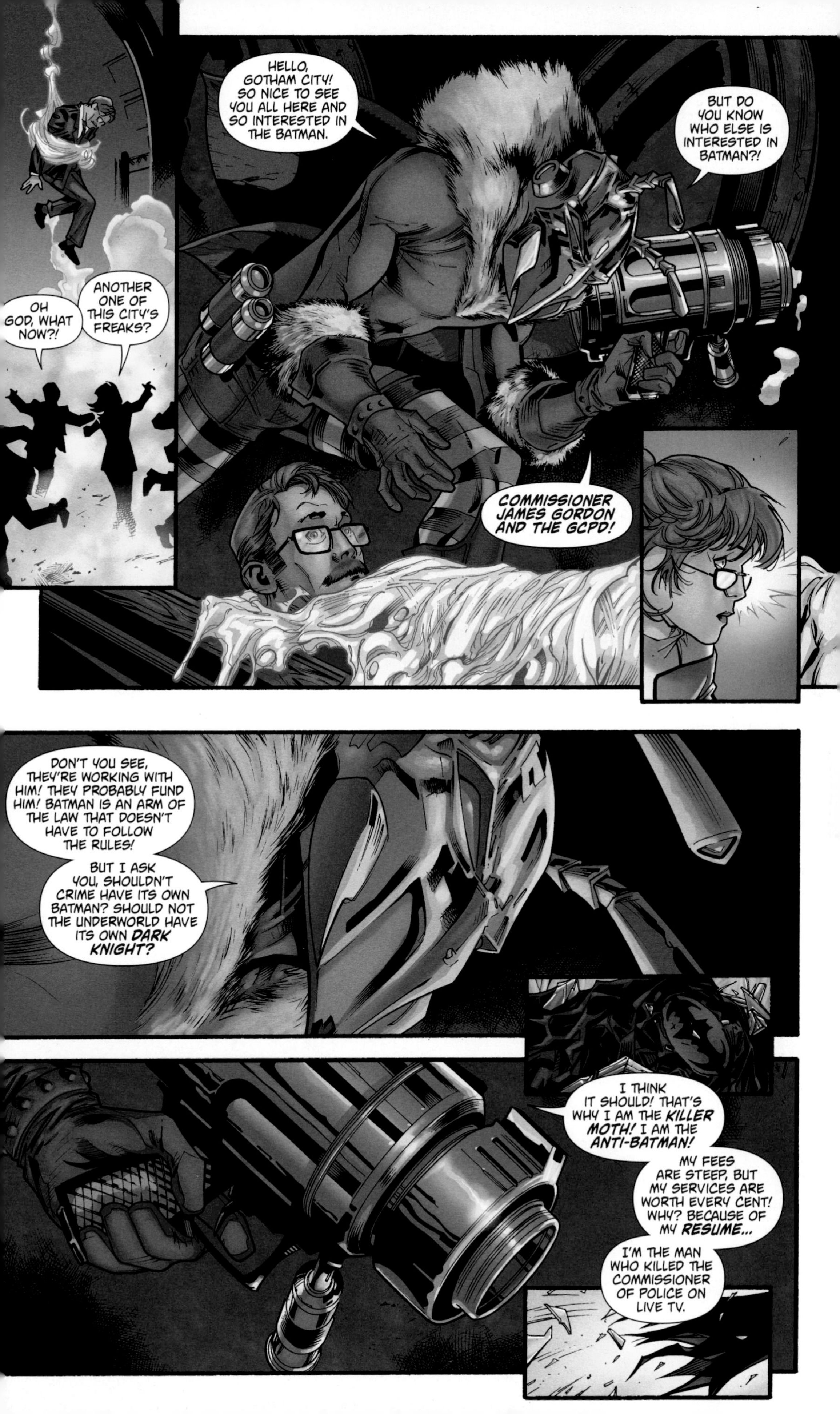

OH GOD, WHAT NOW?!
ANOTHER ONE OF THIS CITY'S FREAKS?
HELLO, GOTHAM CITY! SO NICE TO SEE YOU ALL HERE AND SO INTERESTED IN THE BATMAN.
BUT DO YOU KNOW WHO ELSE IS INTERESTED IN BATMAN?!
COMMISSIONER JAMES GORDON AND THE GCPD!
DON'T YOU SEE, THEY'RE WORKING WITH HIM! THEY PROBABLY FUND HIM! BATMAN IS AN ARM OF THE LAW THAT DOESN'T HAVE TO FOLLOW THE RULES!
BUT I ASK YOU, SHOULDN'T CRIME HAVE ITS OWN BATMAN? SHOULD NOT THE UNDERWORLD HAVE ITS OWN DARK KNIGHT?
I THINK IT SHOULD! THAT'S WHY I AM THE KILLER MOTH! I AM THE ANTI-BATMAN!
MY FEES ARE STEEP, BUT MY SERVICES ARE WORTH EVERY CENT! WHY? BECAUSE OF MY RESUME...
I'M THE MAN WHO KILLED THE COMMISSIONER OF POLICE ON LIVE TV.

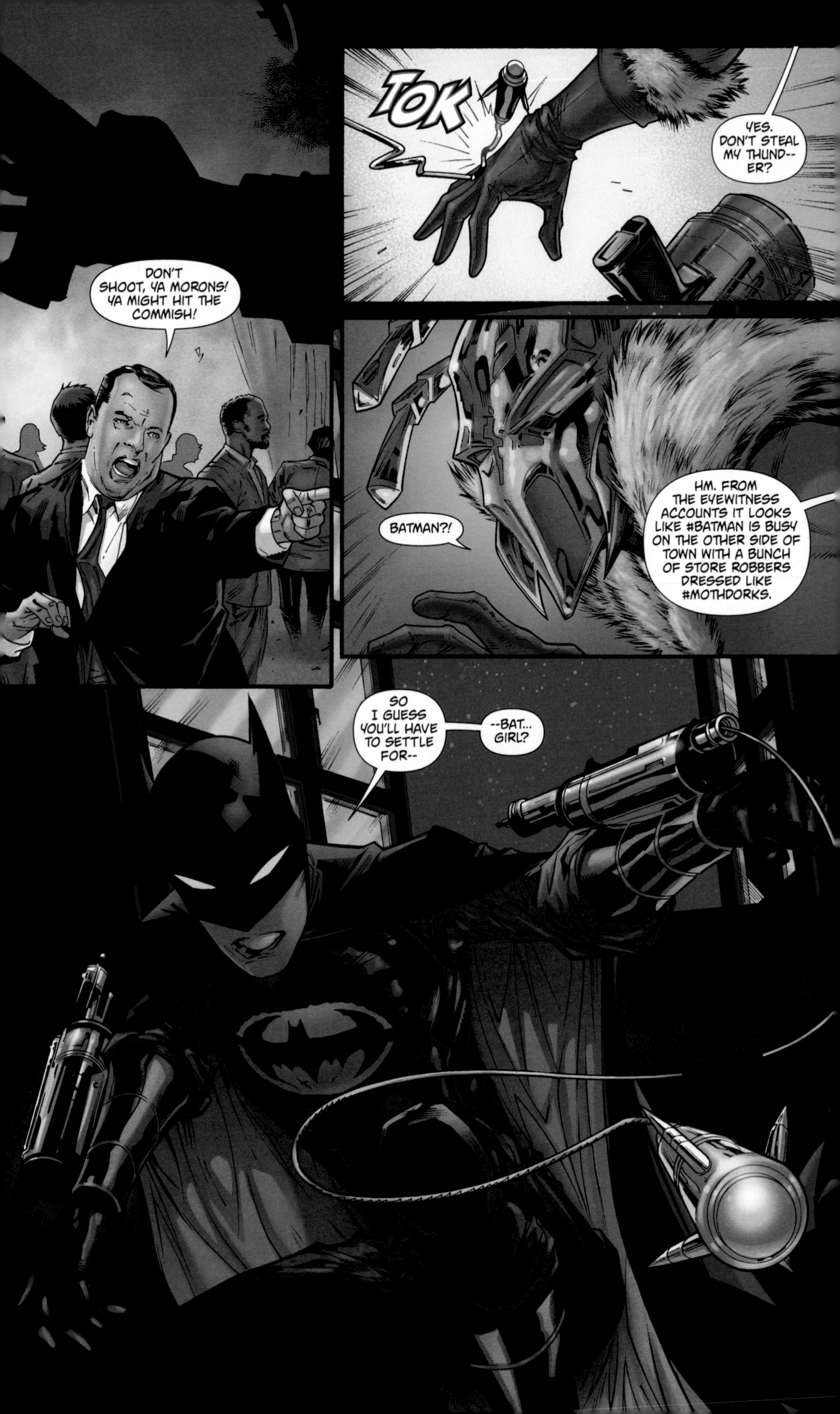
TOK
YES. DON'T STEAL MY THUNDER-- ER?
DON'T SHOOT, YA MORONS! YA MIGHT HIT THE COMMISH!
BATMAN?!
HM. FROM THE EYEWITNESS ACCOUNTS IT LOOKS LIKE #BATMAN IS BUSY ON THE OTHER SIDE OF TOWN WITH A BUNCH OF STORE ROBBERS DRESSED LIKE #MOTHDORKS.
SO I GUESS YOU'LL HAVE TO SETTLE FOR--
--BAT... GIRL?

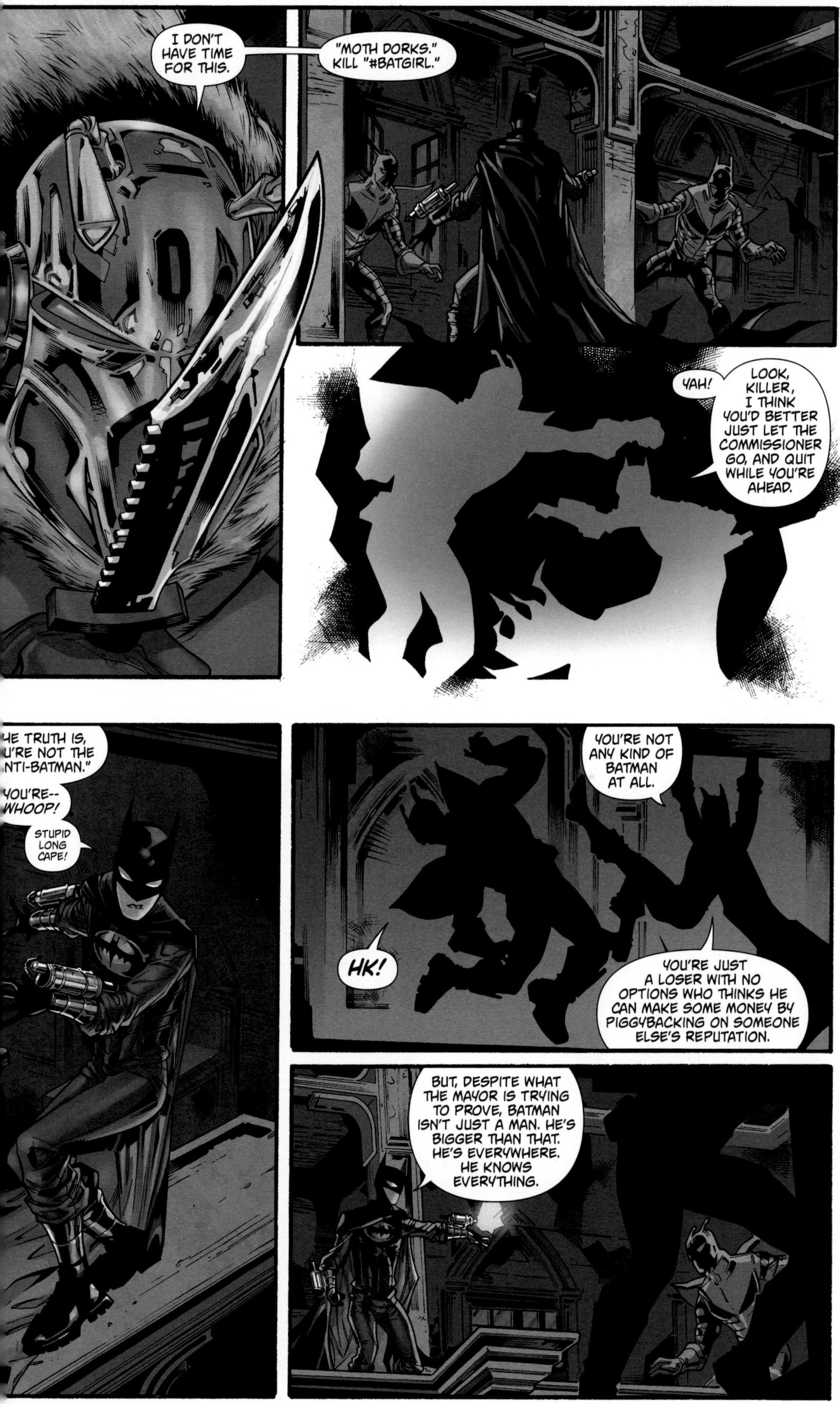
I DON'T HAVE TIME FOR THIS.
"MOTH DORKS." KILL "#BATGIRL."
YAH!
LOOK, KILLER, I THINK YOU'D BETTER JUST LET THE COMMISSIONER GO, AND QUIT WHILE YOU'RE AHEAD.
HE TRUTH IS, U'RE NOT THE NTI-BATMAN."
YOU'RE-- WHOOP!
STUPID LONG CAPE!
YOU'RE NOT ANY KIND OF BATMAN AT ALL.
HK!
YOU'RE JUST A LOSER WITH NO OPTIONS WHO THINKS HE CAN MAKE SOME MONEY BY PIGGYBACKING ON SOMEONE ELSE'S REPUTATION.
BUT, DESPITE WHAT THE MAYOR IS TRYING TO PROVE, BATMAN ISN'T JUST A MAN. HE'S BIGGER THAN THAT. HE'S EVERYWHERE. HE KNOWS EVERYTHING.

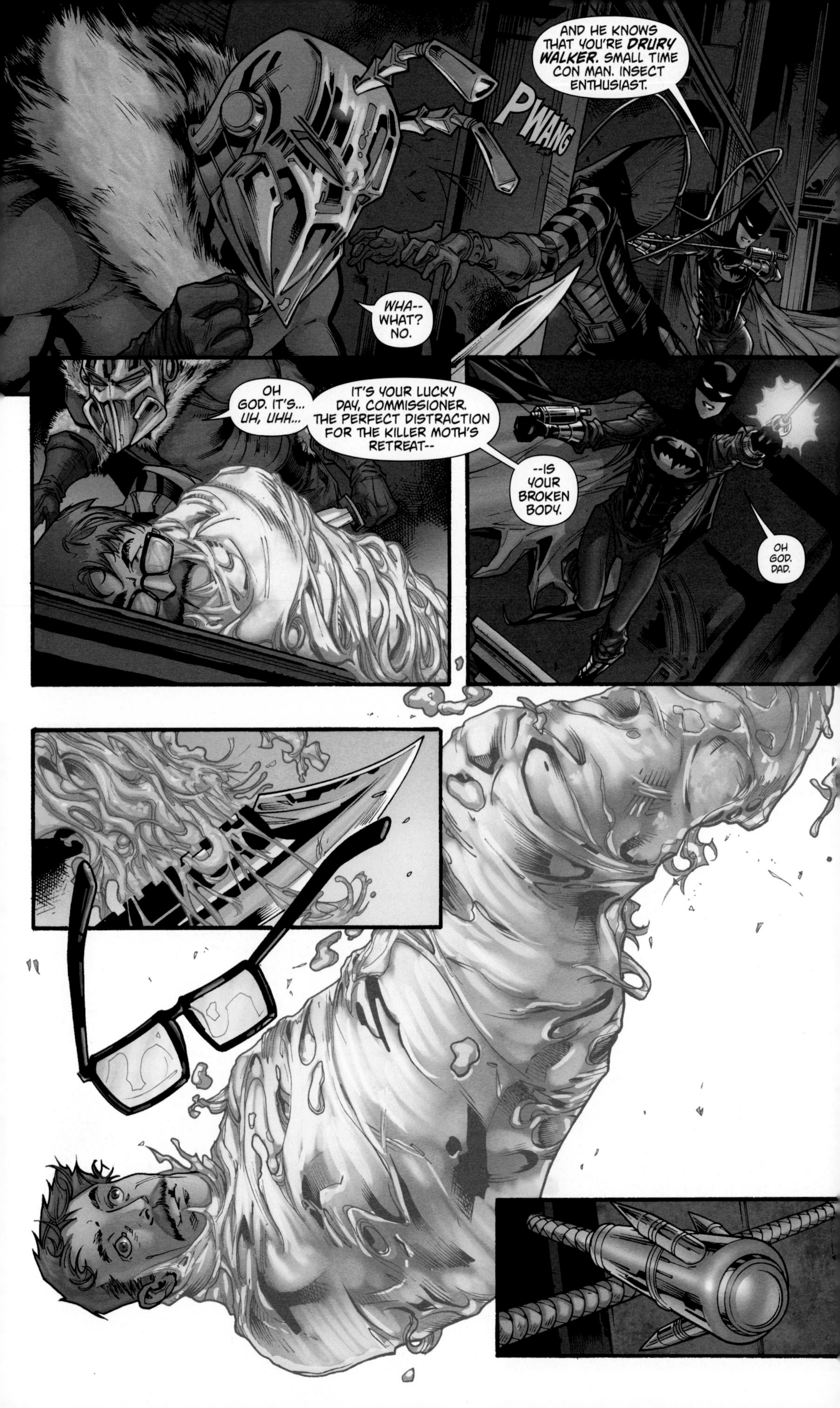
AND HE KNOWS THAT YOU'RE DRURY WALKER. SMALL TIME CON MAN. INSECT ENTHUSIAST.
PWANG
WHA-- WHAT? NO.
OH GOD. IT'S... UH, UHH...
IT'S YOUR LUCKY DAY, COMMISSIONER. THE PERFECT DISTRACTION FOR THE KILLER MOTH'S RETREAT--
--IS YOUR BROKEN BODY.
OH GOD. DAD.

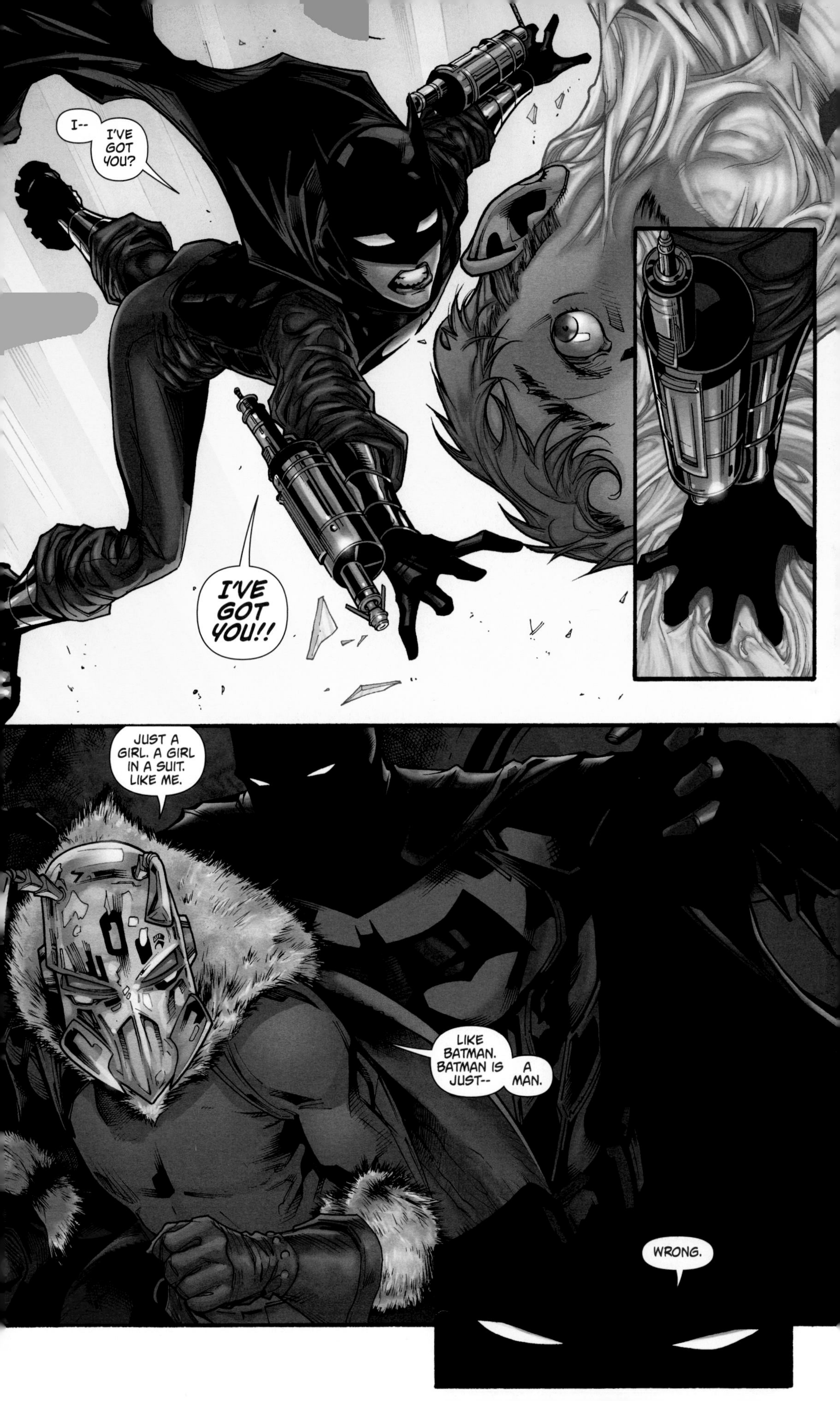
I--
I'VE GOT YOU?
I'VE GOT YOU!!
JUST A GIRL. A GIRL IN A SUIT. LIKE ME.
LIKE BATMAN. BATMAN IS JUST--
A MAN.
WRONG.

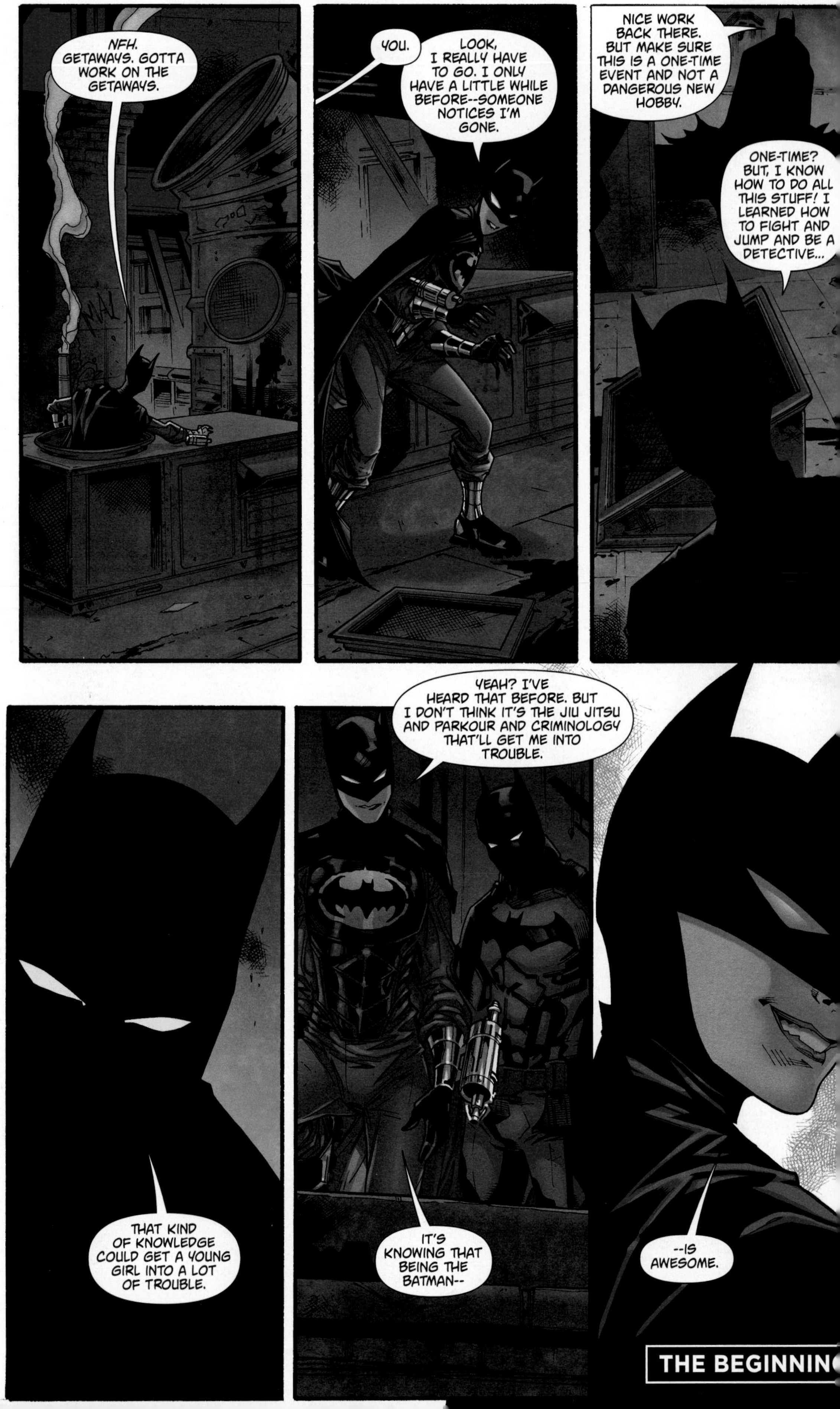
NFH. GETAWAYS. GOTTA WORK ON THE GETAWAYS.
YOU.
LOOK, I REALLY HAVE TO GO. I ONLY HAVE A LITTLE WHILE BEFORE--SOMEONE NOTICES I'M GONE.
NICE WORK BACK THERE. BUT MAKE SURE THIS IS A ONE-TIME EVENT AND NOT A DANGEROUS NEW HOBBY.
ONE-TIME? BUT, I KNOW HOW TO DO ALL THIS STUFF! I LEARNED HOW TO FIGHT AND JUMP AND BE A DETECTIVE...
THAT KIND OF KNOWLEDGE COULD GET A YOUNG GIRL INTO A LOT OF TROUBLE.
YEAH? I'VE HEARD THAT BEFORE. BUT I DON'T THINK IT'S THE JIU JITSU AND PARKOUR AND CRIMINOLOGY THAT'LL GET ME INTO TROUBLE.
IT'S KNOWING THAT BEING THE BATMAN--
--IS AWESOME.
THE BEGINNING

BATMAN

ARKHAM KNIGHT

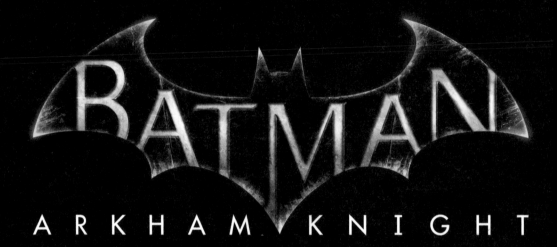